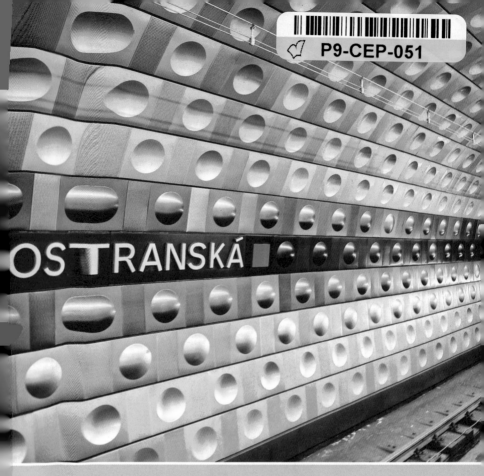

OSTRANSKÁ

THE ROUGH GUIDE TO
PRAGUE

This tenth edition updated by
Marc Di Duca

ROUGH
GUIDES

P9-CEP-051

Contents

Introduction to
Prague

With almost a thousand years of architecture virtually untouched by natural disaster or war, few other cities anywhere in Europe truly compare to Prague. Straddling the slow-moving River Vltava, with a steep wooded hill to one side, the city retains much of its medieval layout and the street facades remain smothered in a rich mantle of Baroque, Rococo and Art Nouveau, most of which successfully escaped the vanities and excesses of twentieth-century development.

For forty years the city lay hidden behind the Iron Curtain, seldom visited by Westerners and preserved in the formaldehyde of Communist inertia. All that changed with the end of totalitarian rule in 1989, and now Prague is one of the most popular city-break destinations in Europe, with a highly developed tourist industry and a list of attractions many other places in Central and Eastern Europe can only envy from afar. Its emergence as one of Europe's leading cities has come as a surprise to some – but not the Czechs themselves. After all, Prague was at the forefront of the European avant-garde for much of the twentieth century, boasting a Cubist movement second only to the one in Paris and, between the wars, a modernist architectural flowering to rival Germany's Bauhaus.

Today Prague is back at the heart of Europe, where it has always felt it belonged – no longer an Eastern Bloc city but a cultured Western-leaning metropolis. It is more than a quarter of a century since the fall of Communism, and an entire generation has grown up feeling very much part of a wider, united continent. The Czech capital has changed in recent years, and mostly for the better – boasting more restaurants, new hotels and improved roads – but with the Czech koruna riding (too) high and prices rising across the board, it is no longer the budget destination it once was. The new-millennium stag and hen parties may have largely moved on to pastures new – to the relief of many – but one thing you can be sure of is that the beer is still cheaper, and better, in this beautiful old city than anywhere else in Europe.

ABOVE STAROMĚSTSKÉ NÁMĚSTÍ (OLD TOWN SQUARE)

What to see

With a population of just one and a quarter million, Prague (Praha to the Czechs) is relatively small as capital cities go. It originally developed as four separate self-governing towns and a Jewish ghetto, whose individual identities and medieval street plans have been preserved, to a greater or lesser extent, to this day. Almost everything of any historical interest lies within these compact central districts, the majority of which are easy to explore quickly on foot. Only in the last hundred years has Prague spread beyond its ancient perimeter, and its suburbs now stretch across the hills for miles on every side.

Prague is divided into two unequal halves by the **River Vltava**. The steeply inclined left bank is dominated by the castle district of **Hradčany**, which contains the city's most obvious sight: Pražský hrad or **Prague Castle** (known simply as the Hrad in Czech), where you'll find the cathedral, the old royal palace and gardens, and a host of museums and galleries. Squeezed between the castle hill and the river are the picturesque seventeenth-century palaces and crooked lanes of **Malá Strana**. This neighbourhood of hidden courtyards and secret walled gardens is home to the Czech parliament and some embassies, and dominated by the green dome and tower of the **church of sv Mikuláš**, the city's finest piece of Baroque architecture. At the southern end of Malá Strana, a funicular railway carries you away from the cramped streets to the top of **Petřín** hill, Prague's most central leafy escape, with a wonderful view across the river and historic centre.

The city's labyrinth of twisting streets is at its most bamboozling in the original medieval hub of the city, **Staré Město** – literally, the "Old Town" – on the right bank of the Vltava. Karlův most, or **Charles Bridge**, its principal link with the opposite bank, is easily the most popular historical monument, and the best place from which to view Prague Castle. Staré Město's other great showpiece is its main square, **Staroměstské náměstí (Old Town Square)**, where you can view Prague's famous astronomical clock and its hourly mechanical show. Enclosed within the boundaries of Staré Město is the former Jewish quarter, or **Josefov.**

HISTORIC HOUSE SYMBOLS

One of the most appealing features of Prague's old residences is that they often retain their old **house symbols**, carved into the gables, on hanging wooden signs or inscribed on the facade. The system originated in medieval times and still survives today, especially on pubs, restaurants and hotels.

Some signs were deliberately chosen to draw custom to the business of the house, like **U zeleného hroznu** (The Green Bunch of Grapes), a wine shop in the Malá Strana; others, like **U železných dveří** (The Iron Door), simply referred to a distinguishing feature of the house, often long since disappeared. Stone clocks, white Indians, golden tigers and trios of black eagles are harder to explain, but were probably just thought up by the owners of various long-since defunct establishments as memorable symbols for a largely illiterate populace.

In the 1770s, the imperial authorities introduced a numerical system, with each house in the city entered onto a register according to a strict chronology. Later, however, the conventional system of progressive street numbering was introduced, so don't be surprised if seventeenth-century pubs like **U medvídků** (*The Little Bears*) have two numbers in addition to a house sign, in this case nos. 7 and 345. The former, Habsburg, number is written on a red background; the latter, modern, number on blue.

The ghetto walls have long since gone and the whole area was remodelled at the turn of the twentieth century, but various synagogues, a medieval cemetery and a town hall survive as powerful reminders of a community that has existed here for more than a millennium.

South and east of the Old Town is the large sprawling district of **Nové Město** ("New Town"), whose main arteries make up the city's commercial and business centre. The heart of Nové Město is **Václavské naměstí (Wenceslas Square)**, focus of the political upheavals of the modern-day republic. Further afield lie various **suburbs**, most of which were developed only in the last hundred years or so. One exception is **Vyšehrad**, which was among the original fortress settlements of the newly arrived Slavs more than a thousand years ago and whose cemetery is now the final resting place of leading Czech artists of the modern age, including composers Smetana and Dvořák. To the east is the eminently desirable residential suburb of **Vinohrady**, peppered with gentrified parks and squares, and neighbouring **Žižkov**, whose two landmarks – the Žižkov monument and the futuristic TV tower – are visible from far and wide.

Nineteenth-century suburbs also sprang up to the north of the city centre in **Holešovice**, now home to Prague's main modern art museum, **Veletržní palác**. The area boasts two huge swathes of greenery: the Letná plain, overlooking the city, and the Stromovka park, beyond which lie the chateau of **Troja** and the zoo. Further west, leafy interwar suburbs like **Dejvice** and **Střešovice**, dotted with modernist family villas, give an entirely different angle on Prague.

Prague's outer suburbs, especially to the south where most of the population lives, are more typical of the old Eastern Bloc, dominated by bleak high-rise housing estates known locally as *paneláky*. However, once you're clear of the city limits, sleepy, provincial **Bohemia** (Čechy) makes itself felt. Many locals own a *chata*, or country cottage, somewhere in these rural backwaters, and every weekend the roads are jammed with folk heading for the hills. Few places are more than an hour from the city by public transport, however, making

SIGHTSEEING BY PUBLIC TRANSPORT

If there's one thing every visitor would like to take home with them from Prague, it's the public transport system. The **metro** – one of the few legacies of the Soviet period that the locals are truly grateful for – is clean and constantly expanding, while the much-loved cream and red trams negotiate the city's cobbles and bridges with remarkable dexterity. You can have a lot of fun with a 24-hour travel pass (see p.22). Hopping on **tram #22** from Národní třída gets you a free tour of the city, crossing the river, ploughing through picturesque Malá Strana and taking on a couple of impressive hairpin bends before ending up outside the gates of Prague Castle. Alternatively, for a few extra crowns, you can catch **tram #91**, an old 1930s tramcar with a conductor, which takes a circuitous route through the city centre en route to or from Prague Castle. Travel passes also cover the city's **funicular**, which will whisk you to the top of Petřín hill, home to the mirror maze and miniature Eiffel Tower. Even more fun are the summer-only **boat services and tourist steamers** (see p.24), which allow a particularly relaxing way to watch the city's main sights slide idly by.

day-trips relatively easy. The most popular destinations are the castles of **Karlštejn** and **Konopiště**, both surrounded by beautiful wooded countryside. Alternatively you can head north, away from the hills and the crowds, to the wine town of **Mělník**, perched high above the confluence of the Vltava and Labe (Elbe) rivers. Further north is **Terezín**, the wartime Jewish ghetto that is a living testament to the Holocaust. One of the most popular day-trips is to the medieval silver-mining town of **Kutná Hora**, 60km to the east, which boasts a glorious Gothic cathedral and a macabre ossuary.

When to go

Lying at the heart of central Europe, Prague has a continental climate: winters can be bitterly cold, summers correspondingly baking. The best times to visit, in terms of weather, are late spring and early autumn. Summer in the city can be stifling, but the real reason for avoiding the peak season is that it can get uncomfortably crowded in the centre – finding a place to eat in the evening, let alone securing a room, can become a trial. If you're looking for good weather, April is the earliest you can guarantee at least some sunny days, and October is the last warm month. The city looks beautiful under winter's snowy blanket, though it does get very cold, and it can also fall prey to "inversions", which smother the city in a hazy grey smog for a week or sometimes more.

LEFT SMÍCHOV

19

things not to miss

It's not possible to see everything Prague has to offer on a short trip – and we don't suggest you try. What follows is a subjective selection of the city's highlights, from Art Nouveau masterpieces to medieval backstreets, from elegant *pasáže* to traditional pubs. All highlights are colour-coded by chapter and have a page reference to take you straight into the Guide, where you can find out more.

1 STAROMĚSTSKÉ NAMĚSTÍ (OLD TOWN SQUARE)

Page 80

Prague's busy showpiece square, dominated by the Old Town Hall, and best known for its astronomical clock.

2 VELETRŽNÍ PALÁC (TRADE FAIR PALACE)

Page 139

The city's main modern art gallery is housed in a functionalist masterpiece.

3 MALÁ STRANA'S PALACE GARDENS

Page 61

Hidden behind the palaces of Malá Strana, these terraced gardens are the perfect inner-city escape.

4 JOSEFOV

Page 90

Six synagogues, a town hall and a medieval cemetery survive from the city's fascinating former Jewish ghetto.

5 OBECNÍ DŮM

Page 109

The largest and most impressive Art Nouveau building in Prague houses a café, a bar, two restaurants, exhibition spaces and a concert hall.

13

14

15

16

17

18

Itineraries

From the Hrad to Vyšehrad, Smíchov to Žižkov, the Czech capital is best enjoyed on your own two feet. The following itineraries will give you the essence of this beguiling city – a good pair of shoes and sense of direction are all that's required.

DAY ONE IN PRAGUE

❶ **Prague Castle** Start at Prague's skyline-dominating castle crammed with reminders of the country's past. Reckon on at least half a day to see everything at a gallop. **See p.33**

❷ **Lunch** Hradčany has limited options, so head downhill into Malá Strana for more choice, perhaps a meat-heavy platter at the medieval *U krále Brabantského* (see p.177), Prague's oldest tavern, a light snack at *U knoflíčků* (see p.176), a typical Czech *cukrárna*, or a stylish stop at *Café de Paris* (see p.176).

❸ **Sv Mikuláš** Visit Prague's premier Baroque church, not forgetting to climb the belfry from where the Communist secret police once spied on the US Embassy. **See p.82**

❹ **Kampa island** Stroll along the largest of the Vltava's islands to admire the view of the right bank and Charles Bridge. **See p.64**

❺ **Petřín** Take the funicular railway from Újezd up Petřín hill for a clamber up the tower, a miniature version of the Eiffel Tower. **See p.66**

❻ **Dinner** The *Klášterní pivovar* within the Strahov Monastery serves hearty pub food. **See p.187**

DAY TWO IN PRAGUE

❶ **Charles Bridge** Walk across Prague's iconic Gothic bridge, surely the finest of its kind in central and Eastern Europe. **See p.69**

❷ **Old Town Square** From the bridge, go with the tourist flow along the old coronation route

to Prague's grandest square, where crowds of visitors gather on the hour to watch the astronomical clock do its thing. **See p.80**

❸ **Lunch** Avoid the touristy restaurants on Old Town Square and head to Josefov where *Kolonial* (see p.180), *U Golema* (see p.180) or *Kolkovna* (see p.190) are popular.

❹ **Jewish Museum** Take a whirlwind tour of the synagogues and the Old Jewish Cemetery belonging to this unique museum. **See p.91**

❺ **Wenceslas Square** Amble through the Old Town's crooked streets to Můstek for a wander up the capital's bustling square-boulevard. **See p.101**

❻ **Dinner** At the end of a hard day's sightseeing, the beer and filling Czech dishes at the *Novoměstský pivovar* hit the spot. **See p.190**

BUDGET PRAGUE

Prague may no longer strictly be a budget destination, but you can spend time here without putting too much pressure on your wallet.

❶ **Hop on a tram** For just the price of a 32Kč ticket, tram #22 provides a top-notch sightseeing tour. **See p.23**

❷ **Malá Strana Gardens** Many of Malá Strana's gardens are free, including the Prague Castle Gardens (see p.45), the Valdštejnská zahrada (see p.60) and the Vojanovy sady (see p.61). Petřín hill (see p.66) can also be seen at no cost – if you're prepared to walk.

ABOVE CHARLES BRIDGE **RIGHT** SV MIKULÁŠ, MALÁ STRANA

❸ Lunch At a traditional *cukrárna* or bakery you can easily put together a tasty light lunch of open sandwiches (*chlebíčky*), soup and pastries for less than 150Kč. *U knofličků*, near the lower station of the Petřín funicular, is superb. **See p.176**

❹ Charles Bridge You don't need a ticket to enjoy Prague's top Gothic structure to the full. Take a good look at the statue groups as you go, but mind the dive-bombing seagulls! **See p.69**

❺ Prague's churches Almost all of the churches, including the magnificent church of sv Jakub near the Old Town Square, are free. **See p.158**

❻ Astronomical clock The Apostles' hourly show is one of the city's classic experiences. **See p.81**

❼ Dinner *Beas* (see p.177) is a vegetarian canteen where you can fill up on basmati rice and vegetable curry for a pittance. Otherwise pubs outside the city centre such as *U Houbaře* (see p.192) do cheap evening mains.

ART NOUVEAU PRAGUE

The curvaceous sculptural decoration and floral motifs of the turn-of-the-twentieth-century Art Nouveau movement had an immense effect on the art and architecture of the Czech capital. The following itinerary offers the highlights in a day.

❶ Hlavní nádraží Take the metro to Prague's main railway station, where renovation has brought the old station building back to its former glory. The *Fantova kavárna* will be a top Art Nouveau coffee stop when it reopens following a revamp. **See p.108**

❷ Grand Hotel Evropa Walk or take the metro to Wenceslas Square and the ornate *Grand Hotel Evropa*. Under renovation, it is set to reopen as a swish period-piece hotel. **See p.170**

❸ Obecní dům Prague's stellar Art Nouveau attraction is the handiwork of just about every leading Czech Art Nouveau artist of the period. The most illustrious of the lot is Alfons Mucha, who designed the stunning Primátorský sál. **See p.109**

❹ Lunch The Obecní dům is the ideal spot for an Art Nouveau lunch, either in the *Francouzská restaurace* (see p.182) or the cellar *Plzeňská restaurace* (see p.182), both of which are turn-of-the-twentieth-century masterpieces in their own right.

❺ Mucha Museum The Primátorský sál in the Obecní dům is just a sample of the amazing works produced by Alfons Mucha. Get the full picture at this superb art museum. **See p.108**

❻ Josefov Saunter through the Old Town and across the Old Town Square into the old Jewish neighbourhood of Josefov, which has the highest concentration of Art Nouveau buildings in the city centre. **See p.90**

❼ Masarykovo nábřeží Heading south from the most Legií, the embankment provides a nonstop parade of neo-Gothic and Art Nouveau mansions. Hlahol (no. 16) is the best of the lot. **See p.118**

PRAGUE TRAM

Basics

Getting there

**Unless you're coming from a neigh-
bouring European country, the quickest
and easiest way to get to Prague is by
plane. There are direct flights from just
about every European capital city, with
flight times from London just under two
hours. There are also one or two nonstop
flights from North America, though you'll
get a much wider choice – and often lower
fares – if you fly via London or another
European gateway.**

With most airlines, how much you pay depends
on how far in advance you book and how much
demand there is during that period – the earlier
you book, the cheaper the prices.

Another option, if you're travelling from Britain
or elsewhere in Europe, is to go by **train**, **bus** or **car**.
These take considerably longer than a plane and
may not work out that much cheaper, but it's
undoubtedly better for the environment.

Flights from the UK and Ireland

You can fly **direct to Prague** from many regional
airports across Britain and Ireland, including from
Bristol and Belfast, or from Dublin, Liverpool or
Birmingham. The most competitive fares are normally
with the **budget airlines** such as Smartwings and
Jet2. If you book far enough in advance or can be
flexible about your dates, you can get returns from
London to Prague for as little as £60 (taxes included
but usually extra for luggage). From Ireland, return
airfares start at around €80 return from Dublin.

Flights from the US and Canada

Delta and Czech Airlines offer **nonstop flights** from
New York to Prague. You'll get a much wider choice
of flights and ticket prices, though, if you opt for an
indirect flight with one or two changes of plane,
allowing you to depart from any number of North
American cities and travel via one of the major
European gateways.

Flying time from New York direct to Prague is
about eight hours. **Fares** depend very much on the
flexibility of the ticket and on availability, with a
New York–Prague direct return costing $1000–1500.

Flights from Australia and New Zealand

Flight times from **Australia and New Zealand** to
Prague are twenty hours or more, depending on
routes and transfer times. There's a wide variety of
routes; those touching down in southeast Asia are
the fastest and cheapest on average. Given the length
of the journey, you might be better off including a
night's stopover in your itinerary – indeed, some
airlines include one in the price of the flight.

The cheapest direct scheduled flights to London
are usually to be found on one of the Asian airlines.
Average **return fares** (including taxes) from eastern
gateways to London are Aus$1500–2000 in low
season (Oct–April), Aus$2000–2500 in high season
(May–Sept). Fares from Perth or Darwin cost around
Aus$200 less. You'll then need to add Aus$100–200
onto all these for the connecting flight to Prague.
Return fares from Auckland to London range
between NZ$2000 and NZ$3000 depending on the
season, route and carrier.

Trains

You can travel **by train** from London to Prague
overnight in around twenty hours. Fares start at
around £140 return but depend on the route you
take and how far in advance you book. To reach
Prague by train you first have to take the **Eurostar**
from London St Pancras to **Paris**. From there,
take the TGV to Zurich from where there is an
overnight sleeper to Prague arriving around 11am
the following day. Other routes go via Brussels,
Cologne and Regensburg or Munich.

Although you can crash out on the seats, it makes
sense to book a **couchette**, which costs an extra £15
one way in a six-berth compartment, rising to £25 in a
three-berth compartment. Couchettes are mixed-sex
and allow little privacy; for a bit more comfort, you

can book a bed in a single-sex two-berth **sleeper** for around £50.

Fares for continental rail travel are relatively flexible, so it's worth shopping around for the best deal, rather than taking the first offer you find. Tickets are usually valid for two months and allow as many stopovers as you want on the specified route. If you're travelling with one or more companions, you may be eligible for a further discount.

The cheapest way to book tickets is usually **online**, but you may have to use several websites to get the best deals. For more details, visit the superb website ⓦ seat61.com.

Buses

One of the cheapest ways to get to Prague is by **bus**. There are daily direct services from London's Victoria Station. Coaches tend to depart in the evening, arriving eighteen hours or so later in Prague's main bus terminal, Florenc, in the early afternoon. The journey is bearable (just about), with short breaks every three to four hours. Prices between companies vary only slightly; best value is Student Agency (see opposite), who offer a one-way ticket on their daily service for as little as 900Kč.

Driving

With two or more passengers, **driving to Prague** can work out relatively inexpensive. However, it is not the most relaxing option, unless you enjoy pounding along Belgian and German motorways for the best part of 15 hours.

Eurotunnel operates a 24-hour train service carrying vehicles and their passengers from Folkestone to Calais. At peak times, services run every ten minutes, with the journey lasting 35 minutes. Off-peak fares in the high season start at £150 return per vehicle (passengers included). The alternative is to catch one of the **ferries** between Dover and Calais/Dunkirk or Newhaven and Dieppe. Prices vary enormously but if you book in advance, summer fares can be as little as £80 return per carload. Journey times are usually around ninety minutes. If you're travelling from north of London, it might be worth taking one of the longer ferry journeys from Newcastle, Hull or Harwich. To find the cheapest fares across the Channel, check out ⓦ directferries.co.uk.

Once you've made it onto the Continent, you have some **1000km of driving** ahead of you. Theoretically, you could make it in twelve hours solid, but realistically it will take you longer. The most direct route

from Calais is via Brussels, Liège (Luik), Cologne (Köln), Frankfurt, Würzburg and Nuremberg (Nürnberg), entering the Czech Republic at the **Waidhaus–Rozvadov** border crossing. **Motorways** in Belgium and Germany are free, but within the Czech Republic you need to buy the relevant vignette (*dálniční známka*), a sticker available from all border crossings and petrol stations: a ten-day sticker costs 310Kč, a month-long one costs 440Kč. If you're travelling by car, you'll need proof of ownership and proof of third-party insurance. You also need a red warning triangle and reflective jacket in case you break down, a first-aid kit, a set of replacement bulbs and a set of replacement fuses, all of which are compulsory in the Czech Republic. From 1 November until 31 March your car must be equipped with winter tyres.

AGENTS AND OPERATORS

ČEDOK ⓦ cedok.com. Former state-owned tourist board offering flights, accommodation and package deals.

ebookers ⓦ ebookers.com. Low fares on an extensive selection of scheduled flights and package deals.

Martin Randall Travel ⓦ martinrandall.com. Small-group cultural tours, led by experts on art, archeology or music.

North South Travel ⓦ northsouthtravel.co.uk. Friendly, competitive travel agency, offering discounted fares worldwide. Profits are used to support projects in the developing world, especially the promotion of sustainable tourism.

STA Travel ⓦ statravel.com. Worldwide specialists in independent travel; also student IDs, travel insurance, car rental, rail passes, bus tickets and more. Good discounts for students and under-26s.

Trailfinders ⓦ trailfinders.com. One of the best-informed and most efficient agents for independent travellers.

Travel CUTS ⓦ travelcuts.com. Canadian youth and student travel firm.

USIT ⓦ usit.ie. Ireland's main student and youth travel specialists.

RAIL CONTACTS

Deutsche Bahn ⓦ bahn.com. Competitive discounted fares for any journey from London across Europe, with very reasonable prices for journeys passing through Germany.

Eurostar ⓦ eurostar.com. Latest fares and youth discounts (plus online booking) on the Eurostar service, plus competitive add-on fares from the rest of the UK.

Idos ⓦ idos.cz. The most widely used online timetable in the Czech Republic, giving train times across the continent.

Man in Seat 61 ⓦ seat61.com. The world's finest train website, full of useful tips and links for rail travel anywhere in the world.

National Rail ⓦ nationalrail.co.uk. First stop for details of all train travel within the UK – fares, passes, train times and delays due to engineering works.

Rail Europe ⓦ raileurope.co.uk. SNCF-owned information and ticket agent for all European passes and journeys from London. It also has an office at 193 Piccadilly, London, W1J 9EU.

Train Tours 4U Ⓦ traintours4u.co.uk. Rail specialist offering competitive prices on international tickets from the UK.

Trainseurope Ⓦ trainseurope.co.uk. Agent specializing in discounted international rail travel.

BUS CONTACTS

Busabout Ⓦ busabout.com. Busabout includes Prague (and the South Bohemian town of Český Krumlov) on its North Loop.

Eurolines UK Ⓦ eurolines.co.uk. Tickets can also be purchased from any National Express agent.

Student Agency Ⓦ studentagency.cz. Despite the name, anyone can travel with this excellent Moravia-based company, which runs a very cheap daily bus service between London and Prague.

FERRY CONTACTS

DFDS Seaways Ⓦ dfdsseaways.co.uk. Newcastle to Amsterdam and Newhaven to Dieppe.

Eurotunnel Ⓦ eurotunnel.com. Folkestone to Calais through the Tunnel.

P&O Ⓦ poferries.com. Dover to Calais and Hull to Rotterdam and Zeebrugge.

Stena Line Ⓦ stenaline.co.uk. Harwich to Hook of Holland.

Entry requirements

Citizens of the US, Canada, Australia and New Zealand need only a full **passport** to enter the Czech Republic. Most EU citizens can enter on their national ID cards and, as the Czech Republic is a Schengen country, these are rarely checked on the border (but everyone must still have valid ID with them at all times). EU citizens can stay as long as they like; US citizens, Canadians, Australians and New Zealanders can stay up to ninety days. Citizens of many other countries require a **visa**, obtainable from a Czech embassy or consulate in the country of application (see Ⓦ mvcr.cz for a list). Visa requirements change often for non-EU nationals and it is always advisable to check the current situation.

CZECH EMBASSIES ABROAD

Australia 8 Culgoa Circuit, O'Malley, Canberra ACT (Ⓣ 02 6290 1386, Ⓦ mzv.cz/canberra).

Canada 251 Cooper St, Ottawa (Ⓣ 613 562 3875, Ⓦ mzv.cz /ottawa).

Ireland 57 Northumberland Rd, Ballsbridge, Dublin (Ⓣ 01 668 1135, Ⓦ mzv.cz/Dublin).

South Africa 936 Pretorius St, Arcadia, Pretoria 0083 (Ⓣ 012 431 2380, Ⓦ mzv.cz/Pretoria).

UK 26 Kensington Palace Gardens, London (Ⓣ 020 7243 1115, Ⓦ mzv.cz/london).

US 3900 Spring of Freedom St NW, Washington DC (Ⓣ 202 274 9100, Ⓦ mzv.cz/washington).

EMBASSIES AND CONSULATES IN PRAGUE

Australia Klimentská 10, Nové Město (Ⓣ 221 729 260; metro Náměstí Republiky).

Canada Ve Struhách 2, Dejvice (Ⓣ 272 101 800, Ⓦ canada.cz; metro Hradčanská).

Ireland Tržiště 13, Malá Strana (Ⓣ 257 011 280, Ⓦ embassyofireland.cz; metro Malostranská).

New Zealand Vaclavske Namesti 11, Nové Město (Ⓣ 234 784 777; metro Můstek).

South Africa Ruská 65, Vršovice (Ⓣ 267 311 114, Ⓦ saprague.cz; metro Flora).

UK Thunovská 14, Malá Strana (Ⓣ 257 402 111, Ⓦ gov.uk; metro Malostranská).

US Tržiště 15, Malá Strana (Ⓣ 257 022 000, Ⓦ usembasy.cz; metro Malostranská).

Arrival

Prague is one of Europe's smaller capital cities, with a population of just 1.28 million. The airport lies around 10km northwest of the city centre, with only a bus link or taxi to get you into town. Both international train stations and the main bus terminal are linked to the centre by the fast and efficient metro system.

By plane

Prague's Václav Havel Airport (**Ruzyně Airport**; Ⓣ 220 111 888, Ⓦ prg.aero) is connected to the city by minibus, bus and taxi. The cheapest way to get into town is on **local bus #119** (daily 5am–midnight; every 15–20min; 20min), which stops frequently and terminates at Nádraží Veleslavín metro station. You can buy your ticket from the public transport (DP) information desk in arrivals (daily 7am–10pm), or from the nearby machines. If you're going to use public transport while in Prague, you might as well buy a pass immediately (see p.23). If you arrive between midnight and 5am, you can catch the hourly **night bus #510** to Divoká Šárka, the terminus for night tram #51, which will take you on to Národní in the centre of town. Another cheap alternative is **Linka AE** (Airport Express), a nonstop bus shuttle to Praha hlavní nádraží (daily 7am–9pm; every 30min; 60Kč).

If you're thinking of taking a **taxi** from the airport, make sure you choose the official airport taxi companies Taxi Praha (Ⓣ 220 414 414, Ⓦ taxi14007.cz) and Fix Taxi (Ⓣ 220 113 892, Ⓦ airportcars.cz), as Prague taxi drivers still have a reputation for wild overcharging. Both companies have desks at arrivals and the journey to the city centre should cost around 400–500Kč.

The metro will one day be extended as far as the airport, but this has proved a difficult project for the city to kick-start.

By train and bus

International trains arrive either at the old Art Nouveau **Praha hlavní nádraží**, on the edge of Nové Město and Vinohrady, or at the unprepossessing **Nádraží Holešovice** (Praha-Holešovice), which lies in an industrial suburb north of the city centre. At both stations you'll find exchange outlets and accommodation agencies. Both stations are on metro lines, and Hlavní nádraží is only a five-minute walk from Václavské náměstí (Wenceslas Square).

Domestic trains usually wind up at **Praha hlavní nádraží** or the central **Masarykovo nádraží** on Hybernská, a couple of blocks east of Náměstí Republiky. Slower trains and various provincial services arrive at a variety of obscure suburban stations: trains from the southwest pull into Praha-Smíchov (metro Smíchovské nádraží); trains from the east arrive at Praha-Vysočany (metro Českomoravská); trains from the west at Praha-Dejvice (metro Hradčanská); and trains from the south very occasionally rumble into Praha-Vršovice.

If you're catching a **train out of Prague**, don't leave buying your ticket until the last minute, as the queues can be slow, and make sure you check which station your train is departing from. You can buy **international train tickets** (*mezinárodní jízdenky*) at either Praha hlavní nádraží or Praha-Holešovice.

Virtually all long-distance international and domestic services terminate at Prague's main **bus terminal**, Florenc (often ÚAN Florenc in timetables; metro Florenc), on the eastern edge of Nové Město. There's a new building with clean cafés and free wi-fi, and a less impressive old part.

City transport

The centre of Prague, where most of the city's sights are concentrated, is reasonably small and best explored on foot. At some point, however, in order to cross the city quickly or reach some of the more widely dispersed attractions, you'll need to use the cheap and very efficient public transport system.

The public transport network, or **dopravní podník** (**DP**; 🌐 dpp.cz), includes the metro, trams and buses. We've included a transport system map in the Guide, and you can get a clear picture of the various lines on the city maps given out at DP offices.

Tickets and passes

Most Prague folk buy monthly passes, and to avoid having to understand the complexities of the single ticket system, you too are best off buying a **travel pass** (*časová jízdenka*) for either 24 hours (*1 den*; 110Kč) or 3 days (*3 dny*; 310Kč); no photos or ID are needed. Punch the ticket to validate it when you first use it. For a monthly (*měsíční*; 550Kč), quarterly (*čtvrtletní*; 1480Kč) or yearly (*roční*; 3650Kč) pass you need ID and a passport-sized photo. All passes are available from **DP travel information offices** (see box opposite), and the 24-hour pass is also available from ticket machines in metro stations.

Single tickets can be bought from a tobacconist (*tabák*), street kiosk, newsagent, Prague City Tourism office or any place that displays the DP sticker. If you can't find one of those outlets, you'll need to master the complicated-looking **ticket machines**, found inside all metro stations and at some bus and tram stops. Despite the multitude of buttons on the machines, for a **single ticket** (*lístek* or *jízdenka*) in the two central zones (*2 pásma*), there are just two

---

WALKING TOURS

Walking tours can cover a lot of ground in a relatively short time in Prague, showing you aspects of the city you might not notice strolling by yourself. The "free walk" concept arrived in the city a few years ago – you tip the guide at the end if you are satisfied. However paid walks given by professional guides are always a better option with smaller groups and no pressure at the end to donate.

Prague Walks ☎ 608 339 099, 🌐 praguewalks.com. Runs group and private walks including themed ambles such as a Žižkov pub tour, a Communism walk and a classical music tour. Prices start at around 500Kč per person.
Discover Prague ☎ 731 067 775, 🌐 discover-prague.com.

Operates professionally guided walks (from 300Kč) themed around the Royal Way, beer and twentieth-century history, as well as bike and segway tours. Note that segways were banned from the historical centre in 2016 so any tour using this mode of transport will steer well clear of the Old Town.

TRAVEL INFORMATION OFFICES

To get free maps (as well as to buy tickets and passes), head for the **DP** information offices:

Airport terminals Daily 7am–9pm.
Anděl metro Daily 7am–9pm.
Hradčanská metro Mon–Fri 6am–8pm, Sat 9.30am–5pm.
Main railway station (Praha hlavní nádraží) Mon–Fri 6am–10pm, Sat & Sun 7am-9pm.
Můstek metro Daily 7am–9pm.
Nádraží Veleslavín metro Mon–Fri 6am–8pm, Sat 9.30am–5pm.

basic choices. The 24Kč version (*krátkodobá*) allows you to travel for up to thirty minutes on trams, buses or metro. The 32Kč version (*základní*) is valid for ninety minutes. Discounted tickets, or *zvýhodněna*, are available for children aged 6–15; under-6s travel free. All of the above tickets are also valid on the Petřín funicular.

To buy a ticket you must press the appropriate button – press it once for one ticket, twice for two, and so on, after which you insert your money. Your change comes out with the ticket. These rather complex machines are being gradually replaced with vastly simpler touchscreen versions that are even appearing on board trams. When you enter the metro, or board a tram or bus, you must validate your ticket by placing it in one of the electronic machines to hand. There are no barriers, but rather unpleasant plain-clothes inspectors (*revizoři*) make random checks and will issue an **on-the-spot fine** of 800Kč to anyone caught without a valid ticket or pass; controllers should show you their ID (a small metal disc) and give you a receipt (*paragon*).

By metro

Prague's futuristic, Soviet-built **metro** is fast, smooth and ultraclean (daily 5am–midnight; every 2min during peak hours, every 4–10min in the evening). Its three lines intersect at various points in the city centre and the route plans are easy to follow.

Stations are fairly discreetly marked above ground with the metro logo in green (line A), yellow (line B) or red (line C). Blue line D is a work in progress and will be for several years to come. Once inside the metro, it's worth knowing that *výstup* means exit and *přestup* will lead you to one of the

connecting lines at an interchange. The digital clock at the end of the platform tells you what time it is and how long it is until the next train.

By tram

The electric **tram** (*tramvaj*) system, in operation since 1891, negotiates Prague's hills and cobbles with remarkable dexterity. Modern Škoda low-floor trams are being introduced, but much of the fleet (traditionally decked out in red and cream) dates back to the Communist era. After the metro, trams are the fastest and most efficient way of getting around (every 6–8min at peak times; every 5–15min at other times) – timetables posted at every stop (*zastávka*) list the departure times from that stop. Note that stops are often named after the side streets and not the main street along which they run. Note, too, that it is the custom for younger folk (and men of all ages) to vacate their seat when an older woman enters the carriage.

Tram #22, which runs from Vinohrady to Hradčany via the centre of town and Malá Strana, offers a good way to orientate yourself and a cheap way of sightseeing, though you should beware of pickpockets. **Night trams** (*noční tramvaje*; #51–58; roughly every 30–40min midnight–4.30am) run different routes from daytime ones; they all pass at some point along Lazarská in Nové Město where you can change.

By bus

You'll rarely need to get on a **bus** (*autobus*) within Prague itself, since most of them keep well out of the centre of town. If you're intent on visiting the zoo or staying in some of the city's more obscure suburbs (or camping in Troja), though, you may need to use them: they operate similar hours to the trams (though services are generally less frequent); route numbers are given in the text where appropriate. **Night buses** (*noční autobusy*; midnight–5am) run hourly from Náměstí Republiky.

Outside Prague, you're more likely to find yourself using buses, though timetables are designed around the needs of commuters, and tend to fizzle out at the weekend. Most services depart from suburban bus terminals in order to keep diesel-burning vehicles out of the city centre; buses to Lidice (see p.163), for example, depart from metro Dejvická. For most minor routes, simply buy your ticket from the driver; for popular long-distance routes, and for travel at peak times, it's best to book your seat in advance.

Bus **timetables** (Ⓦidos.cz) are more difficult to figure out than train ones, as there are no maps to help you out. In the detailed timetables displayed at the main bus station, each service is listed separately, so you may have to scour several time-tables before you discover when the next bus is. A better bet is to look at the departures and arrivals board. Make sure you check on which day the service runs; many run only on certain days (see box below). Minor bus stops are marked with a rusty metal sign saying *zastávka*. If you want to get off, say "*Vystupuju*"; "at the next stop" is "*na příští zastávce*".

By train

The most relaxing way to take a day-trip from Prague is by **train** (*vlak*), run, for the most part, by Czech Railways (**České dráhy** or **ČD**; ☎221 111 122, Ⓦcd.cz). Trains marked "Os" (*osobní*) are local services, which stop at just about every station; those marked "R" (*rychlík* or *spěšný*) are faster, stopping only at major towns. Fast trains are further divided, in descending order of speed, into "SC" (SuperCity) – for which you must pay a supplement – "EC" (EuroCity) or "IC" (InterCity) and "Ex" (Expres).

To buy a **ticket**, simply state your destination – return fares (*zpáteční*) are slightly less than double and two or more people travelling together get a discount (*sleva pro skupiny*).

Large train stations have a simple airport-style arrivals and departures board, which includes information on delays under the heading *zpoždění*. Many stations have poster-style displays of arrivals (*příjezd*) and departures (*odjezd*), the former on white paper, the latter on yellow, with fast trains printed in red. All but the smallest stations also have a comprehensive display of **timetables**; small stations may simply have a board with a list of departures under the title *směr* (direction) followed by a town. Note that a platform, or *nástupiště*, is usually divided into two *kolej* (tracks) on either side.

TIMETABLE ABBREVIATIONS

Czech bus timetables – and to a lesser extent train timetables – include the following crucial information:
jezdí jen v... only running on...
nejezdí v... not running on...

Followed by a date or a symbol:
Cross or "N" Sunday
"S" Saturday
Two crossed hammers Weekdays

By ferry and boat

Though few would regard them as a part of the public transport system, a handful of small summer **ferry services** (*přívoz*) on the Vltava operate between the islands and the riverbanks (daily 6am–10pm; every 30min). In the summer the PPS (*Pražská paroplavební společnost*; ☎224 930 017, Ⓦparoplavba.cz) also runs regular **boat trips** on the River Vltava from just south of Jiráskův most on Rašínovo nábřeží. Three or four boats a day in summer run to Troja (see p.144) in the northern suburbs.

The PPS also offers boat trips around Prague on board a 1930s paddle steamer. Another option is to hop aboard the much smaller boats run by Pražské Benátky/Prague-Venice (☎776 776 779, Ⓦprazske benatky.cz), which depart year round for a thirty-minute meander over to the Čertovka by Kampa island. The boats leave from the north side of Charles Bridge on the Staré Město bank.

By taxi

Taxis come in all shapes and sizes, and, theoretically at least, are relatively cheap. However, Prague taxi drivers have been known to overcharge and although the situation is slightly better than it was, say, fifteen years ago, it does still happen, and regularly. Officially, the initial **fare** on the meter should be around 40Kč plus 28Kč/km within Prague and 6Kč/min waiting time. It's far cheaper to have your hotel or pension call a taxi for you – you then qualify for a cheaper rate – than to hail one or pick one up at the taxi ranks. A cab company with one of the best reputations in the city is **AAA Taxi** (☎14014, Ⓦaaataxi.cz), which has metered taxis all over Prague, though they no longer operate as official carrier to/from the airport.

By car

Negotiating cobbles, trams and traffic jams, and trying to find somewhere to park, makes **driving** by far the worst option for getting around Prague and this mode of transport should probably be avoided by the uninitiated. If you do have to get behind the wheel, bear in mind the **rules of the road** (even if no one else does). This means driving on the right (introduced by the Nazis in 1939); sticking to the speed limit (50kph/30mph) in built-up areas; wearing a seat belt; allowing no under-12s in the front seat; and keeping headlights on at all times. Watch out for restricted streets (signalled by a blank circular sign with a red border) and give way to pedestrians crossing the road when turning left or right, even when you've been given a green light; drivers are also supposed to give way to pedestrians at zebra crossings, though they usually take some persuading. You must also give way to trams, and, if there's no safety island at a tram stop, must stop immediately and allow passengers to get on and off.

The other big nightmare is **parking**. There are three colour-coded parking zones, with pay-and-display meters: the orange zone allows you to park for up to two hours; the green zone allows you up to six hours; the recently widely extended blue zone is for locals only. Illegally parked cars will either be clamped or even towed away – if this happens, phone ☎158 to find out the worst. If you're staying outside the centre, you'll have no problems; if you're at a hotel in the centre, they'll probably have a few parking spaces reserved for guests, though whether you'll find one vacant is another matter.

By bike

Cycling is still seen as more of a leisure activity in the Czech Republic than a means of transport, and in Prague the combination of hills, cobbled streets, tram lines and noxious air is enough to put most people off. **Bike rental** is still not that widespread, but if you're determined to cycle, head for City Bike, Královdorská 5, Staré Město (☎776 180 284, Ⓦcitybike-prague.com; metro Náměstí Republiky) or Praha Bike, Dlouhá 24, Staré Město (☎732 388 880, Ⓦprahabike.cz; metro Náměstí Republiky); both also organize group rides. A bike (*kolo*) needs a half-price ticket to travel on the metro or the train (they're not allowed on trams and buses); they travel in the guard's van on trains, and in the last carriage of the metro.

The media

The full range of foreign newspapers is sold at kiosks on Wenceslas Square and elsewhere. They're generally a day old, but you can buy the European edition of the *Guardian* on the day of issue (it arrives on the streets of Prague around mid-morning), and the *International Herald Tribune* – which contains a distilled English version of the *Frankfurter Allgemeine Zeitung* – is widely available the same day.

The *Prague Post* (Ⓦpraguepost.com) is an **English-language weekly** aimed at the expat community, but good for visitors, too; it's a quality paper with strong business coverage and a useful pull-out listings section. Of the **magazines**, you'll find the best coverage of contemporary Czech politics in English in the *New Presence/Přítomnost* (Ⓦpritomnost.cz), a bilingual current affairs magazine, directly inspired by the Masaryk-funded *Přítomnost*, which was one of the leading periodicals of the First Republic. Various arty magazines run by expats have come and gone over the years; it's worth calling in at an English-language book-store (see p.208) for the latest offerings.

Czechs aren't huge news readers, but there are some (rather thin) newspapers on sale. Left-wing *Právo*, formerly the official mouthpiece of the Communist Party (when it was known as *Rudé právo* or "Red Justice"). Its chief competitor is *Mladá fronta Dnes*, former Communist youth movement paper, now a very popular right-wing daily and the mouthpiece of oligarch populist Andrej Babiš. *Lidové noviny* (the best-known *samizdat* or underground publication under the Communists and the equivalent of *The Times* under the First Republic) is now a populist centre-right daily, while the orange-coloured *Hospodářské noviny* is the Czech equivalent of the *Financial Times* or *Wall Street Journal*. The country's most popular newspaper is post-Communist *Blesk* (*Lightning*), a sensationalist tabloid with lurid colour pictures, naked women and populist politics. If all you want is yesterday's (or, more often than not, the day before yesterday's) international sports results, pick up a copy of the daily *Sport*.

TV and radio

Česká televize's two state-owned **TV channels**, ČT1 and ČT2, have both been eclipsed as far as ratings go by the commercial channel Nova (best known for its short-lived striptease weather programme) and, to a lesser extent, Prima, which exists on a diet of dubbed American imports. ČT2 is your best bet for interesting music programmes and foreign films with subtitles.

On the **radio** the state-run Český rozhlas broadcasts numerous stations including ČR1 (94.6FM), mainly made up of current affairs programmes; ČR2 (91.2FM), which features more magazine-style programming; and ČR3 Vltava (105FM), a culture and arts station that plays a fair amount of classical music. The three top commercial channels are Evropa 2 (88.2FM), Rádio Bonton (99.7FM) and Kiss 98 (98.1 FM), which dish out pop music. More interesting is Radio 1 (91.9FM), which plays a wide range of alternative music.

Festivals

Prague's annual festive calendar is surprisingly light compared with most European capitals, with just a handful of arts events, in addition to the usual religious festivities and public holidays (see p.29).

A festival calendar

JANUARY & FEBRUARY

Epiphany (Den tří králů) On Jan 6, the letters K + M + B (for Kašpar, Melichar and Baltazar) followed by the date of the new year are chalked on doorways across the capital to celebrate the "Day of the Three Kings" when the Magi came to worship Christ.

Masopust or Carnavale (Shrove Tuesday) Ⓦ **carnevale.cz.** The approach of Masopust (the Czech version of carnival) is celebrated locally in the Žižkov district of Prague, where there are five days of parties, concerts and parades; more mainstream events take place under the umbrella of Carnevale, in the city centre.

MARCH & APRIL

Easter (Velikonoce) The age-old ritual of whipping girls' calves with braided birch twigs tied together with ribbons (*pomlázky*) is still practised outside Prague. To prevent such a fate, the girls are supposed to offer the boys a coloured Easter egg and pour a bucket of cold water over them. In the city centre you'll see *pomlázky* and Easter eggs on sale, but precious little actual whipping.

Days of European Film (Dny evropského filmu) Ⓦ **eurofilmfest.cz.** Held over two weeks in April, this is the nearest Prague comes to a film festival: a fortnight of arty European films shown at various screens across the capital.

"Burning of the Witches" (pálení čarodějnic) On April 30 Halloween comes early to the Czech Republic; bonfires are lit across the country, and old brooms thrown out and burned as everyone celebrates the end of the long winter.

MAY

International Book Fair and Literary Festival Ⓦ **svetknihy.cz.** Usually held in mid-May at the Výstaviště fairgrounds (see p.26), and attracting an impressive array of international literary talent. Discussions and readings are often in English.

Prague Spring (Pražské jaro) Ⓦ **festival.cz.** Established in 1946, this is the biggest annual arts event and the country's most prestigious international music festival. It begins on or around May 12, the anniversary of Smetana's death, with a procession from his grave in Vyšehrad to the Obecní dům where the composer's *Má vlast* (*My Country*) is performed in the presence of the president, and finishes on June 2 with a rendition of Beethoven's Ninth Symphony. Tickets for the festival sell out fast.

Prague International Marathon Ⓦ **runczech.com.** Runners from more than fifty countries come to run through the cobbled streets and over Charles Bridge in mid-May.

World Roma Festival (Khamoro) Ⓦ **khamoro.cz.** International festival of Roma music, dance and film, plus seminars and workshops, in late May.

Czech Beer Festival Ⓦ **ceskypivnifestival.cz.** The Czechs test their theory that they produce the best beer in the world at this two-week event in late May. It's held at LetnáC; admission is just 100Kč for all 17 days.

JUNE & JULY

Respect Festival Ⓦ **respectfestival.cz.** World music weekend held at various venues across the city throughout June, including Akropolis and the Štvanice island.

Dance Prague (Tanec Praha) Ⓦ **tanecpraha.cz.** An established highlight of Prague's cultural calendar, this international festival of modern dance takes place throughout the city over three weeks in June.

Bohemia Jazz Fest Ⓦ **bohemiajazzfest.cz.** Held in mid-July on the city's Old Town Square, this annual jazz bash has become one of the biggest music events in the country.

SEPTEMBER & OCTOBER/NOVEMBER

Burčák Ⓦ **strunypodzimu.cz.** At the end of September for a couple of weeks, temporary stalls across the city sell the year's partially fermented new wine, known as *burčák*, a misty, heady brew.

Strings of Autumn (Struny podzimu) Held over more than two months from late September until mid November, this established event includes a mixed bag of music with a programme featuring everything from jazz to classical music, early music to world music.

DECEMBER

Christmas markets Christmas markets selling gifts, food and mulled wine (*svařák*) are set up at several places around the city in December; the biggest ones are on Wenceslas Square and the Old Town Square. Temporary ice rinks are also set up at various locations.

Eve of St Nicholas On the evening of December 5, numerous trios, dressed up as St Nicholas (*svatý Mikuláš*), an angel and a devil, roam the streets, the angel handing out sweets and fruit to children who've been good, while the devil rattles his chains and dishes out coal and potatoes to those who've been naughty. The Czech St Nicholas has white hair and a beard, and dresses not in red but in a white priest's outfit, with a bishop's mitre.

Bohuslav Martinů Festival Ⓦ **martinu.cz.** Annual festival of music in late November/early December celebrating the least-known of the big four Czech composers.

Christmas Eve (Štědrý večer) December 24 is traditionally a day of fasting, broken only when the evening star appears, signalling the beginning of the Christmas feast of carp, potato salad, schnitzel and sweetbreads. Only after the meal are the children allowed to open their presents, which miraculously appear beneath the tree, thanks not to Santa Claus, but to Baby Jesus (*Ježíšek*).

Travel essentials

Addresses

The street name is always written before the number in Prague **addresses**. The word for street (*ulice*) is either abbreviated to *ul.* or missed out altogether – Celetná ulice, for instance, is commonly known as Celetná. Other terms often abbreviated are *náměstí* (square), *třída* (avenue) and *nábřeži* (embankment), which become *nám.*, *tř.* and *nábř.* respectively. Prague is divided into numbered **postal districts** (see p.166) – these are too large to be very much help in orientation, so in this Guide we have generally opted for the names of the smaller historic districts as they appear on street signs, for example Hradčany, Nové Město, Smíchov and so on.

Children

Despite the city's generally friendly attitude to kids and babies, you'll see very few **children** in museums and galleries or in pubs, restaurants or cafés. Apart from the mirror maze (see p.67), the Railway Kingdom (see p.150), the aquarium in Výstaviště (see p.142) and the zoo (see p.144), there aren't very many attractions specifically aimed at kids. The Hrad (see p.33) and the Petřín funicular (see p.66) usually go down well, as does a ride on a tram.

Climate

Prague's **continental climate** can lead to dramatically hot summers and very cold winters. High summer (June–Aug) should be avoided, as sightseeing can be a sticky, uncomfortable affair. Late spring and early autumn are more comfortable but winters, especially January and February, can be bitter.

Costs

Accommodation can be relatively expensive in Prague and many cafés and restaurants charge prices that hover just below the central European average. That said, beer is still cheap, and museums, galleries and clubs tend to be affordable. At the bottom end of the scale, if you stay in a hostel and stick to pubs and takeaways, you could get by on a minimum of £30/US$40 a day, while if you stay in cheapish hotels and eat in inexpensive restaurants, you could manage on £50/US$60 a day.

Most sights and some cinemas and theatres offer **concessions** for senior citizens, the unemployed, full-time students and children under 16, with under-5s being admitted free almost everywhere – proof of eligibility will be required in most cases. **Youth/student ID cards** soon pay for themselves in savings. Full-time students are eligible for the International Student Identity Card or **ISIC** (Ⓦisic.org), which entitles the bearer to special air, rail and bus fares, and discounts at museums, theatres and other attractions. For people under 25 the International Youth Travel Card, or **IYTC** – available from budget travel operators, including STA (see p.20) –costs the same as the ISIC and carries the same benefits.

Crime and personal safety

The Czech papers may be full of the latest robbery, mafia shooting or gory murder out in the sticks, but the **crime rate** in Prague is quite low compared with most European or North American cities. Pickpockets are the biggest hassle, especially in summer around the most popular tourist sights and on the trams and metro. Illegal moneychangers have also reappeared in recent years.

There are two main types of **police**: the *Policie*, the national force, who wear white shirts, navy blue

AVERAGE TEMPERATURES (°C), HOURS OF SUNSHINE AND MONTHLY RAINFALL

	Jan	Feb	Mar	Apr	May	Jun	Jul	Aug	Sep	Oct	Nov	Dec
TEMPERATURE												
min °C	-4	-3	-0	2	8	11	12	13	9	3	0	-2
max °C	1	2	8	12	18	21	22	23	18	12	5	1
SUNSHINE												
hours	2	3	4	6	7	7	7	7	5	4	2	2
RAINFALL												
mm	18	17	25	35	58	68	66	64	40	30	28	22

EMERGENCY NUMBERS

Ambulance ☎ 155 or ☎ 112
Fire ☎ 150 or ☎ 112
Police ☎ 158 or ☎ 112

---

jackets and grey trousers, and the *Městská policie*, run by the Prague city authorities, who wear all-black uniforms. There are **police stations** at Jungmannovo náměstí 9 and Bartolomějská 6, Staré Město (metro Národní třída); they should, in theory, be able to provide an English-speaker.

In addition, there are various private **security guards**, who also dress in black, employed mostly by hotels, banks and supermarkets. They are allowed to carry guns, but have no powers of arrest, and you are not legally obliged to show them your ID.

Electricity

The standard continental voltage is 220 volts AC. Most European appliances should work with an adaptor for continental-style two-pin round plugs. North Americans will need this plus a transformer.

Health

EU healthcare privileges apply in the Czech Republic, so EU citizens are entitled to free emergency **hospital** treatment on production of a European Health Insurance Card or **EHIC**. The main hospital is Nemocnice na Homolce, Roentgenova 2, Motol (bus #167), which runs a 24-hour emergency service and should have English-speaking doctors. Nevertheless, all visitors would do well to take out insurance (see below) to cover themselves against medical emergencies. Many medicines are available over the counter at a **pharmacy** (*lekárna*). Most pharmacies are open Monday to Friday 7.30am to 6pm, but some open 24 hours (all pharmacies should have directions to the nearest 24hr pharmacy posted in the window) – try Palackého 5

(☎ 224 946 982) or Belgická 37 (☎ 222 513 396). For an emergency **dentist**, head for Spálená 12, Nové Město (☎ 222 924 268; metro Národní třída).

Insurance

Though Prague is a relatively safe city (see p.27) and EU healthcare privileges (see above) or your private medical plan may apply, an **insurance policy** is a wise precaution to cover against theft, loss and various other travel mishaps. If you are a non-EU citizen, it's worth checking whether you are already covered before you buy a new policy.

Internet

The vast majority of hotels and hostels – and many cafés and bars – have **free wi-fi**. All Student Agency buses (see p.21), the airport and Florenc bus station also offer free connection. Internet cafés are virtually a thing of the past across the Czech Republic.

Laundry

Most upmarket hotels offer a **laundry service** and most hostels have washing machines. Prague's expats tend to head for one of the following laundries, which all have internet access, TV, service washes, self-service machines and sometimes free tea, coffee and wi-fi: **Laundry Kings** (Dejvická 16, Dejvice; ☎ 233 343 743, ⓦ laundry.czweb.org; metro Hradčanská; Mon–Fri 6am–10pm, Sat & Sun 8am–10pm); **Prague Andy's Laundromat** (Korunní 14, Vinohrady; ☎ 222 510 180, ⓦ praguelaundromat .cz; metro Náměstí Míru; daily 8am–9pm).

Left luggage

Prague's main bus and train stations have lockers and/or a 24-hour **left-luggage** office (*úschovna zavazade*), with instructions in English.

ROUGH GUIDES TRAVEL INSURANCE

Rough Guides has teamed up with WorldNomads.com to offer great **travel insurance** deals. Policies are available to residents of over 150 countries, with cover for a wide range of adventure sports, 24hour emergency assistance, high levels of medical and evacuation cover and a stream of travel safety information. Roughguides.com users can take advantage of their policies online 24/7, from anywhere in the world – even if you're already travelling. And since plans often change when you're on the road, you can extend your policy and even claim online. Roughguides.com users who buy travel insurance with WorldNomads.com can also leave a positive footprint and donate to a community development project. For more information go to ⓦ roughguides.com/travel-insurance.

Lost property

The main train stations have **lost property** offices – look for the sign *ztráty a nálezy* – and there's a central municipal one at Karoliny Světlé 5 (Mon & Wed 8am–5.30pm, Tues & Thurs 8am–4pm, Fri 8am–2pm; ☎ 224 235 085). If you've lost your passport, get in touch with your embassy (see p.21).

Maps

The best maps of Prague are produced by Kartografie Praha, whose popular 1:20,000 booklet (*plán města*) covers the whole city and includes the tram and bus routes, too. It's easy enough to get hold of maps once you've arrived in Prague, from the tourist office, bookstores or your hotel.

Money

The currency is the **Czech crown** or *koruna česká* (abbreviated to Kč or CZK). At the time of going to press there were roughly 32Kč to the pound sterling, 27Kč to the euro and around 20Kč to the US dollar. For up-to-date exchange rates, consult ⓦ xe.com.

Notes come in 100Kč, 200Kč, 500Kč, 1000Kč and 2000Kč (and less frequently 5000Kč) denominations; **coins** as 1Kč, 2Kč, 5Kč, 10Kč, 20Kč and 50Kč. Notes of 2000Kč and 5000Kč are rarely used for transactions of less than 200Kč. Banks are open Monday to Friday from 8am to 5pm, often with a break at lunchtime. ATMs can be found across the city.

Opening hours and public holidays

Though some shops are closed on Sunday, many in the centre (including main supermarkets and department stores) remain open; it's worth noting, though, that some shops are closed on Saturday afternoons. Traditional **pubs** tend to close by 11pm and rarely serve food after 9pm, but many **restaurants** stay open until at least 11pm or midnight. There are plenty of late-night **bars** where you can continue drinking until the early hours.

We have detailed full opening hours of **museums**, **galleries** and other attractions in the Guide. Some of the more central **churches** operate in much the same way as museums and occasionally even have an entry charge. Most, however, are kept locked, with perhaps just the vestibule open, allowing you at least a glimpse of the interior, opening fully only for worship in the early morning (around 7am or 8am on weekdays, more like 10am on Sundays) and/or the evening (around 6pm or 7pm).

National **public holidays** (*Státní svátek*) have always been a potential source of contention for the Czechs. May Day, a nationwide compulsory march under the Communists, remains a public holiday, though only the skinheads, anarchists and die-hard Stalinists take to the streets nowadays. Of the other *slavné májové dny* (Glorious May Days), as they used to be known, May 5, the beginning of the 1945 Prague Uprising, was binned a long time ago, and VE Day is now celebrated as it is with the Western Allies on May 8, and not on May 9, as it was under the Communists, and still is in Russia. September 28, the feast day of the country's patron saint, St Wenceslas, is now Czech State Day. Strangely, however, October 28, the day on which the First Republic was founded in 1918, is still celebrated, despite being a "Czechoslovak" holiday (and, for a while, under the Communists, Nationalization Day).

NATIONAL HOLIDAYS

Jan 1 New Year's Day (Nový rok)
Easter Mon (Velikonoční pondělí)
May 1 May Day (Svátek práce)
May 8 VE Day (Den osvobození)
July 5 Introduction of Christianity (Den slovanských věrozvěstů Cyrila a Metoděje)
July 6 Death of Jan Hus (Den upálení mistra Jana Husa)
Sept 28 Czech State Day (Den české státnosti)
Oct 28 Foundation of the Republic (Den vzniku samostatného československého státu)
Nov 17 Battle for Freedom and Democracy Day (Den boje za svobodu a demokracii)
Dec 24 Christmas Eve (Štědrý den)
Dec 25 Christmas Day (Vánoce)
Dec 26 St Stephen's Day (Den sv Štěpana)

Phones

Most **public phones** take only phone cards (*telefonní karty*), available from post offices, tobacconists and some shops (prices vary). Best value are the **prepaid phone cards** that give you a phone number and a code to enter. There are instructions in English, and if you press the appropriate button the language on the digital read-out will change to English.

The **dialling tone** is a short pulse followed by a long one; the **ringing tone** is long and regular; **engaged** is short and rapid (not to be confused with the connecting tone, which is very short and

---

PHONING HOME FROM PRAGUE

Australia ☎0061 + area code minus zero + number.
Ireland ☎00353 + area code minus zero + number.
New Zealand ☎0064 + area code minus zero + number.
South Africa ☎00 + 27 + area code + number.
UK ☎0044 + area code minus zero + number.
US & Canada ☎001 + area code + number.

---

rapid). The standard Czech response is *prosím*; the word for "extension" is *linka*. If you have any problems, ring ☎1181 to get through to international information.

Smartphones bought for use in Europe, Australia and New Zealand should work fine, though a mobile bought for use in the US is unlikely to work unless it's a tri-band phone. Czech SIM cards can be bought from supermarkets, tobacconists and mobile phone shops for as little as 200Kč and usually come with the same amount of credit as they cost. However, the virtual abolition of roaming charges for EU phones across the EU means you can use a SIM card from another EU country as you would at home.

There are no separate **city/area codes** in the Czech Republic. To **call Prague from abroad**, use your international access code, then the code for the Czech Republic (☎420) and then the number. All Prague **phone numbers** have nine digits.

Post

Outbound **post** is pretty reliable, with letters or cards taking around five working days to Britain and Ireland, and one week to ten days to North America or Australasia. You can buy **stamps** from newsagents, tobacconists and some kiosks, as well as at post offices. Postal charges at the time of going to print were 32Kč for postcards within Europe and 37Kč to North America (check ⓦceska posta.cz for the latest).

The **main post office** (*hlavní pošta*) is at Jindřišská 14, Nové Město (daily 2am–midnight), just off Wenceslas Square; take a ticket and wait for your number to come up. There's a quieter branch at Hybernská 15 (Mon–Fri 8am–8pm, Sat 9am–1pm) next to Masarykovo train station.

Time

The Czech Republic is in **Central European Time** (CET), one hour ahead of Britain and six hours ahead of EST, with the clocks going forward in spring for summer time and back again in autumn. Generally speaking, Czechs use the **24-hour clock**.

Tipping

Tipping is normal practice in cafés, bars and restaurants, but less so in taxis. This is usually done by simply rounding up the total. For example, if the waiter tots up the bill and asks you for 127Kč, you should hand him a 200Kč note and say "take 150Kč".

Tourist information

In Prague, the main **tourist office** is **Prague City Tourism**, whose main branch is within the Staroměstská radnice on Staroměstské náměstí (daily 9am–7pm; ⓦ praguewelcome.cz). There are also offices at Rytířská 12, Staré Město (metro Můstek), on Wenceslas Square and at the airport. Prague City Tourism staff speak English, but their helpfulness varies enormously; however, they can usually answer most enquiries, organize accommodation, and sell maps, guides and theatre tickets. You will see countless green "i" signs around Prague, all of which belong to private tour companies who want to sell you something. The only official, impartial offices are those belonging to Prague City Tourism.

USEFUL WEBSITES

CzechTourism ⓦ czechtourism.com. The Czech Republic's official tourism website belonging to the national tourist board.

Expats ⓦ expats.cz. Fantastic online resource for anyone staying in Prague: visitor information, news, listings and message boards galore.

Fleet Sheet ⓦ fsfinalword.cz. Daily one-page digest of the day's Czech news, sent as an email.

Language ⓦ locallingo.com. Great resource for learning Czech online.

Living Prague ⓦ livingprague.com. Personal online guide to the city by an English expat who has been living in the capital for over two decades.

Maps ⓦ mapy.cz. This site will provide you with a thumbnail map to help you find any hotel, restaurant, pub, shop or street in Prague (and elsewhere in the Czech Republic).

Prague Experience ⓦ pragueexperience.com. Heaps of info on all aspects of staying in the Czech capital.

Prague Post ⓦ praguepost.com. Very useful for the latest news and general tourist information.

Prague TV ⓦ prague.tv. Not a TV station at all, but a great online source for listings and news about Prague, updated daily.

Radio Prague Ⓦ radio.cz. Czech Radio's informative English-language site, with updated news and weather as audio or text.

Seznam Ⓦ seznam.cz. The Czech Republic's biggest web portal.

Welcome to the Czech Republic Ⓦ czech.cz. Basic information on the country in English, and on the worldwide network of Czech centres, which promote Czech culture abroad.

Travellers with disabilities

Disabled access in the Czech Republic has a long way to go, although attitudes are changing and some legislation has been put in place. Transport is a major problem. Buses and old trams are inaccessible for wheelchairs, though many metro stations now have facilities for people with disabilities, and the two train stations (Hlavní nádraží and nádraží Holešovice) have self-operating lifts. Prague's cobbles and general lack of ramps also make life hard on the streets.

For a list of wheelchair-friendly hotels, restaurants, metro stations and so forth, order the various specialized **guidebooks** published by the Prague Wheelchair Association (Pražská organizace vozíčkářů), Benediktská 6, Staré Město (☎ 224 827 210, Ⓦ pov.cz). The association can organize an airport pick-up if you contact it well in advance, and can help with transporting wheelchairs.

Hradčany

Dominating Prague's skyline, Pražský hrad (Prague Castle) is the Czech capital's top sight and a must-see for any visitor. Widely considered the largest castle complex in the world, the Hrad is a vast built-up area occupying a promontory above the River Vltava and is, of course, a UNESCO World Heritage Site. There's been a castle of some kind here since at least the late ninth century, and since then whoever has had control of the Hrad has exercised authority over the Czech Lands. It continues to serve as the main residence of the Czech president, as well as providing a home to several museums, galleries and Prague's most important place of worship, the sky-punching Gothic Cathedral of St Vitus.

1

HRADČANY HIGHLIGHTS

St Vitus Cathedral A mishmash of styles, Prague's main church took a millennium to complete. See p.38
Zlatá ulička A lane of quaint miniature cottages where Kafka once wrote. See p.43
U černého vola Hradčany's last authentic Czech pub. See p.187
Strahov Monastery libraries Two of Prague's most ornately decorated Baroque libraries. See p.52
Šternberský palác Baroque palace housing the Czech Republic's finest collection of European art. See p.49
Villa Richter Elegant restaurant on the hillside leading to the Hrad. See p.176

The Hrad makes up much of the district of **HRADČANY**, a tiny part of the capital whose inhabitants traditionally worked for their masters in the castle. Even now, despite the odd restaurant and *pivnice* (pub) in among the palaces (and even in the Hrad itself), there's very little activity here beyond the stream of tourists who trek through the castle and the civil servants who work either for the president or the government, whose departmental tentacles spread right across Hradčany and down into neighbouring Malá Strana. This makes it a very peaceful and attractive area where it's easy to lose the crowds and enjoy a leisurely stroll.

ARRIVAL AND DEPARTURE   HRADČANY

Stretched out along a high spur above the River Vltava, Hradčany shows a suitable disdain for the public transport system. There's a choice of approaches from Malá Strana, all of which involve at least some walking, and one option of arriving by tram.

On foot From Malostranská metro station, most people take the steep short cut up the Staré zámecké schody, which brings you into the castle from its east end. A better approach, though, is further west, up the stately Zámecké schody, where you can stop and admire the view before entering the castle via the main gates. From April to October, you might consider coming up through Malá Strana's wonderful terraced gardens (see p.45), which are connected to the castle gardens (Palácové zahrady).

By tram The alternative to all this climbing is to take tram #22 from Malostranská metro station, which tackles the steep hairpin bends of Chotkova with ease, and deposits you either at the Pražský hrad stop outside the Královská zahrada (Royal Gardens) to the north of the castle, or, if you prefer, at the Pohořelec stop outside the gates of the Strahovský klášter (monastery), at the far western edge of Hradčany.

Pražský hrad (Prague Castle)

Viewed from Charles Bridge, **PRAŽSKÝ HRAD** (known to the Czechs simply as the **Hrad**) stands aloof from the rest of the city, protected not by bastions and castellated towers, but by a rather austere palatial facade – an "immense unbroken sheer blank wall", as Hilaire Belloc described it – above which rises the great (neo-)Gothic mass of St Vitus Cathedral. It's the picture-postcard image of Prague, and is spectacularly lit up at night, though for the Czechs the castle has been an object of disdain as much as admiration, its alternating fortunes mirroring the shifts in the nation's history. The golden age of Charles IV and Rudolf II and the dark ages of the later Habsburgs, interwar democracy and Stalinist terror – all have emanated from the Hrad. When the first posters appeared in December 1989 demanding "HAVEL NA HRAD" ("Václav Havel to the Castle"), they weren't asking for his re-incarceration. Havel's occupancy of the Hrad was the sign that the reins of government had finally been wrested from the Communist regime.

INFORMATION   PRAŽSKÝ HRAD

Opening hours The castle precinct is open daily (April–Oct 5am–midnight; Nov–March 6am–11pm). Most individual sights within the precinct all keep the same hours (daily: April–Oct 9am–5pm; Nov–March 9am–4pm), but there are exceptions.

Admission You can wander freely through most of the

1

streets, courtyards and gardens of the castle and watch the Changing of the Guard without a ticket. Of the paying sights, you can only visit each one once on any one ticket, but in any order; there's a handy map on the back of each ticket. The Lobkovický palác, Výstava Svatovítského pokladu and temporary exhibitions, such as those held in Císařská konírna and Jízdárna, all have different opening hours and separate admission charges.

Tickets For the sights within the castle, including the cathedral, there are two main types of ticket available. The velký okruh, or long tour (350Kč), gives you entry to most sights, including the Old Royal Palace, the Basilica of sv Jiří, the Prague Castle Picture Gallery, the Story of Prague Castle exhibition, St Vitus Cathedral, the Rosenberg Palace and the Golden Lane. The malý okruh, or short tour (250Kč), only covers the Old Royal Palace, the Basilica of sv Jiří, the Cathedral of St Vitus and the Golden Lane. Tickets to some of the individual sights are also available. Tickets are valid for two days and available from several places, including the main information centre in the third courtyard, opposite the cathedral, where you can also rent an English-language audio-guide (350Kč for 3hr).

Contact details ☎ 224 372 423, ⓦ hrad.cz, ⓦ kulturana hrade.cz.

The first courtyard

The **first courtyard** (první nádvoří), which opens onto Hradčanské náměstí, is guarded by Ignaz Platzer's bloodcurdling *Battling Titans* – two gargantuan figures, one on each of the gate piers, wielding club and dagger and about to inflict fatal blows on their respective victims. Below them usually stand a couple of impassive presidential sentries, dressed according to the weather and now protected from a photographing public by a set of railings. The hourly **Changing of the Guard** (Střídání stráží) is a fairly subdued affair, but every day at noon there's a much more elaborate ceremony, accompanied by a brass ensemble which appears at the first-floor windows to play local rock star Michal Kocáb's specially commissioned, gentle, modern fanfare.

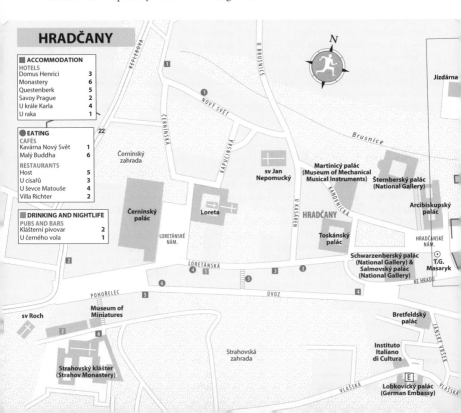

HRADČANY

■ **ACCOMMODATION**
HOTELS
Domus Henrici	3
Monastery	6
Questenberk	5
Savoy Prague	2
U krále Karla	4
U raka	1

● **EATING**
CAFÉS
Kavárna Nový Svět	1
Malý Buddha	6

RESTAURANTS
Host	5
U císařů	3
U ševce Matouše	4
Villa Richter	2

■ **DRINKING AND NIGHTLIFE**
PUBS AND BARS
Klášterní pívovar	2
U černého vola	1

The second courtyard

Passing through the early Baroque Matyášova brána (Matthias Gate), originally a freestanding triumphal arch in the middle of the long-since defunct moat, but now set into one of Pacassi's featureless wings, you reach the **second courtyard** (druhé nádvoří). A grand stairway leads to the presidential apartments in the south wing (off limits to the public), while to the north you can peek in at the beautiful Neoclassical lines of Josip Plečnik's Hall of Columns, which leads to the two grandest reception rooms in the entire complex: the **Španělský sál** (Spanish Hall) and the **Rudolfova galerie** (Rudolf Gallery) in the north wing. Sadly, both are generally out of bounds, though concerts are occasionally held in the Španělský sál. Both rooms were redecorated in the 1860s with lots of gilded chandeliers and mirrors for Emperor Franz-Joseph I's coronation as King of Bohemia, though in the end he decided not to turn up. Under the Communists, the Rudolfova galerie was the incongruous setting for Politburo meetings; Czech presidents use the Španělský sál for grand state receptions.

Encircled by monotonous Pacassi plasterwork, the courtyard itself is really just a through-route to the cathedral, with an early Baroque stone fountain, the **Kohlova kašna**, and a wrought-iron well grille the only obvious distractions. The striking gilded sculpture of a winged leopard by Bořek Šípek, at the entrance to the east wing, is a postmodern homage to Plečnik (see p.37). Occupying the southeast corner of the courtyard is Anselmo Lurago's **chapel of sv Kříž**, whose richly painted interior now houses the **Výstava Svatovítského pokladu** (St Vitus Treasury Exhibition; daily 10am–6pm) a gleaming display of monstrances, chalices, elaborately embroidered church vestments and many other treasures amassed by the cathedral since the eleventh

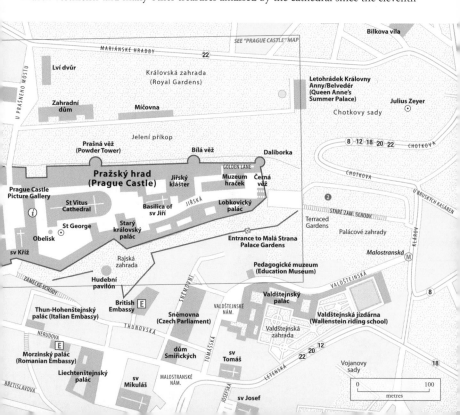

PRAŽSKÝ HRAD (PRAGUE CASTLE)

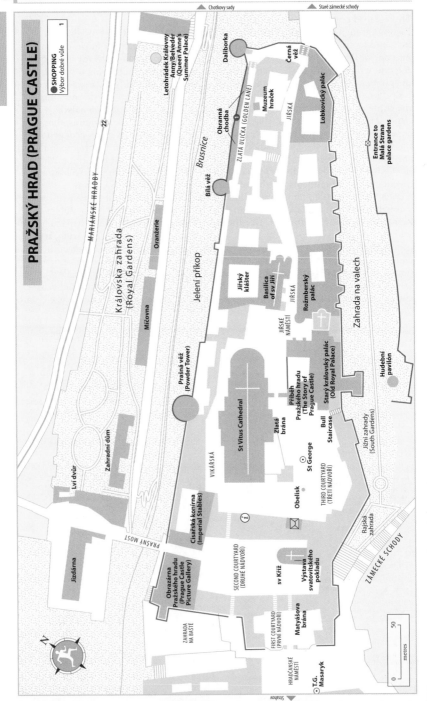

SHOPPING
Výbor dobré vůle 1

Chotkovy sady
Staré zámecké schody

Letohrádek Královny Anny/Belveder (Queen Anne's Summer Palace)
Daliborka
Černá věž
MARIÁNSKÉ HRADBY
22
Oranžérie
Brusnice
Obranná chodba
ZLATÁ ULIČKA (GOLDEN LANE)
Museum hraček
Lobkovický palác
JIŘSKÁ
Bílá věž
Entrance to Malá Strana palace gardens
Královská zahrada (Royal Gardens)
Míčovna
Jelení příkop
Jiřský klášter
Basilica of sv Jiří
Rožmberský palác
JIŘSKÉ NÁMĚSTÍ
JIŘSKÁ
Zahrada na valech
Zahradní dům
Prašná věž (Powder Tower)
St Vitus Cathedral
Zlatá brána
Příběh Pražského hradu (The Story of Prague Castle)
Starý královský palác (Old Royal Palace)
Hudební pavilón
Lví dvůr
VIKÁŘSKÁ
St George
Bull Staircase
Jižní zahrady (South Gardens)
Jizdárna
Císařská konírna (Imperial Stables)
Obelisk
THIRD COURTYARD (TŘETÍ NÁDVOŘÍ)
Rajská zahrada
ZÁMECKÉ SCHODY
PRAŠNÝ MOST
SECOND COURTYARD (DRUHÉ NÁDVOŘÍ)
sv Kříž
Výstava svatovítského pokladu
Obrazárna Pražského hradu (Prague Castle Picture Gallery)
ZAHRADA NA BAŠTĚ
FIRST COURTYARD (PRVNÍ NÁDVOŘÍ)
Matyášova brána
HRADČANSKÉ NÁMĚSTÍ
T.G. Masaryk
Strahov

N

0   50
metres

PLEČNIK: POSTMODERN BEFORE HIS TIME

1

Born in Ljubljana, **Josip Plečnik** (1872–1957) graduated in carpentry and furniture design from his secondary school in Graz before studying under the great Viennese architect Otto Wagner at the Viennese Academy of Fine Arts. He moved to Prague in 1911 and was appointed chief architect to Prague Castle shortly after the foundation of the First Republic. Despite having the backing of the leading Czech architect Jan Kotěra, and of President Masaryk himself, controversy surrounded him as soon as the appointment was announced; his non-Czech background and his quirky, eclectic style placed him at odds with the architectural establishment of the day. In fact, it wasn't until thirty years after his death, following a major retrospective exhibition at the Pompidou in Paris in 1986, that his work was brought to a wider audience. In the 1990s, Plečnik's style, which happily borrows elements from any number of genres from Classical to Assyrian architecture, proved to be an inspiration to a new generation of postmodern architects.

Plečnik's most conspicuous contributions to the castle are the **fir-tree flag poles** in the first courtyard and the granite obelisk in the third courtyard, but his light-hearted touch can be seen throughout the Hrad and its gardens: check out the jokey palm tree with roped-on copper leaves outside the Jízdárna; the **Bull Staircase**, which leads down to the Zahrada na valech; or the impressive **Sloupová síň** (Hall of Columns), which contains the stairs going up to the **Španělský sál**, and can be peeked at through the glass doors between the first and second courtyards. Sadly, much of Plečnik's work – in particular the president's private apartments – remains hidden from public view.

century. The most interesting exhibit is probably Charles IV's gold reliquary cross in which a piece of the Holy Cross and a thorn from Christ's crown of thorns were kept. On the opposite side of the courtyard are the former **Císařská konírna** (Imperial Stables), which still boast their original, magnificent Renaissance vaulting dating from the reign of Rudolf II, and are now used to house temporary exhibitions.

Obrazárna Pražského hradu (Prague Castle Picture Gallery)

Daily: April–Oct 9am–5pm; Nov–March 9am–4pm • 100Kč, or included in the velký okruh ticket (see p.34) • ☎ 224 373 531, Ⓦ kulturanahrade.cz

Remnants of the imperial collection, begun by the Habsburg Emperor Rudolf II (see box, p.44), are housed in the five rooms of the **Obrazárna Pražského hradu**, on the north side of the second courtyard. However, the best of what Rudolf amassed was either taken as booty by the marauding Saxons and Swedes or sold off by his successors. Of the many surreal portraits by **Giuseppe Arcimboldo** that Rudolf once owned, only one now remains in Prague: *Vertumnus* (Autumn), a portrait of Rudolf himself as a collage of fruit, with his eyes as cherries, cheeks as apples and hair as grapes. The rest of the collection is patchy, but it does contain one or two masterpieces, and visiting the gallery is a great way to escape the castle crowds.

In the first room, Heintz the Elder, one of Rudolf's many court painters, provides an unusually upbeat take on the Last Judgement, with a party atmosphere prevailing. The illusionist triple portrait of Rudolf (when viewed from the left), and his Habsburg predecessors (when viewed from the right), by Paulus Roy, is representative of the sort of tricksy work that appealed to the emperor. There are other good royal portraits here, and in the adjacent room, including several by **Cranach the Elder** and one by **Holbein** of Lady Vaux, wife of a poet from the court of Henry VIII.

Immediately down the stairs is one of the collection's finest paintings, **Rubens**' richly coloured *Assembly of the Gods at Olympus*, featuring a typically voluptuous Venus and a slightly fazed Jupiter. Elsewhere, there's an early, very beautiful *Young Woman at her Toilet* by **Titian**. **Veronese**'s best offering is his portrait of Jakob König, a German art dealer in Venice who worked for Rudolf II among others, and who was also a personal friend of the artist. Look out, too, for **Tintoretto**'s *Flagellation of Christ*, a late work in which the artist makes very effective and dramatic use of light, and the bust of Rudolf II by **Adriaen de Vries**, which rather unflatteringly emphasizes the Habsburg line's protruding lower lip.

1

TWO CASTLE ARCHITECTS

The site of today's Prague Castle has been successively built on since the Přemyslid princes erected the first castle here in the ninth century, but two architects in particular bear responsibility for its appearance today. The first is **Nicolò Pacassi**, court architect to Empress Maria Theresa (1740–80), whose austere restorations went hand in hand with the deliberate running down of the Hrad until it was little more than an administrative barracks. For the Czechs, his grey-green eighteenth-century cover-up, which hides a variety of much older buildings, is unforgivable. Less apparent, though no less controversial, is the hand of **Josip Plečnik** (see box, p.37), the Slovene architect who was commissioned by T.G. Masaryk, president of the newly founded Czechoslovak Republic, to restore and modernize the castle in his distinctive style in the 1920s. Most of his work can be found in the interior of the building, primarily in the state rooms where the public is not normally permitted, though his rather incongruous early twentieth-century features do interrupt Pacassi's bland facades at various points.

St Vitus Cathedral

April–Oct Mon–Sat 9am–5pm, Sun noon–5pm; Nov–Feb Mon–Sat 9am–4pm, Sun noon–5pm • Accessible only with Prague Castle tickets (see p.34) • Ⓦ katedralasvatehovita.cz

St Vitus Cathedral, the nation's largest, is squeezed so tightly into the Hrad's third courtyard that it's impossible to get an overall impression of this chaotic edifice, never mind a decent photograph (tourists often lie down on the ground in an attempt to fit the building into their viewfinders). Its asymmetrical appearance is the product of a long and chequered history, for although the foundation stone was laid in 1344, the cathedral was not completed until 1929 – exactly one thousand years after the death of Bohemia's most famous patron saint, Wenceslas.

Brief history

The site of today's cathedral was originally a sacrificial altar to the heathen fertility god **Svantovit**, which partly explains why the first church, founded in 929 by Prince Václav, was dedicated to St Vitus (svatý Vít). Vitus allegedly exorcized the Emperor Diocletian's son and was thereafter known as the patron saint of epileptics and of sufferers from the convulsive disorder Sydenham's chorea (hence the popular name of the illness, St Vitus' dance). The inspiration for the medieval cathedral came from **Emperor Charles IV** (1346–78), who, while still only heir to the throne, not only wangled an independent archbishopric for Prague, but also managed to gather together the relics of St Vitus.

Inspired by the cathedral at Narbonne in France, Charles commissioned the Frenchman **Matthias of Arras** to start work on a similar structure. Matthias died eight years into the job in 1352, with the cathedral barely started, so Charles summoned **Peter Parler** (Petr Parléř in Czech), a gifted 23-year-old from a family of great German masons, to continue the work. For the next 46 years, Parler imprinted his slightly flashier, more inventive *SonderGotik* ("Unusual Gothic") style on the city, but the cathedral advanced no further than the construction of the choir and the south transept before his death in 1399.

Little significant work was carried out during the next four centuries and the half-built cathedral became a highly visible symbol of the Czechs' frustrated aspirations to nationhood. Not until the Czech national revival, or *národní obrození*, of the nineteenth century did building begin again in earnest, with the foundation, in 1859, of the **Union for the Completion of the Cathedral**. A succession of architects, including the arch-neo-Gothicizer Josef Mocker and later Kamil Hilbert, oversaw the completion of the entire west end and, with the help of countless other Czech artists and sculptors, the building was transformed into a treasure-trove of Czech artistic expression. The cathedral was finally given an official opening ceremony in 1929, though work, in fact, continued right up to and beyond World War II.

The exterior

Prague's soot-laden air has made it harder to differentiate between the two building periods. Close inspection, however, reveals that the **western facade**, including the twin spires, sports the rigorous if unimaginative work of the neo-Gothic restorers (their besuited portraits can be found below the rose window), while the **eastern section** – best viewed from the Belvedere – shows the cathedral's original Gothic roots. The south door, known as the Zlatá brána (see p.41), is also pure Parler. Oddly then, it's above the south door that the cathedral's tallest steeple reveals the most conspicuous stylistic join: Pacassi's Baroque topping resting absurdly on a Renaissance parapet of light stone, which is itself glued onto the blackened body of the original squat Gothic tower – a far cry indeed from the commanding steeple envisaged by Charles IV.

The nave

It's difficult not to be impressed by the sheer height of the cathedral **nave**. This is the newest part of the building and, consequently, is adorned with primarily twentieth-century furnishings. The most arresting of these are the modern **stained-glass windows**, which on sunny days send shafts of rainbow light into the nave. The effect is stunning, though entirely out of keeping with Parler's original concept, which was to have almost exclusively Gothic clear-glass windows. The most unusual windows are those by František Kysela, which look as though they have been shattered into hundreds of tiny pieces, a mosaic-like technique used to brilliant effect in the kaleidoscopic rose window over the west door with its *Creation of the World* (1921). Another great window is Max Švabinský's *Day of Judgement* from 1939, which stars the Archangel Michael in green, jewel-encrusted armour brandishing a blood-red sword. Portraits of various Czech rulers feature among the chosen ones; the damned, meanwhile, are being thrown headlong into Hell's lava flow.

In keeping with its secular nature, two of the works from the time of the First Republic were paid for by financial institutions. Arguably the most famous – the *Cyril and Methodius* window in the third chapel in the north wall – was commissioned from none other than Art Nouveau artist **Alfons Mucha** by the Banka Slavie, while on the opposite side of the nave, the window *Those Who Sow in Tears Shall Reap in Joy* was sponsored by a Prague insurance company.

One of the most striking later additions to the cathedral is František Bílek's **wooden altar**, in the north aisle; its anguished portrait of Christ on the cross breaks free of the neo-Gothic strictures that hamper other works inside.

The chancel

There's a one-way system in the **chancel**, so head off to the north choir aisle. Following the ambulatory round, make sure you check out the high-relief seventeenth-century wooden panelling between the arcading on the right, which glories in the flight of the "Winter King", Frederick of the Palatinate (he's depicted crossing the Charles Bridge), following the disastrous Battle of Bílá hora in 1620. The remains of various early Czech rulers are scattered throughout the side chapels, most notably those of Přemysl Otakar I and II, in the Saxon Chapel (the fifth one along), whose limestone tombs are the work of Peter Parler and his workshop; you can also pay your respects to Rudolf II's internal organs, buried in the chapel vault.

Causing a tourist traffic jam slap bang in the middle of the ambulatory, close to the Saxon Chapel, is the perfect Baroque answer to the medieval chapel of sv Václav, the **Tomb of sv Jan of Nepomuk**, plonked here in 1736. It's a work of grotesque excess, designed by Johann Bernhard Fischer von Erlach's son, Johann Michael, and sculpted in solid silver with free-flying angels holding up the heavy drapery of the baldachin. On the lid of the tomb, back-to-back with Jan of Nepomuk himself, a cherub points to the martyr's severed tongue (see box, p.72). The tomb of St Adalbert (sv Vojtěch), one of the four patron saints of Bohemia, lies in humble contrast opposite.

1

GOOD KING WENCESLAS

There's very little substance to the story related in the nineteenth-century English Christmas carol, *Good King Wenceslas*, by J.M. Neale, itself a reworking of the medieval spring song *Tempus adest floridum*. For a start, **Václav** was only a duke and never a king (though he did become a saint); he wasn't even that "good", except in comparison with the rest of his family; Prague's St Agnes fountain, by which "yonder peasant" dwelt, wasn't built until the thirteenth century; and he was killed a good three months before the Feast of Stephen (Boxing Day) – the traditional day for giving to the poor, hence the narrative of the carol.

Born in 907, Václav inherited his title at the tender age of 13. His Christian grandmother, **Ludmila**, was appointed regent in preference to Drahomíra, his pagan mother, who subsequently had Ludmila murdered in a fit of jealousy in 921. On coming of age in 925, Václav became duke in his own right and took a vow of celibacy, intent on promoting Christianity throughout the dukedom. Even so, the local Christians didn't take to him, and when he began making conciliatory overtures to the neighbouring Germans, they persuaded his pagan younger brother, **Boleslav the Cruel**, to do away with him. On September 20, 929, Václav was stabbed to death by Boleslav at the entrance to a church in the Bohemian town of Stará Boleslav. The cult of the righteous king spread rapidly across Bohemia and Václav became one of the four patron saints of the Czech Lands, the other three being St Ludmila, St Adalbert (sv Vojtěch) and St Procopius (sv Prokop).

Between the tomb of sv Jan of Nepomuk and the chapel of sv Václav, Bohemia's one and only Polish ruler, Vladislav Jagiello, built a **Royal Oratory**, connected to his bedroom in the royal palace by a covered bridge. The balustrade sports heraldic shields from Bohemia's (at the time) quite considerable lands, while the hanging vault is smothered in an unusual branch-like decoration, courtesy of Benedikt Ried, the German mason appointed by Vladislav Jagiello as his court architect. To the left, the statue of a miner is a reminder of just how important Kutná Hora's silver mines were in funding such artistic ventures.

Chapel of sv Václav

Of the cathedral's 22 side chapels, the elaborate **Chapel of sv Václav**, by the south door, is by far the main attraction. Although officially dedicated to St Vitus, spiritually the cathedral belongs as much to the Přemyslid prince Václav, or Wenceslas, of "Good King" fame (see box above), the country's patron saint, who was killed by his pagan brother, Boleslav the Cruel. Ten years later, in 939, Boleslav repented, converted and apparently transferred his brother's remains to this very spot. Charles, who was keen to promote the cult of Wenceslas in order to cement his own Luxembourgeois dynasty's rather tenuous claim to the Bohemian throne (though actually he was a half-Přemyslid from his mother's line), had Peter Parler build the present chapel on top of the original grave; the lion's head **door-ring** set into the north door is said to be the one to which Václav clung before being killed. The chapel's rich, almost Byzantine, decoration is like the inside of a jewel casket: the gilded walls are inlaid with approximately 1372 semiprecious Bohemian stones (corresponding to the year of its creation and symbolizing the New Jerusalem from the Book of Revelation – Charles IV loved this kind of numerical symbolism), set around ethereal fourteenth-century frescoes of the Passion; meanwhile, the tragedy of Wenceslas unfolds above the cornice in the later paintings of the Litoměřice school, dating from 1509.

Though a dazzling testament to the golden age of Charles IV's reign, it's not just the chapel's artistic merit that draws visitors. A door in the south wall gives access to a staircase leading to the coronation chamber (very rarely open to the public), which houses the **Bohemian crown jewels**, including the gold crown of St Wenceslas, studded with some of the largest sapphires in the world. Closed to the public since 1867, the door is secured by seven different locks, the keys kept by seven different people, starting with the president himself – like the seven seals of the holy scroll from Revelation. The tight security is partly to prevent any pretenders to the throne trying on the headgear, an allegedly fatal act: the Nazi *Reichsprotektor* Reinhard Heydrich tried it, only to suffer the inevitable consequences (see box, p.119). Replicas of the crown jewels are on display in the Old Royal Palace (see p.41) and occasionally at other locations within the Hrad.

Imperial Mausoleum, Royal Crypt and Great Tower

Great Tower Daily 10am–6pm • 150Kč – not included in Prague Castle tickets price

It's worth taking a look at the sixteenth-century marble **Imperial Mausoleum**, situated in the centre of the choir and surrounded by a fine Renaissance grille on which numerous cherubs are irreverently larking about. It was commissioned by Rudolf II and contains the remains of his grandfather Ferdinand I, his Polish grandmother and his father Maximilian II, the first Habsburgs to wear the Bohemian crown. Unfortunately the tomb is effectively roped off and difficult to appreciate from afar.

Rudolf himself rests beneath them, in one of the two pewter coffins in the somewhat cramped **Royal Crypt** (Královská hrobka), whose entrance is beside the Royal Oratory. Rudolf's coffin (at the back, in the centre) features yet more cherubs, brandishing quills, while the one to the right contains the remains of Maria Amelia, daughter of the Empress Maria Theresa. A number of other Czech kings and queens are buried here, too, reinterred in incongruously modern 1930s sarcophagi, among them the Czechs' favourite King George of Poděbrady, Charles IV and, sharing a single sarcophagus, all four of his wives. The exit from the crypt brings you out in the centre of the nave.

For great views over the castle and the city, climb the gruelling 287 steps of the **Great Tower** (věž), the entrance to which is in the south aisle.

The third courtyard

The Hrad's **third courtyard** (třetí nádvoří) is ripe with examples of Pacassi's tedious plastercraft and cookie-cutter windows. Here Plečnik's granite **monolith** is, in fact, a stunted and unfinished obelisk, originally designed to complement the granite bowl in the Jižní zahrady (South Gardens). Close by is a replica fourteenth-century **bronze statue** and fountain, executed by a couple of Transylvanian Saxon sculptors, depicting a diminutive St George astride a disturbingly large horse (actually two hundred years younger than the rest of the ensemble), slaying an extremely puny dragon – the original is in Old Royal Palace (see p.41).

Also in the third courtyard is Parler's **Zlatá brána** (Golden Gate), decorated with a remarkable fourteenth-century mosaic of the Last Judgement, which has been restored to reveal something of its original, rich colouring – it remains to be seen how it fares in Prague's polluted air. For the moment, you can clearly see the angels helping the dead out of their tombs, and the devils dragging off the wicked by a golden rope towards the red flames of Hell. On the opposite side of the courtyard is Plečnik's **Bull Staircase**, which leads down to the Jižní zahrady, or South Gardens (see p.45).

Starý královský palác (Old Royal Palace)

Daily: April–Oct 9am–5pm; Nov–March 9am–4pm • Accessible only with Prague Castle tickets (see p.34)

On the east side of the castle's third courtyard, just across from the cathedral's Zlatá brána, the **Starý královský palác** was home to the princes and kings of Bohemia from the eleventh to the sixteenth century. It's a multi-tiered sandwich of royal apartments, built one on top of the other by successive generations, but left largely unfurnished and unused for the past three centuries. The original Romanesque palace of Soběslav I now forms the cellars of the present building, above which Charles IV built his own Gothic chambers; these days you enter at the third and top floor, built at the end of the fifteenth century.

1

THE SECOND DEFENESTRATION

After almost two centuries of uneasy coexistence between Catholics and Protestants, matters came to a head over the succession to the throne of the Habsburg archduke Ferdinand, a notoriously intolerant Catholic. On **May 23, 1618**, a posse of more than one hundred Protestant nobles, led by Count Thurn, marched to the chancellery for a showdown with **Jaroslav Bořita z Martinic** and **Vilém Slavata**, the two Catholic governors appointed by Ferdinand I. After a "stormy discussion", the two councillors (and their personal secretary, Filip Fabricius) were thrown out of the window. As a contemporaneous historian recounted: "No mercy was granted them and they were both thrown dressed in their cloaks with their rapiers and decoration head first out of the western window into a moat beneath the palace. They loudly screamed ach, ach, oweh! and attempted to hold onto the narrow window-ledge, but Thurn beat their knuckles with the hilt of his sword until they were both obliged to let go." All three survived the fall, landing in a medieval dung heap below, but the event is generally regarded as the lighting of the blue touch paper of the Thirty Years' war.

Vladislavský sál (Vladislav Hall)

Immediately beyond the antechamber is the bare expanse of the cavernous **Vladislavský sál**, the work of Benedikt Ried. Thought to have been the world's largest secular indoor space when newly built in 1502, it displays some remarkable, sweeping rib vaulting that forms floral patterns on the ceiling, the petals reaching almost to the floor. It was here that the early Bohemian kings were elected, and since 1918 every president from Masaryk onwards has been sworn into office in the hall. In medieval times, the space was also the backdrop for balls, banquets, markets, feasts and jousting tournaments, which explains the ramp-like **Riders' Staircase** in the north wing (now the exit). At the far end of the hall, to the right, there's an outdoor **viewing platform** (closed in winter), from which you can enjoy one of the best views across the city. You can also look down onto the chapel of **Všech svatých**, which Parler added to Charles IV's palace, but which had to be rebuilt after the 1541 fire, and has since been Baroqueified. The only interest here is in the remains of the Czech patron saint, Prokop (Procopius), in an eighteenth-century wooden tomb by the north wall.

   In the southwest corner of the hall, you can gain access to the **Bohemian Chancellery** (Česká kancelář), scene of Prague's **second defenestration** (see box above). On the other side of the Vladislavský sál, to the right of the Riders' Staircase, a door leads into the vaulted room of the **Diet**, whose (purely decorative) ribs imitate those of the main hall. The room is laid out as if for a seventeenth-century session of the Diet: the king on his throne, the archbishop to his right, the judiciary to his left, the nobility facing him, and representatives from towns across Bohemia (with just one collective vote) confined to the gallery by the window. However, the main attraction is the case containing replicas of the Czech **crown jewels**, which usually stands here. A staircase to the left of the Riders' Staircase takes you up to the sparsely furnished rooms of the New Land Rolls, whose walls are tattooed with coats of arms.

Příběh Pražského hradu (The Story of Prague Castle)

Daily: April–Oct 9am–5pm; Nov–March 9am–4pm • 140Kč, or included in the velký okruh ticket (see p.34) • Ⓦ pribeh-hradu.cz

A slightly longwinded but engaging exhibition, **The Story of Prague Castle** is housed in the palace's subterranean Gothic and Romanesque chambers. Things kick off in the classically chronological Eastern European fashion with dusty mammoth bones and prehistoric finds that prove the castle promontory has been inhabited for at least five thousand years. Things then take on a more thematic tone with one or two exceptional items, such as the Vyšehrad Codex, an illuminated manuscript made for the coronation of Vratislav II, first king of Bohemia, in 1086, and the zlatá bula Sicilská (Golden Bull of Sicily), a decree issued by the Holy Roman Emperor in 1212, which made the title of Czech king hereditary. Also look out for the section on King Otakar Přemysl II,

1

a monarch many Czechs regard as their greatest home-grown ruler (as opposed to the foreign Charles IV), the historically charged chain mail and helmet that may have belonged to sv Václav, the grave robes of several Přemyslids and the very impressive grave jewels of the Habsburgs.

Sv Jiří
Daily: April–Oct 9am–5pm; Nov–March 9am–4pm • Accessible only with Prague Castle tickets (see p.34)

Don't be fooled by the russet-red Baroque facade of the **Basilica of sv Jiří**, which dominates Jiřské náměstí; inside you'll discover one of Prague's most beautiful Romanesque building, meticulously scrubbed clean and restored to re-create something like the honey-coloured stone basilica that replaced the original tenth-century church in 1173. The double staircase to the chancel, a rather conspicuous late Baroque addition, now provides a perfect stage for chamber music concerts. The choir vault contains a rare early thirteenth-century painting of the New Jerusalem from Revelation – not to be confused with the very patchy sixteenth-century painting on the apse – while to the right of the chancel, only partially visible, are sixteenth-century frescoes of the **burial chapel of sv Ludmila**, grandmother of St Wenceslas, who was murdered by her daughter-in-law in 921 (see box, p.40), thus becoming Bohemia's first Christian martyr and saint. There's a replica of the recumbent Ludmila, which you can inspect at close quarters, in the south aisle. Also worth a peek is the Romanesque crypt, beneath the choir, which contains a macabre sixteenth-century green wax statue of Vanity, whose shrouded, skeletal body is crawling with snakes and lizards.

Zlatá ulička (Golden Lane)
Daily: April–Oct 9am–5pm; Nov–March 9am–4pm • Accessible only with Prague Castle tickets (see p.34)

As you head away from the basilica along Jiřská, a small lane on the left leads to the **Zlatá ulička**, a seemingly blind alley of miniature cottages in pastel colours, built in the sixteenth century for the 24 members of Rudolf II's castle guard. The contrast in scale with the rest of the Hrad makes this by far the most popular sight in the entire complex, and during the day, at least, the whole street is mobbed. The lane takes its name from the goldsmiths who followed (and modified the buildings) a century later. By the nineteenth century, it had become a slum, attracting artists and craftsmen, its two most famous inhabitants being Jaroslav Seifert, the Czech Nobel-prize-winning poet, and **Franz Kafka**. Kafka's youngest sister, Ottla, rented no. 22, and during the winter of 1916 he came here in the evenings to write short stories. Finally, in 1951, the Communists kicked out the remaining residents and turned most of the houses into souvenir shops for tourists. The souvenir shops are now morphing into a kind of sanitized open-air museum with mocked-up period interiors – no. 27 is a herbalist's cottage, no. 26 once again belongs to a seamstress, no. 16 is now a Renaissance-era tavern and no. 15 a goldsmith's workshop. However the most fascinating interior is that of no. 12, a dwelling that once belonged to cinematographer Joseph Kazda, where between 1948 and 1952 an art society (whose members included Jan Werich and Jiří Trnka) met for film screenings. The tiny **cinema** here shows a loop of Kazda's silent black-and-white footage of Prague.

Obranná chodba, Bílá věž and Daliborka

At 24 Zlatá ulička, you can climb a flight of stairs to the **Obranná chodba** (defensive corridor), which is lined with wooden shields, suits of armour and period costumes. The **Bílá věž** (White Tower), at the western end of the corridor, was the city's main prison from Rudolf's reign onwards – a reconstructed torture chamber underlines the fact. Edward Kelley, the English alchemist, was locked up here by Rudolf for failing to turn base metal into gold, while the emperor's treasurer hanged himself by his gold cord on the treasury keys after being accused of embezzlement.

1

RUDOLF II – ALCHEMY, ASTROLOGY AND ART

In 1583 **Emperor Rudolf II** (r. 1576–1611) switched the imperial court from Vienna to Prague. This was to be the first and last occasion in which Prague would hold centre stage in the Habsburg Empire, and as such is seen as something of a second golden age for the city (the first being under Emperor Charles IV). Bad-tempered, paranoid and probably insane, Rudolf had little interest in the affairs of state – instead, he holed up in the Hrad and indulged his personal passions of alchemy, astrology and art. Thus, Rudolfine Prague played host to an impressive array of international artists, including the idiosyncratic **Giuseppe Arcimboldo**, whose surreal portrait heads were composed entirely of objects. The astronomers **Johannes Kepler** and **Tycho Brahe** were summoned to Rudolf's court to chart the planetary movements and assuage Rudolf's superstitions, and the English alchemists **Edward Kelley** and **John Dee** were employed in order to discover the secret of the philosopher's stone, the mythical substance that would transmute base metal into gold.

Accompanied by his **pet African lion**, Otakar, Rudolf spent less and less time in public, hiding out in the Hrad, where he "loved to paint, weave and dabble in inlaying and watchmaking", according to novelist Angelo Maria Ripellino. With the Turks rapidly approaching the gates of Vienna, Rudolf spent his days amassing exotic curios for his strange and vast **Kunst- und Wunderkammer**, which contained such items as "two nails from Noah's Ark…a lump of clay out of which God formed Adam…and large mandrake roots in the shape of little men reclining on soft velvet cushions in small cases resembling doll beds". Though he sired numerous bastards he refused to marry, since he had been warned in a horoscope that a legitimate heir would rob him of the throne. He was also especially wary of the numerous religious orders that inhabited Prague at the time, having been warned in another horoscope that he would be killed by a monk. In the end, he was relieved of his throne by his younger brother, **Matthias**, in 1611, and died the following year, the day after the death of his beloved lion.

In the opposite direction, the **Daliborka** tower, once another miserable place of imprisonment, is now packed with various instruments of torture. The tower is named for its first prisoner, the young Czech noble Dalibor z Kozojed, accused of supporting a peasants' revolt at the beginning of the fifteenth century. According to legend, he learned to play the violin while imprisoned here, and his music could be heard all over the castle until his execution in 1498 – a tale that inspired Smetana's opera *Dalibor*.

Prašná věž (Powder Tower)

Vikářská • Daily: April–Oct 9am–5pm; Nov–March 9am–4pm • 70Kč

The **Prašná věž** or Mihulka, on Vikářská, the street that runs along the north side of the cathedral, once served as the workshop of gunsmith and bell-founder Tomáš Jaroš. The tower's original name comes from the lamprey (*mihule*), an eel-like fish supposedly bred here for royal consumption, though it's actually more noteworthy as the place where Rudolf's team of alchemists (including Kelley) were put to work trying to discover the secret of the philosopher's stone (see box above). The tower now houses an exhibition on the **Hradní stráž** (Castle Guard), which was established in 1918. Due to the vicissitudes of Czech history, the guards' uniforms have changed numerous times since they first went on duty in the Czechoslovak Legion in 1918.

Rožmberský palác

Jiřská • Daily: April–Oct 9am–5pm; Nov–March 9am–4pm • Accessible only with the velký okruh ticket (see p.34)

For the first time in its history, the **Rožmberský palác** is now open to the public, having been in the hands of the Ministry of the Interior since 1918. It was built by the powerful Rožmberk family in the sixteenth century; in 1600 Rudolf II gained possession in exchange for what is now the Schwarzenberský palác on Hradčanské náměstí (see p.48). The Holy Trinity Chapel, with its wonderful trompe l'oeil frescoes, survives from those days, but the rest of the rooms have been decked out with period furniture to evoke the period from 1753, when the palace became the Institute of Noblewomen (Ústav šlechtičen), a sort of retirement home for aristocratic ladies founded by Empress Maria Theresa. However, the wonderful views from the windows over the Vltava bridges somewhat steal the show.

Lobkovický palác
Jiřská 3 • Daily 10am–6pm; classical concerts 1pm • 275Kč • ☎ 233 312 925, ⓦ lobkowicz.com

The **Lobkovický palác** was appropriated from the aristocratic Lobkowicz family in 1939 and again in 1948 before being handed back in 2002. It now displays an impressive selection of the family's prize possessions (with audio-guide accompaniment by US-born William Lobkowicz himself), including an armoury and a vast art collection. Among them are a portrait of the 4-year-old Infanta Margarita Teresa (possibly by Velázquez), niece and first wife of Emperor Leopold I. The family has a long history of musical patronage (most notably of Beethoven, who dedicated two of his symphonies to the seventh prince), and the original working manuscripts by Mozart and Beethoven on show are pretty impressive. Other highlights include Pieter Brueghel the Elder's sublime *Haymaking* from the artist's famous cycle of seasons, and two views of London by Canaletto. There's a decent **café** in the courtyard and classical music **concerts** held daily at 1pm in the Baroque concert hall (tickets (390–490Kč are available online or from the desk situated near the café).

The Castle Gardens
Daily: April & Oct 10am–6pm; May & Sept 10am–7pm; June & July 10am–9pm; Aug 10am–8pm • Free

The **Castle Gardens** are among the city's loveliest, particularly in terms of views. The Jižní zahrady (South Gardens) enjoy wonderful vistas over the city and link up the terraced gardens of Malá Strana (see p.55), while the Královská zahrada (Royal Gardens) allow a better view of the cathedral and the Vltava's bridges.

Jižní zahrady (South Gardens)
For a superlative view over the city – not to mention a chance to inspect some of Plečnik's quirky additions to the castle – head for the **Jižní zahrady**, accessible via the architect's copper-canopied Bull Staircase on the south side of the third courtyard. Originally laid out in the sixteenth century, but thoroughly remodelled in the 1920s by Josip Plečnik, the first garden you come to from the Bull Staircase, the **Zahrada na valech** (Garden on the Ramparts), features an observation terrace and colonnaded pavilion, below which is an earlier eighteenth-century **Hudební pavilón** (Music Pavilion). Two sandstone obelisks beneath the windows of the Old Royal Palace record the arrival of Slavata and Martinic following their defenestration (see box, p.42). In the opposite direction, beyond the Baroque fountain, lies the smaller **Rajská zahrada** (Paradise Garden), on whose lawn Plečnik plonked an ornamental forty-ton granite basin suspended on two small blocks. From here, a quick slog up the monumental staircase will bring you out onto Hradčanské náměstí.

Královská zahrada (Royal Gardens)
It's worth taking a stroll through the north gate of the second courtyard and across the **Prašný most** (Powder Bridge), erected in the sixteenth century to connect the newly established royal gardens with the Hrad (the original wooden structure has long since been replaced). Below lies the steep wooded **Jelení příkop** (Stag Ditch), once used by the Habsburgs for growing figs and lemons and storing game for the royal hunts, but now accessible to the public.

Beyond the bridge is the entrance to the most verdant of the castle's gardens, the **Královská zahrada**, founded by Emperor Ferdinand I in the 1530s on the site of a former vineyard. Burned down by the Saxons and Swedes during the Thirty Years' War, and blown up by the Prussians, the gardens were only saved from French attack in 1741

1

by the payment of thirty pineapples. Today, these are some of the best-kept gardens in the capital, with fully functioning fountains and immaculately cropped lawns. Consequently, it's a very popular spot, though more a place for admiring the azaleas and almond trees than lounging around on the grass. It was here that tulips brought from Turkey were first acclimatized to Europe before being exported to the Netherlands, and every spring there's an impressive display.

At the main entrance to the gardens is the **Lví dvůr** (Lion's Court), now a restaurant but originally built by Rudolf II to house his private zoo, which included leopards, lynxes, bears, wolves and lions, all of whom lived in heated cages to protect them from the Prague winter. Rudolf was also responsible for the Renaissance ball-game court, known as the **Míčovna** (occasionally open to the public for concerts and exhibitions), built into the south terrace and tattooed with sgraffito by his court architect Bonifaz Wolmut. If you look carefully at the top row of allegorical figures on either side of the sandstone half-columns, you can see that the figure of Industry, between Justice (Justicia) and Loyalty (Fides), is holding a hammer and sickle and a copy of the Five-Year Plan, thoughtfully added by Communist restorers in the 1950s. Incidentally, the guarded ochre building to the right of the Míčovna, the **Zahradní dům**, was built as a summerhouse by Kilian Ignaz Dientzenhofer only to be destroyed during the Prussian bombardment of 1757. It was restored by Pavel Janák, who added the building's two modern wings on a postwar whim of the ill-fated President Beneš; it's now a presidential hideaway.

Letohrádek královny Anny/Belvedér (Queen Anne's Summer Palace)
Open only for exhibitions and concerts

At the eastern end of the Royal Gardens is Prague's most celebrated Renaissance legacy, the **Letohrádek královny Anny**, sometimes referred to as the **Belvedér**, a delicately arcaded summerhouse topped by an inverted copper ship's hull, built by Ferdinand I for his wife, Anne – though she didn't live long enough to see it completed. It was designed by the Genoese architect Paolo della Stella, one of the many Italian masons who settled in Prague in the sixteenth century, and is decorated with a series of lovely figural reliefs depicting scenes from mythology. The palace is mainly used for summertime exhibitions by contemporary artists. At the centre of its miniature formal garden is the **Zpívající fontána** (Singing Fountain), built shortly after the summerhouse and named for the musical sound the drops of water used to make when falling in the metal bowls below. From the garden terrace, you also have an unrivalled view of the cathedral.

Chotkovy sady
Adjacent to the Belvedér is the seldom-visited **Chotkovy sady**, Prague's first public park, founded in 1833 by the ecologically minded city governor, Count Chotek. The atmosphere here is a lot more relaxed than in the nearby Královská zahrada, and you can happily stretch out on the grass and soak up the sunshine, or head for the south wall, which enjoys an unrivalled view of the bridges and islands of the Vltava. At the centre of the park there's a bizarre, melodramatic, grotto-like memorial to the Romantic poet **Julius Zeyer** (1841–1901), in which life-sized characters from Zeyer's works, carved in white marble, emerge from the blackened rocks amid much drapery.

Bílkova vila
Mieckiewiczova 1 • Tues–Sun 10am–6pm • 120Kč • ☎ 233 323 631, ⓦ ghmp.cz

Hidden behind its overgrown garden at Mieckiewiczova 1, the **Bílkova vila** honours one of the most original of all Czech sculptors, **František Bílek** (1872–1941). Born in a part of South Bohemia steeped in the Hussite tradition, Bílek lived a monkish life, spending years in spiritual contemplation, reading the works of Hus and other Czech reformers. The Bílkova vila was built in 1911 to the artist's own design, intended as both a "cathedral of

CLOCKWISE FROM TOP RIVER VLTAVA AND THE HRAD (P.33); LORETA (P.51); GOLDEN LANE (P.43) >

1

art" and the family home. At first sight, it appears a strangely mute red-brick building, out of keeping with the extravagant Symbolist style of Bílek's sculptures. It's meant to symbolize a cornfield, with the front porch supported by giant sheaves of corn; only a sculptural group, depicting the fleeing Comenius and his followers, in the garden, gives a clue as to what lies within.

Inside, the brickwork gives way to bare stone walls lined with Bílek's religious sculptures, giving the impression that you've walked into a chapel rather than an artist's studio: "a workshop and temple", in Bílek's own words. In addition to his sculptural and relief work in wood and stone, often wildly expressive and spiritually tortured, there are also ceramics, graphics and a few mementoes of the sculptor's life. His work is little known outside his native country, but his contemporary admirers included Franz Kafka, Julius Zeyer and Otakar Březina, whose poems and novels provided the inspiration for much of his art. The living quarters have been restored and opened to the public, with much of the original wooden furniture, designed and carved by Bílek himself, still in place. Check out the dressing table for his wife, shaped like some giant church lectern, and the wardrobe decorated with a border of hearts, a penis, a nose, an ear and an eye plus the sun, stars and moon.

Hradčanské náměstí

Hradčanské náměstí fans out from the castle gates, surrounded by the oversized palaces of the old Catholic nobility. Though some of these palaces house major collections belonging to the **National Gallery**, for the most part it's a tranquil space that's generally ignored by the tour groups marching through intent on the Hrad. The one spot everyone heads for is the ramparts in the southeastern corner, by the top of the Zámecké schody, which provide an incomparable view over the red rooftops of Malá Strana, past the famous green dome and tower of the church of sv Mikuláš and beyond to Charles Bridge and the spires of Staré Město. Few people make use of the square's central lawn, which is heralded by a giant green wrought-iron lamppost decked with eight separate lamps from the 1860s, and, behind it, a Baroque plague column, with saintly statues by Ferdinand Maximilian Brokof.

Until the great fire of 1541, the square was the hub of Hradčany, lined with medieval shops and stalls but with no real market as such. After the fire, the developers moved in; the showiest palace on the square is the **Schwarzenberský palác**, one of the National Gallery venues. At no. 2, another Schwarzenberg pile, the **Salmovský palác**, served as the Swedish embassy until the 1970s when the dissident writer Pavel Kohout took refuge here. Frustrated in their attempts to force him out, the Communists closed the embassy down – today it is now another branch of the National Gallery. Nearby, a statue of the country's founder, **T.G. Masaryk**, unveiled in 2000, keeps a watchful eye on today's less exemplary inhabitants of the Hrad. On the opposite side of the square, just outside the castle gates, the sumptuous vanilla-coloured **Arcibiskupský palác** has been seat of the archbishop of Prague since the beginning of the Roman Catholic Church's suzerainty over the Czechs, following the Battle of Bílá hora. The Rococo exterior hints at the even more extravagant furnishings inside; the interior is open to the public only on Maundy Thursday (the Thursday before Easter).

Salmovský palác – Czech nineteenth-century art

Hradčanské náměstí 2 • Tues–Sun 10am–6pm • 220Kč • ⓦ ngprague.cz

The National Gallery's **Czech nineteenth-century art collection** resides in the **Salmovský palác**. The majority of the works displayed are pretty unexceptional, though due to the proximity of Prague's headlining sights, things here are always blissfully peaceful and crowd-free.

Look out for Antonín Machek's eye-catching series of 32 naive scenes depicting Bohemian rulers from Krok to Ferdinand IV, and numerous pieces by members of the

1

influential **Mánes family**, including Antonín Mánes, whose success in getting the Czech countryside to look like Italy gave birth to Romantic Czech landscape painting. Three of his offspring also took up the brush: Quido specialized in idealized peasant genre pictures; Amálie obeyed her father's wishes and restricted herself to a little gentle landscape painting; Josef was the most successful of the trio, much in demand as a portrait artist, and one of the leading exponents of patriotically uplifting depictions of national events (he himself took part in the 1848 disturbances in Prague). **Mikuláš Aleš**, whose sgraffito designs can be seen on many of the city's nineteenth-century buildings, is underrepresented, though you can admire his decorative depiction of the historical meeting between George of Poděbrady and Matthias Corvinus.

Schwarzenberský palác – Czech Baroque art
Hradčanské náměstí 2 • Tues–Sun 10am–6pm • 220Kč • ℗ ngprague.cz

The powerful Lobkowicz family replaced seven houses on the south side of the square with an over-the-top sgraffitoed pile now known as the **Schwarzenberský palác** after its last aristocratic owners. For a brief period, it belonged to the Rožmberk family, whose last in line, Petr Vok, in 1601 held the infamous banquet that proved fatal to the Danish astronomer Tycho Brahe. So as not to offend his host, Tycho refrained from leaving the table before Vok, only to burst his bladder, after which he staggered off to his house in Nový Svět, where he died five days later. The palace now houses the National Gallery's vast collection of **Czech Baroque art**, which is of only limited interest to the nonspecialist. Chronologically, the collection begins on the second floor, where you can get a brief glimpse of the overtly sensual and erotic tastes of Rudolf II, who enjoyed works such as Hans von Aachen's sexually charged *Suicide of Lucretia* and Josef Heintz's riotous orgy in his *Last Judgement*. The paltry remains of Rudolf's *Kunstkammer* are pretty disappointing, but the adjacent room contains some superb woodcuts by Dürer, Holbein and Altdorfer among others, including some wonderfully imaginative depictions of Satan and the Whore of Babylon. The rest of the gallery, which is spread over three floors, is given over to the likes of Karel Škréta and Petr Brandl, whose paintings and sculptures spearheaded the Counter-Reformation and fill chapels and churches across the Czech Lands. Perhaps the most compelling reason to wade through the gallery is to admire the vigorous, gesticulating sculptures of Matthias Bernhard Braun and Ferdinand Maximilian Brokof.

Šternberský palác – European art
Hradčanské náměstí 15 • Tues–Sun 10am–6pm • 220Kč • ℗ ngprague.cz

A passage alongside the archbishop's palace from Hradčanské náměstí leads to the early eighteenth-century **Šternberský palác**, which houses the National Gallery's vast **European art** collection. This ranges mainly from the **fourteenth to the eighteenth centuries**, but excludes works by Czech artists of the period, which you'll find in the Schwarzenberský palace (see above) and in the Anežský klášter (see p.85). The handful of masterpieces makes a visit worthwhile, and there's an elegant café in the courtyard. To see the National Gallery's more impressive nineteenth- and twentieth-century European art collection, you need to pay a visit to the Veletržní palác (see p.139).

First floor
The tour route begins on the **first floor** with **Tuscan** religious art, most notably a series of exquisite miniature triptychs by Bernardo Daddi, plus several striking triangular-framed portraits of holy figures by Pietro Lorenzetti, including a very fine *St Anthony Abbot*, with long curly hair and beard. Before you move on, take a detour to the side room 11, which contains Orthodox icons from Venice, the Balkans and Russia. Moving swiftly into the gallery's large **Flemish** collection, it's worth checking out Dieric Bouts's *Lamentation*, a complex composition crowded with figures in medieval garb. Other works worth seeking out are Caroto's effeminate *St John the Evangelist on Patmos*, in room 10, St John lazily dreaming of the apocalypse, and the two richly coloured

1

Bronzino portraits in room 12. One of the most eye-catching works is Jan Gossaert's *St Luke Drawing the Virgin*, in room 13, an exercise in architectural geometry and perspective that once hung in the cathedral.

Second floor

The huge **second floor** is best taken at a canter by non-experts. Outstanding works here include **Tintoretto**'s *St Jerome* (room 17), a searching portrait of old age; a wonderfully rugged portrait of a Spanish guerilla leader from the Peninsular War by **Goya** (room 22); and a mesmerizing *Praying Christ* by **El Greco** (room 23). Be sure, too, to have a look at the Činský kabinet (room 35), a small oval chamber smothered in gaudy Baroque chinoiserie, and one of the palace's few surviving slices of original decor. Elsewhere, there is a series of canvases by the **Brueghel** family (room 26), **Rembrandt**'s *Scholar in his Study* (room 29) and **Rubens**' colossal *Murder of St Thomas* (room 30), with its pink-buttocked cherubs hovering over the bloody scene. Nearby, in the vast (and uneven) Dutch section, there's a wonderful portrait of an arrogant "young gun" named Jasper by **Frans Hals** (room 31).

Ground floor

The **ground floor** galleries contain one of the most prized paintings in the whole collection: the *Feast of the Rosary* by **Albrecht Dürer**, in room 1, depicting, among others, the Virgin Mary, the Pope, the Holy Roman Emperor and even a self-portrait of Dürer himself (top right). This was one of Rudolf II's most prized acquisitions (he was an avid Dürer fan), and was transported on foot across the Alps to Prague (he didn't trust wheeled transport with such a precious object). Also in this room are several superb canvases by Lucas Cranach the Elder. The only other ground-floor room worth the footwork is room 3, where Hans Raphons's *Passion Altar – Christ in Purgatory* features some wicked devils, especially the green she-devil with cudgel.

Martinický palác – Museum of Mechanical Musical Instruments

Hradčanské náměstí 8 • Open only for events • ⓦ martinickypalac.cz

Compared to the other palaces on the square, the **Martinický palác**, at no. 8, is a fairly modest affair, built in 1620 by one of the councillors who survived the second defenestration (see box, p.42). Its rich sgraffito decoration, which continues in the inner courtyard, was only discovered during restoration work in the 1970s. On the facade, you can easily make out Potiphar's wife making a grab at a naked and unwilling Joseph. The interior boasts many Renaissance elements but is only open for events such as weddings and corporate bashes.

Nový Svět

Nestling in a shallow dip in the northwest corner of Hradčany, **Nový Svět** (meaning "New World", though nothing to do with Dvořák) provides a glimpse of life on a totally different scale from Hradčanské náměstí. Similar in many ways to the Golden Lane in the Hrad, this cluster of brightly coloured cottages, which curls around the corner into Černínská, is all that's left of Hradčany's medieval slums, painted up and sanitized in the eighteenth and nineteenth centuries. Despite having all the same ingredients for mass tourist appeal as Golden Lane, it remains remarkably undisturbed, save for a few swish wine bars, the odd hotel and a large outdoor summer theatre.

Černínský palác

Loretánské náměstí 5 • Not open to the public

Up the hill from Nový Svět, Loretánské náměstí is dominated by the phenomenal 135m-long facade of the **Černínský palác**, decorated with thirty Palladian half-columns and supported by a swathe of diamond-pointed rustication. For all its grandeur – it's the largest palace in Prague, for the sake of which two whole streets were demolished – it's a pretty brutal building, commissioned in the 1660s by Count Humprecht Jan Černín, one-time imperial ambassador to Venice and a man of monumental self-importance. After quarrelling with the master of Italian Baroque, Giovanni Bernini, and disagreeing with Prague's own Carlo Lurago, Count Černín settled on Francesco Caratti as his architect, only to have the finished building panned by critics as a tasteless mass of stone. The grandiose plans, which were nowhere near completion when the count died, nearly bankrupted future generations of Černíns, who were eventually forced to sell the palace in 1851 to the Austrian state, which converted it into military barracks.

Since the First Republic, the palace has housed the **Ministry of Foreign Affairs**, and during the war it briefly acted as the Nazi *Reichsprotektor*'s residence. On March 10, 1948, it was the scene of Prague's third defenestration. Just a week or so after the Communist coup, **Jan Masaryk**, the only son of the founder of the Republic, and the last non-Communist in Gottwald's cabinet, plunged 15m to his death from the top-floor bathroom window of the palace. Whether it was murder or suicide (he had been suffering from depression, partly induced by the country's political path) will probably never be satisfactorily resolved, but for most people Masaryk's death cast a dark shadow over the new regime. An eponymously titled 2017 Czech blockbuster examines his last months, with Czech actor of bit-part Hollywood fame Karel Roden playing the lead role.

Loreta

Loretánské náměstí 7 • Daily: April–Oct 9am–5pm; Nov–March 9.30am–4pm • 150Kč • ☎ 220 516 740, ⓦ loreta.cz

The facade of the **Loreta**, an elaborate Baroque pilgrimage complex immediately opposite the Černínský palác on Loretánské náměstí, was built by the Dientzenhofers, a Bavarian family of architects, in the early part of the eighteenth century, and is the perfect antidote to Caratti's humourless Černínský palác nearby. It's all whimsical flourishes and dandy twirls, topped by a tower that lights up like a Chinese lantern at night, and by day clanks out the hymn *We Greet Thee a Thousand Times* on its 27 Dutch bells (it also puts on special performances of other tunes from time to time).

Santa Casa

The Loreta's facade and cloisters, which were built to shelter pilgrims from the elements, are, in fact, just the outer casing for the focus of the complex, the **Santa Casa**. This is the oldest part of the Loreta, founded by Kateřina Lobkowicz in 1626 and smothered in a rich mantle of stucco depicting the building's miraculous transportation from the Holy Land. Legend has it that the Santa Casa (the Virgin Mary's home in Nazareth), under threat from the heathen Turks, was transported by a host of angels to a small village in Dalmatia and from there, via a number of brief stop-offs, to a small laurel grove (*lauretum* in Latin) in northern Italy (it was later moved to a hilltop in Italy's Le Marche province where it is still a major place of Catholic pilgrimage). News of the miracle spread across the Catholic lands, prompting a spate of copycat shrines, and during the Counter-Reformation the cult was actively encouraged in an attempt to broaden the popular appeal of Catholicism. The Prague Loreta was one of fifty built in the Czech Lands alone, each of the shrines following an identical design, with pride of place given to a lime-wood statue, the *Black Madonna and Child*, encased in silver. Sadly only a handful remain standing today, the Prague Loreta being the best preserved of those that survived.

Narození Páně (Church of the Nativity)

Behind the Santa Casa, the Dientzenhofers built the much larger church of **Narození Páně**, which is like a mini-version of sv Mikuláš down in Malá Strana. There's a high cherub count, plenty of gilding and a lovely organ replete with music-making angels and putti.

1

On either side of the main altar are glass cabinets containing the fully clothed and wax-headed standing skeletons of Spanish saints Felicissimus and Marcia and, next to them, paintings of St Apollonia – who had her teeth smashed in during her martyrdom and is now invoked for toothache – and St Agatha, carrying her severed breasts on a dish. As in the church, most of the saints honoured in the **cloisters** are women. Without doubt, the weirdest of the lot is St Wilgefortis (Starosta in Czech), whose statue stands in the final chapel of the cloisters. Daughter of the king of Portugal, she was due to marry the king of Sicily, despite having taken a vow of virginity. God intervened and she grew a beard, whereupon the king of Sicily broke off the marriage and her father had her crucified. Wilgefortis thus became the patron saint of unhappily married women, and is depicted bearded on the cross (and easily mistaken for Christ in drag).

Treasury

You can get some idea of the Loreta's serious financial backing in the **treasury** (on the first floor of the west wing), much ransacked over the years but still stuffed full of gold. Most folk come here to gawp at the master exhibit, an outrageous Viennese silver monstrance called the **Prague Sun** (Pražské slunce), designed by Fischer von Erlach in 1699 and studded with 6222 diamonds taken from the wedding dress of Countess Kolovrat, who made the Loreta sole heir to her fortune.

Strahovský klášter (Strahov Monastery)

Strahovské nádvoří 1• ⓦ strahovmonastery.cz

The arcaded street-cum-square of Pohořelec, west of Loretánské náměstí, leads to the chunky remnants of the eighteenth-century zigzag fortifications that mark the edge of the old city, as defined by Charles IV back in the fourteenth century. On the south side of Pohořelec is the **Strahovský klášter**, founded in 1140 by the Premonstratensian order. Strahov was one of the lucky few to escape Joseph II's 1783 dissolution of the monasteries, a feat it managed by declaring itself a scholarly institution – the monks had, in fact, amassed one of the finest libraries in Bohemia. It continued to function until shortly after the Communists took power, when, along with all other religious establishments, it was closed down and most of its inmates thrown into prison; following the events of 1989, the white-robed monks returned.

The Baroque entrance to the monastery is topped by a statue of **sv Norbert**, twelfth-century founder of the Premonstratensian order of clerical monks, whose relics were brought here in 1627. Just inside the cobbled outer courtyard is a tiny deconsecrated church built by Rudolf II and dedicated to **sv Roch**, protector against plagues, one of which had very nearly rampaged through Prague in 1599; it's now a private art gallery. The other church in this peaceful little courtyard is the still functioning twelfth-century monastery church of **Nanebezvetí Panny Marie**, which was given its last remodelling in Baroque times by Anselmo Lurago – it's well worth a peek for its colourful frescoes relating to St Norbert's life.

Leaving the monastery through the narrow doorway in the eastern wall, you enter the gardens and orchards of the **Strahovská zahrada**, from where you can see the whole city in perspective. The gardens form part of a wooded hill known as Petřín, and the path to the right contours round to the Stations of the Cross that lead up to the miniature Eiffel Tower aka the Petřínská rozhledna (see p.67).

The monastery libraries

Daily 9am–noon & 1–5pm • 120Kč • ☏ 233 107 718

The real reason most visitors head to Strahov is to see the monastery's two ornate **libraries**; the entrance for both is to the right as you enter the outer courtyard. The first library you come to is the later and larger of the two, the **Filosofický sál** (Philosophical Hall), built in some haste in the 1780s in order to accommodate the books and bookcases from Louka monastery in Moravia that failed to escape Joseph's decree. The tall walnut bookcases touch the library's lofty ceiling, which is busily decorated with frescoes by the Viennese painter Franz Maulbertsch on the theme of the search for truth. Don't miss the collection of curios exhibited in the glass cabinets outside the library, which features shells, turtles, crabs, lobsters, dried-up sea monsters, butterflies, beetles, plastic fruit and moths. There's even a pair of whales' penises displayed alongside a narwhal horn, several harpoons and a model ship. The other main room, seventy years older than the Philosophical Hall, is the low-ceilinged **Teologický sál** (Theological Hall), studded with ancient globes, its wedding-cake stucco framing frescoes on a similar theme. The library's oldest book, the ninth-century gem-studded Strahov Gospel, is displayed outside. Look out, too, for the cabinet of books documenting Czech trees, each of which has the appropriate type of bark on its spine.

Strahovská obrazárna (Strahov Picture Gallery)
Daily 9am–11.30 & noon–5pm • 120Kč

An archway on the far side of the monastery contains the ticket office for the monastery's art gallery, the **Strahovská obrazárna**, situated above the cloisters and accessible from the door on the right, beyond the ticket office. The gallery's collection of religious art, church plate and reliquaries, reassembled in the early 1990s after it was broken up by the authorities in the late 1940s, is a mere fraction of the monastery's total. The items displayed may not be to everyone's taste, but include the odd gem from Rudolf II's collection – not least a portrait of the emperor himself by Hans von Aachen, plus a superb portrait of Rembrandt's elderly mother by Gerrit Dou. There are also a few paintings by Baroque masters Brandl and Škréta.

Muzeum miniatur (Museum of Miniatures)
Daily 9am–5pm • 100Kč • ⓦ muzeumminiatur.cz

The Strahov Monastery is the unlikely home of the **Muzeum miniatur**, in the northeastern corner of the main courtyard. Displayed in this small museum are forty or so works by **Anatoly Konyenko**, a Russian who holds the record for constructing the smallest book in the world, a thirty-page edition of Chekhov's *Chameleon*. Among the other miracles of miniature manufacture are a (real, though dead) flea bearing golden horseshoes; scissors; a key and lock; the Lord's Prayer written on a human hair; and a caravan of camels passing through the eye of a needle.

MALÁ STRANA ROOFTOPS

Malá Strana

Malá Strana, Prague's picturesque "Little Quarter", gathered around the Baroque masterpiece that is the Church of sv Mikuláš, sits below the castle and is, in many ways, the city's most enchanting district. Its peaceful, often steep, eighteenth-century backstreets have changed very little since Mozart strolled them during his frequent visits to Prague between 1787 and 1791. Despite the quarter's minuscule size – a square of roughly 600 by 600 metres squeezed in between the river and Hradčany – it's easy enough to lose the crowds, most of whom rarely stray from the prescribed route linking Charles Bridge with the castle. Its streets conceal a host of delightfully peaceful terraced gardens, as well as the wooded hill of Petřín, which together provide the perfect urban escape when Prague is at its busiest.

MALÁ STRANA HIGHLIGHTS

Sv Mikuláš Prague's finest example of baroque church architecture. See p.58
Café Savoy Coffee and cakes amid authentic Austro-Hungarian splendour. See p.176
U Hrocha A typical, ungentrified Czech pub in the heart of the district. See p.188
Franz Kafka Museum The lowdown on Prague's most famous writer. See p.62
Petřínská rozhledna This mini Eiffel Tower provides the best views of Malá Strana. See p.67
John Lennon Wall The capital's most famous piece of graffiti that's added to daily. See p.62

2

Long before the Přemyslid king Otakar II decided to establish a German community on the Vltava's left bank in 1257, a mixture of Jews, merchants and monks had settled on the slopes below the castle. But, as with Hradčany, it was the **fire of 1541** – which devastated the entire area – and the **expulsion of the Protestants** after 1620 that together had the greatest impact on the visual and social make-up of the quarter. In place of the old Gothic town, the newly ascendant Catholic nobility built opulent palaces here, though generally without quite the same destructive glee as up in Hradčany.

In 1918, the majority of these buildings became home to the chief foreign embassies in Czechoslovakia and remain so to this day. After 1948 the rest of the district's real estate was turned into flats to alleviate the postwar housing shortage. Things have come full circle again with property in Malá Strana now among the most sought-after in Prague. Yet despite all the changes, the new hotels and the souvenir shops, much of Malá Strana remains relatively undisturbed and and it's easy to escape the urban hustle here. The island of **Kampa**, in particular, is one of the most peaceful stretches of riverfront in Prague.

Malostranské náměstí

Malá Strana's epicentre has always been the sloping, cobbled **Malostranské náměstí**, which is dominated and divided into two by the church of sv Mikuláš (see p.58). Trams and cars hurtle across it, regularly dodged by a procession of people – some heading up the hill to the Hrad, others pausing for coffee and cakes at the numerous bars and restaurants hidden in the square's arcades and Gothic vaults. The most famous (and the most central) of the cafés was the **Malostranská kavárna**, established in 1874, an occasional haunt of Kafka, Brod, Werfel and friends in the 1920s, and now, perhaps inevitably, a *Starbucks*. On every side, Neoclassical facades line the square, imitating the colour and grandeur of those of Hradčanské and Staroměstské náměstí. The square is due a gentrifying facelift in the coming years; the scruffy car park that used to blight one side is already a thing of the past.

Lichtenštejnský palác

Malostranské náměstí 258/13 • ☎ 257 534 206, ⊗ hamu.cz • Tram #12, #20 or #22 to Malostranské náměstí

The largest Baroque facade to be added to Malostranské náměstí is the **Lichtenštejnský palác**, occupying the entire west flank. Today it's home to the university music and dance faculty (HAMU), as well as being a concert venue, art gallery and café, but the pleasing frontage hides a history linked to repression: first as the home of Karl von Liechtenstein, the man who pronounced the death sentence on the 27 Protestant leaders in 1621; then as headquarters for the Swedes during the 1648 siege; and later as the base of the Austrian General Windischgrätz, scourge of the 1848 revolution.

Dům Smiřických (Smiřický House)

Malostranské náměstí 18 • Tram #12, #20 or #22 to Malostranské náměstí

On the northeast side of Malostranské náměstí, distinguished by its two little turrets and pistachio-and-vanilla colour scheme, is the **dům Smiřických** where the Protestant posse met in 1618 to decide how to get rid of Emperor Ferdinand's Catholic governors: whether to attack them with daggers, or, as they eventually attempted to do, kill them by throwing them out of the window (see box, p.42).

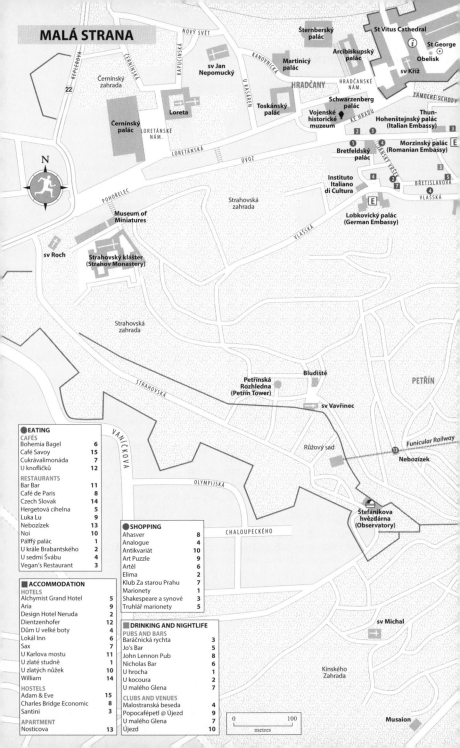

MALÁ STRANA

● EATING

CAFÉS
Bohemia Bagel	6
Café Savoy	15
Cukrávalimonáda	7
U knoflíčků	12

RESTAURANTS
Bar Bar	11
Café de Paris	8
Czech Slovak	14
Hergetová cihelna	5
Luka Lu	9
Nebozízek	13
Noi	10
Pálffý palác	1
U krále Brabantského	2
U sedmi Švábu	4
Vegan's Restaurant	3

■ ACCOMMODATION

HOTELS
Alchymist Grand Hotel	5
Aria	9
Design Hotel Neruda	2
Dientzenhofer	12
Dům U velké boty	4
Lokál Inn	6
Sax	7
U Karlova mostu	11
U zlaté studně	1
U zlatých nůžek	10
William	14

HOSTELS
Adam & Eve	15
Charles Bridge Economic	8
Santini	3

APARTMENT
Nosticova	13

● SHOPPING
Ahasver	8
Analogue	4
Antikvariát	10
Art Puzzle	9
Artěl	6
Elima	2
Klub Za starou Prahu	7
Marionety	1
Shakespeare a synové	3
Truhlář marionety	5

■ DRINKING AND NIGHTLIFE

PUBS AND BARS
Baráčnická rychta	3
Jo's Bar	5
John Lennon Pub	8
Nicholas Bar	6
U hrocha	1
U kocoura	2
U malého Glena	7

CLUBS AND VENUES
Malostranská beseda	4
Popocafépetl @ Újezd	9
U malého Glena	7
Újezd	10

0   100
metres

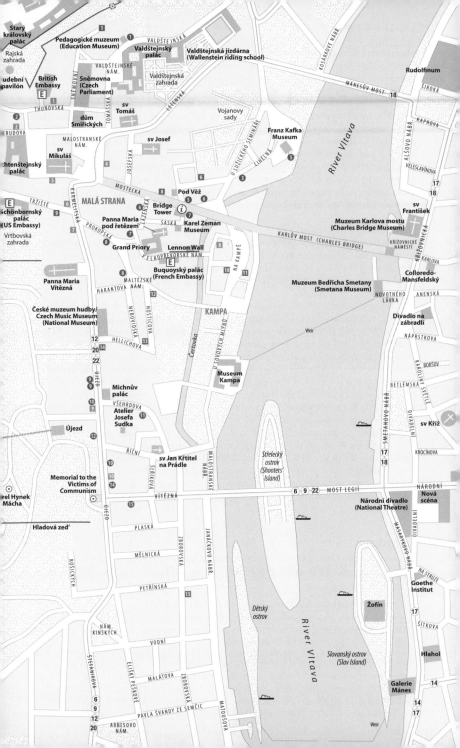

Sněmovna (Czech Parliament)

Sněmovní 4 • ☎ 257 174 117, ⓦ psp.cz • Tram #12, #20 or #22 to Malostranské náměstí

Sněmovní, the side street that runs alongside the western facade of the Dům Smiřických, takes its name from the **Sněmovna**, the Neoclassical palace that served as the provincial Diet in the nineteenth century, the National Assembly of the First Republic in 1918, the Czech National Council after federalization in 1968 and, since 1993, as home to the Chamber of Deputies, the (more important) lower house of the **Czech Parliament**. No one would deny that this is a cramped and hard-to-access location and former Finance Minister (and possible future Prime Minister) Andrej Babiš has touted the megalomaniacal idea of creating a purpose-built, out-of-town government quarter. Only groups can take a free, prearranged guided tour (in Czech only) of the parliament, but anyone can wander into the public gallery to watch the sluggish wheels of Czech coalition politics turn.

Sv Mikuláš (St Nicholas)

Malostranské náměstí • **Church** Daily: March–Oct 9am–5pm; Nov–Feb 9am–4pm • 70Kč **Belfry** Daily: April–Sept 10am–10pm; March & Oct 10am–8pm; Nov–Feb 10am–6pm • 90Kč • ☎ 257 534 215, ⓦ stnicholas.cz • Tram #12, #20 or #22 to Malostranské náměstí

Dominating the Malá Strana skyline is the **church of sv Mikuláš**, or **St Nicholas**, easily Prague's most magnificent Baroque building, and one of the last great structures to appear on the left bank.

Nothing about the relatively plain west facade prepares you for the High Baroque **interior**, dominated by the nave's vast fresco by Johann Lukas Kracker, which portrays some of Mikuláš' more fanciful miraculous feats. Along with his role as Santa Claus, he is also depicted here rescuing sailors in distress, saving women from prostitution by throwing them bags of gold and reprieving from death three unjustly condemned men. Even given the overwhelming proportions of the nave, the dome at the far end of the church remains impressive, thanks, more than anything, to its sheer height. Leering over you as you gaze up at the dome are four terrifyingly oversized and stern Church Fathers; one brandishes a gilded thunderbolt, while another garrottes a devil with his crozier, leaving no doubt as to the gravity of the Jesuit message.

Exhibitions are occasionally staged in the church's gallery, which gives you a great chance to look down on the nave and get closer to the frescoes. For fine views over Malá Strana climb the 215 steps of the **belfry**, which never actually belonged to the church and was used as a fire watchtower. During the decades of Communist rule the views came in handy for Prague's secret police who used the belfry to spy on the nearby Western embassies (especially the comings and goings at the US Embassy) and dissident activity around Malá Strana. It's now part of the Prague City Museum.

Nerudova

The most important of the various cobbled streets leading up to the Hrad from Malostranské náměstí is **Nerudova**, part of the Royal Way that leads from

---

THE CHURCH OF SV MIKULÁŠ – A FAMILY AFFAIR

Begun in 1702 the church of sv Mikuláš was the most prestigious commission of **Christoph Dientzenhofer**, a German immigrant from a dynasty of Bavarian architects, and is, without doubt, his finest work. For the Jesuits, who were already ensconced in the adjoining college, it was their most ambitious project yet in Bohemia, and the ultimate symbol of their stranglehold on the country. When Christoph died in 1722, the project stayed in the family with son Kilian Ignaz Dientzenhofer, along with Kilian's son-in-law, Anselmo Lurago, left to finish the project, which they did with a masterful flourish, adding the giant green dome and tower – now among the most characteristic landmarks on Prague's left bank. Sadly for the Jesuits, they were able to enjoy the finished product for just twenty years before they were banished from the Habsburg Empire in 1773.

JAN NERUDA AND MALÁ STRANA

Nerudova is named after the Czech journalist and writer **Jan Neruda** (1834–91), who was born at *U dvou sluncŭ* (The Two Suns), at no. 47, an inn sporting twin Dutch gables at the top of the street; Neruda later lived for ten years at no. 44, now the classy *Hotel Neruda*. His *Tales from Malá Strana* (*Povídky malostranské*) immortalized Bohemian life on Prague's left bank, though he's perhaps best known outside the Czech Republic via the Chilean Nobel Prize-winner, Pablo Neruda, who took his pen name from the lesser-known Czech.

the Nové Město – and hence its permanent occupation by tourists and increasing tackiness.

Many of the Baroque houses that line the steep climb up to the Hrad retain their medieval barn doors, and most are adorned with their own peculiar house signs (see box, p.6). At the bottom of the street are two of Nerudova's fancier buildings: no. 5 is the **Morzinský palác**, now the Romanian embassy, its doorway designed by Giovanni Santini and supported by two Moors (a pun on the owner's name) sculpted by Brokof; diagonally opposite, no. 20 is the **Thun-Hohenštejnský palác** (also by Santini), now the Italian embassy, with two giant eagles by Braun holding up the portal. Further up the street, according to Prague folklore Casanova and Mozart are believed to have met at a ball given by the aristocrat owners of no. 33, the **Bretfeldský palác**, in 1791, when Mozart was in town for the premiere of *La Clemenza di Tito* (see box, p.65).

Halfway up the hill, Nerudova ends at a crossroads where it meets the cobbled hairpin of Ke Hradu, which the royal coronation procession used to ascend.

Tržiště

Running (very) roughly parallel to Nerudova – and linked to it by several picturesque side streets and steps – is **Tržiště**, which sets off from just south of Malostranské náměstí. Halfway up on the left is the **Schönbornský palác**, which has been the US embassy for decades. The entrance, and the renowned gardens, are watched over by CCTV and sometimes twitchy Czech policemen – a far cry from the dilapidated palace in which Kafka rented an apartment in March 1917, and where he suffered his first bout of the tuberculosis that was to kill him. Don't even think about getting your camera out here.

Lobkovický palác

Vlašská 19 • Tram #12, #20 or #22 to Malostranské náměstí

Since its construction in 1702 by Count Přehořovský z Kvasejovic, the refined **Lobkovický palác** (not to be confused with the palace of the same name in Hradčany) has served many purposes including Czech Education Ministry, Masaryk Academy and Chinese embassy – its latest tenant is the German embassy. The best views are from the rear – you'll have to approach it from Petřín (see p.66). The gardens are not open to the public, but you should be able to see David Černý's 1991 sculpture *Quo Vadis?*, a gold Trabant on legs, erected in memory of the fleeing East Germans (see box below).

EAST GERMANS GO OVER THE WALL

In the summer of 1989, several thousand East Germans climbed over the garden wall of the West German embassy compound to demand West German citizenship, which had been every German's right since partition. The neighbouring streets were soon jam-packed with abandoned Trabants, as the beautiful **Lobkovický palace gardens** became a muddy **refugee camp**. Eventually the Czechoslovak government gave in and organized special sealed trains to take the East Germans – cheered on their way by thousands of Praguers – over the Iron Curtain, thus prompting the exodus that eventually brought down the Berlin Wall.

Valdštejnský palác

Valdštejnské náměstí • Sat & Sun: April, May & Oct 10am–5pm; June–Sept 10am–6pm • Free • ☎ 257 075 707, Ⓦ senat.cz • Metro Malostranská

To the north of Malostranské náměstí, up Tomášská, lies the **Valdštejnský palác**, which takes up the whole of the eastern side of Valdštejnské náměstí and Valdštejnská. As early as 1621, **Albrecht von Waldstein** (Wallenstein) started to build a palace that would reflect his status as commander of the Imperial Catholic armies of the Thirty Years' War. By buying, confiscating and then destroying 26 houses, three gardens and a brick factory, he succeeded in ripping apart a densely populated area of Malá Strana to make way for one of the first, and largest, Baroque palaces in the city. The Czech upper house, or **Senát**, is now housed here, and at weekends you can visit several of the frescoed Baroque rooms they use.

Valdštejnská zahrada (Wallenstein Garden)

Letenská April, May & Oct Mon–Fri 7.30am–6pm (to 7pm June–Sept), Sat & Sun from 10am • Free • Metro Malostranská

The Valdštejnský palác's formal gardens, the **Valdštejnská zahrada** (accessible from the palace's main entrance, from the piazza outside Malostranská metro and also from a doorway in the palace walls along Letenská), are a good place to take a breather from the city streets. The focus of the gardens is the gigantic Italianate **sala terrena**, a monumental loggia decorated with frescoes of the Trojan Wars, which stands at the end of an avenue of bronze sculptures by Adriaen de Vries. The originals, which were intended to form a fountain, were taken off as booty by the Swedes in 1648 and now adorn the royal gardens in Drottningholm. In addition, there are a number of peacocks, a carp pond, the mother of all grottos and an old menagerie, which is now home to a mini-parliament of eagle owls.

Valdštejnská jízdárna (Wallenstein Riding School)

Valdštejnská 3 • Tues–Sun 10am–6pm • 150Kč • ☎ 257 073 136, Ⓦ ngprague.cz • Metro Malostranská

At the northern end of the Valdštejnská zahrada, the palace's former riding school, **Valdštejnská jízdárna**, is now part of the **National Gallery** – the space is used for temporary exhibitions of fine art and photography. The riding school is accessible only from the courtyard of the nearby Malostranská metro station.

Pedagogické muzeum (Education Museum)

Valdštejnská 20 • Tues–Sun 10am–12.30pm & 1–5pm • 60Kč • ☎ 257 533 455, Ⓦ pmjak.cz • Metro Malostranská

A palace opposite the Senate on Valdštejnská houses the **Pedagogické muzeum**, one of the Czech Republic's oldest museums, holding a permanent exhibition on the history of education in the Czech Lands. Despite a revamp in the late noughties, the museum is a fairly dry affair, although you do get to learn about the Czech teacher **Jan Amos Komenský** (1592–1670) – known in English as John Comenius – who was forced to leave his homeland after the victory of Waldstein's Catholic armies, eventually settling in Protestant England. Komenský's educational methods are taken for granted now but they were revolutionary for their time: among other things, he believed in universal education, in relating education to everyday life, teaching in the vernacular and learning languages through conversation. He is known in the Czech Lands as the "Teacher of the Nations" and every Czech will expect you to have heard of him.

Sv Tomáš

Josefská 8 • Mon–Sat 11.30am–1pm, Sun 4–6pm • ☎ 257 530 556 • Tram #12, #20 or #22 to Malostranské náměstí

To the northeast of Malostranské náměstí, just before the tramlines running along Letenská squeeze under a set of flying butresses, the priory **church of sv Tomáš** (St Thomas) stands in its Baroque finery, demanding attention. Destroyed in the Hussite wars, it was rebuilt by Kilian Ignaz Dientzenhofer in the 1720s and the rich burghers of Malá Strana spared no expense, as is clear from the ornate interior, with its dinky little dome and fantastically colourful frescoes by Václav Vavřinec Reiner. They also bought a couple of

ALBRECHT VON WALDSTEIN

Albrecht von Waldstein (known to the Czechs as Albrecht z Valdštejna, and to the English as Wallenstein – the name given to him by the German playwright Schiller in his tragic trilogy) was the most notorious warlord of the Thirty Years' War. If the imperial astrologer Johannes Kepler is to be believed, this is all because he was born at 4pm on September 14, 1583. According to Kepler's horoscope, Waldstein was destined to be greedy, deceitful, unloved and unloving. Sure enough, at an early age he tried to kill a servant, for which he was expelled from his Lutheran school. Recuperating in Italy, he converted to Catholicism (an astute career move) and married a wealthy widow who conveniently died shortly after the marriage. Waldstein used his new fortune to cultivate a friendship with Prince Ferdinand, heir to the Habsburg Empire, who in turn thought that a rich, tame Bohemian noble could come in handy.

During the Thirty Years' War, Waldstein offered his services (and an army of thousands) to Emperor Ferdinand free of charge, but with the right to plunder as he saw fit – within five years of the **Battle of Bílá hora** in 1620 (see box, p.147), Waldstein owned a quarter of Bohemia. By 1630, he was a duke, and earned the right to keep his hat on in the imperial presence as well as the more dubious honour of handing the emperor a napkin after he had used his fingerbowl. However, at this point Ferdinand grew wary of Waldstein's ambition, and relieved him of his command.

The following year, the Saxons occupied Prague, and the emperor was forced to reinstate Waldstein. Ferdinand couldn't afford to do without the supplies from Waldstein's estates, but knew he was mortgaging large chunks of the empire to pay for his services. More alarmingly, there were persistent rumours that Waldstein was about to declare himself king of Bohemia and defect to the French enemy. In 1634, Waldstein openly rebelled against Ferdinand, who immediately hatched a plot to murder him, sending a motley posse including English, Irish and Scottish mercenaries to the border town of **Cheb** (**Eger**), where they cut the general down in his nightshirt as he tried to rise from his sickbed. Some see him as the first man to unify Germany since Charlemagne, others see him as a wily Czech hero. In reality he was probably just another ambitious, violent man, as his stars had predicted.

Rubens for the tall main altarpiece (the originals are now in the hands of the Národní galerie) and two dead saints, St Just and St Boniface, whose gruesome clothed skeletons lie in glass coffins on either side of the nave, by the second pillar. A few traces of the church's Gothic origins can be seen in the vaulted chapel at the eastern end of the north aisle.

Palácové zahrady (Palace Gardens)

Valdštejnská 12–14 • Daily: April & Oct 10am–6pm; May & Sept 10am–7pm; June & July 10am–9pm; Aug 10am–8pm • 100Kč • ☎ 257 214 817, Ⓦ palacove-zahrady.cz • Metro Malostranská

One of Malá Strana's most hidden secrets is the steeply terraced **palácové zahrady**, hidden away behind the Baroque facades on Valdštejnská on the slopes below the castle. There are five small, interlinking gardens in total, dotted with little pavilions and terraces hung with vines, all commanding splendid views over Prague. If you're approaching from below, you can enter either via the Ledeburská zahrada on Valdštejnské náměstí, or the Kolowratská zahrada on Valdštejnská, both of which connect with the other palace gardens. You can also exit or enter via the easternmost garden, the Malá Fürstenberská zahrada, which joins up with the Zahrada na valech (see p.45) beneath the Hrad itself.

Vojanovy sady (Vojanovy Gardens)

U lužického semináře 17 • Daily: April–Sept 8am–7pm; Oct–March 8am–5pm • Free • ☎ 257 531 839, Ⓦ vojanovysady.cz • Tram #12, #20 or #22 to Malostranské náměstí

The **Vojanovy sady**, securely concealed behind a ring of high walls off U lužického semináře, was originally a monastic garden belonging to the Carmelites. Now the space is an informal public park, with weeping willows and lots of grass on which to picnic; outdoor art exhibitions and occasional concerts also take place here.

Franz Kafka Museum

Cihelná 2b · Daily 10am–6pm · 200Kč · ☎ 257 535 373, ⓦ kafkamuseum.cz · Tram #12, #20 or #22 to Malostranské náměstí

The Prague tourist industry is rather obsessed with Kafka, emblazoning his image on everything from fridge magnets to T-shirts. For the more serious literary fan, the **Franz Kafka Museum** is hidden away in a courtyard off Cihelná (a former medieval brickyard), in front of which you'll find David Černý's amusing and much-photographed fountain which is made up of two gentlemen urinating into a pool in the shape of the Czech Republic. Highlights of the exhibition, a well-curated and sophisticated rundown of Kafka's life and works (see p.98), include photos of the old ghetto into which he was born, an invoice from his father's shop bearing the logo of a jackdaw (*kavka* in Czech), copies of Kafka's job applications and his requests for sick leave, one of his reports on accident prevention in the workplace and facsimiles of his pen sketches. Upstairs, audiovisuals and theatrical trickery are employed to explore the torment, alienation and claustrophobia Kafka felt throughout his life and expressed through his writings.

Vrtbovská zahrada (Vrtbovská Gardens)

Karmelitská 25 · April–Oct daily 10am–6pm · 65Kč · ⓦ vrtbovska.cz · Tram #12, #20 or #22 to Malostranské náměstí

On the corner of Karmelitská and Tržiště stands the entrance to another of the most elusive of Malá Strana's many Baroque gardens, the **Vrtbovská zahrada**, founded on the site of the former vineyards of the Vrtbovský palác in 1720. Laid out on Tuscan-style terraces, dotted with ornamental urns and statues of the gods by Matthias Bernhard Braun, the gardens twist their way up the lower slopes of Petřín Hill to an observation terrace, from where there's a spectacular rooftop perspective of the city.

Maltézské náměstí

Tram #12, #20 or #22 to Malostranské náměstí

From the trams and traffic of Karmelitská, it's a relief to cut across to the calm restraint of cobbled **Maltézské náměstí**, one of a number of delightful little squares between here and the river, with a plague column at the north end. The square takes its name from the Order of the Knights of St John of Jerusalem (or Maltese Knights), who in 1160 founded the nearby church of **Panna Maria pod řetězem** (St Mary Below-the-Chain), so called because it was the Knights' job to guard the Judith Bridge. The original Romanesque church was pulled down by the Knights themselves in the fourteenth century, but only the chancel and towers had been successfully rebuilt by the time of the Hussite Wars. The two bulky Gothic towers are still standing and the apse is now thoroughly Baroque, but the nave remains unfinished and open to the elements.

Velkopřevorské náměstí

Tram #12, #20 or #22 to Hellichova

The Knights who built the church of St Mary Below-the-Chain still own the building and the adjacent Grand Priory, which backs onto **Velkopřevorské náměstí**, a pretty little square to the south, which sometimes echoes to the sound of music from the nearby Prague conservatoire. On one side of the square, behind a row of lime trees, is the apricot-coloured Rococo **Buquoyský palác**, built for a French aristocratic family and appropriately enough now the French embassy.

Opposite the palace is the famous **John Lennon Wall**, where Prague's youth established an ad hoc graffiti shrine to the ex-Beatle after his violent death in 1980. The running battle between police and graffiti artists continued throughout the 1990s, with the Maltese Knights (whose wall it is) taking an equally dim view of the mural and whitewashing on a couple of occasions. The scribblings were obliterated again during an illegal street-art stunt

CLOCKWISE FROM TOP MUSEUM KAMPA (P.64); ENTRANCE TO MALÁ STRANA FROM CHARLES BRIDGE; PALACE GARDENS (P.61) >

in 2014, but you'd hardly know today. Another shrine has developed to the east, on the bridge over the **Čertovka**, where couples have attached various **padlocks** to the railings.

Kampa

Tram #12, #20 or #22 to Hellichova

Heading for **Kampa**, the largest of the Vltava's islands, with its cafés, old mills and serene riverside park and playground, is the perfect way to escape the crowds on Charles Bridge, from which it can be accessed easily via a stone flight of steps. The island is separated from the left bank by Prague's "Little Venice", a thin strip of water called **Čertovka** (Devil's Stream), which used to power several mill-wheels and whose banks bear absolutely no resemblance at all to La Serenissima. In contrast to the rest of the left bank, the fire of 1541 had a positive effect on Kampa, since the flotsam from the blaze effectively stabilized the island's shifting shoreline. Nevertheless, Kampa was still subject to frequent flooding right up until the Vltava was dammed in the 1950s. Only in the great flood of 2002 did water again reach the second floor of some buildings.

For much of its history, the island was the city's main washhouse, a fact commemorated by the church of **sv Jan Křtitel Na Prádle** (St John the Baptist at the Cleaners) on Říční, beyond the island's southernmost tip. It wasn't until the sixteenth and seventeenth centuries that the Nostitz family, who owned Kampa, began to develop the northern half of the island; the southern half was left untouched, and today remains as a quite scruffy public park, but one with riverside views across to Staré Město. To the north, the oval main square, **Na Kampě**, once a pottery market, is studded with slender acacia trees and cut through by the Charles Bridge.

Museum Kampa

U Sovových mlýnů 2 · Daily 10am–6pm · 240Kč · ☎ 257 286 147, ⓦ museumkampa.cz · Tram #12, #20 or #22 to Hellichova

Housed in a stylishly converted riverside watermill, the **Museum Kampa** is dedicated to the private art collection of Jan and Meda Mládek. As well as temporary exhibitions, this smart modern gallery displays the best of the Mládeks' permanent collection, including a vast series of works by the Czech artist **František Kupka** (1871–1957), in international terms the most important Czech painter of the twentieth century. Apprenticed to a saddler who initiated him into spiritualism, Kupka became a medium and took up painting, eventually moving to Paris in 1895. He secured his place in art history by being (possibly) the first artist in the Western world to exhibit abstract paintings, but though his psychedelic paintings were influential in the 1960s, abstract art was frowned upon by the Communist regime and Kupka was pretty much ignored by his native country from 1948 to 1989. Works here encompass early Expressionist watercolours such as the *Study for Water Bathers* (1907), transitional pastels including *Fauvist Chair* (1910) and more abstract paintings, such as the seminal *Cathedral* and *Study for Fugue in Two Colours* (both c.1912).

The gallery also displays a good selection of works by the sculptor **Otto Gutfreund** (1889–1927), who started out as an enthusiastic Cubist, producing dynamic, vigorous portraits such as *Viki* (1912). After World War I, when he joined the French Foreign Legion but was interned for three years for insubordination, Gutfreund switched to depicting everyday folk in bright colour, as in *Trade* and *Lovers*, in a style that prefigures Socialist Realism. His life was cut short when he drowned while swimming in the Vltava.

Panna Maria Vítězná

Karmelitská 9 · Mon–Sat 8.30am–7pm, Sun 8.30am–8pm · Free · ⓦ pragjesu.info · Tram #12, #20 or #22 to Hellichova

The rather plain **church of Panna Maria Vítězná** was begun in early Baroque style by German Lutherans in 1611, and later handed over to the Carmelites after the Battle of Bílá hora. Although there are chalices, monstrances and a Rococo crown studded with diamonds and pearls to admire, the main reason for a visit is to see the **Pražské Jezulátko** effigy, Prague's most popular piece of Catholic kitsch.

Pražské Jezulátko

The **Pražské Jezulátko**, or Bambino di Praga, is a 45cm-high wax effigy of the infant Jesus as a precocious 3-year-old, enthroned in a glass case, which was donated by one of the Lobkowicz family's Spanish brides in 1628. Credited with miraculous powers, the Pražské Jezulátko became an object of international pilgrimage equal in stature to the Santa Casa in Loreta (see p.51), similarly inspiring a whole series of replicas. It continues to attract visitors (mainly noisy Italian and Spanish school parties) and boasts a vast personal wardrobe of expensive swaddling clothes – approaching a hundred separate outfits at the last count – changed ten times a year by the Carmelite nuns. A minuscule **museum**, up the spiral staircase in the south aisle, contains a tiny selection of his velvet and satin overgarments.

2

České muzeum hudby (Czech Music Museum)

Karmelitská 2 • Wed–Mon 10am–6pm • 120Kč • ☎ 257 257 777, ⓦ nm.cz • Tram #12, #20 or #22 to Hellichova

Part of the National Museum, **České muzeum hudby**, the city's under-visited music museum, is housed in a former Dominican nunnery. Temporary exhibitions are held on the ground floor of the magnificently tall main hall (formerly the nunnery church), while the permanent collection begins upstairs. The first exhibition kicks off with a cut-and-splice medley of musical film footage alongside a display of electric guitars and an early Tesla synthesizer. Next up is August Förster's pioneering quarter-tone grand piano from 1924 – you can even listen to **Alois Hába**'s microtonal *Fantazie no. 10* composed for, and performed on, its three keyboards. After this rather promising start, the museum settles down into a conventional display of old central European instruments from a precious Baumgartner clavichord and an Amati violin to Neapolitan mandolins and a vast contrabass more than 2m high. There are several violins made by the craftsmen who once lived on nearby Nerudova (once called Loutnařská, or "Lute-makers' Street") and an intriguing folk section with zithers, bagpipes, Slovak *fujara* (a shepherd's flute) and the odd barrel organ. What saves the collection from being as exhausting as it is exhaustive is the fact that you can hear many of the instruments on display being put through their paces at listening posts in each room. Top-notch lectures and concerts are also held here, in the main hall.

MOZART IN PRAGUE

Mozart made the first of several visits to Prague with his wife Constanze in 1787, staying with his friend and patron Count Thun in what is now the British embassy (Thunovská 14). A year earlier, his opera *The Marriage of Figaro*, which had failed to please the critics in Vienna, had been given a rapturous reception at Prague's Nostitz Theatre, now the Stavovské divadlo (see p.85), and on his arrival in 1787 Mozart was already flavour of the month. As he wrote in his diary: "Here they talk about nothing but *Figaro*. Nothing is played, sung or whistled but *Figaro*. Nothing, nothing but *Figaro*. Certainly a great honour for me!" Encouraged by this, he chose to premiere his next opera, *Don Giovanni*, later that year, in Prague rather than Vienna. He arrived with an incomplete score in hand, and wrote the overture at the Dušeks' Bertramka villa in Smíchov, dedicating it to the "good people of Prague". Apart from a brief sojourn while on a concert tour, Mozart's fourth and final visit to Prague took place in 1791, the year of his death. The climax of the stay was the premiere of his final opera, *La Clemenza di Tito*, commissioned for the coronation of Leopold II as king of Bohemia (and completed whilst on the coach from Vienna to Prague). The opera didn't go down quite as well as the previous ones – the empress is alleged to have shouted "German hogwash" from her box. Nevertheless, four thousand people turned out for the composer's memorial service, held in Malá Strana's church of sv Mikuláš to the strains of his *Requiem Mass*.

Michnův palác

Újezd 40 • Ⓦ sokol.eu • Tram #6, #9, #12, #20 or #22 to Újezd

The **Michnův palác** was built by nobleman Pavel Michna z Vacínova, though the facade and gateway still incorporate Renaissance elements of the earlier summer palace built by the Kinský family around 1580. From 1787 the building was used as an armoury, falling into disrepair until it was bought in 1921 by the Czech nationalist sports movement **Sokol**, made into its headquarters and renamed Tyršův dům after one of its founders, Miroslav Tyrš. Set up in 1862, in direct response to the German Turnverband physical education movement, Sokol (Czech for "falcon") played an important role in the Czech national revival (*národní obrození*). As well as having branches in almost every village across the land (most Czech settlements have a crumbling Sokolovna), it organized mass extravaganzas of synchronized gymnastics every six years from 1882 onwards. The Communists outlawed Sokol (as the Nazis had also done) and, in its place, established a tradition of similar spectacles called **Spartakiáda**, held every five years in the Strahov stadium behind Petřín. In the 1990s, the Spartakiáda, indelibly tainted by their political past, were once more replaced by events that the reformed Sokol organized, though the movement is now a tiny, fringe organization. A small but interesting exhibition details what today's Sokol gets up to.

Atelier Josefa Sudka (Josef Sudek's studio)

Újezd 30 • Tues–Sun noon–6pm • 10Kč • ☎ 251 510 760, Ⓦ sudek-atelier.cz • Tram #6, #9, #12, #20 or #22 to Újezd

Hidden behind the buildings on the east side of Újezd, an extension of Karmelitská, is a faithful reconstruction of **Josef Sudek's studio**, a cute little wooden garden structure, where the great photographer lived with his sister from 1927. Sudek moved out to Úvoz 24 in 1958, but he used this place as a darkroom to the end of his life. The twisted tree in the garden will be familiar to those acquainted with the numerous photographic cycles he based around the studio. The building has a few of Sudek's personal effects and is now used for temporary exhibitions of other photographers' works.

Memorial to the Victims of Communism

Corner of Vítězná and Újezd • Tram #6, #9, #12, #20 or #22 to Újezd

In 2002, the Czechs finally erected a **Memorial to the Victims of Communism** at the foot of Petřín hill, where Újezd meets Vítězná. The location has no particular resonance with the period, but the memorial itself has an eerie quality, especially when it's lit up at night. It consists of a series of statues, self-portraits by sculptor Olbram Zoubek, standing on steps that lead down from Petřín hill behind, each in varying stages of disintegration. The inscription at the base of the monument reads "205,486 convicted, 248 executed, 4500 died in prison, 327 annihilated at the border, 170,938 emigrated". Most Czechs are unaware that such a monument even exists.

Petřín

Funicular railway Daily 9am–11.30pm; every 10–15min • ☎ 257 320 814 • Public transport tickets and travel passes valid

The hilly wooded slopes of **Petřín**, distinguished by the Rozhledna, a scaled-down version of the Eiffel Tower, make up the largest green space in the city centre. The tower is just one of several exhibits that survive from the 1891 Prague Exhibition whose modest legacy also includes the 510m-long **funicular railway** (*lanová dráha*), which makes its trundling ascent from a station just off Újezd. The original funicular was powered by a simple but ingenious system whereby two carriages, one at either end of the steep track, were fitted with large water tanks that were alternately filled at the top and emptied at the bottom. As the carriages pass each other at the halfway station of Nebozízek, you can get out and soak in the view from the restaurant of the same name.

At the top of the hill stands the southernmost perimeter wall of the old city – popularly known as the **Hladová zeď** (Hunger Wall) – which heads northwestwards to the Strahovský klášter and eastwards back down to Újezd. Instigated in the 1460s by Charles IV, it was much lauded at the time (and later by the Communists) as a great public work that provided employment for the burgeoning ranks of the city's destitute (hence its name); in fact, much of the wall's construction was paid for by the expropriation of Jewish property.

sv. Vavřinec (St Lawrence)

Petřínské sady • Easter–Oct Fri 5–6.30pm

If you follow the wall northwest from the funicular, you'll come to the twin-towered **church of sv Vavřinec**, which recalls the German name for Petřín – Laurenziberg. Built on the foundations of a Romanesque chapel, the Baroque church you see today is probably the work of Kilián Ignác Dienzenhofer, but the building itself was erected by the Palliardi family between 1739 and 1745. It's rarely open for visitors.

2

Petřínská Rozhledna (Petřín Tower)

Petřínské sady 633 • Daily: April–Sept 10am–10pm; March & Oct 10am–8pm; Nov–Feb 10am–6pm • 150Kč • ☎ 257 320 112, ⓦ muzeumprahy.cz

Topping Petřín hill is a series of buildings dating back to the 1891 Exhibition. The most celebrated of these is the **Petřínská Rozhledna**, an octagonal interpretation – though a mere fifth of the size – of the Eiffel Tower that shocked Paris in 1889, and a tribute to the city's strong cultural and political links with Paris at the time. It's 299 steps to the top, but the view from the public gallery is terrific in fine weather.

Bludiště

Petřínské sady • Daily: April–Sept 10am–10pm; March & Oct 10am–8pm; Nov–Feb 10am–6pm • 90Kč • ⓦ muzeumprahy.cz

Next to the Petřínská Rozhledna stands the **Bludiště**, a mini neo-Gothic castle complete with mock drawbridge. The first section of the interior features a **mirror maze**, a stroke of silly genius by the exhibition organizers. This is followed by an action-packed, life-sized **diorama** of the victory of Prague's students and Jews over the Swedes on the Charles Bridge in 1648. The humour of the convex and concave mirrors that lie beyond the diorama is so simple that it has both adults and kids giggling away.

Štefánikova hvězdárna (Štefánik Observatory)

Strahovská 205 • Opening hours vary throughout year; see website • 65Kč • ☎ 257 320 540, ⓦ observatory.cz

If you head south from the top of the funicular, you come immediately to the aromatic **Růžový sad** (Rose Garden), whose colour-coordinated rose beds are laid out in front of Petřín's **observatory**, the **Štefánikova hvězdárna**. Established in the mid-1920s when Prague's astronomers began to complain that their viewing positions on the roof of the main railway station and at the top of the Klementinum tower were being rendered useless by light pollution, the observatory is named after one of the founders of the Czechoslovak state in 1918, Slovak Milan Rastislav Štefánik, who was also a professional stargazer. The small astronomical exhibition inside is worth a quick look, and if it's a clear night, a peek through either of the observatory's two powerful telescopes is a treat. The observatory also holds lots of events for children.

Karel Hynek Mácha statue

Downhill from the Štefánikova hvězdárna observatory stands a bust of the leading Czech nineteenth-century Romantic poet **Karel Hynek Mácha**, who penned the poem *Maj* (May), on the subject of unrequited love. In spring, and in particular on May 1, the statue remains a popular place of pilgrimage for courting couples. In fact locally Petřín hill has something of a reputation among young lovers, several songs having been written about its virtues as a place to head for a bit of secluded romance.

Staré Město

Staré Město, literally "Old Town", is Prague's historic heart and second only to the Hrad in tourism terms. Its intricate and often confusing web of narrow lanes radiates medieval charm, though the occasional tour-group bottlenecks lessen the effect somewhat. However, despite the tourist crush, there are still plenty of residential areas and quiet backstreets in which to escape and discover hidden architectural gems. At the Old Town's heart is Staroměstské náměstí, Prague's showpiece main square, easily the most magnificent in Eastern Europe. And linking the area to Malá Strana is Charles Bridge, one of Europe's most impressive medieval structures, which has spanned the often destructively fickle Vltava for more than six centuries.

STARÉ MĚSTO HIGHLIGHTS

Charles Bridge Admire the open-air sculpture gallery on Europe's finest Gothic bridge. See below

Old Town Square The epicentre of Prague's medieval Old Town. See p.80

Gurmet Pasáž Dlouhá Artisan food court set against a backdrop of typical Prague functionalist architecture. See box, p.180

Astronomical Clock Watch the show this ornate clock performs on the hour. See box, p.81

Lehká hlava Experience Prague's best vegetarian restaurant. See p.178

U zlatého tygra No-nonsense Prague pub where writer Bohumil Hrabal once drank. See p.190

While exploring Staré Město, most visitors unwittingly retrace the **královská cesta**, the traditional route of the coronation procession from one of Prague's medieval gateways, the Prašná brána (see p.109), up to the Hrad. Established by the Přemyslids, the route was followed, with a few minor variations, by every king until the Emperor Ferdinand IV in 1836, the last of the Habsburgs to bother having himself crowned in Prague.

Merchants and craftsmen began settling in what is now Staré Město as early as the tenth century, and in the mid-thirteenth century it was granted town status, with jurisdiction over its own affairs. During the Counter-Reformation, the victorious Catholic nobles built fewer large palaces here than on the left bank, leaving the medieval street plan pretty much intact with the exception of the Klementinum (the Jesuits' powerhouse) and the Jewish Quarter, Josefov, which was largely reconstructed in the late nineteenth century (see p.90). Like so much of Prague, however, Staré Město is still, on the surface, overwhelmingly Baroque, built literally on top of its Gothic predecessor to guard against the floods that plagued the town.

Karlův most (Charles Bridge)

Tram #17, #18 or #24 to Karlovy lázně

Charles Bridge, or **Karlův most** – which for more than four hundred years was the only link between the two halves of Prague – is one of the city's most familiar monuments. Completed in 1402 by the court architect Peter Parler, it's an impressive chunk of medieval engineering, aligned slightly askew between two hefty Gothic gateways, but its fame is due almost entirely to the magnificent, mostly Baroque, **statues** (additions to the original structure) that punctuate its length. Individually, only a few of the works are outstanding, but taken collectively, set against the backdrop of the Hrad, the effect is impressive. The bridge is a perennially popular place to hang out: the crush of sightseers never abates during the day, when the niches created by the bridge-piers are occupied by souvenir hawkers and buskers, but at night things calm down a bit, and the views are, if anything, even more spectacular. Catching the bridge in the early hours of a snowy morning is sheer magic.

Brief history

Karlův most was begun by **Charles IV** in 1357 to replace an earlier structure, the **Judith Bridge** (Juditin most), which had been swept away by one of the Vltava's frequent floods. Given its strategic significance, it comes as no surprise that the bridge has played an important part in Prague's history: in 1648 it was the site of the last battle of the Thirty Years' War, fought between the besieging Swedes and an ad hoc army of Prague's students and Jews; in 1744 the invading Prussians were defeated at the same spot; and in 1848 it formed the front line between the revolutionaries on the Staré Město side and the reactionary forces on the left bank.

For its first four hundred years it was known simply as the Prague or **Stone Bridge** – only in 1870 was it officially named after its patron. Since 1950, the bridge has been closed to vehicles; incredibly a tram line once ran across it. Prague's most famous

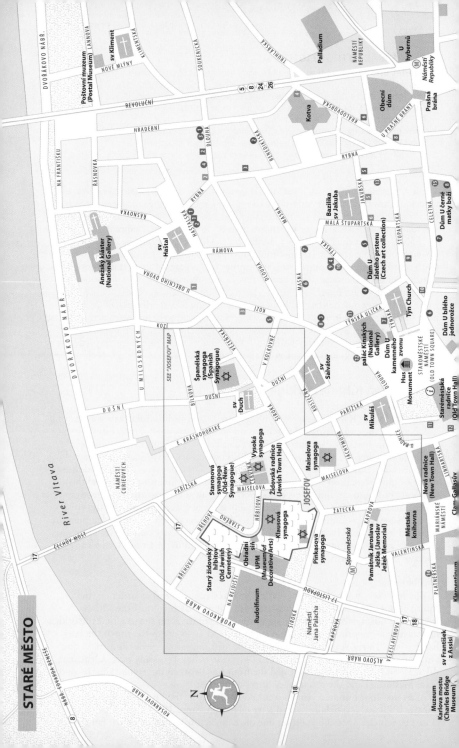

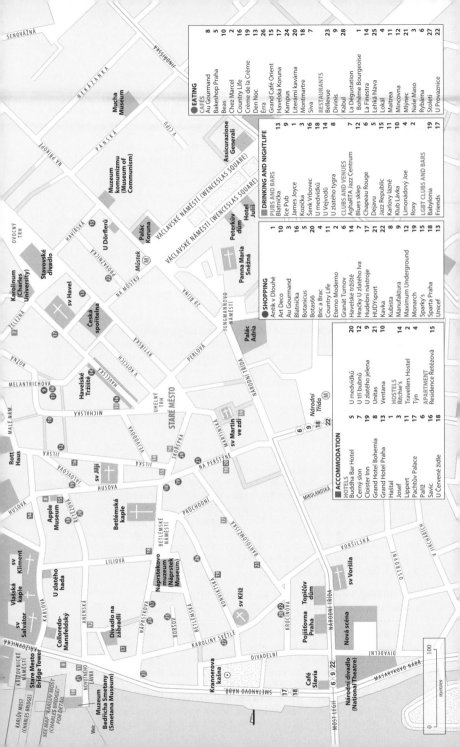

ST JOHN OF NEPOMUK

Where Emperor Charles IV sought to promote Václav (Wenceslas) as the nation's preferred saint, the Jesuits, with Habsburg backing, replaced him during the Counter-Reformation with another Czech martyr, **John of Nepomuk** (Jan Nepomucký). The latter had been arrested, tortured, and then thrown – bound and gagged – off Charles Bridge in 1393 on the orders of Václav IV, allegedly for refusing to divulge the secrets of the queen's confession. A cluster of stars was said to have appeared over the spot where he drowned, hence the halo of stars on every subsequent portrayal of the saint. The Jesuits, in order to ensure his canonization, exhumed his corpse and produced what they claimed to be his tongue – alive and licking, so to speak (it was in fact his very dead brain).

The more prosaic reason for John of Nepomuk's death was simply that he was caught up in a dispute between the archbishop and the king over the appointment of the abbot of Kladruby, and backed the wrong side. John was tortured on the rack along with two other priests, who were then made to sign a document denying that they had been maltreated; John, however, died before he could sign, and his dead body was secretly dumped in the river. The Vatican finally admitted this in 1961, some 232 years after his canonization.

landmark was last threatened by the river it spans in 2002 when water almost reached the tops of the arches in the biggest **flood** the city had seen in a century, but it survived to celebrate its 650th birthday in 2007.

Malostranské mostecké věže (Malá Strana bridge towers)

Karlův most • April–Sept daily 10am–10pm; March & Oct daily 10am–8pm; Nov–Feb daily 10am–6pm • 90Kč

Forming the entrance to Charles Bridge, on the Malá Strana side, are two unequal bridge towers, **Malostranské mostecké věže**, connected by a castellated arch. The smaller, stumpy tower was once part of the original Judith Bridge (named after the wife of Vladislav I, who built it in the twelfth century); the taller of the two, crowned by one of the pinnacled wedge-spires more commonly associated with the right bank, contains a small exhibition, but it's the bird's-eye views from the balcony that most come for.

The statues

A bronze **crucifix** has stood on Charles Bridge since its construction, but the first sculpture wasn't added until 1683, when **St John of Nepomuk** appeared (see box above). His **statue** was such a propaganda success that the Catholic church authorities ordered another 21 to be erected between 1706 and 1714. These included works by Prague's leading Baroque sculptors, led by Matthias Bernhard Braun and Ferdinand Maximilian Brokof. The sculptures, many of them crafted in sandstone, have weathered badly over the years and have mostly been replaced by copies; to see the originals, and several slightly controversial statues whose subjects fell out of favour and were removed, visit the Lapidárium (see p.143).

Staroměstská mostecká věž (Staré Město bridge tower)

Karlův most • Daily: April–Sept 10am–10pm; March & Oct 10am–8pm; Nov–Feb10am–6pm • 90Kč • ☎ 224 220 569

The **Staroměstská mostecká věž**, part of the Prague City Museum, is arguably the finest of the three towers on Charles Bridge, built entirely for show and not for defensive purposes. The western facade was wrecked in the battle of 1648 but the eastern facade is still encrusted in Gothic cake-like decorations from Peter Parler's workshop along with a series of mini-sculptures. The central figures are St Vitus, flanked by Charles IV on the right and his son, Václav IV, on the left; above stand two of Bohemia's patron saints, Adalbert and Sigismund. The severed heads of twelve of the Protestant leaders were suspended from the tower in iron baskets following their execution on Staroměstské náměstí in 1621, and all but one remained there until the Saxons passed through the capital ten years later. The tower's permanent exhibition is of little interest – the real attraction lies in the views from the roof.

Křižovnické náměstí

Tram #17, #18 or #24 to Karlovy lázně

Pass under the Staré Město bridge tower and you find yourself in **Křižovnické náměstí**, an awkward space hemmed in by its constituent buildings and, with cars and trams hurtling across the east side of the square, a hazardous spot for unwary pedestrians. Hard by the bridge tower is a nineteenth-century cast-iron statue of **Charles IV** (see box below), erected on the five hundredth anniversary of his founding of the university. There's a **museum** devoted to Charles Bridge here, plus two striking **churches** that are definitely worth exploring.

Muzeum Karlova mostu (Charles Bridge Museum)

Křižovnické náměstí 3 • Daily: May–Sept 10am–8pm; Oct–April 10am–6pm • 170Kč • ☎ 731 455 512, ⓦ muzeumkarlovamostu.cz • Tram #17, #18 or #24 to Karlovy lázně

The **Muzeum Karlova mostu** just off Charles Bridge houses an exhibition on the bridge's history. Anyone with an interest in stonemasonry and engineering will enjoy it; the archive film footage is interesting for anyone. From the museum it's possible to access the underground spaces beneath the **Church of František z Assisi**, the original Gothic building whose foundations were laid in 1252 by Anežka Přemyslovna, daughter of King Přemysl Otakar I, later St Anežka (St Agnes).

Notice the series of numbers above the entrance to the museum – 135797531. This palindrome gives the auspicious moment, to the minute, chosen for Charles IV

CHARLES IV (1316–78)

There may be more legends and intrigue associated with the reign of Rudolf II (see box, p.44), but it was under **Emperor Charles IV** (Karel IV to the Czechs) that Prague enjoyed its true golden age. In just over thirty years, Charles transformed the city into the effective capital of the Holy Roman Empire, establishing its archbishopric, its university, a host of monasteries and churches, an entire new town (Nové Město), plus several monuments that survive to this day – most notably St Vitus Cathedral, and, of course, Charles Bridge (Karlův most).

Born in Prague in 1316 (and christened Václav), Charles was the only son of King John of Luxembourg and Queen Eliška, daughter of Přemyslid King Václav II. Suspecting his wife of plotting to dethrone him, King John imprisoned her and Charles, the young heir spending his first three years in dungeons at Křivoklát and Loket castles. In 1323, he was despatched to the fashionable court of his uncle Charles IV of France, to keep him out of any further trouble and complete his education – he never saw his mother again. In France he was given the name Charles and married off to Blanche de Valois, the first of his four wives.

In 1346, his father (by then totally blind) was killed at the **Battle of Crécy**, and Charles, who escaped with just a wound, inherited the Czech crown. He immediately busied himself with building up his Bohemian power base, and within two years had himself elected **Holy Roman Emperor**. Fluent in Czech, French, German, Latin and Italian, Charles used his international contacts to gather a whole host of foreign artists to his new capital, most famously persuading the Italian man of letters, **Petrarch**, to pay a visit.

Though later chroniclers tried to paint Charles as chaste and pure, even he admitted in his autobiography that he had strayed in his youth: "seduced by the perverted people, we were perverted by the perverts", he wrote of his Italian sojourn. And just as Rudolf II created his *Kunst- und Wunderkammer*, Charles also spent much of his spare time amassing a bizarre **collection of relics** to ensure a smooth passage into the afterlife. He cajoled and blackmailed his way into obtaining part of the whip used in the Passion, two thorns from Christ's crown, a few drops of milk from the Virgin Mary and one of Mary Magdalene's breasts, all beautifully encased in reliquaries designed by Prague's finest goldsmiths.

3

THE CHARLES BRIDGE STATUES

(1) St Cosmas and St Damian Paid for by the university medical faculty. Jesus is flanked by these twin martyrs, both dressed in medieval doctors' garb – they were renowned for offering their medical services free of charge.

(2) St Wenceslas Added by Czech nationalists in the nineteenth century.

(3) St Vitus Brokof's St Vitus is depicted as a Roman legionary, his foot being gently nibbled by one of the lions that went on to devour him in a Roman amphitheatre.

(4) The founders of the Trinitarian Order One of the most striking sculptural groups, again by Brokof: St John of Matha, the hermit Felix of Valois and his pet stag, plus, for some unknown reason, St Ivan, whose good works included ransoming persecuted Christians – three petrified souls can be seen through the prison bars below – from the infidels, represented by a bored Turkish jailer and his rabid dog.

(5) St Philip Benizi Amid the blackened sandstone, the lightly coloured figure of the (at the time) only recently canonized Servite friar stands out as the only marble statue. At his feet sits the papal crown, which he turned down when it was offered to him in 1268.

(6) St Adalbert Prague's second bishop, the youthful cleric who was hounded out of the city on more than one occasion by the blissfully pagan citizens of Prague.

(7) St Cajetan Another (at the time) recently canonized saint; founder of the Theatine Order, he stands in front of a column of cherubs sporting a sacred heart.

(8) St Lutgard One of the most successful statues, sculpted by Braun when he was just 26 years old. The blind Flemish Cistercian nun is depicted in the middle of her celebrated vision, in which Christ appeared so that she could kiss his wounds.

(9) St Augustine & (10) St Nicholas of Tolentino Sponsored by the Augustinians; St Nicholas of Tolentino, one of St Augustine's followers, is depicted dishing out bread to the poor.

(11) St Jude Thaddaeus The apostle and patron saint of people in dire straits holds the club with which the pagans beat him to death.

(12) St Vincent Ferrer The recently restored Dominican friar stands over one of his converts to self-flagellation. The inscription below lists his miraculous achievements, including the conversion of 2500 Jews, forty resurrections and the exorcism of seventy demons. He is joined, somewhat inexplicably, by Bohemia's best-loved hermit, **St Procopius**.

(13) Roland If you look over the side of the bridge by (12), you'll see a rather sorry-looking nineteenth-century sculpture of Roland – Bruncvík in Czech – brandishing his miraculous golden sword (the real thing is said to be embedded in the bridge, to be used in case of municipal emergency). The original, erected to protect the rights of the Staré Město over the full extent of the bridge, was destroyed in 1648.

(14) St Anthony of Padua & (15) St Francis of Assisi The Franciscan pier – St Francis is a lifeless nineteenth-century figure accompanied by two angels.

(16) St John of Nepomuk (see box, p.72). The bridge's earliest and most popular sculpture. The only bronze statue, it's now green with age, the gold-leaf halo of stars and palm branch gently blowing in the breeze. St John's appearance here in 1683 was part of the Jesuits' campaign to have him canonized; the statue inspired hundreds of copies, which adorn bridges throughout central Europe. On the base, there's a bronze relief depicting his martyrdom, the figure of John now extremely worn through years of being touched for good luck.

(17) St Ludmila A rather androgynous version of Bohemia's first martyr holds the veil with which she was strangled. Standing alongside is her grandson, **St Wenceslas**, depicted as a young child; his future martyrdom is recounted in the bas-relief.

(18–21) St Francis Borgia (19) These two piers are occupied by glum nineteenth-century space-fillers: a trio of Bohemian saints – **Norbert**, **Sigismund** and **Wenceslas** (18) – **John the Baptist** (20) and **St Christopher** (21). Between piers 18 and 20 a small bronze cross set into the wall and a relief above wall level marks the spot where John of Nepomuk was dumped in the river; touch it and you're guaranteed to return to the city.

(22) St Cyril and St Methodius In 1890, the two Jesuit statues on this pier were swept away by a flood: the statue of the order's founder, St Ignatius Loyola, was replaced with the most recent additions to the bridge (in 1938), these ninth-century missionaries who introduced Christianity to the Slavs.

(23) St Francis Xavier The Jesuit missionary survived the order's unpopularity and his statue was replaced by a copy after it was swept away. One of the more unusual sculptural groups, the saint, who worked in India and the Far East, is held aloft by three Moorish and two "Oriental" converts; Brokof placed himself on the saint's left side.

(24) St Anne Mary's mother with Jesus and Mary.

(25) Joseph With a slightly older Jesus at his feet, this is a nineteenth-century replacement for another Brokof, this time destroyed by gunfire during the 1848 revolution.

(26) The Crucifixion Where the original fourteenth-century crucifix stood alone on the bridge for years. The gold-leaf, Hebrew inscription, "Holy, Holy, Holy is Our Lord of the Multitude", from the Book of Isaiah, was added in 1696, paid for by a Prague Jew who was ordered to do so by the city court, having been found guilty of blasphemy before the cross. The city's Jewish community persuaded the local council to erect a plaque here, explaining that the charges were drummed up and the inscription designed to humiliate Prague's Jews. Apart from Christ himself, all the figures, and the Pietà opposite **(27)**, were added in the nineteenth century.

(28) The Dominicans placed their founder, **St Dominic**, and their other leading light, **St Thomas Aquinas**, beside the **Madonna**; in≈among the cherubs is a dog with a burning torch in his mouth, a reference to the vision of Dominic's mother.

(29) St Barbara The patron saint of miners, whose beautifully sculpted hands so impressed Kafka, is accompanied by **St Margaret** and **St Elizabeth**.

(30) The Madonna presides over the kneeling figure of **St Bernard**, and a bubbling mass of cherubs mucking about with the instruments of the Passion – the cock, the dice and the centurion's gauntlet.

(31) St Ivo The patron saint of lawyers, flanked by Justice and a prospective client, stands with an outstretched hand, into which Prague law students traditionally place a glass of beer after their finals.

(32) At the very end of the bridge stands **Charles IV** himself, a work by Dresden sculptor Hähnel, erected in 1848.

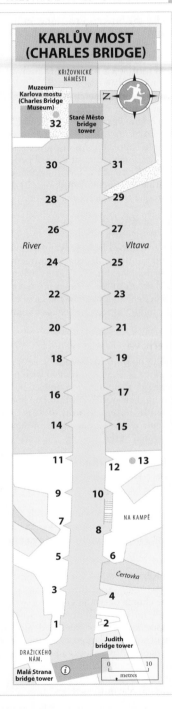

KARLŮV MOST (CHARLES BRIDGE)

3

to lay the bridge's first stone: in the year 1357, on the ninth day of the seventh month, at 5.31am. The Czechs' most illustrious monarch was fond of this sort of symbolism.

Sv František z Assisi (St Francis of Assisi)

Tram #17, #18 or #24 to Karlovy lázně

The half-brick **church of sv František z Assisi** was built in the 1680s to a design by Jean-Baptiste Mathey for the Czech Order of Knights of the Cross with a Red Star, the original gatekeepers of the old Judith Bridge. Founded in the thirteenth century, the order reached the zenith of its power in the seventeenth century, during which its monks supplied most of the archbishops of Prague.

The church's interior is a real period piece, dominated by its huge dome, decorated with a fresco of the Last Judgement by Václav Vavřinec Reiner, and smothered in rich marble and gilded furnishings; its design served as a blueprint for numerous subsequent Baroque churches in Prague.

Sv Salvátor (St Saviour)

Tram #17, #18 or #24 to Karlovy lázně

Over the road from sv František z Assisi is the **church of sv Salvátor**, its facade prickling with saintly statues that are attractively illuminated after dark. Founded in 1593, but not completed until 1714, sv Salvátor marks the beginning of the Jesuits' rise to power and is part of the Klementinum complex (see opposite). Like many of their churches, its design copies that of the Gesù church in Rome; it's worth a quick look, if only for the bubbly stucco and delicate ironwork in its triple-naved interior.

Karlova

Running from Křižovnické náměstí all the way to Malé náměstí, the narrow street of **Karlova** is invariably packed with people winding their way towards Staroměstské náměstí, their attention divided between checking out the souvenir shops and not losing their way. With Europop blaring from several shops, jesters' hats and puppets in abundance, and an army of Russian touts and over-enthusiastic Balkan shopkeepers, the place can feel oppressive in the height of summer, and is, in many ways, better savoured in the evening.

Vlašská kaple (Italian Chapel)

Karlova 1 • Open during services, concerts and exhibitions • Metro Staroměstská

At the first wiggle in Karlova, you come to the **Vlašská kaple**, which served the large community of Italian masons, sculptors and painters who settled in Prague during the Renaissance period, and is still, strictly speaking, the property of the Italian state. The present Vlašská kaple is a tiny oval Baroque chapel completed in 1600; sadly it's rarely open except during services and for the occasional exhibition and concert.

Sv Kliment

Karlova 1 • Open during services only • Metro Staroměstská

The **church of sv Kliment**, next to the Vlašská kaple and accessible via the same portal, is a minor gem of Prague Baroque by Dientzenhofer, with statues by Braun. There's a spectacular set of frescoes depicting the life of St Clement (whose martyrdom involved being lashed to an anchor and hurled into the Black Sea). The unusual spiky golden iconostasis was added in the 1980s by its owners since the late 1960s, the Greek Catholic church, who observe Orthodox rites but recognize the Pope as the head of their church. Services are held mornings and evenings in Ukrainian and Old Church Slavonic.

U zlatého hada (The Golden Serpent)

Liliova 17 • Metro Staroměstská

On the opposite side of Karlova to Vlašská kaple and sv Kliment, at the junction with Liliová, the former café **U zlatého hada** is where the Armenian Deomatus Damajan opened the city's first coffeehouse in 1708. According to legend, the café was always full, not least because Damajan had a red-wine fountain inside. It is now a café-restaurant, though sadly minus the fountain and original furnishings.

Apple Museum

Husova 21 • Daily 10am–10pm • 290Kč • ☎ 777 560 062, ⓦ applemuseum.com • Metro Staroměstská

Just off Karlova, the medieval lanes of Prague's Old Town provide an unlikely location for one of the world's best computer technology museums. Established in 2015 using private collections, the **Apple Museum** is unmissable, even for those with an aversion to iMacs and iPads. Guided – aptly – by your smartphone, the exhibition is the definitive Apple collection with everything from Steve Jobs' New Balance trainers and the very first Apple I computer to chunky 1990s printers and a section on Pixar, founded by Jobs in 1986. The rows of boxy early computers and more recent, flashier touchscreen technology are interspersed with the history of Apple, mainly focusing on Steve Jobs' departure from the company, his return in 1997 and his untimely death in 2011.

3

Klementinum

Křižovnická 190 • Daily 6am–11pm; 50min tours of the interior daily 10am–6pm • 220Kč • ☎ 733 129 252, ⓦ klementinum.com • Metro Staroměstská

As they stroll down Karlova, few tourists notice the **Klementinum**, the vast former Jesuit College on the north side of the street. In 1556, Ferdinand I summoned the Jesuits to Prague to help bolster the Catholic cause in Bohemia, handing them the church of sv Kliment which Dientzenhofer later rebuilt (see opposite). Initially, the Jesuits proceeded with caution, but once the Counter-Reformation set in, they were put in control of the entire university and provincial education system. From their secure base at sv Kliment, they began to establish space for a great Catholic seat of learning in the city by buying up the surrounding land, demolishing more than thirty old town houses and eventually occupying an area second in size only to the Hrad. In 1773, not long after the Klementinum was finally completed, the Jesuits were turfed out of the country and the building was donated to the university. Renovation work has been ongoing for years here, so be prepared for tours to miss out sections of the complex or not to run at all.

The Klementinum houses the **Národní knihovna** (National Library) and its millions of books, including the world's largest collection of works by the early English reformer, Yorkshireman John Wycliffe, whose writings had an enormous impact on the fourteenth-century Czech religious community, inspiring preachers such as Hus to speak out against the social conditions of the time. There's a side entrance beside the church of sv Salvátor, but the **main entrance** is inconspicuously placed just beyond the church of sv Kliment: both of them let you into a series of plain but tranquil courtyards. Here and there, sections of the original building have been left intact; the most ornate parts are now open to the public.

A TOWERING RECORD

As any Prague resident will proudly tell you, the **Astronomical Tower** within the Klementinum complex is the only place in the world that has been monitoring and recording meteorological data since 1775. What they may not know is that until 1928 the tower was also used to tell the citizens of Prague when it was noon: a man would wave a flag from the tower and a cannon would be fired from Petřín Hill.

Nearby is the visitors' entrance, where you must sign up for a **guided tour** in order to see inside. On the ground floor is the **Zrcadlová kaple** (Mirrored Chapel), which with its fake marble, gilded stucco and mirror panels boasts fine acoustics and is often used for concerts. Upstairs, in the **Barokní sál** (Baroque Library), a long room lined with leather tomes, note the ceiling, decorated with one continuous illusionistic fresco praising secular wisdom, and the wrought-iron gallery balustrade held up by wooden barley-sugar columns. Roughly at the centre of the Klementinum complex is the Jesuits' **Astronomická věž** (Astonomical Tower), from which you can enjoy a fantastic view over the city centre.

Mariánské náměstí and around

Opposite the southeastern corner of the Klementinum, the Renaissance corner house **U zlaté studné** (The Golden Well) stands out like a wedge of cheese; its thick stucco reliefs of assorted saints were commissioned in 1701 by the owner in gratitude for having been spared the plague. A short diversion here, down Seminářská, brings you out onto **Mariánské náměstí**, generally fairly deserted compared with heaving Karlova.

Nová radnice (New Town Hall)
Mariánské náměstí 2 • Metro Staroměstská

The rather severe **Nová radnice**, on the east side of Mariánské náměstí, is home to the city council. It's hard to believe that it was built by Osvald Polívka, architect of the exuberant Art Nouveau Obecní dům (see p.109). The most striking features are the two gargantuan figures that stand guard at either corner, by the sculptor of the Hus Monument, Ladislav Šaloun. The one on the left, looking like Darth Vader, is the "Iron Knight", mascot of the armourers' guild; to the right is the grotesquely caricatured sixteenth-century Jewish sage and scholar, **Rabbi Löw** (see box, p.93). Löw was visited by Death on several occasions, but escaped his clutches until he reached the ripe old age of 97, when the Grim Reaper hid in a rose innocently given to him by his granddaughter.

Clam-Gallasův palác
Husova 20 • Exhibitions Tues–Sun 10am–6pm • ☎ 236 003 135, ⓦ ahmp.cz • Metro Staroměstská

Despite its size – it occupies the ground space of a good five or six old houses – the Baroque **Clam-Gallasův palác** is easy to overlook in the tight space of Husova. It's a typically lavish affair by the Viennese architect Fischer von Erlach, with big and burly Atlantes supporting the portals. Obscure but interesting historical and cultural exhibitions take place here, organized by the Prague City Archives; evening concerts allow you to climb the grandiose staircase and have a peek at the sumptuous Baroque ceremonial rooms.

Malé náměstí
Metro Staroměstská

Traditionally the last stop on the way from Charles Bridge to Staroměstské náměstí is diminutive **Malé náměstí**, originally settled by French merchants in the twelfth century. The square was also home to the first apothecary in Prague, opened by a Florentine in 1353; the pharmacy **U zlaté koruny** (The Golden Crown), at no. 13, which boasts a restored Baroque interior, with chandeliers and a few drug jars, is now a jewellers'. However the square's best-known building is the russet-red, neo-Renaissance **Rott Haus**, originally an ironmonger's shop founded by V.J. Rott in 1840, whose facade is smothered in agricultural scenes and motifs inspired by the Czech artist Mikuláš Aleš. At the centre of the square stands a Renaissance fountain, dating from 1560, which retains its beautiful, original wrought-iron canopy, though it's no longer functioning.

Staroměstské náměstí (Old Town Square)

Metro Staroměstská

Dating back to around the tenth century, **Staroměstské náměstí** is easily the most spectacular square in Prague, the city's traditional epicentre and its oldest open space. It has had at least seven names over its thousand-year history, only gaining its current moniker in 1895. Most of the brightly coloured houses look solidly eighteenth century, but their Baroque facades hide considerably older buildings. From the eleventh century onwards, this was the city's main marketplace, known simply as Velké náměstí (Great Square), to which all roads in Bohemia led, and where merchants from all over Europe gathered. When the five towns that made up Prague were united in 1784, it was the **town hall** here that was made the seat of the new city council, and for the next two hundred years this grand piazza (along with Wenceslas Square) witnessed the country's most violent demonstrations and battles. Nowadays, its cobbles swarm with tourists all year round: in summer cafés spread out their tables, in winter there's a Christmas market, and every day people pour in to watch the town hall's astronomical clock chime, to sit on the benches in front of the **Hus Monument** and to have a drink in this historic showpiece.

Staroměstská radnice (Old Town Hall)

Staroměstské náměstí 1 • **Interiors** Mon 11am–7pm, Tues–Sun 9am–7pm **Tower** Mon 11am–10pm, Tues–Sun 9am–10pm • 250Kč • 📞 236 002 629, Ⓦ staromestskaradnicepraha.cz • Metro Staroměstská

It wasn't until the reign of King John of Luxembourg (1310–46) that Staré Město was allowed to build its own town hall, now known as the **Staroměstská radnice**. Short of funds, the citizens decided against a new structure, buying a corner house on the square instead and simply adding an extra floor; later on, they added the east wing, with its graceful Gothic oriel and obligatory wedge-tower. Gradually, over the centuries, the neighbouring merchants' houses to the west were incorporated into the building, so that now it stretches all the way across to the richly sgraffitoed **Dům U minuty**, which juts out into the square.

On May 8, 1945, on the final day of the Prague Uprising, the Nazis still held on to Staroměstské náměstí, and in a last desperate act set fire to the town hall's neo-Gothic **east wing**, which stretched almost to the church of sv Mikuláš. The tower and oriel chapel were rebuilt immediately, but only a crumbling fragment remains of the east wing; the rest of it is marked by the stretch of grass to the north. Embedded in the wall of the tower is a plaque marked "Dukla", and a case containing a handful of earth from the Slovak pass where some eighty thousand Soviet and Czechoslovak soldiers lost their lives in the first (and most costly) battle to liberate the country in October 1944.

The town hall is a popular place to get married, but visitors can also see the Romano-Gothic **cellars**, and the Gothic **chapel**, designed by Peter Parler, which has patches of medieval wall painting, plus a couple of relatively unexciting municipal chambers. You can also see the Apostles on the square's **astronomical clock** (see box opposite) close up – huge crowds gather just before the clock strikes the hour to watch them filing out. Fewer enjoy the real treat here – a clamber up the almost 70m-tall **tower** for a panoramic sweep across Prague's spires; tickets are available on the third floor. Climbing the tower also gets you a

---

HEADS ROLL IN THE OLD TOWN

Set into the paving on the western side of the Old Town Hall (Staroměstská radnice), **27 white crosses** commemorate one of the bloodiest days ever seen on the Old Town Square. On June 21, 1621, 27 Protestant leaders, condemned to death on the orders of Emperor Ferdinand II following the Battle of Bílá hora, were publicly executed here by the Prague executioner Jan Mlydář. Twenty-four enjoyed the nobleman's privilege and had their heads lopped off; the three remaining commoners were hanged, drawn and quartered. Mlydář also chopped off the right hand of three of the nobles, and hacked off the tongue of the rector of Prague University, Johannes Jessenius. The severed heads were then displayed on the Charles Bridge for all to see.

THE ASTRONOMICAL CLOCK

For many visitors, a major highlight of the Old Town is the *orloj* or **astronomical clock**, which has been gleaming on the south wall of the Old Town Hall (Staroměstská radnice) since the early fifteenth century. The working figures were added in 1490 by a **Master Hanuš** who, legend has it, was then blinded with a red-hot poker by the town councilors to make sure he couldn't repeat the feat anywhere else. In retaliation, he groped his way around the clock, succeeded in stopping it, and then promptly died of a heart attack – the clock stayed broken for more than eighty years.

Today, a crowd of tourists gathers every hour (9am–9pm) in front of the tower to watch a mechanical dumbshow by the clock's assorted figures, which all had to be re-carved by a local puppeteer after World War II: the Apostles shuffle past the top two windows, bowing to the audience, while perched on pinnacles below are the four threats to the city as perceived by the medieval mind – Death carrying his hourglass and tolling his bell, the Jew with his moneybags (since 1945 minus his stereotypical beard), Vanity admiring his reflection and a turbaned Turk shaking his head. Beneath the moving figures, four characters representing Philosophy, Religion, Astronomy and History stand motionless throughout the performance. Finally, a cockerel pops out and flaps its wings to signal that the show's over; the clock then chimes the hour.

The complex **clock face** tells three different sets of time: the golden hand points to a double set of Roman numerals from I to XII, and when the hand points to the top XII, it's noon (**Central European Time**); it also points to the outer ring of Gothic numbers from 1 to 24, which can rotate independently, and when the hand points to 24 it is sunset (**Old Bohemian Time**); finally, the numbers from 1 to 12 immediately below the Roman numerals divide the day into twelve hours, however many normal hours of daylight there are, and the golden sun tells you what time of day it is (**Babylonian Time**). The clock also charts – as the medieval astronomer saw it – the movements of the sun and planets around the earth, and the movement of the sun and moon through the signs of the zodiac; therefore, if you know how, you can determine the date. The revolving dial below the clock face is decorated with bucolic paintings of the "cycle of twelve idylls from the life of the Bohemian peasant", plus the signs of the zodiac, by **Josef Mánes**, a leading light in the Czech national revival. Around the edge, yet another pointer shows what day of the month and week it is, and, more importantly, what saint's day it is (and therefore when it's a holiday).

The *orloj* last had a service in the 1980s, so don't be disappointed in coming years if you find a video mapping project in its place as the clock gets a much-needed overhaul.

3

peek at the vast **model** of contemporary Prague, on the fourth floor, made over the course of twenty years out of cardboard and plexiglass by Vlastimil Slíva and Jiří Straka. The whole caboodle has recently received some much-needed renovation with a completely reopening set for May 2018.

Hus Monument

Metro Staroměstská

The last major feature added to the Old Town Square is the colossal **Hus Monument**, a turbulent sea of blackened bodies – the oppressed to his right, the defiant to his left – out of which rises the majestic moral authority of Jan Hus himself (see box, p.88), gazing into the horizon. For the sculptor Ladislav Šaloun, a maverick who received no formal training, the monument was his life's work, commissioned in 1900 when the Art Nouveau-style Vienna Secession was at its peak, but strangely old-fashioned by the time it was completed in 1915. It would be difficult to claim that it blends in with its Baroque surroundings, yet this has never mattered to the Czechs, for whom its significance goes far beyond aesthetics.

The Austrians refused to hold an official unveiling of the statue; in protest, on July 6, 1915, the five hundredth anniversary of the death of Hus, the people of Prague smothered the monument in flowers. Since then it has been a powerful symbol of Czech nationalism: in March 1939 it was draped in swastikas by the invading Nazis, and in August 1968 it was shrouded in funeral black by locals as a protest against the

Soviet invasion. The inscription along the base is a quote from the will of Comenius, one of Hus's later followers, and includes Hus's most famous dictum, *Pravda vítězí* (Truth Prevails), words which appear (somewhat ironically in president Zeman's case, many might say) on the Czech president's official banner under the Czech coat of arms.

Sv Mikuláš

Staroměstské náměstí • Mon–Sat 10am–4pm, Sun noon–4pm • Free • Ⓦ svmikulas.cz • Metro Staroměstská

The destruction of the east wing of the town hall in 1945 rudely exposed Kilian Ignaz Dientzenhofer's **church of sv Mikuláš**, built in just three years between 1732 and 1735. The original was founded by German merchants in the thirteenth century, and served as Staré Město's parish church until the Týn church was completed. Later, it was handed over to the Benedictines, who commissioned Dientzenhofer to replace it with the present building. His hand is clearly evident: the south facade is decidedly luscious – Braun's blackened statuary pop up at every cornice – promising an interior to surpass even its sister church of sv Mikuláš (see p.58) in Malá Strana, which Dientzenhofer built with his father immediately afterwards. Inside, however, the space is considerably smaller, theatrically organized into a series of interlocking curves. It's also rather plainly furnished, partly because it was closed down by Joseph II and turned into a storehouse for grain and furniture. Instead, your eyes are drawn sharply upwards to the impressive stuccowork, the wrought-iron galleries and the trompe l'oeil frescoes on the dome. The acoustics are superb, and the church hosts regular **concerts**.

Palác Kinských – Asian art

Staroměstské náměstí 12 • Tues–Sun 10am–6pm • 150Kč • ☎ 224 301 122, Ⓦ ngprague.cz • Metro Staroměstská

The largest secular building on Old Town Square is the Rococo **Palác Kinských**, designed by Kilian Ignaz Dientzenhofer and built by his son-in-law Anselmo Lurago. In the nineteenth century it had a German *Gymnasium* at the rear, attended by, among others, Franz Kafka (whose father ran a haberdashery shop on the ground floor). However, the palace is perhaps most infamous as the venue for the fateful speech by the Communist prime minister, Klement Gottwald, who walked out onto the grey stone balcony one snowy February morning in 1948, flanked by Party honchos, to address thousands of enthusiastic supporters who packed the square below. This was the beginning of *Vítězný únor* (Victorious February), the bloodless coup that brought the Communists to power and sealed the fate of the country for the next 41 years. Today the building is partially in the care of the **National Gallery**, which displays the best of its 13,000-piece collection of **Asian art** here along with temporary exhibitions on Oriental themes.

Dům U kamenného zvonu (House at the Stone Bell)

Staroměstské náměstí 13 • Tues–Sun 10am–8pm • 120Kč • ☎ 224 828 245, Ⓦ ghmp.cz • Metro Staroměstská

Until the 1970s, **Dům U kamenného zvonu** was much like any other of the merchant houses that line Old Town Square – covered in a thick icing of Baroque plasterwork and topped by an undistinguished roof gable. In the process of restoration, however, it was controversially stripped down to its Gothic core, which uncovered the original honey-coloured stonework and simple wedge roof, and it now serves as a central venue for cutting-edge modern art exhibitions, lectures and concerts organized by the **Galerie hlavního města Prahy** (City Gallery Prague).

Dům U bílého jednorožce (House at the White Unicorn)

Staroměstské náměstí 20 • Metro Staroměstská

Rather than a white unicorn, the sixteenth-century house sign on the **Dům U bílého jednorožce** actually depicts a one-horned ram. Bedřich Smetana opened a music academy here in 1848 and this was also the site of Prague's most famous *salon*, run by Berta Fanta. Prague German writers Franz Kafka, Max Brod and Franz Werfel attended, as did **Albert Einstein**, who worked in Prague for a number of years before World War I.

Týn church

Staroměstské náměstí 604 • Mon–Sat 10am–1pm & 3–5pm, Sun 10am–noon • Donation requested • ☎ 222 318 186 •
Metro Staroměstská

Staré Město's most impressive Gothic structure, the mighty **Týn church** (Chrám Matky
boží před Týnem), is far more imposing than the main square's church of sv Mikuláš.
Its two irregular towers, bristling with baubles, spires and pinnacles, rise like giant
antennae above the arcaded houses that otherwise obscure its facade, and are
spectacularly lit up at night. Like the nearby Hus Monument, the Týn church, begun
in the fourteenth century under Charles IV, is a source of Czech national pride. In an
act of defiance, George of Poděbrady, the last Czech and the only Hussite king of
Bohemia, adorned the high stone gable with a statue of himself and a giant gilded
kalich (chalice), the mascot of all Hussite sects. The church remained a hotbed of
Hussitism until the Protestants' crushing defeat at the Battle of Bílá hora, after which
the chalice was melted down to provide the newly ensconced statue of the Virgin Mary
with a golden halo, sceptre and crown.

Despite being one of the main landmarks of Staré Město, it's well-nigh impossible to
appreciate the church from anything but a considerable distance, since it's boxed in by
the houses around it, some of which are actually built right against the walls. To reach
the **entrance**, take the third arch on the left, which passes under the Venetian gables
of the former Týn School. The church's high-vaulted, narrow nave is bright white,
punctuated at ground level by black and gold Baroque altarpieces. One or two original
Gothic furnishings survive, notably the fifteenth-century baldachin, housing a winged
altar in the north aisle, and, opposite, the pulpit, whose panels are enhanced by some
sensitive nineteenth-century icons. Behind the pulpit, you'll find a superb, winged altar
depicting John the Baptist, dating from 1520, and executed by the artist known as
Master I.P. To view the north portal and canopy, which bears the hallmark of Peter
Parler's workshop, you must go back outside and head down Týnská.

The pillar on the right of the chancel steps contains the red marble **tomb of Tycho
Brahe**, the famous Danish astronomer who arrived in Prague wearing a silver and gold
false nose, having lost his own in a duel over a woman in Rostock. Court astronomer
to Rudolf II for just two years, Brahe laid much of the groundwork for Johannes
Kepler's later discoveries – Kepler getting his chance of employment when Brahe died
of a burst bladder after one of Petr Vok's notorious binges in 1601.

Týn (Ungelt)

Metro Staroměstská

Just off Týnská, the alleyway north of the Týn church, lies the picturesque cobbled
courtyard of **Týn**, previously known by its German name, Ungelt (meaning "No
Money", a pseudonym used to deter marauding invaders), which, as the trading base
of German merchants, was one of the first settlements on the Vltava. A hospice,
church and hostel were built for the merchants, and by the fourteenth century the
area had become a successful international marketplace; soon afterwards the traders
moved up to the Hrad, and the court was transformed into a palace. The complex
has since been restored, and is now a pretty place in which to stroll; the Dominicans
have moved back into one section, while the remainder houses shops, cafés, pubs,
restaurants and a hotel.

Dům U zlatého prstenu (House of the Golden Ring)

Týnská 6 • Daily 9am–8pm • 150Kč • ☎ 224 827 022, 🖰 muzeumprahy.cz • Metro Staroměstská

Heading along Týnská you soon arrive at a handsome Gothic townhouse, the **Dům U
zlatého prstenu**, which in 2016 passed into the hands of the Prague City Museum
after spending a quarter of a century as a gallery. A brand-new exhibition, opened to
coincide with the seven-hundredth anniversary of the birth of Emperor Charles IV,

examines the way Prague was transformed in the fourteenth century into a Gothic showpiece during the reign of the Czechs' most illustrious ruler. Exhibits look at Charles IV's plans for the city and the reality of what was achieved. The unrivalled highlight is the virtual model of fourteenth-century Prague showing all of Charles' additions, including the romantically named Cattle Market, the Dobytčí trh, now known as Karlovo náměstí, the largest in Europe when established.

Celetná

Metro Můstek/Náměstí Republiky

Celetná, whose name comes from the bakers who used to bake a particular type of small loaf (*calty*) here in the Middle Ages, leads east from Staroměstské náměstí direct to the Prašná brána, one of the original gateways of the old town. It's one of the oldest streets in Prague, lying along both the former trade route from the old town market square and the *králová cesta*, the route the kings of Bohemia once took to their coronation at the Hrad. Its buildings were smartly refaced in the Baroque period, and their pastel plasterwork is now crisply maintained. Dive down one of the covered passages to the left and into the backstreets and you'll soon lose the crowds.

Dům U Černé Matky boží (House at the Black Madonna)

Ovocný trh 19 · Tues 10am–7pm, Wed–Sun 10am–6pm · 150Kč · ☎ 778 543 902, ⓦ upm.cz · Metro Náměstí Republiky

Two-thirds of the way along Celetná, at the junction with Ovocný trh, stands the **Dům U Černé Matky boží**, built as a department store in 1911–12 by Josef Gočár and one of the best examples of Czech Cubist architecture in Prague. Czech Cubism was a short-lived style whose most surprising attribute, in this instance, is its ability to adapt existing Baroque motifs: Gočár's house sits much more happily among its eighteenth-century neighbours than, for example, the functionalist shop opposite – one of Gočár's later designs from the 1930s. On the second and third floors you'll find the reinstated Museum of Cubism, a branch of the Museum of Decorative Arts, where you can admire some extremely rare art, ceramics and furniture from the interwar period by stellar names such as Emil Filla, Josef Čapek (brother of Karel Čapek), Josef Chochol and Josef Gočár. Enjoy a post-museum coffee in swish, First Republic-style at the recreated Cubist **café** on the first floor (see p.178).

Bazilika sv Jakuba

Malá Štupartská 6 · Sat–Thurs 9.30am–noon & 2–4pm, Fri 9.30am–noon & 2–3pm · Free · Metro Náměstí Republiky

Concealed in the backstreets north of Celetná is the Franciscan **Basilica of sv Jakub**, or **St James**, with its distinctive stucco portal on Malá Štupartská. The church's massive Gothic proportions – it has the longest nave in Prague after the cathedral – make it a favourite venue for organ recitals, Mozart masses and other concerts. After the great fire of 1689, Prague's Baroque artists remodelled the entire interior, adding huge pilasters, a series of colourful frescoes and more than twenty side altars. The most famous of these is the tomb of the count of Mitrovice, in the northern aisle, designed by Fischer von Erlach and Prague's own Maximilian Brokof.

The church has close historical links with the **butchers of Prague**, who were given a chapel in gratitude for their defence of the city in 1611 and 1648. Hanging high up on the west wall, on the right as you enter, is a thoroughly decomposed human forearm (it looks like a piece of old rope hanging from a chain). It has been there for more than four hundred years, ever since, as legend would have it, a thief tried to steal the jewels of the Madonna from the high altar. As the thief reached out, the Virgin supposedly grabbed his arm and refused to let go. The next day the congregation of butchers had no option but to lop it off, and it has hung there as a warning ever since.

Anežský klášter (Convent of St Agnes) – medieval art

U Milosrdných 17 • Tues–Sun 10am–6pm • 220Kč • ☎ 221 879 216, ⓦ ngprague.cz • Tram #5, #8, #24 or #26 to Dlouhá třída

North of sv Jakub through the backstreets, the **Anežský klášter**, Prague's oldest surviving Gothic building, stands within a stone's throw of the river as it loops around to the east. It was founded in 1233 as a Franciscan convent, and takes its name from Anežka (Agnes), youngest daughter of Přemysl Otakar I, who left her life of regal privilege to become the convent's first abbess. Anežka took her vows seriously, living on a diet of raw onions and fruit with long periods of fasting, and in 1874 she was beatified to try and combat the spread of Hussitism among the Czechs. She was officially canonized, an event which finally took place on November 12, 1989, when Czech Catholics were invited to a special Mass at St Peter's in Rome. An old Czech prophecy claimed that "There will be peace and prosperity in Bohemia upon the canonization of Agnes" – four days later the Velvet Revolution kicked off.

The convent itself has enjoyed a chequered history. It was used as an arsenal by the Hussites, and eventually closed down in 1782 by Joseph II, who turned it into a place where the Prague poor could live and set up their own workshops. The whole neighbourhood remained a slum area until well into the twentieth century, and its restoration only finally took place in the 1980s.

The convent now provides a fittingly atmospheric setting for the **National Gallery's medieval art collection**, in particular the art that flourished under the patronage of Charles IV.

Medieval art collection

The **medieval art** exhibition is arranged chronologically, starting with a remarkable silver-gilt casket from 1360 used to house the skull of sv Ludmila. The nine panels from the altarpiece of the Cistercian monastery at Vyšší Brod in South Bohemia, from around 1350, are among the finest in central Europe; the panel depicting the Annunciation is particularly rich in iconography. The real gems of the collection, however, are the six panels by **Master Theodoric**, who created more than one hundred such paintings for Charles IV's castle chapel at Karlštejn. These larger-than-life, half-length portraits of saints, Church Fathers and so on are full of intense expression and rich colour, their depictions spilling onto the embossed frames.

The three late fourteenth-century panels by the **Master of Třeboň** show an ever-greater variety of balance, delicacy and depth, and the increasing influence of Flemish paintings of the period. The quality of the works in the gallery's largest room is pretty uneven, so head straight to the end of the room where you'll find Cranach's superb *Portrait of a Young Lady Holding a Fern*. Beyond are a couple of smaller rooms, where you'll find two unusual carved wooden bust reliquaries of saints Adalbert and Wenceslas. For a glimpse of some extraordinary draughtsmanship, check out the woodcuts by Cranach the Elder, Dürer and the lesser-known Hans Burgkmair – the seven-headed beast in Dürer's *Apocalypse* cycle is particularly stiking. One oil painting that stands out is Albrecht Altdorfer's colourful, languid *Martyrdom of St Florian*. Finally, don't miss the superb sixteenth-century wood sculptures by **Master I.P.**, including an incredibly detailed *Christ the Saviour and the Last Judgement*, in which Death's entrails are in the process of being devoured by a frog.

You exit via the Gothic cloisters and the bare church that serves as a resting place for, among others, Václav I (1205–53) and Anežka herself.

Stavovské divadlo (Estates Theatre)

Ovocný trh 1 • Tours 200Kč; call in advance for English-language tours • ☎ 224 902 231, ⓦ narodni-divadlo.cz • Metro Můstek

Dominating **Ovocný trh**, site of the old fruit market, is the lime-green and dirty-white **Stavovské divadlo**. Built in the early 1780s for the entertainment of Prague's large and powerful German community, the theatre is one of the finest Neoclassical buildings in

Prague, reflecting the pumped-up self-confidence of its former patrons. But the Stavovské divadlo also has its firm place in Czech history, too, for it was here that the Czech national anthem, *Kde domov můj?* (*Where Is My Home?*), was first performed, as part of the comedy *Fidlovačka* by J.K. Tyl. It is also something of a place of pilgrimage for **Mozart** fans, since it is the only opera house left standing in which Mozart actually performed. Indeed, it was here, rather than in the hostile climate of Vienna, that the composer chose to premiere both *Don Giovanni* and *La Clemenza di Tito*.

Karolinum (Charles University)

Ovocný trh 3 • ☎ 224 491 251, Ⓦ cuni.cz • Metro Můstek

On the north side of the Stavovské divadlo is the historical home of **Charles University**, the **Karolinum**, established by Charles IV in 1348 as the first university in the Czech Lands. Although it was open to all nationalities, with instruction in Latin, it wasn't long before disputes between the various "nations" came to a head. In 1408, Václav IV issued the Decree of Kutná Hora, which gave the Bohemian "nation" – both Czech- and German-speaking – a majority vote in the university. In protest, the other "nations" upped and left for Leipzig, the first of many ethnic problems that continued to bubble away throughout the university's six-hundred-year history until the forced and violent expulsion of all German-speakers after World War II.

To begin with, the university had no fixed abode; it wasn't until 1383 that Václav IV bought the present site of the Karolinum. All that's left of the original fourteenth-century building is the Gothic oriel window that juts out from the south wall; the rest was trashed by the Nazis in 1945. The twentieth-century main entrance is a modern red-brick curtain wall building by Jaroslav Fragner, set back from the street and inscribed with the original Latin name "Universitas Karolina". Just a couple of small departments and the chancellor's office and administration are now housed here, with the rest spread over the length and breadth of the city. However, this is still where students are sworn into the university and go through their graduation ceremony. The heavily restored Gothic vaults, on the ground floor of the south wing, are now used as a contemporary **art gallery**.

Sv Havel

Havelská • Mon, Tues, Thurs & Sat 11am–noon, Wed & Fri 3–4.30pm, Sun 8am–noon • ☎ 222 318 186 • Metro Můstek

Generally overlooked by tourists, the **church of sv Havel** has an undulating Baroque facade designed by Santini. The name of the church has, of course, no relation to the playwright-president but is dedicated to the Irish monk, St Gall. It was built in the thirteenth century to serve the German-speaking community who had been invited to Prague partly to replace the Jewish traders killed in the city's 1096 pogrom. Between 1380 and 1390 none other than future saint John of Nepomuk served as parish priest here. During the re-catholization of the Czech Lands in the eighteenth century the church was handed over to the Carmelites, who redesigned the interior, now usually only visible through an iron grille.

Havelské tržiště (Havelské market)

Havelská • Mon–Sat 7am–6.30pm, Sun 8am–6pm • Metro Můstek

Extending the length of Havelská, **Havelské tržiště** is the last surviving open-air bazaar in the historical city centre. It was originally run by the German community, and stretched all the way from Ovocný trh to Uhelný trh, taking in a couple of other streets as well at its zenith. It was once a fruit and veg market, but today souvenirs have taken over, pushing out all other produce except for a small amount of outrageously priced fruit. However, don't be put off as some of the mementos on sale here are of a better quality than in Prague's countless souvenir shops.

Sv Martin ve zdi (St Martin-in-the-Wall)

Martinská 8 • Summer Mon–Sat 2–4pm • ⓦ www.martinvezdi.eu • Metro Můstek

The Havelská market runs west into **Uhelný trh**, which gets its name from the *uhlí* (coal) that was sold here in medieval times. South of Uhelný trh, down Martinská, the street miraculously opens out to make room for the twelfth-century **church of sv Martin ve zdi**. It's still essentially a Romanesque structure, adapted to suit Gothic tastes a century later. Closed down in 1784 by Joseph II and turned into a warehouse, shops and flats, the church was bought and restored by the city council in 1904; they added the creamy neo-Renaissance tower, and eventually handed the church over to the Czech Brethren. For them, it has a special significance as the place where communion "in both kinds" (bread and wine), one of the fundamental demands of the Hussites, was first administered to the whole congregation, in 1414. There's very little to see inside, which is just as well as most of the year it's open only for services and concerts which are listed on the church's website.

Bartolomějská

3

Metro Národní třída

Around the corner from sv Martin ve zdi is the gloomy, sterile **Bartolomějská** street, dominated by a tall, grim-looking building on its south side, which served as the main interrogation centre of the **Communist secret police**, the Státní bezpečnost, or StB. As in the rest of Eastern Europe, the accusations (often unproven) and revelations of who exactly collaborated with the StB caused the downfall of leading politicians right across the political spectrum. The building is now back in the hands of the Franciscan nuns who occupied the place prior to 1948, and its former police cells now serve as rooms.

Betlémská kaple

Betlémské náměstí 4 • Daily: April–Oct 10am–7pm; Nov–March 10am–6pm • 60Kč • ☎ 224 248 595, ⓦ bethlehemchapel.eu • Metro Národní třída

The irregular but attractive Betlémské square is named after the **Betlémská kaple**, whose high wooden gables face onto the normally quiet piazza. The chapel was founded in 1391 by religious reformists, who, denied the right to build a church, proceeded instead to erect the largest chapel in Bohemia, with a total capacity of three thousand. Sermons were delivered not in the customary Latin, but in Czech – a truly revolutionary concept at the time. From 1402 to 1413 **Jan Hus** (see box, p.88) preached here, regularly pulling in more than enough commoners to fill the chapel. Hus was eventually excommunicated for his outspokenness, found guilty of heresy and burnt at the stake at the Council of Constance in 1415.

The chapel continued to attract reformists from all over Europe for another two centuries. The Anabaptist **Thomas Müntzer** preached here in the sixteenth century, having fled to Prague from Zwickau – he later became one of the leaders of the German Peasants' War. Of the original building, only the three outer walls remain, with restored patches of the biblical scenes, used to get the message across to the illiterate congregation. The rest is a scrupulous Communist-era reconstruction by Jaroslav Fragner, using the original plans and a fair amount of imaginative guesswork. The initial reconstruction work was carried out after the war, the Communists keen to portray Hus as a Czech nationalist and social critic as much as a religious reformer, and, of course, to dwell on the revolutionary Müntzer's later appearances here.

Náprstkovo muzeum (Náprstek Museum)

Betlémské náměstí 1 • Tues–Sun 10am–6pm • 100Kč • ☎ 224 497 500, ⓦ nm.cz • Metro Národní třída

At the western end of Betlémské náměstí stands the **Náprstkovo muzeum**, whose founder, Czech nationalist **Vojta Náprstek**, was inspired by the great Victorian

3

JAN HUS

The legendary preacher – and Czech national hero – **Jan Hus** was born in the small village of Husinec in South Bohemia around 1372. From a childhood of poverty, he enjoyed a steady rise through the Czech education system, taking his degree at the Karolinum in the 1390s, and eventually being ordained as a deacon and priest around 1400. Although without doubt an admirer of the English religious reformer **John Wycliffe** (and the Lollards), Hus was by no means as radical as many of his colleagues who preached at the Betlémská kaple. Nor did he actually advocate many of the more famous tenets of the heretical religious movement that took his name: **Hussitism**. In particular, he never advocated giving communion "in both kinds" (bread and wine) to the general congregation.

In the end, it wasn't the disputes over Wycliffe, whose books were burnt on the orders of the archbishop in 1414, that proved Hus's downfall, but an argument over the sale of indulgences to fund the inter-papal wars that prompted his unofficial trial at the **Council of Constance**. Having been guaranteed safe conduct by Emperor Sigismund himself, Hus naïvely went to Constance to defend his views, and was burnt at the stake as a heretic on July 6, 1415. The Czechs were outraged, and Hus became a national hero overnight, inspiring thousands to rebel against the authorities of the day. In 1999, Pope John Paul II expressed "deep regret" over his death, but refused to pardon Hus – however, the anniversary of Hus's death (July 6) is a **Czech national holiday**.

---

museums of London while in exile following the 1848 revolution. On his return, he turned the family brewery into a museum, initially intending it to concentrate on the virtues of industrial progress. However, Náprstek's interests gradually shifted towards anthropology and it is his **ethnographic collections** that are now displayed in the museum, the original technological exhibits having long since been carted off to the Národní technické muzeum (see p.137). Despite the fact that the museum could clearly do with an injection of cash, it still manages to put on some truly excellent temporary ethnographic exhibitions on the ground floor. The permanent collection begins on the first floor, where you'll find the skeleton of a fin-whale more than 20m long suspended from the ceiling. Underneath it there's a range of exhibits from the Americas, with everything from Inuit furs and Apache smoking pipes decorated with porcupine quills and beads, to toy skeletons on bicycles from Mexico and Amazonian shrunken heads. Upstairs, the much smaller display of items from Australia and Oceania includes some remarkable sculptures.

Sv Jiljí

Husova 8 • ☎ 224 218 440 • Metro Národní třída

One building that might catch your eye between Betlémské náměstí and Karlova is the **church of sv Jiljí** (St Giles). The outward appearance of the building suggests another Gothic masterpiece, but the interior is decked out in the familiar black baroque excess of the eighteenth century, with huge gilded acanthus-leaf capitals and barley-sugar columns galore. The **frescoes** by Václav Vavřinec Reiner (who is buried in the church) are full of praise for his patrons, the Dominicans, who took over the church after the Protestant defeat of 1620. They were expelled, in turn, after the Communists took power, only to return following the events of 1989. Reiner's paintings also depict the unhappy story of **St Giles** himself, a ninth-century hermit who is thought to have lived somewhere in Provence. Out one day with his pet deer, Giles and his companion were chased by the hounds of King Wanda of the Visigoths. The hounds were rooted to the spot by an invisible power, while the arrow from the hunters struck Giles in the foot as he defended his pet – the hermit was later looked upon as the patron saint of cripples. Sunday services here (9.30am and noon) are in Polish.

Divadlo na zábradlí (Theatre on the Balustrade)

Anenské náměstí 5 • ⓦ nazabradli.cz • Tram #17, #18 or #24 to Karlovy lázně

The **Divadlo na zábradlí** was founded in 1958 by Czech actors Jiří Suchý and Ivan Vyskočil, among others. As well as championing mime as a genre, the venue was also at the centre of Prague's absurdist theatre scene in the 1960s, with Václav Havel himself working first as a stagehand and later as resident playwright. Later, it became something of a refuge for film directors of the Czech New Wave who couldn't get their work shown in the cinema, and it remains one of Prague's more innovative small theatres.

Muzeum Bedřicha Smetany (Smetana Museum)

Novotného lávka 1 • Wed–Mon 10am–5pm • 50Kč • ⓦ nm.cz • Tram #17, #18 or #24 to Karlovy lázně

The gaily decorated neo-Renaissance building at the very end of Novotného lávka, on the riverfront itself, was once the city's waterworks. It now houses, among other things, the **Muzeum Bedřicha Smetany**, on the first floor. Litomyšl-born Bedřich Smetana (1824–84), despite having German as his mother tongue, was without doubt the most nationalist of all the great Czech composers, taking an active part in the 1848 revolution and the later national revival movement. He enjoyed his greatest success as a composer with *Prodaná nevěsta* (*The Bartered Bride*), but he was forced to give up conducting in 1874 with the onset of deafness, and eventually died of syphilis in a mental asylum. Unfortunately, the museum fails to capture much of the spirit of the man, concentrating instead on items such as his spectacles and the garnet jewellery of his first wife. Still, the views across to the castle are good, and you get to wave a laser baton around in order to listen to his music.

Outside, beneath the large weeping willow that droops over the embankment, and surrounded by touristy café tables, the **statue** of the seated Smetana is rather unfortunately placed, with his back towards one of his most famous sources of inspiration, the River Vltava.

Krannerova kašna

Park Národního probuzení, Smetanovo nábřeží • Metro Národní třída

A short stroll south along the embankment brings you to a small park centred on the **Krannerova kašna**, an enormous, elaborate and lugubrious neo-Gothic memorial sheltering a bronze statue of the Emperor Franz I (1792–1835), one of the few Habsburg monuments to survive the nationalist outpouring that accompanied the foundation of Czechoslovakia in 1918. The ground plan of the monument is in the shape of an eight-pointed star and, bizarrely, the plinth also functions as a fountain with water gushing from its foundations.

OLD JEWISH CEMETERY

Josefov

Since the fall of Communism in 1989, Prague's old Jewish ghetto, or Josefov, has become one of the city's top sights – year-round the streets are thronged with tourists trekking from one synagogue to another on self-guided tours. But the synagogues, the town hall and the medieval cemetery are but scraps of what once existed here. At the end of the nineteenth century, a period of great economic growth for the Habsburg Empire, it was decided that Prague should be turned into a beautiful bourgeois city, modelled on Paris. What you see today are the remnants of the ghetto following the consequent *asanace* or "sanitization", when Josefov's notoriously malodorous backstreets and alleyways were replaced with block after block of luxurious five-storey Art Nouveau blocks.

JOSEFOV HIGHLIGHTS

Staronová synagoga Prague's oldest and most mysterious synagogue. See below
UPM Check out this unrivalled repository of Czech design. See p.99
Old Jewish Cemetery Ancient crooked gravestones, Hebrew inscriptions and an eerie atmosphere. See p.94
Dinitz One of Prague's more authentic kosher restaurants. See p.180
Rudolfinum Once the Czech Parliament, this grand riverside building is now home to the Czech Philharmonic. See p.98

In any other European city occupied by the Nazis in World War II, what little that was left of the old ghetto would have been demolished. But, although thousands of Prague's Jews were transported to the new ghetto in Terezín and eventually to Auschwitz, the Prague ghetto was preserved under the Nazis in order to provide a record of the communities they had destroyed. By this grotesque twist of fate, Jewish artefacts from Czechoslovakia and beyond were gathered here, and now make up one of the richest collections of Judaica in Europe, and one of the most fascinating sights in Prague.

Geographically, **Josefov** lies within the Staré Město, to the northwest of Staroměstské náměstí, between the main square and the river. The warren-like street plan of the old ghetto has long since disappeared, and through the heart of Josefov now runs the ultimate bourgeois avenue, **Pařížsk**, a riot of turn-of-the-twentieth-century sculpturing, spikes and turrets, its ground floor premises occupied by absurdly upmarket shops. If Josefov can still be said to have a main street, it's really the parallel street of **Maiselova**, named after the community's sixteenth-century leader. The sheer volume of tourists visiting Josefov has brought with it the inevitable rash of souvenir stalls, flogging dubious "Jewish" souvenirs, and, it has to be said, the whole area is now something of a tourist trap. Yet to skip this part of the old town is to miss out on an entire slice of the city's cultural history.

Also included in this chapter are the sights around **náměstí Jana Palacha**, adjacent to, but strictly speaking outside, the Jewish quarter, most notably the city's excellent **Museum of Decorative Arts** (UPM).

INFORMATION

Tickets All the major sights of Josefov – five synagogues and the cemetery, defined as the Jewish Museum (ⓦ jewishmuseum.cz) – are covered by an all-in-one 500Kč ticket, valid for one day only and available from any of the quarter's numerous ticket offices. If you don't want to visit the Staronová synagoga, the ticket costs just 330Kč.

Opening hours Hours are the same across all the sights belonging to the Jewish Museum (Mon–Fri & Sun: April–Oct 9am–6pm; Nov–March 9am–4.30pm). In order to try to regulate the flow of visitors, at peak times there is a timed entry system. This gives you around twenty minutes at each sight, but don't worry too much if you don't adhere rigidly to your timetable.

Staronová synagoga (Old-New Synagogue)

Červená 2 • Mon–Fri & Sun: April–Oct 9am–6pm; Nov–March 9am–4.30pm; the synagogue closes early on Fri, and all day during Jewish holidays • Jewish Museum ticket (see above) 500Kč, otherwise 200Kč • Metro Staroměstská

As you walk down Maiselova, it's impossible to miss the steep, sawtooth brick gables of the **Staronová synagoga** or Altneuschul, called the Old-New Synagogue because when it was built it was indeed very new, though it eventually became the oldest synagogue in Josefov. Begun in the second half of the thirteenth century, it is, in fact, the oldest functioning synagogue in Europe, one of the earliest Gothic buildings in Prague, and still the religious centre for Prague's remaining Orthodox Jews. Since the law prevented Jews from becoming architects, the synagogue is thought to have been constructed by the builders working on the Franciscan convent of sv Anežka, or St Agnes (see p.85).

Its five-ribbed vaulting is unique in Bohemia; the extra, purely decorative rib was added to avoid any hint of a cross.

To get to the **main hall**, you must pass through one of the two low vestibules from which women watch the proceedings through narrow slits. Above the entrance is an elaborate tympanum covered in the twisting branches of a vine tree, its twelve bunches of grapes representing the tribes of Israel. The simple interior is mostly taken up with the elaborate wrought-iron cage enclosing the *bimah* in the centre. In 1354, Charles IV granted Jews a red flag inscribed with a Star of David – the first such community in the world known to have adopted the symbol. The red standard on display was a gift from Emperor Ferdinand II for helping fend off the Swedes in 1648.

North of the synagogue is one of the many statues in Prague that were hidden from the Nazis for the duration of the war: an anguished statue of **Moses** by František Bílek.

Pařížská ulice

ⓦ parizskaulice.cz • Metro Staroměstská

Running arrow-straight from the Old Town Square to Čechův Bridge across the Vltava, **Pařížská ulice** (Paris Street) represents the most serious alteration to this part of Josefov brought about by the late nineteenth-century *asanace* (see box, p.94). Sliced unswervingly through the ghetto, the only building to survive here was the Staronová synagoga itself. The new street was originally named Mikulášská třída, after the church which stands at the Old Town Square end, but this was changed in 1926 to reflect the avenue's similarity to the boulevards of the French capital. Indeed, the city authorities were planning another boulevard to run straight from Wenceslas Square to Letná, obliterating a large chunk of the Old Town in the process. Thankfully this was deemed too expensive and never even begun. Today Pařížská is lined with excruciatingly

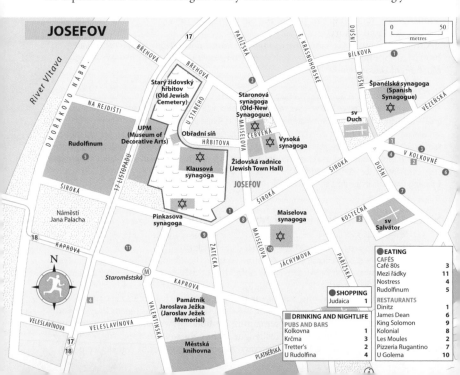

THE GOLEM

Legends concerning the animation of unformed matter (which is what the Hebrew word **golem** means), using the mystical texts of the Kabbala, were around long before Frankenstein started experimenting with corpses. Two hungry fifth-century rabbis may have made the most practical golem when they sculpted a clay calf, brought it to life and then ate it, but the most famous is undoubtedly **Rabbi Löw**'s giant servant made from the mud of the Vltava, who was brought to life when the rabbi placed a *shem* in its mouth, a tablet with a magic Hebrew inscription.

There are numerous versions of the tale, though the earliest invoking Rabbi Löw appeared only in the nineteenth century. In some, **Yossel**, the golem, is a figure of fun, flooding the rabbi's kitchen rather in the manner of Disney's Sorcerer's Apprentice; others portray him as the guardian of the ghetto, helping Rabbi Löw in his struggle with the anti-Semites at Rudolf II's court. In almost all versions, however, the golem finally runs amok. One particularly appealing tale is that the golem's rebellion was because Löw forgot to allow his creature to rest on the Sabbath. He was conducting the service when news of its frenzy arrived, and he immediately ran out to deal with it. The congregation, reluctant to continue without him, merely repeated the verse in the psalm the rabbi had been reciting until Löw returned. This explains the peculiarity at the **Staronová synagoga** (Old-New Synagogue) where a line in the Sabbath service is repeated even today. In all the stories, the end finally comes when Löw removes the *shem* once and for all, and carries the remains of his creature to the attic of the Staronová synagoga, where they have supposedly resided ever since (a fact disputed by the pedantic journalist Egon Erwin Kisch, who climbed in to check).

The legends are amended at each telling, and have proved an enduringly popular theme for generations of artists and writers. **Paul Wegener**'s German Expressionist film versions (1914–20) and the dark psychological novel of **Gustav Meyrink** (1915) are probably two of the most powerful treatments. Meyrink's golem lives in a room which has no windows and no doors, emerging to haunt the streets of Prague every 33 years – by which reckoning, it's long overdue a reappearance.

4

expensive boutiques – if you are Burberry or Bvlgari looking for exclusive Prague retail space, this is where you want to be. Rents on this street are the highest in the Czech Republic, property prices astronomical by Czech standards. Needless to say, you no longer hear much Czech spoken along its length.

Židovská radnice (Jewish Town Hall)

Maiselova 18 • Mon–Fri & Sun: April–Oct 9am–6pm; Nov–March 9am–4.30pm • Jewish Museum tickets (see p.91) 330Kč/500Kč • Metro Staroměstská

Just south of the Staronová synagoga stands the **Židovská radnice**, one of the few such buildings in Europe to survive the Holocaust. Founded and funded as a town hall by Maisel in the sixteenth century, it was later rebuilt as the creamy-pink Rococo building you see now, and today houses the offices of Prague's Jewish community. The belfry, permission for whose construction was granted by Ferdinand III, has a clock on each of its four sides, plus a Hebrew clock stuck on the north gable which, like the Hebrew script, goes "backwards". Adjacent to the town hall is the **Vysoká synagoga** (High Synagogue), whose dour grey facade belies its rich interior; it's now one of only two synagogues in Josefov still used for religious services and is normally closed to the public.

Maiselova synagoga

Maiselova 8 • Mon–Fri & Sun: April–Oct 9am–6pm; Nov–March 9am–4.30pm • Jewish Museum tickets (see p.91) 330Kč/500Kč • Metro Staroměstská

Founded and paid for entirely by Mordecai Maisel, the neo-Gothic **Maiselova synagoga**, set back from the neighbouring houses on Maiselova, was, in its day, one of the most ornate synagogues in Josefov. Nowadays, its bare, whitewashed,

> ### KLUB ZA STAROU PRAHU
>
> Around six hundred houses were demolished in the great Josefov *asanace*, the biggest incursion into the medieval fabric of the Czech capital ever to be permitted by the city authorities. The same fate awaited the Old Town and Malá Strana, the overzealous planners looking to transform medieval Prague into a kind of *fin de siècle* Paris on the Vltava. However, even in the late nineteenth century, many Prague dwellers recognized the value of their city's heritage and launched a campaign to stop the destruction. This led to the creation of one of Prague's most important civic movements - the **Klub za starou Prahu** (Old Prague Club; ⓦ zastarouprahu.cz) which to this day highlights the excesses of unscrupulous developers across the city and calls out corrupt city councillors whose actions threaten the integrity of this most precious city.

turn-of-the-twentieth-century interior houses an exhibition on the history of the Czech-Jewish community up until the 1781 Edict of Tolerance. Along with glass cabinets filled with gold and silverwork, Hanukkah candlesticks, Torah scrolls and other religious artefacts, there's also one of the antiquated Renaissance-era ruffs that had to be worn by all unmarried males from the age of 12, and a copy of Ferdinand I's 1551 decree enforcing the wearing of a circular yellow badge.

Pinkasova synagoga

Široká 3 · Mon–Fri & Sun: April–Oct 9am–6pm; Nov–March 9am–4.30pm · Jewish Museum tickets (see p.91) 330Kč/500Kč · Metro Staroměstská

Jutting out at an angle on the south side of the Old Jewish Cemetery (see below) with its entrance on Široká, the **Pinkasova synagoga** was built in the 1530s for the powerful Horovitz family, and has undergone countless restorations over the centuries. In 1958, it was transformed into a chilling **memorial** to the 77,297 Czech Jews killed during the Holocaust. The memorial was closed shortly after the 1967 Six Day War – due to damp, according to the Communists – and remained so, allegedly because of problems with the masonry, until it was finally painstakingly restored in the 1990s. All that remains of the synagogue's original decor today is the ornate *bimah* surrounded by a beautiful wrought-iron grille, supported by barley-sugar columns, behind which there's a chilling list of the death camps of Eastern Europe.

Of all the sights of the Jewish quarter, the Holocaust memorial is perhaps the most moving, with every bit of wall space taken up with the carved stone list of victims, stating simply their name, birth date and date of death or transportation to the camps. It is the longest epitaph in the world, yet it represents a mere fraction of those who died in the Nazi concentration camps. Upstairs, in a room beside the women's gallery, there's also a harrowing exhibition of **children's drawings** from the Jewish ghetto in Terezín; most of the children were killed in the camps – surely wartime Bohemia's most distressing story.

Starý židovský hřbitov (Old Jewish Cemetery)

U Starého Hřbitova · Mon–Fri & Sun: April–Oct 9am–6pm; Nov–March 9am–4.30pm · Jewish Museum tickets (see p.91) 330Kč/500Kč · Metro Staroměstská

At the heart of Josefov is the **Starý židovský hřbitov**, established in the fifteenth century and used until 1787. There are an estimated 100,000 people buried here (far outnumbering the 12,000 headstones), one on top of the other, six palms apart, and as many as twelve layers deep. The enormous numbers of visitors has meant that the **graves** themselves were roped off in the 1990s, and a one-way system introduced: you enter from the Pinkasova synagoga, on Široká, and leave by the Klausová synagoga. Get to the Old Jewish Cemetery before the crowds – a difficult task for much of the year – and it can be a poignant reminder of the ghetto, its inhabitants subjected to inhuman overcrowding even in death. The rest of Prague recedes beyond the tall ash trees and cramped perimeter walls, the crooked, haphazard headstones and Hebrew inscriptions casting a powerful spell.

Each headstone bears a symbol denoting the profession or tribe of the deceased: a pair of hands for the Cohens; a pitcher and basin for the Levites; scissors for a tailor; a violin for a musician. On many graves you'll spot pebbles, some holding down *kvitlech* or small messages of supplication. The greatest number of these sits on the grave of Rabbi Löw (see box, p.93), who is buried by the wall directly opposite the entrance, followed closely by the rich Renaissance tomb of Mordecai Maisel, some 10m to the southeast. The oldest grave, dating from 1439, belongs to the poet Avigdor Karo, who lived to tell the tale of the 1389 pogrom.

Immediately on your left as you leave the cemetery is the **Obřadní síň**, a lugubrious neo-Renaissance house built in 1906 as a ceremonial hall by the Jewish Burial Society. Appropriately enough, it's now devoted to an exhibition on Jewish traditions of burial and death, though it would probably be more useful if you could visit it before heading off into the cemetery rather than after.

Klausová synagoga

U Starého hřbitova • Mon–Fri & Sun: April–Oct 9am–6pm; Nov–March 9am–4.30pm • Jewish Museum tickets (see p.91) 330Kč/500Kč • Metro Staroměstská

Close to the entrance to the Starý židovský hřbitov (Old Jewish Cemetery) is the **Klausová synagoga**, a late seventeenth-century building, founded in the 1690s by Mordecai Maisel on the site of three small prayer rooms in what was then a notorious red-light district. The relatively ornate Baroque interior contains a rich display of religious objects such as prayer books, Torah scrolls, skullcaps, Hanukkah lamps and other items associated with particularly significant points in Jewish life such as birth, circumcision, bar mitzvahs and weddings.

Španělská synagoga (Spanish Synagogue)

Vězeňská 1 • Mon–Fri & Sun: April–Oct 9am–6pm; Nov–March 9am–4.30pm • Jewish Museum tickets (see p.91) 330Kč/500Kč • Metro Staroměstská

The most elaborate building belonging to the Jewish Museum is the **Španělská synagoga**, built on a site once occupied by Prague's Alt Schul or Old Synagogue. Begun in 1868, the Spanish Synagogue is by far the most ornate in Josefov, the breathtaking, gilded Moorish interior deliberately imitating the Alhambra (hence its name). Every available surface is smothered with a profusion of floral motifs and geometric patterns, in vibrant reds, greens and blues, which are repeated in the huge stained-glass windows.

The synagogue now houses an interesting **history exhibition** telling the story of Prague's Jews from the time of the 1781 Edict of Tolerance to the Holocaust. Lovely, slender, painted cast-iron columns hold up the women's gallery, where displays include a fascinating set of photos depicting the old ghetto at the time of its demolition. There's a section on Prague's German-Jewish writers, including Kafka, and information on the Nazis' plans for a museum and on the Holocaust. In the **zimní synagoga** on the first floor, you can see various silver religious artefacts, just a fraction of the six thousand pieces collected here, initially for Prague's Jewish Museum, founded in 1906, and later under the Nazis. Also worth a peek are the changing Jewish art exhibitions at the **Galerie Roberta Guttmanna** (Mon–Fri & Sun: April–Oct 9am–6pm; Nov–March 9am–4.30pm; 40Kč), around the back of the synagogue at U staré školy 3.

JEWISH SETTLEMENT IN PRAGUE

Jews probably settled in Prague as early as the tenth century and, initially at least, are thought to have settled on both sides of the river. In 1096, at the time of the first crusade, the first recorded pogrom took place, an event that may have hastened the formation of a closely knit "Jewish town" within Staré Město during the twelfth century. It wasn't until much later that Jews were actually herded into a **walled ghetto** (and several centuries before the word "ghetto" was actually first coined in Venice), sealed off from the rest of the town and subjected to a curfew. Jews were also subject to laws restricting their choice of profession to moneylending and the rag trade; in addition, some form of visible identification, a cap or badge (and even, at one time, a ruff), remained a more or less constant feature of Jewish life until the Enlightenment.

STATUTA JUDAEORUM

In 1262, Přemysl King Otakar II issued a **Statuta Judaeorum**, which granted the Jews their own religious and civil self-administration. In effect, however, the Jews were little more than the personal property of the king, and though Otakar himself appears to have been genuine in his motives, later rulers used the *Statuta* as a form of blackmail, extorting money whenever they saw fit. In 1389, during one of the worst **pogroms**, three thousand Jews were massacred over Easter, some while sheltering in the Staronová synagoga (Old-New Synagogue) – an event commemorated every year thereafter on Yom Kippur. In 1541, a fire ripped through Hradčany and Malá Strana and a Jew was tortured into "confessing" the crime. The Bohemian Estates immediately persuaded Emperor Ferdinand I to **expel the Jews** from Prague. In the end, however, a small number of families were allowed to remain.

GOLDEN AGE

By contrast, the reign of Rudolf II (1576–1612) was a time of economic and cultural prosperity for the community, which is thought to have numbered up to ten thousand, making it by far the largest Jewish community in the Diaspora. The Jewish mayor, **Mordecai Maisel**, Rudolf's minister of finance, became one of the richest men in Bohemia and a symbol of success for an entire generation; his money bought and built the Jewish quarter a town hall, a bath house, pavements and several synagogues. This was the "golden age" of the ghetto: the time of **Rabbi Löw**, the severe and conservative chief rabbi of Prague, who is now best known as the legendary creator of the Jewish Frankenstein's monster, or "golem" – though, in fact, the story of Rabbi Löw and the golem first appeared only in the nineteenth century (see box, p.93).

Amid the violence of the Thirty Years' War, the Jews enjoyed an unusual degree of protection from the emperor, who was heavily dependent on their financial acumen and their loans. In **1648**, Prague's Jews, along with the city's students, repaid their imperial bosses by repelling the marauding Swedes on Charles Bridge, for which they won the lasting respect of Ferdinand III (1637–57).

JOSEPH II AND REFORM

Things went into reverse again during the eighteenth century, until in 1744 Empress Maria Theresa used the community as a scapegoat for her disastrous war against the Prussians, and ordered the expulsion of all Jews from Prague. She allowed them to return in 1748, though only after much pressure from the guilds. It was the enlightened **Emperor Joseph II** (1780–90) who did most to lift the restrictions on Jews. His 1781 Edict of Tolerance ended the dress codes, opened up education to all non-Catholics and removed the gates from the ghetto. In 1850, the community paid him homage by officially naming the ghetto **Josefov**, or Josefstadt.

The downside to Joseph's reforms was that he was hellbent on **Jewish assimilation**. The use of Hebrew or Yiddish in business transactions was banned, and Jews were ordered to

Náměstí Jana Palacha

Kaprova and Široká emerge from Josefov at **náměstí Jana Palacha**, previously known as náměstí Krasnoarmejců (Red Army Square) and embellished with a flowerbed in the shape of a red star (now replaced by the circular vent of an underground car park) in memory of the Soviet dead who were temporarily buried here in May 1945. It was probably this, as much as the fact that the building on the east side of

Germanize their names (there were 109 names permitted for men and 35 for women). However, it wasn't until the social upheavals of **1848** that Jews were given equal status within the Empire and allowed officially to settle outside the confines of the ghetto – concessions that were accompanied by a number of violent anti-Semitic protests on the part of the Czechs.

FROM 1848 TO THE FIRST REPUBLIC

From 1848 the ghetto went into terminal **decline**. The more prosperous Jewish families began to move to other districts of the city, leaving behind only the poorest Jews and strictly Orthodox families, who were rapidly joined by the Prague underclass: gypsies, beggars, prostitutes and alcoholics. By 1890, only twenty percent of Josefov's population were Jewish, yet it was still the most densely populated area in Prague, with a staggering 186,000 people crammed into its streets. The ghetto had become a carbuncle in the centre of bourgeois Prague, a source of disease and vice: in the words of Gustav Meyrink, a "demonic underworld, a place of anguish, a beggarly and phantasmagorical quarter whose eeriness seemed to have spread and led to paralysis."

The ending of restrictions and the **destruction of the ghetto**, which began in 1893, increased the pressure on Jews to assimilate, a process that brought with it its own set of problems. Prague's Jews were split roughly half and half between predominantly German- or Yiddish-speakers and Czech-speakers. Yet since some two-thirds of Prague's German population were Jewish, and all Jews had been forced to take German names by Joseph II, all Jews were seen by Czech nationalists as a Germanizing influence. Tensions between the country's German-speaking minority and the Czechs grew steadily worse in the run-up to World War I, and the Jewish community found itself caught in the firing line – "like powerless stowaways attempting to steer a course through the storms of embattled nationalities", as one Prague Jew put it.

THE FINAL DECADES

Despite several anti-Semitic riots in the years before and after the war, the foundation of the new republic in 1918, and, in particular, its founder and first president, T.G. Masaryk, whose liberal credentials were impeccable, were welcomed by most Jews. For the first time in their history, Jews were given equal rights as a recognized ethnic group, though only a minority opted to be registered as Jewish. The **interwar period** was probably the nearest Prague's Jewish community came to a second "golden age", a time most clearly expressed in the now famous flowering of its *Deutsche Prager Literatur*, led by German-Jewish writers such as Franz Werfel, Franz Kafka, Max Brod and Rainer Maria Rilke.

After the **Nazis occupied Prague** on March 15, 1939, the city's Jews were subject to an increasingly harsh set of regulations, by which they were barred from most professions, placed under curfew and compelled to wear a yellow Star of David. In November 1941, the first transport of Prague Jews set off for the new ghetto in **Terezín**, 60km northwest of the city. Of the estimated 55,000 Jews in Prague at the time of the Nazi invasion, more than 36,000 died in the camps. Many survivors emigrated to Israel and the US. Of the eight thousand who registered as Jewish in the Prague census of 1947, a significant number joined the Communist Party, only to find themselves victims of Stalinist **anti-Semitic purges** during the 1950s.

It's difficult to calculate exactly how many Jews now live in Prague – around a thousand were officially registered as such prior to 1989 – though their numbers have undoubtedly been bolstered by those Czech Jews who have rediscovered their roots and, more significantly, by the new, if small influx of Jewish Americans and Israelis. The controversy over Jewish property – most of which was seized by the Nazis, and therefore not covered by the original restitution law – has been resolved, allowing the community to reclaim, among other things, the six synagogues, the town hall and the Old Jewish Cemetery.

4

the square is the Faculty of Philosophy, where Jan Palach (see p.106) was a student, that prompted the new authorities to make the first of the street name changes here in 1989 (there's a bust of Palach on the corner of the building). By coincidence, the road that intersects the square from the north is called **17 listopadu** (17 November), originally commemorating the day in 1939 when the Nazis closed down all Czech institutions of higher education, but now also commemorating the events on that

ON KAFKA'S TRAIL

Prague never lets go of you…this little mother has claws. We ought to set fire to it at both ends, on Vyšehrad and Hradčany, and maybe then it might be possible to escape.

Franz Kafka, "Letter to Oskar Polak" (December 2, 1902)

Franz Kafka was born on July 3, 1883, above the *Batalion Schnapps* bar on the corner of Maiselova and Kaprova (only the portal remains and his bust stands outside). He lived almost his entire life within a short walk of his birthplace. His father was a small businessman from a Czech-Jewish family of kosher butchers (Kafka himself was a lifelong vegetarian), his mother from a wealthy German-Jewish family of merchants. The family owned a haberdashery shop, located at various premises on or near Staroměstské náměstí. In 1889 they moved out of Josefov and lived for the next seven years in the beautiful Renaissance Dům U minuty, next door to the Staroměstská radnice (Old Town Hall), during which time Kafka attended the Volksschule on Masná (now a Czech primary school), followed by a spell at an exceptionally strict German *Gymnasium*, at the back of the palác Kinských.

At 18, he began a law degree at the German half of the Karolinum, which was where he met his lifelong friend and posthumous biographer and editor, **Max Brod**. Kafka spent most of his working life in the field of **accident insurance**, until he retired through ill health in 1922. Illness and depression plagued him throughout his life and he spent many months as a patient at the innumerable spas in central Europe. He was engaged three times (twice to the same woman), but never married, finally leaving home at the age of 31 for bachelor digs on the corner of Dlouhá and Masná, where he wrote the bulk of his most famous work, *The Trial*. He died of **tuberculosis** at the age of 40 in a sanatorium just outside Vienna, on June 3, 1924, and is buried in the Nový židovský hřbitov in Prague's Žižkov district.

As a German among Czechs, a Jew among Germans and an agnostic among believers, Kafka had good reason to live in a constant state of alienation and fear, or *Angst*. Life was precarious for Prague's Jews, and the destruction of the Jewish quarter throughout his childhood had a profound effect on his psyche. It comes as a surprise to many Kafka readers that anyone immersed in so beautiful a city could write such claustrophobic and paranoid texts; and that, as a member of the **café society** of the time, he could write in a style so completely at odds with his verbose, artistic friends. It's also hard to understand how Kafka could find no publisher for *The Trial* during his lifetime.

After his death, Kafka's works were published in Czech and German and enjoyed brief critical acclaim before the Nazis **banned** them. Even after the war, Kafka, along with most German-Czech authors, was deliberately overlooked in his native country. In addition, his account of the terrifying brutality and power of bureaucracy over the individual, though not in fact directed at totalitarian systems as such, was too close to the bone for the Communists. The 1962 **Writers' Union** conference at Liblice finally broke the official silence on Kafka, one of many small events that kicked off the Prague Spring. In the immediate aftermath of the 1968 Soviet invasion, the Kafka bust was removed from Josefov, and his books remained unpublished in Czechoslovakia until 1990.

Having been *persona non grata* in his homeland for most of the last century, and despite the fact that the vast majority of Czechs do not consider him a Czech writer at all, Kafka now suffers from overexposure in Prague due to his popularity with Western tourists. You'll see his image plastered across everything from T-shirts to mugs to key rings, but the **Kafka Museum** (see p.62) in Malá Strana is a worthwhile stop for anyone with a more serious interest in one of Prague's more intriguing figures.

date in 1989 (see p.115). Along 17 listopadu you will find a couple of other large university faculties and the Prague Conservatory.

Rudolfinum

Alšovo nábřeží 12 • ☎ 227 059 227, ⊕ rudolfinum.cz • Tours 200Kč • Metro Staroměstská

The north side of náměstí Jana Palacha is entirely dominated by the **Rudolfinum**, a neo-Renaissance building designed by Josef Zítek and Josef Schulz and opened in 1885. It was originally conceived to house an art gallery, museum and concert hall for the Czech-speaking community. However, in 1918 it became the seat of the new Czechoslovak parliament, which it remained until 1938 when it was closed down by the Nazis. According to author Jiří Weil, the Germans were keen to rid the building's balustrade of its statue of the Jewish composer Mendelssohn. However, since none of the statues was actually named, they decided to remove the one with the largest nose; unfortunately for the Nazis, this turned out to be Wagner, Hitler's favourite composer. In 1946, the Rudolfinum returned to its original artistic purpose and it's since been sandblasted back to its erstwhile woody-brown hue. Now one of the capital's main concert venues and exhibition spaces, it's home to the **Czech Philharmonic** and a first-floor café, worth a visit for its wonderfully grand decor (see p.199). **Tours** of the building run in English up to five times a month in the afternoon (check the website for exact dates and times).

UPM (Museum of Decorative Arts)

17 listopadu • Ⓦ upm.cz • Metro Staroměstská

The **UPM**, or Umělecko-průmyslové museum, installed in one of Josef Schulz's worthy late nineteenth-century creations, is richly decorated in mosaics, stained glass and sculptures, and counts among Prague's best museums. Literally translated, this is a **Museum of Decorative Arts**, though the translation hardly does justice to what is one of the most fascinating museums in the capital. From its foundation in 1885 through to the end of the First Republic, the UPM received the best that the Czech modern movement had to offer – from Art Nouveau to the avant-garde – and consequently its collection is unrivalled.

In recent years the UPM has undergone a complete rebuild. Reopening is expected at some point in 2018, when there will be more clearly defined curation of the museum's **collections**, which include textiles and richly embroidered religious vestments from the fifteenth to the eighteenth centuries, lacework down the ages, costumes spanning three centuries, impressive displays of glass, ceramic and pottery – for many the highlight of the entire UPM – plus furniture, jewellery, curios, Czech photography, interwar prints, works by Josef Sudek, avant-garde graphics by Karel Teige, book designs by Josef Váchal and some of Alfons Mucha's famous turn-of-the-twentieth-century Parisian advertising posters.

4

Památník Jaroslava Ježka (Jaroslav Ježek Memorial)

Kaprova 10 • Tues 1–6pm • 20Kč • ☎ 257 257 739, Ⓦ nm.cz • Metro Staroměstská

If you happen to be in the Josefov area on a Tuesday afternoon, it's worth taking the opportunity to visit the **Památník Jaroslava Ježeka**, which occupies one room of the first-floor flat of the avant-garde composer **Jaroslav Ježek** (1906–42). It's a great way to escape the crowds, hear some of Ježek's music and admire the Modrý pokoj (Blue Room), with its functionalist furniture and grand piano, in which he spent many hours composing.

ART NOUVEAU DETAIL AT PRAGUE MAIN STATION

Nové Město

The Nové Město, Prague's New Town, was certainly new when founded in 1348 by Emperor Charles IV to link the Old Town with Vyšehrad. Three times bigger than the Old Town, it lacks the crooked web of lanes and thoroughfares of its older neighbours, but its medieval origins are still much in evidence, despite many nineteenth- and twentieth-century alterations and embellishments. The Nové Město is where you'll find many of Prague's major hotels, cinemas, nightclubs, fast-food outlets and department stores, and has a much more lived-in feel than other parts of the historical centre. This is most evident on the quarter's main square, the elongated Václavské náměstí (Wenceslas Square), which has provided the backdrop for many pivotal moments in Czech history.

5

NOVÉ MĚSTO HIGHLIGHTS

Wenceslas Square More of a boulevard than a square, this is the epicentre of the Czech world. See below

National Theatre The Czechs' main stage was built using donations from across the land. See p.115

Obecní dům Art Nouveau masterpiece containing concert halls and stylish eateries. See p.109

Slavia Prague's most famous café, the erstwhile haunt of famous dissidents. See p.183

Pivovarský dům Superb micro-brewery and one of the best places to sample hearty Czech cuisine. See p.190

Large market squares, wide streets and a level of town planning far ahead of its time were employed by Charles IV to transform Prague into the new capital city of the Holy Roman Empire. However, Nové Město was incomplete when Charles died, and quickly became the city's poorest quarter after Josefov, fertile ground for Hussites and radicals throughout the centuries.

In the second half of the nineteenth century the authorities set about a campaign of slum clearance similar to that inflicted on the Jewish quarter; only the churches and a few important historical buildings were left standing, but Charles's street layout survives pretty much intact. The leading architects of the day began to line the **wide boulevards** with ostentatious examples of their work, which were eagerly snapped up by the new class of status-conscious businessman – a process that has continued into this century, making Nové Město the most architecturally varied area of Prague.

The obvious starting point is **Wenceslas Square** (Václavské náměstí), hub of the modern city, and somewhere you will inevitably pass through again and again. The two principal, partially pedestrianized streets that lead off it are **Na příkopě** and 28 října, which becomes **Národní třída**. These streets together form the *zlatý kříž* or "golden cross", Prague's commercial axis and for over a century the most expensive slice of real estate in the capital. The *zlatý kříž* and the surrounding streets also contain some of Prague's finest late nineteenth-century, Art Nouveau and early twentieth-century architecture.

The rest of Nové Město, which spreads out northeast and southwest of Wenceslas Square, is much less explored, and for the most part still heavily residential. A few specific sights are worth singling out for attention – the museum devoted to **Dvořák** on Ke Karlovu, the **Mánes** art gallery on the waterfront, and the memorial to the Czechoslovak parachutists off Karlovo náměstí, for example – but the rest is decidedly less exciting than all that's gone before. However, if your ultimate destination is Vyšehrad, you can easily take in some of the more enjoyable bits of southern Nové Město en route.

Václavské náměstí (Wenceslas Square)

Metro Můstek/Muzeum

The natural pivot around which modern Prague revolves, **Václavské náměstí** (Václavák in slangy Czech) is more of a wide, gently sloping boulevard than a square as such. It's scarcely a conventional – or even convenient – space in which to hold mass demonstrations, yet for the last 160 years or more it has been the natural focus of political protest in Prague (see box, p.104).

Despite the square's medieval origins, its oldest building dates only from the eighteenth century, and the vast majority are much younger. As the city's money moved south of Staré Město during the Industrial Revolution, so the square became the **architectural showpiece** of the nation, and it is now lined with self-important six- or seven-storey buildings, representing every artistic trend of the past hundred years, from neo-Renaissance and Art Nouveau to Socialist Realism and tasteless 1990s excess. However, lying outside the UNESCO-protected Old Town, this is also where some of the worst crimes of post-Communist architecture have been perpetrated, the most

NOVÉ MĚSTO

N

DRINKING AND NIGHTLIFE

PUBS AND BARS

American Bar	1
Branický sklípek	9
Bredovský dvůr	4
Novoměstský pivovar	10
Pivovarský dům	16
Potrefená husa	15
Cellarius	14
U Fleků	12
U havrana	14
U Pinkasů	3
Výloha Bar	17

CLUBS AND VENUES

Lucerna	8
Lucerna music bar	7
Nebe	11
Reduta	6
Studio 54	2
Vagon	5
LGBT CLUB AND BAR	
JampaDampa	13

SHOPPING

Academia	11
Antikvariát Dlážděné	3
Baťa	8
Bazar	18
Bontonland	7
Čalový krámek	9
Centrum Fotoškoda	10
Česká mincovna	5
The Globe	17
Hras	12
Jan Pazdera	13
Kant	16
Koh-I-Noor	4
Kotva	1
Moser	6
Palladium	2
Phono.cz	15

Florenc
Florenc Bus Station
Muzeum Prahy (City of Prague Museum)
Ministry of Transport
sv Petr
Bílá labuť
Banka legii
Masarykovo nádraží
Poštovní muzeum (Postal Museum)
Novomlýnská vodárenská věž (water tower)
sv Kliment
Náměstí Republiky
Palladium
Lidový dům
U Hybernů
Jubilejní synagoga
Praha hlavní nádraží (Prague main train station)
Hlavní Nádraží
Vrchlického sady
Obecní dům
Kotva
Prašná brána
Živnostenská banka
Mucha Museum
Jindřišská věž
sv Jindřich
Grand Hotel Evropa
Hotel
Assicurazione Generali
Debenhams
Melantrich
Dům černé matky boží
Muzeum komunizmu (Museum of Communism)
Palác Koruna
Peterkův dům
Hotel Juliš
Panna Maria Sněžná
Františkánská zahrada
Palác Adria
My národní
Anežský klášter (National Gallery)
Haštal
sv Jakub
Bazilika sv Jakub
Stavovské divadlo
Dům U zlatého prstenu (Czech art collection)
Týn Church
Dům U bílého jednorožce
Karolinum (Charles University)
sv Havel
U Dörflerů
Můstek
sv Jiljí
Spanělská synagoga (Spanish Synagogue)
Staronová synagoga
Maiselova synagoga
sv Mikuláš
palác Kinských (National Gallery)
Staroměstské náměstí (OLD TOWN SQUARE)
Staroměstská radnice (Old Town Hall)
Nová radnice (New Town Hall)
Betlémská kaple
sv Kliment
Náprstkovo muzeum (Náprstek Museum)
sv Kříž
Topičův dům
Pojišťovna Praha
Pinkasova synagoga
Rudolfinum
Městská knihovna
Klementinum
sv František
sv Salvátor
Josefov
Staré Město
Muzeum Karlova mostu (Charles Bridge Museum)
Staré Mesto Bridge Tower
Bedřicha Smetany (Smetana Museum)
Franz Kafka Museum
Museum Kampa
Kampa
Střelecký ostrov (Shooters' Island)
Café Slavia
Weir

■ **EATING**

CAFÉS
Café 35	22
Cafétérapie	32
Daruma	30
Dhaba Beas	5
Dobrá čajovna	9
Friends Coffee House	16
Góvinda	1
Imperial	4
Louvre	10
Lucerna	14
Marathon	21
Myšák	12
Obecní dům	6
Pekářství Moravec	3
Slavia	11
Svatováclavská cukrárna	29
Tramvaj	13
Velryba	18

RESTAURANTS
Cicala	27
Dnister	31
Dynamo	19
Francouzská restaurace	6
Hybernia	7
Klub Cestovatelů	24
Kmotra	17
Miss Saigon	25
Monarchie	15
Plzeňská restaurace	6
Ryby & Chips	26
U Činny	23
U Šumavy	28
U sádlu	2
Žofín Garden	20
Zvonice	8

■ **ACCOMMODATION**

HOTELS
Alcron	16
Boho Prague	6
Boscolo Prague	7
Central	5
Dancing House Hotel	18
Fusion Hotel	8
Grand Hotel Evropa	12
Harmony	2
Hotel 16 – U sv Kateřiny	20
Icon Hotel	15
Imperial	3
Jungmann	11
Mánes	17
Moods	1
Palace	10
Salvator	4
U Šuterů	13
U svatého Jana	21

HOSTELS
MadHouse	14
Miss Sophie's	19
Rosemary	9

5

VÁCLAVSKÉ NÁMĚSTÍ: A HISTORY OF PROTEST

The history of protest on Prague's main square goes back to the **1848 Revolution**, whose violent denouement began here on June 12 with a peaceful open-air Mass organized by Prague students. On the crest of the nationalist disturbances, the square – which had been known as Koňský trh (Horse Market) since its foundation by Charles IV – was given its present name. Naturally enough, it was one of the rallying points for the jubilant crowds on **October 28, 1918**, when Czechoslovakia's independence was declared. At the lowest point of the Nazi occupation, on **July 3, 1942**, some two weeks after the capture of Reinhard Heydrich's assassins (see box, p.119), more than 200,000 Czechs gathered to swear allegiance to the Third Reich. Just six years later, in **February 1948**, the square was filled to capacity once more, this time with Communist demonstrators enthusiastically supporting the February coup. Then, during the Warsaw Pact invasion of **August 1968**, it was the scene of some of the most violent confrontations between the Soviet invaders and the Czechs, during which the Národní muzeum came under fire – according to the Czechs, the Soviet officer in charge mistook it for the Parliament building, though they were most probably aiming for the nearby Radio Prague building, which was transmitting news of the Soviet invasion out to the West. And it was at the top of the square, on **January 16, 1969**, that Jan Palach set fire to himself in protest at the continuing occupation of the country by Russian troops.

Most famously it was here, during the November 1989 **Velvet Revolution**, that more than 250,000 people crammed into the square night after night, enduring subzero temperatures, to call for the resignation of the Communist Party leaders and to demand free elections. On **November 27, 1989**, the whole of Prague came to a standstill for the two-hour nationwide general strike called by Občanské fórum (Civic Forum), who led the revolution. It was this last mass mobilization that proved decisive – by noon the next day the Communist old guard had thrown in the towel.

Mass protests continued even into the 1990s, most notably with the **Děkujeme, odejděte!** campaign against the perceived Klaus-Zeman stitch-up of the post-Communist political scene, which on one occasion unexpectedly filled the Václavák's 40,000 square metres of cobbles. Both men went on to serve as president.

recent example the huge bulbous roof of the building opposite the National Museum on the left as you look up the square. Recent controversy has surrounded an enormous building on the corner of Opletalova Street which a long campaign of public protest could not save from the developers' demolition gangs. What have remained virtually untouched since the commercial boom of the First Republic are the Václavák's period-piece arcades or **pasáže** (see box, p.106).

If you've no interest in modern architecture, there's less reason to stroll up the square; the shops and restaurants are pretty bland in comparison to other parts of the city centre and most bona fide Czech businesses got out years ago. The square has also yet to shake off entirely the seedy reputation it acquired during the 1990s: prostitution has waned and the discos have mostly closed down, but the petty criminals, dodgy cab drivers and outlet stores remain. The famous sausage stands that dot the square's length have stubbornly held their ground, despite plans for a thorough makeover that the authorities have been promising/threatening for the past fifteen years. The idea is ultimately to rid Wenceslas Square of cars altogether, creating a large open pedestrianized space. However, work is not scheduled to start any time soon.

The most bustling part of Wenceslas Square and a popular place to meet before hitting town is around **Můstek**, the city's most central metro station, at the northern (bottom) end of the square. The name Můstek means "little bridge" – obviously a reference to the ditch that once ran the length of na Příkopě along the end of what became Wenceslas Square.

Palác Koruna

Václavské náměstí 1 • Metro Můstek

The area around Můstek is dominated by the **Palác Koruna**, a hulking wedge of sculptured concrete and gold, built for an insurance company in 1914 by Antonín Pfeiffer, one of many to study under Jan Kotěra. The building is a rare mixture of heavy constructivism and gilded Secession-style ornamentation, but the pièce de résistance is the palace's pearly crown, which lights up at night.

Kysela buildings
Metro Můstek

Opposite Palác Koruna is a recent neo-functionalist glass building, accompanied by two much older functionalist shops from the late 1920s, designed by **Ludvík Kysela** and billed at the time as Prague's first glass curtain-wall buildings. Along with the *Hotel Juliš* (see below), they represent the perfect expression of the optimistic mood of progress and modernism that permeated the interwar republic. The second of the Kysela buildings was constructed in 1929 as a **Baťa** store, one of a chain of functionalist shoe shops built for the Czech shoe magnate, Tomáš Baťa, who was a great patron of avant-garde Czech architecture. Baťa fled the country in 1948, when the Communists nationalized the shoe industry, only to have several of his old stores returned to the family after 1989. Even if you've no intention of buying a pair of Baťas, it's worth taking the lift to the top floor for a bird's-eye view of the square.

Peterkův dům
Václavské náměstí 12 • Metro Můstek

At the turn of the twentieth century, Czech architecture was in the throes of its own version of Art Nouveau, known as **secese** (the Czech word for Secession). One of the earliest practitioners was Jan Kotěra, a pupil of the great architect of the Viennese Secession, Otto Wagner. Kotěra's first work, undertaken at the age of 28, was the **Peterkův dům**, a slender, subdued essay in the new style – though he eventually moved on to a much more brutal modernism.

Hotel Juliš
Václavské náměstí 22 • Metro Můstek

The **Hotel Juliš** is a supreme example of Czech functionalism. It was designed by Pavel Janák, who had already made his name as one of the leading lights of the short-lived Czech Cubist (and later Rondo-Cubist) movement (see p.129).

South of Jindřišská

One of the Communists' most miserable attempts to continue Václavské náměstí's tradition of grand architecture was the former **Družba** (Friendship) department store, now a far-flung branch of Debenhams, which stands like a 1970s reject on the eastern side of the square. Opposite is the former **Melantrich** publishing house (now a branch of Marks & Spencer), whose first floor was occupied for many years by the offices of the Socialist Party newspaper, *Svobodné slovo* (The Free Word). For forty years, the Socialist Party was a loyal puppet of the Communist government, but on the second night of the November 1989 demonstrations, the newspaper handed over its well-placed balcony to the opposition speakers of Občanské fórum (Civic Forum), and later witnessed the historic appearance of Havel and Dubček.

Grand Hotel Evropa and around

Next to the Debenhams building are probably the two most ornate buildings on Václavské náměstí, the Art Nouveau **Grand Hotel Evropa** and its slim neighbour, the *Hotel Meran*. The structures, designed by two of Friedrich Ohmann's disciples, Bendelmayer and Dryák, both feature decor dating from 1903–05; the *Evropa*, in particular, has kept many of its original fittings intact, and its café retains a sumptuous interior, complete with Symbolist art and elaborate brass fittings and light fixtures, all unchanged since the hotel first opened. At the time of research it was receiving a complete and much-needed overhaul and is expected to open as a luxury hotel sometime towards the end of the decade.

5

PRAGUE'S PASÁŽE

Prague has an impressive array of old **shopping arcades**, or *pasáže* as they're known in Czech, the majority of which are located in and around Wenceslas Square and date from the first half of the twentieth century. Compared with the chic *passages* off the Champs-Élysées, Prague's *pasáže* offer more modest pleasures: a few shops, the odd café and, more often than not, a cinema. The king of the lot is the lavishly decorated **Lucerna** *pasáž* at the Palác Lucerna, which stretches all the way from Štěpánská to Vodičkova and contains an equally ornate cinema, café and concert hall. You can continue your indoor stroll on the other side of Vodičkova through the **Světozor** *pasáž*, which boasts another cinema, and a wonderful stained-glass mosaic advertising the old Communist electronics company Tesla.

Palác Lucerna and around

Metro Můstek

Opposite the *Grand Hotel Evropa* stands the sprawling **Palác Lucerna**, one of the more appealing of Václavské náměstí's numerous atmospherically lit *pasáže*, or shopping arcades (see box above). Designed in the early twentieth century in Moorish style by, among others, Havel's own grandfather, it was returned to Havel and his brother after 1989 and was subsequently the focus of much public family squabbling. Suspended from the ceiling in the centre of the arcade is David Černý's parody of the square's equestrian Wenceslas Monument, with the saint astride an upside-down charger.

Apart from a brief glance at the **Hotel Jalta**, built in the Stalinist aesthetic of the 1950s, there's nothing more to stop for south of here, architecturally speaking, until you get to the Wenceslas Monument. However, you might by this point have noticed the two vintage trams beached on short pieces of rail in the central reservation, reminders of the days when trams trundled down the square but now converted into the *Tramvaj* café (see p.182).

The Wenceslas Monument

Metro Muzeum

A statue of St Wenceslas (see box, p.40) has stood at the top of the square since 1680, but the present **Wenceslas Monument**, by the father of Czech sculpture, Josef Václav Myslbek, was only unveiled in 1912, after thirty years on the drawing board. This epicentre of the Czech world is worthy and heroic but pretty unexciting, with the Czech patron saint sitting resolutely astride his mighty steed, surrounded by smaller-scale representations of four other Bohemian saints – his mother Ludmila, Procopius, Adalbert and Agnes – added in the 1920s.

In 1918, 1948, 1968 and again in 1989, the monument was used as a national political notice board, festooned in posters, flags and slogans, and even now it remains the city's favourite soapbox venue (for instance, it was used by Prague's large Ukrainian community during the revolution of 2014).

On October 28, 1939, during the demonstrations here against the Nazi occupation, the medical student **Jan Opletal** was shot when troops opened fire on protesters. Two of Prague's most famous martyrs were fatally wounded close by. On January 16, 1969, the 21-year-old philosophy student **Jan Palach** set himself alight in protest against the continuing occupation of his country by the Soviets; he died from his injuries three days later. **Jan Zajíc** followed Palach's example on February 25, the twenty-first anniversary of the Communist coup. Attempts to lay flowers on this spot on the anniversary of Palach's protest provided an annual source of confrontation with the Communist authorities; Václav Havel received the last of his many prison sentences for just such an action in January 1989. A simple memorial to *obětem komunismu* (the victims of Communism), adorned with flowers, lies close to the monument. Two mounds of cobblestones, and a cross set into the pavement outside the Národní muzeum, mark where Palach and Zajíc ended their lives.

Národní muzeum (National Museum)

5

Václavské náměstí 68 • ⓦ nm.cz • Metro Muzeum

At the top, southern, end of Václavské náměstí sits the broad, brooding hulk of the **Národní muzeum**, built by Josef Schulz in 1890. Deliberately modelled on the great European museums of Paris and Vienna, it dominates the view up the square like a giant golden eagle with outstretched wings. Along with the National Theatre, this is one of the great landmarks of the nineteenth-century Czech national revival, sporting a monumental gilt-framed glass cupola, worthy clumps of sculptural decoration and narrative frescoes from Czech history.

Neglected for decades, still bearing its bullet holes from 1945 and 1968, and slowly being eaten away by Prague's noxious air, the building was closed in 2011 for much-needed renovation. Work on the spanking new National Museum costing 1.6 billion crowns is scheduled to end by 2018, though this may be an optimistic prognosis.

Wilsonova

The southern end of Václavské náměstí displays some of the worst blight that Communist planners inflicted on Prague: above all, the thundering six-lane highway (known as the *magistrála*) that separates Nové Město from the residential suburb of Vinohrady to the east and south, and effectively cuts off the Národní muzeum from Václavské náměstí. Previously known as Vitězného února (Victorious February Street) after the 1948 Communist coup, the road was renamed **Wilsonova** in honour of US President Woodrow Wilson (a personal friend of the Masaryk family), who effectively gave the country its independence from Austria-Hungary in 1918 by backing the proposal for a separate Czechoslovak state. Various ideas have been put forward over the years to ease the crush of cars, lorries and tourist coaches (tunnels, detours) but nothing has ever been implemented and the traffic situation in this part of Prague remains as bad as ever.

Národní muzeum – nová budova (National Museum – new building)

Vinohradská 1 • Daily 10am–6pm • 200Kč • ⓣ 224 497 111, ⓦ nm.cz • Metro Muzeum

The former **Prague Stock Exchange**, alongside the grand Národní muzeum building, only completed in the 1930s but rendered entirely redundant by the 1948 Communist coup, is probably the most famous victim of postwar "reconstruction". The architect Karel Prager was given the task of designing a new "socialist" **Federal Assembly** building on the same site, without destroying the old bourse: he opted for a supremely unappealing bronze-tinted plate-glass structure, supported by concrete stilts and sitting uncomfortably on top of its diminutive predecessor. After the break-up of Czechoslovakia the building hosted Radio Free Europe before being turned over to the **National Museum**, which uses it for **temporary exhibitions**.

Státní opera

Wilsonova 4 • ⓣ 224 901 448, ⓦ narodni-divadlo.cz • Metro Muzeum

Next to the old Parliament building, the **Státní opera** is another of Prague's grandiose facades receiving a long-required facelift after years of exposure to traffic fumes from the *magistrála* that tears past its front entrance, just metres from the building. It was constructed by the Viennese duo Helmer and Fellner, and opened in 1888 as the Neues Deutsches Theater, shortly after the Czechs had built their own national theatre on the waterfront. Always second fiddle to the Stavovské divadlo, though equally ornate inside, it was one of the last great building projects of Prague's once all-powerful German-speaking minority. The velvet-and-gold interior is still as fresh as it was when the Bohemian-born composer Gustav Mahler brought the traffic to a standstill conducting the premiere of his *Seventh Symphony*. It's set to reopen in the summer of 2019.

5 Praha hlavní nádraží (Prague Main Station)

Wilsonova 8 • ⓦ cd.cz • Metro Hlavní nádraží

Designed by Czech architect Josef Fanta and officially opened in 1909 as the Franz-Josefs Bahnhof, Prague's main train station, **Praha hlavní nádraží**, was one of the final architectural glories of the dying Empire. Arriving by metro, or buying tickets in the over-polished subterranean modern section, it's easy to miss the station's surviving Art Nouveau parts. The original entrance on Wilsonova still exudes imperial confidence, with its wrought-iron canopy and naked figurines clinging to the sides of the towers; on the other side of the road, two great glass protrusions signal the new entrance that opens out into the green space of the Vrchlického sady, a grimy gathering point for Prague's numerous down-and-outs. The Art Nouveau sections, including the remarkable *Fantova kavárna*, have been under renovation for years, the seedy 1977 "new" terminal having been half-heartedly revamped as a crass and rather cramped shopping centre a decade ago.

Na příkopě and around

If you head northeastwards from Můstek at the end of Václavské náměstí, you can join those ambling down **Na příkopě** (literally "on the ditch"), a street that traces the course of the old Staré Město ditch, which was filled in in 1760. Na příkopě has been an architectural showcase for more than a century, and formed the backdrop for the weekend *passeggiata* at the end of the nineteenth century.

The south side of Na příkopě features grandiose buildings such as the former **Haas department store** at no. 4, built in 1869–71 by Theophil Hansen, the Danish architect responsible for much of the redevelopment of the Ringstrasse in Vienna. Many of the finest turn-of-the-twentieth-century buildings, including the *Café Corso* and the *Café Français* – once the favourite haunts of Prague's German-Jewish literary set – were torn down and replaced during the enthusiastic construction boom of the interwar republic. At no. 7, the Art Nouveau **U Dörflerů**, from 1905, with its gilded floral curlicues, is one of the few survivors along this stretch. On the north side of the street there are a couple of interesting buildings at **nos 18 and 20**. The latter is now part of the Živnostenka banka, designed by Osvald Polívka over the course of twenty years for the Zemská banka and connected by a kind of Bridge of Sighs suspended over Nekázanka. The style is 1890s neo-Renaissance, though there are Art Nouveau elements, such as Jan Preisler's gilded mosaics and Ladislav Šaloun's attic sculptures. It's worth nipping upstairs to the main banking hall to appreciate the financial might of the Czech capital in the last decades of the Austro-Hungarian Empire.

Muzeum komunismu (Museum of Communism)

Na příkopě 10 • Daily 9am–9pm • 190Kč • ☎ 224 212 966, ⓦ muzeumkomunismu.cz • Metro Můstek

It took an American expat to open Prague's first museum dedicated to the country's troubled Communist past. Situated above a branch of *McDonald's*, and in the same building as a casino, the much-hyped **Muzeum komunismu** can be found (with some difficulty) on the first floor of the Palác Savarin. The exhibition gives a brief and rather muddled rundown of Czech twentieth-century history, accompanied by a superb collection of Communist statues, uniforms and propaganda posters. The overpriced admission aside, the politics are a bit simplistic – the popular postwar support for the Party is underplayed – but it's worth tracking down for the memorabilia alone. There's a mock-up of a Communist classroom, a chilling StB (secret police) room and plenty of film footage of protests throughout the period.

Mucha Museum

Panská 7 • Daily 10am–6pm • 240Kč • ☎ 224 216 415, ⓦ mucha.cz • Metro Můstek

The **Mucha Museum**, housed in the Kaunicky palác, south off Na příkopě down Panská, is dedicated to **Alfons Mucha** (1860–1939), probably the most famous (and popular) of all

Czech artists, at least in the West. Mucha made his name in *fin de siècle* Paris, where he shot to fame in 1895 after designing the Art Nouveau poster *Gismonda* for the actress Sarah Bernhardt. "Le Style Mucha" became all the rage, but the artist himself came to despise this "commercial" period of his work, and in 1910 he moved back to his homeland and threw himself into the national cause, designing patriotic stamps, banknotes and posters for the new republic.

The whole of Mucha's career is covered in the permanent exhibition, and there's a good selection of informal photos taken by the artist himself of his models, and of Paul Gauguin (with whom he shared a studio) playing the harmonium with his trousers down. The only work not represented here is his massive *Slav Epic*, which may or may not be hanging in the Veletržní palace when you arrive in Prague (see p.139), but the excellent half-hour video (in English) covers the decade of his life he devoted to this cycle of nationalist paintings. In the end, Mucha paid for his Czech nationalism with his life; summoned for questioning by the Gestapo after the 1939 Nazi invasion, he died shortly after being released.

Náměstí Republiky and around

Metro Náměstí Republiky

Náměstí Republiky, at the eastern end of Na příkopě, is an amorphous space and a major tram and metro interchange, revamped and pedestrianized around a decade ago. It was at this time that the east side gained **Palladium** (see p.141), Prague's premier city-centre shopping mall, built within an old army barracks and retaining its salmon-pink, crenellated facade. During Advent the square hosts what many regard as the city's best **Christmas market**.

Prašná brána (Powder Gate)

Náměstí republiky 5 • Daily: March & Oct 10am–8pm; April–Sept 10am–10pm; Nov–Feb 10am–6pm • 90Kč • ☎ 725 847 875, ⓦ muzeumprahy.cz • Metro Náměstí Republiky

By far the oldest structure on Náměstí Republiky is the **Prašná brána**, one of the eight medieval gate-towers that once guarded the Staré Město. The present tower was begun by King Vladislav Jagiello in 1475, shortly after he'd moved into the royal court, which was situated next door at the time (on the site of today's Obecní dům). Work stopped when he retreated to Prague Castle to avoid the wrath of his subjects; later on, it was used to store gunpowder – hence the name. The small historical exhibition inside traces the tower's architectural metamorphosis from its earliest days up to its current remodelling, courtesy of the nineteenth-century restorer Josef Mocker. There's always an interesting Prague-themed temporary exhibition on here, but most people ignore the displays and scramble straight up for the modest view from the top.

Obecní dům (Municipal House)

Náměstí Republiky 5 • Daily 10am–8pm • Tours 290Kč • ☎ 222 002 101, ⓦ www.obecni-dum.cz • Metro Náměstí Republiky

Attached to the Powder Gate on Náměstí Republiky, and built on the ruins of the old royal court, the **Obecní dům** is by far the most exciting Art Nouveau building in Prague, and one of the few places that still manages to conjure up the atmosphere of Prague's turn-of-the-twentieth-century café society. Conceived as a cultural centre for the Czech community, it's probably the finest architectural achievement of the Czech national revival, designed by **Osvald Polívka** and **Antonín Balšánek**, and extravagantly decorated inside and out with the help of almost every artist connected with the Czech Secession. From the lifts to the cloakrooms, just about all the furnishings remain as they were when the building was completed in 1911, and every square centimetre of the interior and exterior has been lovingly restored. Appropriately enough, it was here that Czechoslovakia's independence was declared on October 28, 1918.

5

The simplest way of soaking up the interior – peppered with mosaics and pendulous brass chandeliers – is to have a coffee in the cavernous café, or a full meal in the equally spacious *Francouzská restaurace* (see p.182); there's also the cheaper *Plzeňská restaurace* (see p.182) in the cellar, along with the original 1910 *American Bar* (see p.190). Several rooms on the second floor are given over to temporary art exhibitions, while the building's **Smetanova síň**, Prague's largest concert hall, stages numerous concerts, including the opening salvo of the Pražské jaro (Prague Spring Festival) – traditionally a rendition of Smetana's *Má vlast* (My Country) – with the president in attendance.

For a more detailed inspection of the building's spectacular interior you can sign up for one of the regular **guided tours**, in Czech and English, at the modern information centre on the ground floor, beyond the main foyer (or book online). Tours take in the Smetanova síň, plus several rooms normally out of bounds to the public. Highlights include the folksy **Slovácký salónek**, which features a built-in aquarium decorated with gilded snails, the fountain in the mosaic-tiled recess in the **Salónek Boženy Němcové** and the Moorish silk walls and chandeliers of the **Orientální salónek**. The Czechoslovak declaration of independence took place in 1918 in the **Sál Grégrův**, with its mediocre murals depicting the battle between the sexes. The finest room of the lot, though, is the chapel-like **Primátorský sál**, designed by Alfons Mucha, with jewel-encrusted embroidered curtains, stained-glass windows and paintings on the pendentives depicting civic virtues personified by leading figures from Czech history.

Hybernská
Metro Náměstí Republiky

Directly opposite the Obecní dům stands a haughty Neoclassical building, **U hybernů** (The Hibernians), built as a customs office in the Napoleonic period, on the site of a Baroque church that belonged to an order of Irish Franciscans who fled Tudor England (hence its name) – it's currently a theatre. Walk along **Hybernská** from here and you'll pass the Art Nouveau **Hotel Central** on the right. Designed by Dryák and Bendelmayer, who built the *Grand Hotel Evropa* on Wenceslas Square (see p.105), and dating from 1900, it boasts gilded decoration that stands out amid its plainer nineteenth-century neighbours.

Lidový dům
Hybernská 7 • ⓦ cssd.cz • Metro Náměstí Republiky

The headquarters of the country's main centre-left political party, the Czech Social Democratic Party (ČSSD), the **Lidový dům** is a huge Baroque palace built by the famous Carlo Lurago in the 1650s and known as the Losyovský palác until the party acquired the building in 1907. In January 1912 a small backroom in the building was given over to a congress of the exiled Russian Social Democratic Labour Party (RSDLP) with **Lenin** himself in the chair. ČSSD was forcibly amalgamated with the Communist Party shortly after the 1948 coup, after which the palace became the Lenin Museum, its facade decorated with scenes from Lenin's life. These were dismantled in 1990, and when the party regained its independence it took over the Lidový dům once again.

Masarykovo nádraží
Havlíčkova 2 • ⓦ cd.cz • Tram #5, #26 or #29 to Masarykovo nádraží

At the end of Hybernská, a wrought-iron canopy held up by slim green pillars marks the entrance to Prague's second oldest train station, **Masarykovo nádraží**. Opened in 1845, it's a modest, almost provincial affair compared with the opulent Art Nouveau Praha hlavní nádraží, many of its original features surviving intact. Known as Praha střed during the Communist decades, it was renamed after Czechoslovakia's first president in 1990 – his bust adorns the wall on the left as you enter. Despite plans to modernize, the station retains a post-Communist feel, its seedy casino, dirt-cheap bakeries and gooey coffee machines all firmly still in place.

Jindříšská věž

Jindříšská • Daily 10am–7pm, to 6pm Nov–Mar • 120Kč • ☎ 224 232 429, ⓦ jindrisskavez.cz • Metro Můstek

5

South of Masarykovo nádraží, along Dlážděná, is the old hay market, **Senovážné náměstí**, cluttered with parked cars and a couple of bits of sculpture. Its most distinguished feature is the **Jindříšská věž**, the freestanding fifteenth-century belfry of the nearby **church of sv Jindřich** (St Henry), whose digitally controlled, high-pitched bells ring out every fifteen minutes and play an entire medley every four hours. In contrast to every other surviving tower in Prague, the Jindříšská věž has been imaginatively and expensively restored and now contains a café, restaurant, shop, exhibition space and, on the fourth floor, small **museum** on Prague's hundred-plus towers, with a good view across the city's rooftops.

Jubilejní synagoga (Jubilee synagogue)

Jeruzalémská 7 • April–Oct Sun–Fri 11am–5pm • 80Kč • Metro Hlavní nádraží

The **Jubilejní synagoga**, a short way up Jeruzalémská from Senovážné náměstí, was named in honour of the fiftieth year of Emperor Franz-Joseph I's reign in 1908. Built in a colourful Moorish style similar to that of the Španělská synagoga in Josefov, but with a touch of Art Nouveau, the synagogue is definitely worth the thirty-minute guided tour. The Hebrew quote from Malachi on the facade strikes a note of liberal optimism: "Do we not have one father? Were we not created by the same God?"

Na poříčí

Metro Náměstí Republiky/Florenc

Running roughly parallel with Hybernská, to the north of Masarykovo nádraží, is the much busier street of **Na poříčí**, an area that, like sv Havel in Staré Město, was originally settled by German merchants. As a lively shopping street, Na poříčí seems very much out on a limb, as does the cluster of hotels at the end of the street and around the corner in **Těšnov**. The reason behind this is the now defunct Těšnov train station, which was demolished in the 1960s to make way for the monstrous Wilsonova flyover.

   Kafka spent most of his working life as a frustrated and unhappy clerk for the Arbeiter-Unfall-Versicherungs-Anstalt (Workers' Accident Insurance Company), in the grand nineteenth-century building at no. 7. Further along at no. 15, there's more faded *fin de siècle* architecture at the **Café Imperial**, which has miraculously retained its elaborate ceramic tiling from 1914 (see p.182).

Banka legií

Na poříčí 24 • Mon–Fri 9am–5pm • Metro Náměstí Republiky

An unusual piece of corporate architecture, the **Banka legií**, now a branch of the ČSOB, is one of Pavel Janák's rare Rondo-Cubist efforts from the early 1920s. Set into the bold smoky-red moulding is a striking white marble frieze by Otto Gutfreund, depicting the epic march across Siberia undertaken by the Czechoslovak Legion and their embroilment in the Russian Revolution (see p.227). You're free to wander into the main banking hall on the ground floor, which, though marred by the twenty-first-century bank fittings, retains its curved glass roof and distinctive red-and-white marble patterning. The glass curtain-walled **Bílá labuť** (White Swan) department store, opposite, is a good example of the functionalist style that Janák and others went on to embrace in the late 1920s and 1930s.

Muzeum Prahy (City of Prague Museum)

Na poříčí 52 • Tues–Sun 9am–6pm • 120Kč • ☎ 224 816 772, ⓦ muzeumprahy.cz • Metro Florenc

Antonín Balšánek's purpose-built mansion, housing the Muzeum hlavního města Prahy, better known simply as the **Muzeum Prahy**, somehow managed to survive 1960s redevelopment and now stands like a neo-Renaissance beached whale next to the

5

Wilsonova flyover near Florenc bus station. Inside, there's an ad hoc collection of the city's art, a number of antique bicycles and usually an intriguing temporary exhibition on some fascinating aspect of the Czech capital. The museum's prize possession is the incredible **Langweilův model**, a 3D paper representation of Prague's old centre completed by university librarian Antonín Langweil in the 1830s. The model offers a fascinating insight into early nineteenth-century Prague – predominantly Baroque, with the cathedral incomplete and the Jewish quarter "unsanitized" – and, consequently, has served as one of the most useful records for the city's restorers. The most surprising thing is that so little has changed. Langweil spent all his time and money on the model, but could find neither a sponsor nor a buyer. He died in poverty, leaving his family with considerable debts.

Poštovní muzeum (Postal Museum)

Nové mlýny 2 • Tues–Sun 9am–5pm • 50Kč • ☎ 222 312 006, ⓦ postovnimuzeum.cz • Tram #5, #8, #24 or #26 to Dlouhá třída

North of Na poříčí, close to the riverbank of nábřeží Ludvika Svobody, is the **Poštovní muzeum**, housed in the Vávrův dům, an old mill, near one of Prague's many water towers. The first floor contains a series of jolly nineteenth-century wall paintings of Romantic Austrian landscapes, and a collection of drawings on postman themes. The real philately is on the ground floor – a vast international collection of stamps arranged in vertical pull-out drawers. The Czechoslovak issues are historically and artistically interesting, as well as of appeal to collectors. Stamps became a useful tool in the propaganda wars of the last century; even such short-lived ventures as the Hungarian-backed Slovak Soviet Republic of 1918–19 and the Slovak National Uprising of autumn 1944 managed to print off special issues. Under the First Republic, the country's leading artists, notably Alfons Mucha and Max Švabinský, were commissioned to design stamps, some of which are exceptionally beautiful. Other exhibits of interest include smart, brass-buttoned postal uniforms from different ages and a display of period post boxes.

Ministry of Transport

Nábřeží Ludvíka Svobody 12 • ⓦ www.mdcr.cz • Tram #24 to Těšnov

The distinctive, glass-domed 1920s building that now houses the **Ministry of Transport** holds a special place in the country's history. Under the Communists, it was the former headquarters of the Party's Central Committee, where Dubček and his fellow reformers were arrested in August 1968, before being spirited away to Moscow for "frank and fraternal" discussions.

Novomlýnská vodárenská věž (Novomlýnská Water Tower)

Nové mlýny 3A • Tues–Sun 9am–6pm • 120Kč • ⓦ muzeumprahy.cz • Tram #6, #8, #15, #17 or #26 to Dlouhá třída

A short walk from the Ministry of Transport and Revoluční, Prague's newest attraction, the **Novomlýnská vodárenská věž**, is a renovated seventeenth-century water tower that once supplied all of the New Town. The tower has suffered many a trauma including floods and being shot up a few times in various wars (look out for the bullet holes on the outside). It also burnt down twice in its history and thus makes a fitting venue for a new **multimedia exhibition** on Prague's most famous fires, including, of course, the blaze that destroyed the first incarnation of the National Theatre.

Jungmannovo náměstí

Metro Můstek

Heading west from Můstek (see p.104), before hitting Národní třída, you pass through **Jungmannovo náměstí**, named for Josef Jungmann (1772–1847), a prolific writer,

5

translator and leading light of the Czech national revival, whose pensive, seated statue was erected here in 1878. This small, ill-proportioned square boasts an unrivalled panoply of Czech architectural curiosities, ranging from Emil Králíček and Matěj Blecha's unique **Cubist streetlamp** (and seat) from 1912, beyond the Jungmann statue in the eastern corner of the square, to the gleaming, functionalist facade of the former **ARA department store**, built in the late 1920s on the corner of Perlova and ulice 28 října (October 28 Street, commemorating the foundation of the First Republic).

Palác Adria

Národní třída 40 • Metro Můstek

Diagonally opposite the ARA department store is Jungmannovo náměstí's most imposing building, the chunky, vigorously sculptured **Palác Adria**. It was designed in the early 1920s by Pavel Janák and Josef Zasche, with sculptural extras by Otto Gutfreund and a central *Seafaring* group by Jan Štursa. Janák was a pioneering figure in the short-lived, prewar Czech Cubist movement; after the war, he and Josef Gočár attempted to create a national style of architecture appropriate for the new republic. The style was dubbed "Rondo-Cubism" – semicircular motifs are a recurrent theme – though the Palác Adria owes as much to the Italian Renaissance as it does to the new national style.

Constructed for the Italian insurance company Reunione Adriatica di Sicurità – hence its current name – the building's *pasáž* (see box, p.106) retains its wonderful original portal featuring sculptures by Bohumil Kafka, depicting the twelve signs of the zodiac. The theatre in the basement of the building was once a studio for the multimedia **Laterna magika** (Magic Lantern) company. In 1989, it became the underground nerve centre of the Velvet Revolution, when Občanské fórum (Civic Forum) found temporary shelter here shortly after their inaugural meeting on the Sunday following the November 17 demonstration. Against a stage backdrop for Dürenmatt's *Minotaurus*, the Forum thrashed out tactics in the dressing rooms and gave daily press conferences in the auditorium during the crucial fortnight before the Communists relinquished power.

Panna Maria Sněžná

Jungmannovo náměstí 18 • ☎ 224 490 340, ⓦ pms.ofm.cz • Metro Můstek

Right beside the Cubist streetlamp on Jungmannovo náměstí stands the medieval gateway of the Franciscan **church of Panna Maria Sněžná** (St Mary of the Snows), once one of the great landmarks of Wenceslas Square, but now barely visible from any of the surrounding streets. To enter the church, go through the archway beside the Austrian Cultural Institute, behind the statue of Jungmann, and across the courtyard beyond. Like most of Nové Město's churches, the Panna Maria Sněžná was founded by Charles IV, who envisaged a vast coronation church even bigger than St Vitus Cathedral. Unfortunately, the Hussite wars intervened and only the chancel was completed; the result is curious – a church that is short in depth but outstrips the cathedral in height. The 30m-high, prettily painted vaulting – which collapsed on the Franciscans who inherited the half-completed building in the seventeenth century – is magnificent, as is the gold and black early Baroque main altar, Prague's tallest, which touches the ceiling. To get an idea of the intended scale of the finished structure, take a stroll through the **Františkánská zahrada**, south of the church; these gardens make a lovely hideaway from Nové Mesto's bustle and a picnic oasis, marred only by the modern garden furniture.

Národní třída and around

Tram #6, #9, #18, #22 or #24 to Národní třída

The eastern half of **Národní třída** is lined with shops, galleries and clubs, all of which begin to peter out as you near the Vltava. On the north side is an eye-catching duo of Art Nouveau buildings, designed by Osvald Polívka in 1907–08. The first, at no. 7, was built for the **pojišťovna Praha** (Prague Savings Bank), hence the beautiful mosaic lettering

THE MASAKR

5

On the night of **November 17, 1989**, a 50,000-strong, officially sanctioned student demonstration, organized by the students' union SSM (League of Young Socialists), worked its way down Národní with the intention of reaching Wenceslas Square. Halfway down the street they were confronted by the *bílé přílby* (white helmets) and *červené barety* (red berets) of the hated **riot police**. For what must have seemed like hours, there was a stalemate as the students sat down and refused to disperse, some of them handing flowers out to the police. Suddenly, without any warning, the police attacked and what became known as the **masakr** (massacre) began. In the end, no one was actually killed, though it wasn't for want of trying by the police. On the facade of the Kaňkův dům, **Národní 16**, there's a small symbolic bronze relief of eight hands reaching out for help, a permanent shrine in memory of the hundreds who were hospitalized in the violence. This is the rallying point for the annual commemoration on November 17.

above the windows advertising *život* (life insurance) and *kapital* (loans), as well as help with *důchod* (pensions) and *věno* (dowries). Next door, the slightly more ostentatious **Topičův dům**, headquarters of Československý spisovatel, the official state publishers, makes the perfect neighbour, with a similarly ornate wrought-iron and glass canopy.

Sv Voršila

Národní třída • Tram #6, #9, #17, #18 or #22 to Národní divadlo

Towards the river end of Národní třída the **convent and church of sv Voršila** (St Ursula) are distinguished by the rare sight (in this part of town) of two trees – in this case sticking straight out of the base of the white facade. When it was completed in 1678, this was one of the first truly flamboyant Baroque buildings in Prague, and its white stucco and frescoed interior have been restored to their original state.

Knihovna Václava Havla (Havel Library)

Ostrovní 13 • Tues–Sun noon–5pm • Free • ☎ 222 220 112, ⓦ vaclavhavel-library.org • Tram #6, #9, #17, #18 or #22 to Národní divadlo

The **Knihovna Václava Havla** is an excellent exhibition tracing the life of **Václav Havel**, possibly the most famous of Czechs (outside the country's borders at any rate). The display follows the president-playwright from plump bourgeois toddler to well-groomed president via many a black-and-white image of his long-haired dissident days. The walls are panelled with good English translations of speech excerpts, some criticizing his fellow countrymen for their narrow-mindedness (small wonder he became so unpopular in the post-Communist 1990s), and all centred on a library of his works. The main Havel archive is in the same building but is of little real interest to foreign visitors.

Národní divadlo (National Theatre)

Národní 2 • Tours 200Kč • ☎ 224 901 448, ⓦ narodni-divadlo.cz • Tram #6, #9, #17, #18 or #22 to Národní divadlo

Overlooking the Vltava, at the end of Národní, is the gold-crested **Národní divadlo**, proud symbol of the Czech nation. Refused money from the Habsburg state coffers, Czechs of all classes dug deep into their own pockets to raise funds for the venture themselves. The foundation stones, gathered from various historically significant sites in Bohemia and Moravia (plus one sent by expats in America), were laid in 1868 by the historian and politician František Palacký and the composer Bedřich Smetana; the architect, Josef Zítek, spent the next thirteen years on the project. In June 1881, the theatre opened with a premiere of Smetana's opera *Libuše*, but in August of the same year, fire destroyed everything except the outer walls. Within two years the whole thing was rebuilt – even the emperor contributed this time – under the supervision of Josef Schulz, and it opened once again to the strains of *Libuše*. The grand portal on the north side of the theatre is embellished with suitably triumphant allegorical figures, and, inside, every square centimetre is taken up with paintings and sculptures by leading

5

artists of the Czech national revival. Prague City Tourism offices can arrange tours of the interiors for individuals – these run daily in English.

Nová scéna

Národní třída 4 · ☎ 224 931 482, ⓦ novascena.cz · Tram #6, #9, #17, #18 or #22 to Národní divadlo

Standing behind the Národní divadlo, and in dramatic contrast with it, is the theatre's modern extension, the glass cube of the 1983 **Nová scéna**, designed by Karel Prager, the leading (and now much reviled) architect of the Communist era. It's one of those buildings most Praguers love to hate – it was described by one Czech as looking like "frozen piss" – though compared to much of Prague's Communist-era architecture, it's not that bad. It's home to the Laterna Magika, a multimedia theatre company that combines live actors, film and sound in often quite impressive avant-garde performances. Miloš Forman, Jiří Trnka, Jan Švankmajer and several other big hitters of the Czech cultural scene were involved with the Laterna Magika at some point in their careers.

Café Slavia

Tram #6, #9, #17, #18 or #22 to Národní divadlo

Opposite the National Theatre, **Café Slavia** has been a favourite haunt of the city's writers, dissidents and artists (and, inevitably, actors) since the days of the First Republic. The Czech avant-garde movement, Devětsil, led by Karel Teige, used to hold its meetings here in the 1920s; the meetings are recorded for posterity by another of its members, the Nobel prize-winner Jaroslav Seifert, in his *Slavia Poems*. The café has been carelessly modernized since those arcadian days, but it still has a great riverside view and Viktor Oliva's *Absinthe Drinker* canvas on the wall.

Vodičkova and around

Of the many roads that head from Wenceslas Square towards Karlovo náměstí, **Vodičkova** is probably the most impressive. You can catch several trams along this route, but there are a handful of buildings worth checking out on the way so you may choose to walk.

U Nováků

Vodičkova 28 · Metro Můstek

The **U Nováků** building is impossible to miss, thanks to Jan Preisler's mosaic of bucolic frolicking (its actual subject, *Trade and Industry*, is confined to the edges of the picture), and Osvald Polívka's curvilinear window frames and delicate, ivy-like ironwork – look out for the frog-prince holding up a windowsill. Built for the Novák department store in the early 1900s, for the past sixty years it has been a cabaret hall, restaurant and café all rolled into one; sadly, the original interior fittings have long since gone.

Minerva girls' school

Vodičkova 22 · Metro Můstek

Set slightly back from Vodičkova stands the imposing neo-Renaissance **Minerva girls' school**, covered in chocolate-brown sgraffito. Founded in 1866, it was the first such institution in Prague, and was notorious for the antics of its pupils, the "Minervans", who shocked bourgeois Czech society with their experimentations with fashion, drugs and sexual freedom. It is now occupied by a rather more sober junior school and part of the university's pedagogical faculty.

Karlovo náměstí

Metro Karlovo náměstí

The impressive proportions of **Karlovo náměstí**, once Prague's biggest square, are no longer so easy to appreciate, obscured by an unkempt, tree-planted public garden and

MILENA JESENSKÁ

5

The most famous "Minervan" (see opposite) was **Milena Jesenská**, born in 1896 into a Czech family whose ancestry stretched back to the sixteenth century. Shortly after leaving school, she was confined to a mental asylum by her father when he discovered that she was having an affair with a Jew. On her release, she married the Jewish intellectual **Ernst Pollak**, and moved to Vienna, where she took a job as a railway porter to support the two of them. While living in Vienna, she sent her Czech translation of one of **Franz Kafka**'s short stories to his publisher; Kafka wrote back himself, and so began their intense, mostly epistolary, relationship. Kafka described her later as "the only woman who ever understood me", and with his encouragement she took up writing professionally. Tragically, by the time Milena had extricated herself from what turned out to be a disastrous marriage, Kafka, still smarting from three failed engagements with other women, had decided never to commit himself to anyone else; his letters alone survived as a moving testament to their love.

Milena returned to Prague in 1925, and moved on from writing fashion articles to critiques of avant-garde architecture, becoming one of the city's leading journalists. She married again, this time the prominent functionalist architect **Jaromír Krejcar**, but later, a difficult pregnancy and childbirth left her addicted to morphine. She overcame her dependency only after joining the Communist Party, but was to quit after the first of Stalin's show trials in 1936. She continued to work as a journalist in the late 1930s, and wrote a series of articles condemning the rise of Fascism in the Sudetenland.

When the Nazis rolled into Prague in 1939, Milena's Vinohrady flat had already become a centre for resistance. For a while, she managed to hang on to her job, but her independent intellectual stance and provocative gestures – for instance, wearing a yellow star as a mark of solidarity with her Jewish friends – soon attracted the attentions of the Gestapo and, after a brief spell in the notorious Pankrác prison, she was sent to **Ravensbrück**, the women's concentration camp near Berlin, where she died of kidney failure in May 1944.

---

spliced in two by the busy thoroughfare of Ječná. The square was created by Charles IV as Nové Město's cattle market and used by him for the grisly annual public display of his impressive collection of saintly relics; today it actually signals the southern limit of the city's main commercial district and the beginning of predominantly residential southern Prague.

Novoměstská radnice (New Town Hall)

Karlovo náměstí 23 · **Tower** Mid-April to mid-Oct Tues–Sun 10am–6pm · 60Kč · ☎ 224 948 229, ⓦ nrpraha.cz · Metro Karlovo náměstí

The **Novoměstská radnice**, at the northeastern corner of Karlovo náměstí, sports three impressive triangular gables embellished with intricate blind tracery. It was built, like the town hall on Staroměstské náměstí, during the reign of King John of Luxembourg, though it has survived rather better, and is now one of the finest Gothic buildings in the city. It was here that Prague's **first defenestration** took place on July 30, 1419, when the radical Hussite preacher Jan Želivský and his penniless religious followers stormed the building, mobbed the councillors and burghers, and threw twelve or thirteen of them (including the mayor) out of the town hall windows onto the pikes of the Hussite mob below, who clubbed any survivors to death. Václav IV (son of Emperor Charles IV), on hearing the news, suffered a stroke and died two weeks later. So began the long and bloody Hussite Wars. After the amalgamation of Prague's towns in 1784, the building was used as a criminal court and prison. Nowadays, you can visit the site of the defenestration, and climb to the top of the **tower** for a view over central Prague.

Sv Ignác

Ječná 2 · 6am–noon & 3.30–6.30pm · ☎ 221 990 200, ⓦ kostelignac.cz · Metro Karlovo náměstí

During the Counter-Reformation the Jesuits were allowed to demolish 23 houses on the east side of Karlovo náměstí to make way for their huge college (now one of the city's main hospitals) and the accompanying **church of sv Ignác** (St Ignatius), begun in 1665 by

5

Carlo Lurago and finished by Martin Reiner and Paul Ignaz Bayer. The statue of St Ignatius, which sits above the tympanum surrounded by a sunburst, caused controversy at the time, as until then only the Holy Trinity had been depicted in such a way. The church, modelled, like so many Jesuit churches, on the Gesù in Rome, is quite remarkable inside, a salmon-pink and white confection, with lots of frothy stuccowork and an exuberant powder-pink pulpit dripping with gold drapery, cherubs and saints.

Faustův dům (Faust House)

Karlovo náměstí 40 • Metro Karlovo náměstí

At the southern end of Karlovo náměstí is the so-called **Faustův dům**, a salmon-pink and grey late Baroque building with a long and preposterous history of alchemy. An occult priest from Opava owned the house in the fourteenth century and, two hundred years later in 1590, international con-man and Rudolf II's favourite English alchemist Edward Kelley bought it as a base for his attempts to turn worthless metals into gold, though he only spent a year here before being arrested for fraud and imprisoned in Křivoklát Castle. The building is also the traditional setting for the Czech version of the Faust legend, with the arrival one rainy night of a penniless and homeless student, Jan Šťastný (meaning lucky, or in Latin *Faustus*). Finding money in the house, he decides to keep it – only to discover that it was put there by the Devil, who then claims his soul in return. A pharmacy (lekárna) now occupies the ground floor.

Sv Cyril and Metoděj and Heydrich Martyrs' Monument

Corner Resslova and Na Zderaze • **Church** Sat 8–9.30am, Sun 9am–noon **Monument** March–Oct Tues–Sun 9am–5pm; Nov–Feb Tues–Sun 9am–5pm • Free admission • Ⓦ pamatnik-heydrichiady.cz • Metro Karlovo náměstí

Just off Karlovo náměstí, a short way along thundering Resslova, the **Orthodox cathedral of sv Cyril and Metoděj** was constructed by Bayer and Dientzenhofer as a Roman Catholic place of worship in the eighteenth century; since the 1930s it has been the mother ship of the Orthodox Church in the Czech Lands. Amid all the traffic, it's extremely difficult to imagine the scene here on June 18, 1942, when seven **Czechoslovak secret agents** involved in the assassination of Reinhard Heydrich, the most high-profile assassination of World War II (see box opposite), were besieged in the church by hundreds of Waffen SS. Acting on a tip-off by one of the Czech resistance who turned himself in, the Nazis surrounded the church just after 4am and fought a pitched battle for more than six hours, trying explosives, flooding and any other method they could think of (notice the bullet-pocked slit in the exterior south wall) to drive the men out of their stronghold in the crypt. Eventually, all seven agents committed suicide rather than give themselves up. A plaque at street level on the south wall commemorates those who died, and an **exhibition** on the whole affair – the **Heydrich Martyrs' Monument** – is situated in the crypt itself; the entrance is underneath the church steps on Na Zderaze.

The embankment

Grandly confident turn-of-the-twentieth-century apartment blocks line the Vltava's right bank, almost without interruption, for some 2km from the Charles Bridge south to the rocky outcrop of Vyšehrad. It's a long walk, even just along the length of **Masarykovo** and **Rašínovo nábřeží**, but tramlines run the entire stretch. Bridges link the embankment to some of the Vltava's islands such as Střelecký ostrov and Slovanský ostrov (better known as Žofín), oases of leafy calm in Prague's hectic cityscape. The Náplavka, the cobbled roadway that runs from Slovanský ostrov to Vyšehrad has seen a lot of hipster gentrification in recent years and is a hive of skating, strolling and street food in the summer months.

THE ASSASSINATION OF REINHARD HEYDRICH

5

The assassination of **Reinhard Heydrich** in 1942 was the only attempt the Allies ever made on the life of a leading Nazi. It's an incident that the Allies have always billed as a great success in the otherwise rather pitiful seven-year history of the Czech resistance. But, as with all acts of brave resistance during the war, there was a price to be paid. Given that the reprisals meted out to the Czech population were entirely predictable, it remains a controversial, if not suicidal, decision to have made.

The target, Reinhard Tristan Eugen Heydrich, was a talented and upwardly mobile anti-Semite (despite rumours that he was partly Jewish himself), a great organizer and a skilful concert violinist. He was a late recruit to the Nazi Party, signing up in 1931, after having been dismissed from the German Navy for dishonourable conduct towards a woman. However, he swiftly rose through the ranks of the SS to become second in command after Himmler, and in the autumn of 1941 he was appointed **Reichsprotektor** of the puppet state of Böhmen und Mähren – effectively, the most powerful man in the Czech Lands. Although his rule began with brutality, it soon settled into the tried and tested policy that Heydrich liked to call *Peitsche und Zucker* (literally, "whip and sugar").

On the morning of May 27, 1942, as Heydrich was being driven by his personal bodyguard, Oberscharführer Klein, in his open-top Mercedes from his manor house north of Prague to his office in Hradčany, three Czechoslovak agents (parachuted in from England) were taking up positions in the northeastern suburb of Libeň. The first agent gave the signal as the car pulled into Kirchmayer Boulevard (now V Holešovičkách). Another agent, a Slovak called **Gabčík**, pulled out a Sten gun and tried to shoot, but the gun jammed. Rather than driving out of the situation, Heydrich ordered Klein to stop the car and attempted to shoot back. At this point, the third agent, **Kubiš**, threw a hand grenade at the car. The blast injured Kubiš and Heydrich, who immediately leapt out and began firing at Kubiš. Kubiš, with blood pouring down his face, jumped on his bicycle and fled downhill. Gabčík, meanwhile, pulled out a second gun and exchanged shots with Heydrich, until the latter collapsed from his wounds. Gabčík fled into a butcher's, shot Klein – who was in hot pursuit – in the legs and escaped down the backstreets.

Meanwhile, back at the Mercedes, a baker's van was flagged down by a passer-by, but the baker refused to get involved. Eventually, a small truck carrying floor polish was commandeered and Heydrich was taken to the Bulovka hospital. He died eight days later from shrapnel wounds and was given full Nazi honours at his **Prague funeral**; the cortege passed down Wenceslas Square, in front of a crowd of thousands. As the home resistance had forewarned, revenge was quick to follow. The day after Heydrich's funeral, the village of **Lidice** was burnt to the ground and its male inhabitants murdered; two weeks later the men and women of Ležáky suffered a similar fate.

The plan to assassinate Heydrich had been formulated in the early months of 1942 by the Czechoslovak **government-in-exile** in London, without consultation with the Czech Communist leadership in Moscow, and despite fierce opposition from the resistance within Czechoslovakia. Since it was clear that the reprisals would be horrific (thousands were executed in the aftermath), the only logical explanation for the plan is that this was precisely the aim of the government-in-exile's operation – to forge a solid wedge of resentment between the Germans and Czechs. In this respect, if in no other, the operation was ultimately successful.

Hlahol

Masarykovo nábřeží 16 • ☎ 224 934 547, ⓦ hlahol.cz • Tram #6, #9, #17, #18 or #22 to Národní divadlo

Most of the ornate buildings along the waterfront itself are private residential tenements, and therefore inaccessible. One exception is the Art Nouveau concert hall, **Hlahol**, built for the Hlahol men's choir in 1903–06, and designed by the architect of the main train station, Josef Fanta, with a pediment mural by Mucha and statues by Šaloun – check the website or the posters outside the hall for details of upcoming concerts.

5 | Střelecký ostrov

Floating in the middle of the Vltava and accessible from Most Legií (Bridge of the Legions), **Střelecký ostrov**, or Shooters' Island, is so named because it's where the army held their shooting practice, on and off, from the fifteenth until the nineteenth century. Closer to the left bank, it became a favourite spot for a Sunday promenade, and is still popular, especially in summer. The first Sokol festival took place here in 1882 (see p.66), and the first May Day demonstrations in 1890.

Slovanský ostrov

Tram #6, #9, #17, #18 or #22 to Národní divadlo

Quiet **Slovanský ostrov** came about as a result of the natural silting of the river in the eighteenth century. It's commonly known as **Žofín**, after the island's grand 1835 cultural centre named in honour of Sophie, Emperor Franz-Joseph I's mum. By the late nineteenth century the island had become one of the city's foremost pleasure gardens, where, as the composer Berlioz remarked, "bad musicians shamelessly make abominable music in the open air and immodest young males and females indulge in brazen dancing, while idlers and wasters…lounge about smoking foul tobacco and drinking beer." Concerts, balls and other social gatherings still take place in the cultural centre, though generally things are much less raucous than in Berlioz's day. At the northern end of the island the park benches gathered around a statue of the greatest Czech female novelist, **Božena Němcová**, provide a pleasant urban picnic spot. The southern tip is dominated by the onion-domed **Šítek water tower**, which provided a convenient lookout post for the Czech secret police watching over Havel's nearby flat (see below).

Galerie Mánes

Masarykovo nábřeží 250 • Tues–Sun 10am–6pm • ☎ 224 932 938, ⓦ galeriemanes.com • Tram #17 to Jiráskovo náměstí

Spanning the narrow channel between Slovanský Island and the embankment is the striking white functionalist shoebox of the **Galerie Mánes**. Designed in open-plan style by Otakar Novotný in 1930, the art gallery is named after Josef Mánes, a traditional nineteenth-century landscape painter and Czech nationalist, and puts on consistently interesting contemporary exhibitions; in addition there's a café and an upstairs restaurant, suspended above the channel.

Tančící dům (Dancing House)

Jiráskovo náměstí 6 • ⓦ tadu.cz • Tram #17 to Jiráskovo náměstí

South of the Mánes gallery, Masarykovo nábřeží becomes **Rašínovo nábřeží**, named after Alois Rašín, who was sentenced to death for treason during World War I, went on to become the interwar Minister of Finance and was assassinated by an anarchist in 1923. The most striking structure on this part of the embankment is the **Tančící dům** (Dancing House) – popularly known as "Fred and Ginger" and named after the shape of the building's two towers, which vaguely resemble a couple ballroom dancing. (Some less enthusiastic Praguers comment that it looks more like a crushed plastic bottle abutting a cartoon prison.) Designed by the Canadian-born Frank Gehry and the Yugoslav-born Vlado Milunič and built on the site of a tenement accidently destroyed by a stray American bomb during a WWII air raid, it represents the worst excesses of post-Communist architecture that plagued Czech cityscapes in the 1990s: it looms next door to no. 77, an apartment block built at the turn of the twentieth century by Havel's grandfather, where, until the early 1990s, Havel and his first wife, Olga, lived in the top-floor flat. The Dancing House would not get planning permission in today's Prague, which quickly smartened up about its historical heritage in the late 1990s. Part of the building has been turned into a hotel (*Xref*) by former Czech football international, Vladimír Šmicer.

Palacký Monument
Palackého náměstí • Tram #3, #4, #10, #14, #16 or #17 to Palackého náměstí

Around 250m south of the Tančící dům, the buildings retreat for a moment to reveal Stanislav Suchardá's remarkable Art Nouveau **Palacký Monument**, dedicated to František Palacký, the great nineteenth-century Czech historian, politician and nationalist. Like the Hus Monument, which was unveiled three years later, this mammoth project – fifteen years in the making – had missed its moment by the time it was finally completed in 1912, and was met with universal disfavour. The critics have mellowed over the years, and nowadays it's appreciated for what it is – an energetic and inspirational piece of work. Ethereal bronze bodies, representing the world of the imagination, shoot out at all angles, contrasting sharply with the plain stone mass of the plinth and below, the giant, grimly determined, seated figure of Palacký himself, representing the real world.

Výtoň
Rašínovo nábřeží 412 • Tues–Sun 10am–6pm • 60Kč • ☎ 224 919 833 • Tram #3, #7 or #17 to Výtoň

If you continue along the embankment to the very southern edge of Nové Město you'll come to a freestanding square building sunk below the level of the embankment. This is **Výtoň**, an attractive, sixteenth-century former customs house that now houses a pub and a small **museum** telling the history of the Podskalí area – literally "under the rocks", or *vyšehrad* – with a model of the old embankment. There's also a fascinating video of one of the last *voroplavba* (log rafts) to come down the Vltava before the river was dammed in the 1950s.

Emauzy monastery and around
Vyšehradská 49 • **Cloisters** April & Oct Mon–Fri 11am–5pm; May–Sept Mon–Sat 11am–5pm; Nov–March Mon–Fri 11am–2pm • 60Kč • ☎ 224 917 662, Ⓦ emauzy.cz • Metro Karlovo náměstí

Behind Palackého náměstí, the intertwined concrete spires of the **Emauzy monastery** are an unusual modern addition to the Prague skyline. The monastery was one of the few important historical buildings to be damaged in World War II, in this case by an errant Anglo-American bomb. Charles IV founded the monastery for Croatian Benedictines, who used the Old Slavonic liturgy (hence its Czech name, Klášter na Slovanech, or "Monastery at the Slavs"), but after the Battle of Bílá hora it was handed over to the more mainstream Spanish Benedictines, who renamed it after Emmaus. The cloisters, containing some precious Gothic frescoes, are open to visitors.

Sv Jan Nepomucký na skalce (St John of Nepomuk on the Rock)
Vyšehradská • Services Sun 11am • Metro Karlovo náměstí

Rising up behind Emauzy is one of Kilian Ignaz Dientzenhofer's little gems, the **church of sv Jan Nepomucký na skalce**, finished in the late 1730s and with a facade that displays the plasticity of the Bavarian's Baroque style in all its glory. It's one of Prague's most pleasing churches, perched high above Vyšehradská, the tramlines tracing a sweeping curve below. Unfortunately it's closed to visitors, though you might be able to sneak in for the 11am Sunday service, which is held in German.

Botanická zahrada (Botanical garden)
Na Slupi 16 • Daily: Feb & March 10am–5pm; April–Aug 10am–7.30pm; Sept & Oct 10am–6pm; Nov–Jan 10am–3.30pm • Greenhouses 55Kč • ☎ 221 951 883, Ⓦ bz-uk.cz • Tram #6, #18 or #24 to Botanická zahrada

The **Botanická zahrada** belongs to Charles University's botanic garden, laid out in 1897 on a series of terraces. Though far from spectacular, the garden is one of the few patches of green in this part of town, and the 1930s greenhouses (*skleníky*) have been restored to their former glory.

5

U kalicha
Na Bojišti 12–14 • ☎ 224 912 557, ⓦ ukalicha.cz • Metro I.P. Pavlova

The **U kalicha** pub is immortalized in the opening passages of the consistently popular comic novel *The Good Soldier Švejk*, by Jaroslav Hašek. In the story, on the eve of World War I, Švejk (Schweik to the Germans) walks into *U kalicha*, where a plain-clothes officer of the Austro-Hungarian constabulary is sitting drinking and, after a brief conversation, finds himself arrested in connection with the assassination of Archduke Ferdinand. Whatever the pub may have been like in Hašek's day (and even then, it wasn't his local), it's now unashamedly oriented towards reaping in the euros, and about the only authentic thing you'll find inside – albeit at a price – is the beer.

Muzeum Antonína Dvořáka (Dvořák Museum)
Ke Karlovu 20 • Tues–Sun 10am–1.30pm & 2–5pm • 50Kč • ☎ 224 918 013, ⓦ nm.cz • Metro I.P. Pavlova

Set back from the road, the elegant salmon-pink **Vila Amerika** houses the **Muzeum Antonína Dvořáka**, devoted to Czech composer **Antonín Dvořák** (1841–1904), who lived for a time on nearby Žitná. Even if you've no interest in Dvořák, the house itself is a delight, designed for the upwardly mobile Count Michna as a minuscule Baroque summer palace around 1720 and one of Kilian Ignaz Dientzenhofer's most successful secular works. Easily the most famous of all Czech composers, for many years Dvořák had to play second fiddle to Smetana in the orchestra at the Národní divadlo, where Smetana was the conductor. Among the various items of memorabilia are Dvořák's golden honorary degree gown from Cambridge and some furniture from his Žitná flat. However, the tasteful period rooms, with the composer's music wafting in and out and the tiny garden dotted with Baroque sculptures, compensate for what the display cabinets may lack. Occasional concerts take place upstairs, in the *velky sál*, with its trompe l'oeil frescoes.

Muzeum Policie ČR (Czech Police Museum)
Ke Karlovu 1 • **Museum** Tues–Sun 10am–5pm • 30Kč **Go-karts** Thurs 1–3pm, Sat & Sun 10am–noon & 2–4pm • 50Kč • ☎ 224 922 183, ⓦ muzeumpolicie.cz • Tram #3, #10, #14, #16, #18 or #24 to Albertov

At the southern end of Ke Karlovu, the former Augustinian monastery of Karlov is now the **Muzeum Policie ČR**. Under the Communists, the most famous exhibit was undoubtedly Brek, the stuffed German Shepherd Dog who saw twelve years' service on border patrols, intercepted sixty "law-breakers" and was twice shot in action. Brek has been mothballed, and the current exhibition concentrates on road and traffic offences and the force's latest challenges: forgery, drugs and murder. Sadly, there's not much information in English, but it's still mildly diverting, in particular the exhibits on the Iron Curtain, the display of Czech police motorbikes through the ages, the parade of European police uniforms and the gruesome section on forensic science. For the kids, there's a **go-karting** track (*dětské dopravní hřiště*).

Na Karlově
Ke Karlovu 1 • ⓦ kostelnakarlove.com • Tram #3, #10, #14, #16, #18 or #24 to Albertov

The monastic **church of Na Karlově**, founded by Charles IV (of course) and designed in imitation of Charlemagne's tomb in Aachen, is quite unlike any other church in Prague. If it's open, you should take a look at the musty interior, which was remodelled in the sixteenth century by Bonifaz Wohlmut. The stellar vault has no central supporting pillars – a remarkable feat of engineering for its time, and one that gave rise to numerous legends about the architect being in league with the devil. The later Baroque fittings are just as arresting, with polychrome figures dotted about on every cornice – check out Pontius Pilate and Christ above the south door, and beneath them, a set of holy stairs and a subterranean Bethlehem grotto (Betlémské jeskyně).

Vyšehrad and the eastern suburbs

The fortress of Vyšehrad, south of Nové Město, was one of the earliest settlements in Prague, and is by far the most enticing of the city's outlying sights. There's a real mixed bag here – the cemetery contains the remains of Bohemia's artistic elite; the ramparts afford superb views over the river; and below the fortress stand several examples of Czech Cubist architecture. By the end of his reign in 1378, Charles IV had laid out his city on such a grand scale that it wasn't until the mid-nineteenth-century Industrial Revolution that Prague began to spread beyond the boundaries of the medieval town. The first suburbs were planned to the east of the old town, with public parks and grid street plans. Of these eastern districts, Vinohrady and Žižkov best retain their individual late nineteenth-century identities.

VYŠEHRAD AND THE EASTERN SUBURBS

■ DRINKING AND NIGHTLIFE

PUBS AND BARS
Akropolis	7
Demínka	16
Pastička	10
Prague Beer Museum	21
Riegrovy sady	8
U Houdků	6
U růžového sadu	15
Vínečko 33	15
Vinohradský Parlament	20
Žluta Pumpa	22
Zvonařka	23

CLUBS AND VENUES
Fatal	5
Forum Karlín	2
Kongresové centrum Praha	24
Matrix	1
O2 Arena	1
Radost FX	19
U vystřeleného oka	8

LGBT CLUBS AND BARS
Bar 21	13
On Club	17
Piano Bar	12
The Saints	11
Střelec	18
Termix	14

● EATING

CAFÉS
Blatouch	10
Fialová cukrárna	6
Kaaba	5
Radost FX Café	7
Roza K	12

RESTAURANTS
Döner Kebab Žižkov	1
Las Adelitas	14
Mailsi	3
Masala	13
Mrázek	9
Olše	4
Singidunum	8
U Slovanské Lípy	2
Zanzibar	11

■ ACCOMMODATION

HOTELS
Anna	5
Arco	9
Ehrlich	2
Galileo	6/7
Le Palais	10
Vítkov	1
Vyšehrad	11

HOSTELS
Clown and Bard	4
Czech Inn	3
Hostel One	8

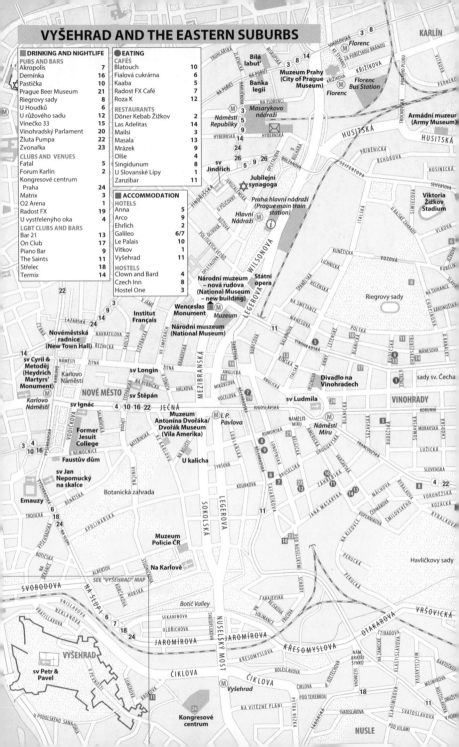

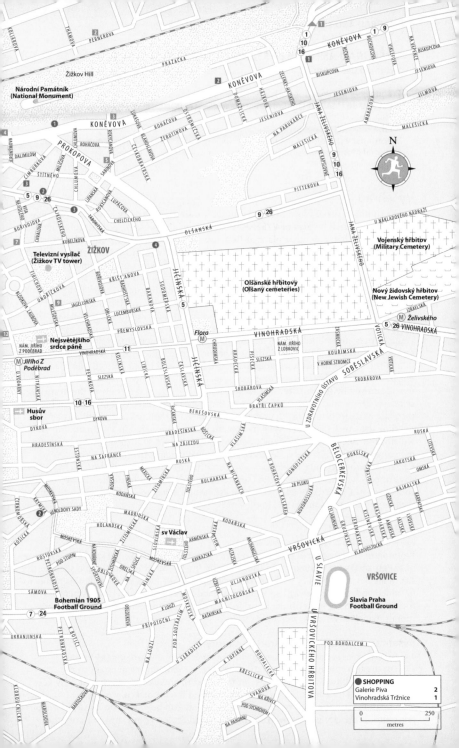

6

VYŠEHRAD AND THE EASTERN SUBURBS HIGHLIGHTS

Vyšehrad Cemetery The final resting place of Czech greats such as Smetana, Dvořák and Mucha. See below

Prague Beer Museum Sample beers from around the country at this no-nonsense pub. See p.193

Most Sacred Heart of Our Lord Prague's wackiest church built by Slovene architect Josip Plečnik. See p.130

Kaaba Funky, retro-styled coffee halt in the heart of Vinohrady. See p.184

Vinohradský parlament The Prague pub dragged into the twenty-first century. See p.192

National Monument Learn about Czechoslovakia's Communist history at this Brutalist complex. See p.134

Vyšehrad

At the southern tip of Nové Město, around 3km south of the city centre, the vertigo-inducing red-brick fortress of **VYŠEHRAD** – literally "High Castle" – has more myths attached to it than any other place in Bohemia. According to Czech legend, this is where the Slav tribes first settled in Prague, where the "wise and tireless chieftain" Krok built a castle – and whence his youngest daughter **Libuše** went on to found Praha (Prague) itself. Archeological evidence doesn't bear the last claim out, but it's clear that **Přemysl Vratislav II** (1061–92), the first Bohemian ruler to bear the title "king", built a royal palace here to get away from his younger brother who was lording it in the Hrad. Within half a century the royals had moved back to Hradčany, into a new palace, after which Vyšehrad began to lose its political significance.

The fortress enjoyed something of a renaissance under Emperor Charles IV, who wished to associate his own dynasty with that of the early Přemyslids. A system of walls was built to link the fortress to the newly founded Nové Město, and it was decreed that the *královská cesta* (royal or coronation route) should begin from here. Those fortifications were destroyed by the **Hussites** in 1420, but the hill was settled again over the next two centuries. In the mid-seventeenth century, the Habsburgs turfed everyone out and rebuilt the place as a fortified barracks, only to tear it down in 1866 to create a public park. By the time the **Czech national revival** movement became interested in Vyšehrad, only the red-brick fortifications were left as a reminder of its former strategic importance; they rediscovered its history and its legends, and gradually transformed it into a symbol of Czech nationhood. Today, Vyšehrad – visited, it has to be said, mostly by Czech day-trippers – makes for one of the most rewarding excursions from the human congestion of the city, a perfect afternoon escape and a great place from which to watch the evening sun set behind the Hrad.

Sv Petr and Pavel

Daily 10am–5.30pm • 50Kč • ☎ 224 911 353 • Metro Vyšehrad

Dominating the skyline of the city's southern suburbs, the blackened sandstone **basilica of sv Petr and Pavel** was rebuilt in the 1880s by Josef Mocker in neo-Gothic style on the site of an eleventh-century basilica. The twin open-work spires were the last elements to be added and are the fortress's most familiar landmark. The seventeen bells play one of fifty melodies every hour on the hour. Inside, you can admire the church's Art Nouveau murals, which cover every available surface.

Vyšehradský hřbitov (Vyšehrad Cemetery)

Daily: March, April & Oct 8am–6pm; May–Sept 8am–7pm; Nov–Feb 8am–5pm • Free • ⓦ slavin.cz • Metro Vyšehrad

One of the first initiatives of the national revival movement was to establish the **Vyšehradský hřbitov**, which spreads out to the north and east of the church of sv Petr and Pavel. It's a measure of the part that artists and intellectuals played in the foundation of the nation, and the high regard in which they are still held, that the most prestigious graveyard in the city is given over to them: no soldiers, no politicians, not even the

Communists managed to muscle their way in here (though there are a few merchants and bankers). Sheltered from the wind by its high walls, lined on two sides by delicate arcades, it's a tiny cemetery (reflecting, as it were, the size of the nation) filled with mostly well-kept graves, many of them designed by the country's leading sculptors. Amazingly, burials still take place here from time to time.

The graves

To the uninitiated only a handful of figures are well known, but for the Czechs the place is alive with great names (there are useful grave plans at the entrances). Ladislav Šaloun's tomb for **Antonín Dvořák** (1841–1904), situated under the arches, is one of the more ostentatious ones, with a mosaic inscription, studded with gold stones, glistening behind wrought-iron railings. **Bedřich Smetana** (1824–84), who died twenty years earlier, is buried in comparatively modest surroundings near the Slavín monument (see p.128). The Pražské jaro festival famously begins with a procession from his grave to the Obecní dům, on the anniversary of his death (May 12).

Other graves that attract (mostly Czech) pilgrims are those of the nineteenth-century writer **Božena Němcová**, in the shadow of the church's east end, and nearby author Jan Neruda from the same era. Playwright **Karel Čapek**, whose final resting place faces

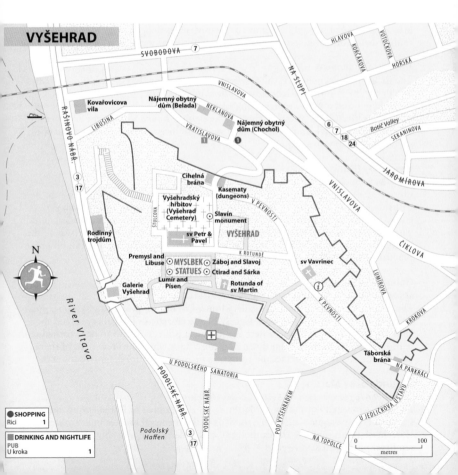

VYŠEHRAD

SHOPPING
Rici 1

DRINKING AND NIGHTLIFE
PUB
U kroka 1

6

VYŠEHRAD CEMETERY AND THE VELVET REVOLUTION

The grave of the Romantic poet **Karel Hynek Mácha** in Vyšehrad Cemetery was the first assembly point for the demonstration on November 17, 1989, which was organized to commemorate the fiftieth anniversary of the Nazi attack on Czech higher education institutions and which triggered the **Velvet Revolution**.

Student protests against the German occupation had reached a peak on October 28, 1939, when violent clashes resulted in the death of medical student Jan Opletal; his funeral, on November 11, was accompanied by more violent disturbances. On November 17, the Nazis took the initiative, executing various student leaders, packing thousands off to the camps and shutting down all Czech higher education institutes. Fifty years later, in 1989, the cemetery was the gathering point for a 50,000-strong crowd, which attempted to march from here to Wenceslas Square, an event that kicked off the Velvet Revolution.

the arcades coined one of the two Czech words to have entered the English language, "robot" (the other is "pistol"). Several graves of lesser-known individuals stand out artistically, too: in particular, František Bílek's towering statue *Sorrow* on the grave of the writer Václav Beneš Třebízský, which aroused a storm of protest when it was first unveiled; Bohumil Kafka's headstone for Dr Josef Kaizl, with a woman's face peeping out from the grave; and Karel Hladík's modern *Cathedral* sculpture, which sits above his own grave. Surprisingly, the grave of Josef Mocker, Bohemia's great nineteenth-century neo-Gothicizer, hasn't a trace of neo-Gothic styling on it at all.

The Slavín monument

The focus of the cemetery is the **Slavín monument**, a big, bulky stele built in 1893 to a design by Antonín Wiehl, covered in commemorative plaques and topped by a sarcophagus and a statue representing Genius. It's the communal resting place of more than fifty Czech artists, including the painter **Alfons Mucha**, the sculptors Josef Václav Myslbek and Ladislav Šaloun, the architect Josef Gočár and the opera singer **Ema Destinnová**.

Kasematy (dungeons)

Daily: Guided tours hourly 10am–4pm • 60Kč

Once you've seen the Vyšehrad Cemetery and the basilica of sv Petr and Pavel the next best thing to do is to head off and explore the **Kasematy**, or dungeons, which you enter via the **Cihelná brána**. After a short guided tour of a section of the underground passageways beneath the ramparts, you enter a vast storage hall that shelters six of the original baroque statues from Charles Bridge. There's also an interesting exhibition on the history of the fortress and Prague's city defences through the ages.

Galerie Vyšehrad

Daily: April–Oct 9.30am–6pm; Nov, Dec & March 9.30am–5pm • 60Kč • Metro Vyšehrad

The **Galerie Vyšehrad**, a small art gallery housed in one of Vyšehrad's bastions, puts on temporary exhibitions of work usually by Czech artists. The gallery stands above **Libušina lázně** (Libuše's bath) where the mythical princess is said to have bathed with her lovers before hurling them down into the Vltava when she grew tired of them. The oblong structure is in fact the ruins of a fifteenth-century defensive tower.

Rotunda of sv Martin

V pevnosti • Only open for services Mon, Wed & Fri 6pm, Sat 8am • Metro Vyšehrad

The over-renovated **Rotunda of sv Martin** – one of a number of Romanesque rotundas scattered across Prague – is the sole survivor of the medieval fortress built by Vratislav II in the eleventh century. The cannon ball embedded in the wall above the portal is a reminder of the Prussian siege of 1757.

Myslbek statues
Metro Vyšehrad

If the weather's good there are few better places in the Czech capital for a picnic than the patch of grass to the south of the basilica of sv Petr and Pavel, where there are regular outdoor concerts on summer Sundays. Dotted about the grass are the gargantuan **Myslbek statues** that used to adorn the nearby bridge, Palackého most. Four couples are dotted across the green, all taken from Prague legends: *Přemysl and Libuše*, the husband-and-wife team who founded Prague and started Bohemia's first royal dynasty, the Přemyslids; *Lumír and Píseň*, the legendary Czech singer and his muse, Song; *Záboj and Slavoj*, two mythical Czech warriors; and *Ctirad and Šárka* (see box, p.146).

6

Cubist villas
Tram #3, #7 or #17 to Výtoň

The most impressive example of Czech Cubist architecture, brilliantly exploiting its angular location, is Chochol's **nájemný obytný dům**, an apartment block at Neklanova 30, begun in 1913 for František Hodek and now housing a restaurant on its ground floor. Further along Neklanova, at no. 2, there's Antonín Belada's **nájemný obytný dům**, with its Cubist facade, and around the corner is the most ambitious project of the lot – Chochol's **Kovařovicova vila**, which backs onto Libušina. From the front, on Rašínovo nábřeží, you can appreciate the clever, slightly askew layout of the garden, designed right down to its zigzag garden railings. Further along the embankment is Chochol's largest commission, the **Rodinný trojdům**, a large building complex with a heavy mansard roof, a central "Baroque" gable with a pedimental frieze and room

---

CZECH CUBISM IN VYŠEHRAD

Even if you harbour only a passing interest in modern architecture, it's worth seeking out the cluster of **Cubist villas** below the fortress in Vyšehrad. Whereas Czech Art Nouveau was heavily influenced by the Viennese Secession, it was Paris rather than the imperial capital that provided the stimulus for the short-lived but extremely productive Czech Cubist movement. In 1911, the **Skupina výtvarných umělců**, or SVU (**Group of Fine Artists**), was founded in Prague, and quickly became the movement's organizing force. Pavel Janák was the SVU's chief theorist, Josef Gočár its most illustrious exponent, but Josef Chochol was the most successful practitioner of the style in Prague.

Cubism is associated mostly with painting, and the unique contribution of its Czech offshoot was to apply the theory to **furniture** and **architecture**. In Vyšehrad alone, Chochol completed three buildings, close to one another below the fortress, using prismatic shapes and angular lines to produce the sharp geometric contrasts of light and dark shadows characteristic of Cubist painting. Outside the Czech Republic, only the preparatory drawings by the French architect Duchamp-Villon for his (unrealized) Maison Cubiste can be considered remotely similar.

The SVU's plans were cut short by World War I, after which Janák and Gočár attempted to establish a specifically Czechoslovak style of architecture incorporating prewar Cubism. The style was dubbed Rondo-Cubism since the prismatic moulding had been replaced by semicircular motifs, but only a few projects got off the ground before Czech architects turned to the functionalist ideals of the international Modernist movement.

CUBIST AND RONDO-CUBIST BUILDINGS OUTSIDE VYŠEHRAD

Prague's unique Cubist and Rondo-Cubist buildings are scattered across the city. Here are five of the best outside Vyšehrad:

Diamant (Králíček) Nové Město. Map p.102
Dům U černé Matky boží (Gočár) Staré Město. See p.84
Janák's Banka legií (Janák) Nové Město. See p.111
Lamppost (Blecha and Králíček) Nové Město. See p.114
Palác Adria (Janák and Zasche) Nové Město. See p.114

enough for three families. Sadly for tourists, all of these properties are private residences and cannot be visited by the public.

ARRIVAL AND INFORMATION VYŠEHRAD

Arrival There are several approaches to the fortress: if you've come by one of the trams (#3, #7, #17) that trundle along the embankment to the Výtoň stop, you can either wind your way up Vratislavova and enter through the Cihelná brána, or take the steep stairway from Rašínovo nábřeží that leads up through the trees to a small side entrance in the west wall. Alternatively, from Vyšehrad metro station, walk west past the ugly Kongresové centrum Praha, and enter through the Táborská brána and Leopoldova brána.

Information centres Between the Táborská brána and Leopoldova brána (daily: April–Oct 9.30am–6pm; Nov–March 9.30am–5pm; ☎ 261 225 304, ⓦ praha-vysehrad.cz) and at the Cihelná brána (same hours; ☎ 242 451 197).

Eating and drinking Vyšehrad is perfect for a picnic, though *Café Citadella* in the southwestern corner of the ramparts is convenient for food and drink, as are the pubs in the streets below the fortress.

Vinohrady

Southeast of Nové Město is the predominantly late nineteenth-century district of **VINOHRADY**, Prague's most resolutely bourgeois suburb, with two spacious parks – **Riegrovy sady**, to the north, and **Havlíčkovy sady**, to the south – and a fabulous array of turn-of-the-twentieth-century apartment buildings, now some of the capital's most expensive flats. In terms of conventional sightseeing, however, the area is definitely low priority, though there are a few places here (and in neighbouring Žižkov) worth a visit, most of them quick and easy to reach by metro.

Náměstí Míru
Metro Náměstí Míru

If Vinohrady has a centre, it's the verdant piazza of **náměstí Míru**, a good introduction to the aspirations of this confident, bourgeois neighbourhood. At its centre stands the brick-built basilica of **sv Ludmila**, designed by Josef Mocker in the late 1880s in a severe neo-Gothic style, though the interior furnishings have the odd flourish of Art Nouveau. In front of the church is a statue commemorating the **Čapek brothers**, writer Karel and painter Josef, both local residents, who together symbolized the golden era of the interwar republic. Karel died of pneumonia in 1938, shortly after the Nazi invasion, while Josef perished in Belsen seven years later. Two more buildings on the square deserve attention, the most flamboyant being the **Divadlo na Vinohradech**, built in 1907, using Art Nouveau and neo-Baroque elements in equal measure. More subdued, but equally ornate inside and out, is the district's former **Národní dům**, a grandiose neo-Renaissance edifice from the 1890s housing a ballroom/concert hall and restaurant.

From náměstí Míru, block after block of tenements, each clothed in its own individual garment of sculptural decoration, form a grid plan of grand avenues stretching eastwards to the city's great cemeteries (see p.132). In good weather, you could stroll your way down Mánesova to Plečnik's church. However, distances are large, and you may prefer to take the metro.

Nejsvětějšího Srdce Páně (Most Sacred Heart of Our Lord)
Náměstí Jiřího z Poděbrad • Open for 40min before services: Mon–Sat 8am & 6pm, Sun 9am, 11am & 6pm • ☎ 222 727 713, ⓦ srdcepane.cz • Metro Jiřího z Poděbrad

Halfway between náměstí Míru and the Olšanské cemeteries, **náměstí Jiřího z Poděbrad** is Vinohrady's second square after náměstí Míru. Dominating the centre of the park-like space is Prague's most celebrated modern church, **Nejsvětějšího Srdce Páně**, built in 1928 by Josip Plečnik, the Slovene architect responsible for much of the interior remodelling of the Hrad (see box, p.38). It's a marvellously eclectic and individualistic work, employing a sophisticated potpourri of architectural styles: a Neoclassical pediment and a great slab

of a clock tower with a giant transparent face in imitation of a Gothic rose window, as well as the bricks and mortar of contemporary Constructivism. Plečnik also had a sharp eye for detail; look out for the little gold crosses inset into the brickwork like stars, inside and out, and the celestial orbs of light suspended above the heads of the congregation. If you can track down the priest, it may just be possible to climb the clock tower.

Husův sbor (Hussite Church)

Dykova 1 • Weekly service Sun 9am • ☎ 222 519 677, Ⓦ hs-vinohrady.cz • Tram #10 or #16 to Vinohradská vodárna

The **Husův sbor**, three blocks south of náměstí Jiřího z Poděbrad, along U vodárny, stands on the corner of Dykova. Built in the early 1930s by Pavel Janák, the church's most salient feature is its freestanding hollow tower, which encloses a corkscrew spiral staircase and is topped by a giant copper chalice, symbol of the Hussite faith. A memorial on the wall commemorates the church's pioneering role in the Prague Uprising against the Nazis in May 1945, when it served as a Czech resistance headquarters.

Sv Václav

Náměstí Svatopluka Čecha • ☎ 271 742 523 • Tram #4 or #22 to Čechovo náměstí

The **church of sv Václav**, built in 1930 by Josef Gočár, is an uncompromising functionalist structure that forms the severe centrepiece of a sloping green square. The main feature is the slender, smoothly rendered 80m-high tower topped with a plain cross. Up to the base of the tower leads a distinctive stepped roof, the entire structure gleaming toothpaste white and often lit up after dark.

Žižkov

They share much the same architectural heritage, but **ŽIŽKOV** is Vinohrady's edgier, poorer twin, a traditionally working-class area that was a Communist Party stronghold between the wars, earning it the nickname "Red Žižkov". Nowadays its peeling turn-of-the-twentieth-century tenements are home to a mixture of less-than-wealthy Czechs, Roma and foreigners. It was until recently something of a nightlife hotspot but this aspect of the neighbourhood has gone a bit grotty in recent years. This leaves the main reason for venturing onto Žižkov's less than pristine streets to visit its two landmarks – ancient (**Žižkov Hill**) and modern (the **TV tower**) – and the city's main **cemeteries**, at the eastern end of Vinohradská.

Televizní vysílač (TV tower)

Mahlerovy sady 1 • Daily 9am–midnight • 230Kč • ☎ 210 320 081, Ⓦ towerpark.cz • Metro Jiřího z Poděbrad

At 216m in height, the **Televizní vysílač**, or TV tower, is the tallest building in Prague. Close up, it's an intimidating piece of futuristic architecture, made all the more disturbing by the addition of several statues of giant babies crawling up the sides, courtesy of artist David Černý. Begun in the 1970s in a desperate bid to jam West German television transmissions, the tower became fully operational only in the 1990s. In the course of its construction, however, the Communists saw fit to demolish part of a nearby Jewish cemetery that had served the community between 1787 and 1891; a small section survives to the northwest of the tower. From the fifth-floor café or the viewing platform on the eighth floor, you can enjoy a **spectacular view** across Prague and beyond. During refurbishment in 2012, for some unexplained reason the operators decided to create what must be Prague's most bizarre hotel – it has a grand total of one room and is imaginatively named *One Room Hotel*.

Olšanské hřbitovy (Olšany cemeteries)

Vinohradská and Jana Želivského • Daily dawn–dusk • Ⓦ www.hrbitovy.cz • Metro Flora or tram #10, #11, #16 or #26 to Mezi Hřbitovy

If you approach from the west, the first and the largest of Prague's vast cemeteries – each of which is bigger than the entire Jewish quarter – is the **Olšanské hřbitovy**, originally

JAROSLAV SEIFERT OF ŽIŽKOV

The Czech Nobel prize-winning poet **Jaroslav Seifert** (1901–86) was born (look for the bust at Bořivojova 104) and bred in the Žižkov district. He was one of the founding members of the Czechoslovak Communist Party, and in 1920 helped found Devětsil, the most daring and provocative avant-garde movement of the interwar republic. Always accused of harbouring bourgeois sentiments, Seifert and several other Communist writers were expelled from the Party when Gottwald and the Stalinists hijacked the Fifth Congress in 1929. After the 1948 coup, he became *persona non grata*, though he rose to prominence briefly during the 1956 Writers' Union congress when he attempted to lead a rebellion against the Stalinists. He was a signatory of Charter 77, and in 1984, amid much controversy, he became the one and only Czech to win the Nobel Prize for Literature.

6

created for the victims of the 1680 plague epidemic. The perimeter walls are lined with glass cabinets, stacked like shoeboxes, containing funeral urns and mementoes, while the graves themselves are a mixed bag of artistic achievements, reflecting the funereal fashions of the day as much as the character of the deceased. The cemeteries are divided into districts and crisscrossed with cobbled streets; at each gate there's a map, and usually an aged janitor ready to point you in the right direction.

The cemeteries' two most famous incumbents are an ill-fitting couple: **Klement Gottwald**, the country's first Communist president, whose remains were removed from the mausoleum on Žižkov Hill in 1962 after the embalming went wrong; and **Jan Palach**, the philosophy student who set light to himself in January 1969 in protest at the Soviet occupation. More than 750,000 people attended Palach's funeral, and, in an attempt to put a stop to the annual vigils at his graveside, he was reburied in his mother's home town of Všetaty, to the north of Prague. His place was taken by an unknown woman, Maria Jedličková, who for the next seventeen years had her grave covered in flowers instead. Finally, in 1990, Palach's body was returned to the Olšany cemeteries; you'll find it just to the east of the main entrance on Vinohradská.

Vojenský hřbitov (Military Cemetery)

Jana Želivského • Daily dawn–dusk • Metro Želivského

To the east of the Olšany cemeteries, and usually totally deserted, is the **Vojenský hřbitov**; the entrance is 200m along Jana Želivského, on the right. Its centrepiece is the monument to the 436 Soviet soldiers who lost their lives on May 9, 1945, during the liberation of Prague, surrounded by a small, tufty meadow dotted with simple white crosses. Nearby, the graves of Czechs who died fighting for the Habsburgs on the Italian front in World War I are laid out in a semicircle. There are even some Commonwealth war graves here, mostly (though not exclusively) British POWs who died in captivity.

Nový židovský hřbitov (New Jewish Cemetery)

Izraelská 1 • April–Oct Mon–Thurs & Sun 9am–5pm, Fri 9am–2pm; Nov–March Mon–Thurs & Sun 9am–4pm, Fri 9am–2pm • 50Kč • ☏ 226 235 248 • Metro Želivského

Immediately south of the Military Cemetery is the **Nový židovský hřbitov**, founded in the 1890s, when the one by the Žižkov TV tower (see opposite) became overcrowded; it was designed to last for a century, with room for 100,000 graves. It's a melancholy spot, particularly so in the eastern section, where large empty allotments wait in vain to be filled by the generation that perished in the Holocaust. In fact, the community is now so small that it's unlikely the graveyard will ever be full. Most people come here to visit **Franz Kafka**'s grave, 400m east along the south wall and signposted from the entrance. He is buried, along with his mother and father (both of whom outlived him), beneath a plain headstone; the plaque below commemorates his three sisters who died in the camps.

Žižkov Hill

Walk or take bus #133, #175 or #207 from Florenc metro station to U Památníku

Žižkov hill (also known as Vítkov hill) is the thin green wedge of land that separates Žižkov from Karlín, the grid-plan industrial district to the north. From its westernmost point, which juts out almost to the edge of Nové Město, is the definitive panoramic view over the city centre. It was here, on July 14, 1420, that the Hussites enjoyed their first and finest victory, the **Battle of Vítkov**, under the inspired leadership of the one-eyed general Jan Žižka (hence the name of the district). Ludicrously outnumbered by more than ten to one, Žižka and his fanatically motivated troops thoroughly trounced Emperor Sigismund and his papal forces.

Armádní muzeum (Army Museum)

U Památníku 2 • Tues–Sun 10am–6pm • Free • ⓦ vhu.cz • Walk or take bus #133, #175 or #207 from Florenc metro station to U Památníku

On the right as you climb Žižkov Hill stands the **Armádní muzeum**, guarded by a handful of tanks, howitzers and armoured vehicles. Czech military victories may be few and far between, but the country has a long history of manufacturing top-class weaponry for world powers (Semtex is probably their most infamous export). The museum covers the period from 1914 to 1945, with a balanced account of both world wars, including the fate of the Czechoslovak Legion, the Heydrich assassination (see box, p.119) and the 1945 Prague Uprising.

Národní památník (National Monument)

U Památníku 1900 • April–Oct Wed–Sun; Nov–March Thurs–Sun 10am–6pm • 120Kč • ⓦ nm.cz • Walk or take bus #133, #175 or #207 from Florenc metro station to U Památníku

The chief reason for ascending Žižkov Hill is to visit the giant concrete **Národní památník**, which houses a fascinating museum on the history of Czechoslovakia from its foundation in 1918 to its disintegration in 1992. Despite its overblown totalitarian aesthetics, inside and out, the monument was actually begun in the late 1920s as a memorial to the Czechoslovak Legion who fought against the Habsburgs – the gargantuan equestrian statue of the mace-wielding Žižka, which fronts the monument, is reputedly the largest in the world. The building eventually became a Communist mausoleum: presidents Gottwald, Zápotocký and Svoboda were all buried here, along with the obligatory Unknown Soldier and various other Party hacks. Gottwald himself was originally pickled and embalmed (à la Lenin), but a fire damaged his corpse so badly that the leader had to be cremated in 1962. In 1990, the remaining bodies were cremated and quietly reinterred in the Olšany cemeteries.

From the south side of the monument, you enter the central hall, which has engaging displays on the great political turning points in **Czech twentieth-century history**: the 1938 Munich Agreement, the 1948 Communist coup, the 1968 Prague Spring and the 1989 Velvet Revolution. Along the sides are cabinets filled with historical artefacts from the Sudetenland, the Sokol, Scout and Communist Pioneer movements, as well as the hiking subculture known as *tramping*. The Kolumbárium where the Communist leaders were once interred now commemorates famous (non-Communist) Czechs of the last century. There's plenty of social realist decor for fans of Communist kitsch – the best stuff is in the marble apsidal Síň osvobození (Liberation Hall), where the **Tomb of the Unknown Soviet Soldier** resides, surrounded by mosaic depictions of heroic World War II combatants. In the basement, you can inspect the state-of-the-art 1950s technology that failed to preserve Gottwald's remains and the remnants of his sarcophagus.

Holešovice and the western suburbs

Prague doesn't begin and end with Charles Bridge, and beyond the Baroque palaces of the Vltava's left bank lie the city's northern and western suburbs, an area most tourists neglect. Spread over a much larger area than those east of the Vltava, the suburbs on this side of the river offer much greater variety; gritty Holešovice and parts of Smíchov date from the late nineteenth century, whereas Dejvice and Střešovice were laid out between the wars as well-to-do garden suburbs. The left bank also boasts a great deal more greenery, including the city's largest public park, Stromovka. In the far west lies Bílá hora, scene of the Czechs' most decisive defeat in battle, the effects of which still reverberate to this day.

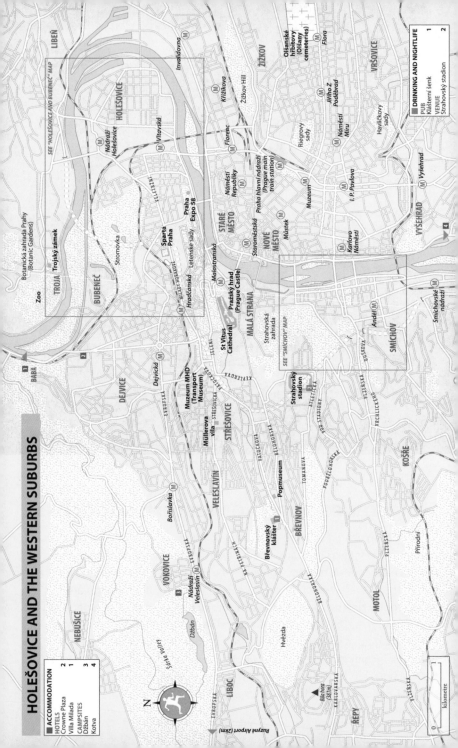

HOLEŠOVICE AND THE WESTERN SUBURBS

SEE "HOLEŠOVICE AND BUBENEČ" MAP

SEE "SMÍCHOV" MAP

Ruzyně Airport (2km)

N

0   1
kilometre

Regions / districts

LIBEŇ
HOLEŠOVICE
ŽIŽKOV
VRŠOVICE
TROJA
BUBENEČ
STARÉ MĚSTO
NOVÉ MĚSTO
MALÁ STRANA
VYŠEHRAD
SMÍCHOV
DEJVICE
STŘEŠOVICE
VELESLAVÍN
VOKOVICE
NEBUŠICE
LIBOC
BŘEVNOV
KOŠÍŘE
MOTOL
ŘEPY

Labelled features

Botanická zahrada Prahy (Botanic Gardens)
Zoo
Trojský zámek
Stromovka
Sparta Praha
Praha Expo 58
Nádraží Holešovice
Vltavská
Invalidovna
Křižíkova
Žižkov Hill
Florenc
Náměstí Republiky
Praha hlavní nádraží (Prague main train station)
Staroměstská
Staroměstská
Můstek
Muzeum
Náměstí Míru
Jiřího z Poděbrad
Flora
Olšanské hřbitovy (Olšany cemeteries)
Havlíčkovy sady
Riegrovy sady
I. P. Pavlova
Karlovo Náměstí
Vyšehrad
Letenské sady
Molostranská
Hradčanská
Pražský hrad (Prague Castle)
St Vitus Cathedral
Strahovská zahrada
Anděl
Smíchovské nádraží
Muzeum MHD (Transport Museum)
Müllerova vila
Popmuseum
Strahovský stadion
Bořislavka
Dejvická
Nádraží Veleslavín
Břevnovský klášter
Bílá hora (381m)
Přírodní
Šárka Valley
Džbán
Hvězda
BABA

Streets

MILADY HORÁKOVÉ
VELETRŽNÍ
EVROPSKÁ
STŘEŠOVICKÁ
PATOČKOVÁ
BĚLOHORSKÁ
NA PETŘINÁCH
KARLOVARSKÁ
PLZEŇSKÁ
VRCHLICKÉHO
POD STADIONY
DROBNÝHO
KEPLEROVA
STROSSMAYEROVÁ
TOMANOVA
ATLETICKÁ
POD STADIONY
PLZEŇSKÁ

HOLEŠOVICE AND THE WESTERN SUBURBS HIGHLIGHTS

National Technical Museum View Czechoslovakia's fleet of yesteryear at this superb museum. See p.137
Trade Fair Palace Prague's best art gallery focusing on nineteenth- and twentieth-century works. See p.139
Hanavský pavilón Art Nouveau pavilion restaurant with city views. See p.185
Prague Zoo One of central Europe's best zoos, accessible by boat along the Vltava. See p.144
Meet Factory Artist David Černý's multipurpose venue in Smíchov. See p.195
Railway Kingdom The largest model railway in the Czech Republic and one of the capital's most popular attractions. See p.150

There are several specific sights in each suburb that can lend structure to your wandering. The most significant attraction is the **Veletržní palác** in **Holešovice**, which houses the country's finest modern art collection. Other sights – for instance the functionalist villas in **Dejvice** and **Střešovice** – are of more specialized interest; some, such as the exquisite Renaissance chateau of **Hvězda**, deserve to be better known, and some areas, like **Smíchov**, give an interesting slice of downtown Prague that most tourists fail to see.

Holešovice and Bubeneč

The late nineteenth- and early twentieth-century districts of **HOLEŠOVICE** and **BUBENEČ**, tucked into a huge U-bend in the Vltava, have little in the way of truly magnificent architecture, but they do have some grandiose apartment blocks and a huge swathe of former factories that are slowly being converted for use as nightclubs, galleries and flats. The neighbourhoods also boast two huge areas of relaxing greenery: to the south, **Letná**, overlooking the city centre, and to the north, **Stromovka**, bordering the Výstaviště trade fair grounds. Holešovice is also home to the **Veletržní palác**, Prague's must-see modern art museum.

Letná
Tram #1, #8, #12, #15, #25 or #26 to Sparta

Hovering above the city, the flat green expanse of the high **Letná** plain has long been the traditional assembly point for invading and besieging armies. It was laid out as a public park in the mid-nineteenth century and used under the Communists as the site of their **May Day parades**. For these, thousands of citizens were dragooned into marching past the south side of the city's main football ground, the Sparta stadium, where the old Communist cronies would take the salute from a giant red podium. In November 1989, the largest demo of the Velvet Revolution took place here, with nearly a million people gathering to support the general strike. In 1990 the road by the football stadium was renamed after Milada Horáková, the Socialist politician executed in a Communist show trial in 1950.

Národní technické muzeum (National Technical Museum)
Kostelní 42 • Mon–Fri 9am–5.30pm, Sat & Sun 10am–6pm • 190Kč • ☎ 220 399 111, ⓦntm.cz • Tram #1, #8, #12, #15, #25 or #26 to Strossmayerovo náměstí

Occupying a seminal functionalist 1930s building on Kostelní, the **Národní technické muzeum** is, despite its rather dull title, a surprisingly engaging place to while away an afternoon. Reopened in 2011 after a complete overhaul, the showpiece hangar-like main hall contains an impressive gallery of motorbikes, Czech and foreign, and a wonderful collection of old planes, trains and automobiles from Czechoslovakia's industrial heyday between the wars when the country's Škoda cars and Tatra soft-top stretch limos were desirable baubles. The oldest car in the collection is Laurin &

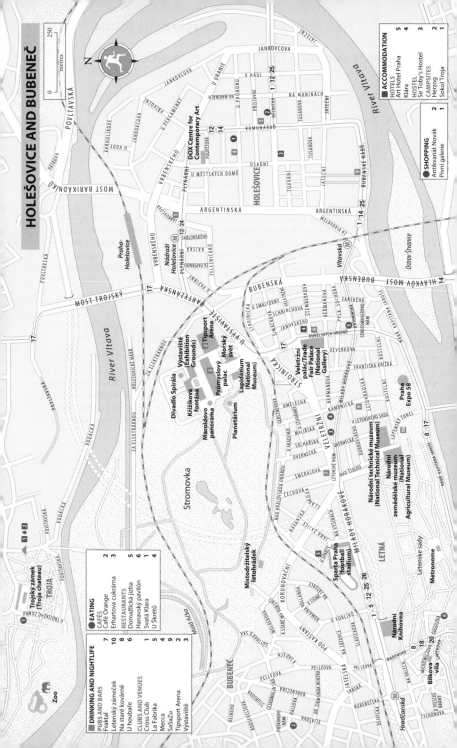

HOLEŠOVICE AND BUBENEČ

N

0 | 250
metres

JANKOVCOVA

DOX Centre for Contemporary Art

HOLEŠOVICE

ARGENTINSKÁ

Praha-Holešovice

Nádraží Holešovice Ⓜ

MOST TROJSKÝ

River Vltava

River Vltava

Stromovka

BUBENSKÁ

HLÁVKŮV MOST

Vltavská Ⓜ

Ostrov Štvanice

Výstaviště (Exhibition Grounds)

Divadlo Spirála

Křížíkova fontána

Maroldovo panorama

Planetárium

Průmyslový palác

Mořský svět

2 Tipsport Arena

Lapidárium (National Museum)

Veletržní palác/Trade Fair Palace (National Gallery)

Praha Expo 58

Národní technické muzeum (National Technical Museum)

Národní zemědělské muzeum (National Agricultural Museum)

Místodržitelský letohrádek

Sparta Praha (football stadium)

LETNÁ

Metronome

Letenské sady

BUBENEČ

Národní knihovna

Bílkova vila

Hradčanská Ⓜ

Zoo

Trojský zámek (Troja chateau)

TROJA

DRINKING AND NIGHTLIFE

PUBS AND BARS
Fraktal	7
Letenský zámeček	10
Na staré kovárně	8
U houbaře	6

CLUBS AND VENUES
Cross Club	1
La Fabrika	5
Mecca	4
SaSaZu	9
Tipsport Arena	2
Výstaviště	3

● EATING

CAFÉS
Café Orange	2
Erhartova cukrárna	3

RESTAURANTS
Domažlická jizba	5
Hanavský pavilón	6
Svatá Klára	1
U Skřetů	4

■ ACCOMMODATION

HOTELS
Art Hotel Praha	5
Klára	4

HOSTEL
Sir Toby's Hostel	3

CAMPSITES
Herzog	2
Sokol Troja	1

● SHOPPING
Antikvariát Novák	2
Pivní galerie	1

LETNÁ'S STALIN MONUMENT

Letná's – indeed Prague's – most infamous monument is one that no longer exists. The **Stalin monument**, the largest in the world, was once visible from almost every part of the city: a 30m-high granite sculpture portraying a procession of Czechs and Russians being led to Communism by the Pied Piper figure of Stalin, but popularly dubbed *tlačenice* (the crush) because of its resemblance to a Communist-era bread queue. Designed by Jiří Štursa and Otakar Švec, it took around six hundred workers five hundred days to erect the 14,200-ton monster. Švec committed suicide shortly before it was unveiled, as his wife had done three years previously, leaving all his money to a school for blind children, since they at least would not have to see his creation. It was eventually revealed to the cheering masses on May 1, 1955, but within a year, Khrushchev had denounced his predecessor. After pressure from Moscow, the monument was blown to smithereens by a series of explosions spread over a fortnight in 1962. All that remains above ground is the statue's vast concrete platform and steps, on the southern edge of the Letná plain, since 1991 graced with a symbolic giant red **metronome**, actually a piece of (now rather tatty) sculpture by Vratislav Novák called *Stroj času* (*Time Machine*); it's a great viewpoint, with the central stretch of the Vltava glistening in the afternoon sun.

7

Klement's 1898 Präsident, more of a motorized carriage than a car; the museum also boasts the oldest Bugatti in the world. Other displays trace the development of early photography and printing, but it's the wheeled wonders most come to see.

Národní zemědělské muzeum (National Agricultural Museum)

Kostelní 44 • Tues–Sun 9am–5pm • 110Kč • ☎ 220 308 200, ⍟ nzm.cz • Tram #1, #8, #12, #15, #25 or #26 to Strossmayerovo náměstí

Occupying a 1930s building, almost identical to that of the National Technical Museum next door, the seldom-visited **Národní zemědělské muzeum** contains probably one of the finest displays of tractors that you're ever likely to see. Among the domestic workhorses by Škoda and Zetor, there's a Lanz Bulldog, one of the most popular interwar German tractors, with its distinctive, easy-to-maintain hot bulb engine, and a very fetching American MrCormick-Deering tractor in lilac and red livery. Several upstairs galleries are given over to temporary exhibitions throughout the year, and outside there's a small city farm with hens, very large rabbits and a couple of Wallachian sheep. The museum often hosts folksy summer events involving national costume and hearty countryside food.

Veletržní palác (Trade Fair Palace) – Nineteenth- and twentieth-century art

Dukelských hrdinů 47 • Tues–Sun 10am–6pm • 250Kč including audio-guide in English • ☎ 224 301 122, ⍟ ngprague.cz • Tram #1, #6, #12, #14, or #17 to Veletržní palác

Situated at the corner of Dukelských hrdinů and Veletržní, some distance from the nearest metro station, **Veletržní palác** gets nothing like the number of visitors it should. Not only does the building house the National Gallery's excellent **nineteenth- and twentieth-century art** collection, but it's also a sight in itself. A seven-storey building constructed in 1928 by Oldřich Tyl and Josef Fuchs, it is Prague's ultimate functionalist masterpiece, not so much from the outside, but certainly inside, where its gleaming white vastness is suitably awesome. Even the normally hypercritical Le Corbusier, who visited the building the year it was completed, was impressed: "Seeing the Trade Fair Palace, I realized how to make large buildings, having so far built only several relatively small houses on a low budget."

The main exhibition hall is once more used for trade fairs, with the Národní galerie confined to the north wing. Nevertheless, the gallery is both big and bewildering, stretching over six floors, and virtually impossible to view in its entirety; the most popular section is the **French art** collection on the third floor. From the ground floor you can stare up at the glass-roofed atrium, a glorious space for wacky modern pieces of art, overlooked by six floors of balconies.

First floor: foreign art

As good a place as any to start is the bluntly entitled **Foreign Art** exhibition that occupies the first floor. There are one or two gems here, beginning with **Gustav Klimt**'s mischievous *Virgins*, a mass of naked bodies and tangled limbs painted over in psychedelic colours, plus one of the square landscapes he enjoyed painting during his summer holidays in the Salzkammergut.

Egon Schiele's mother came from the South Bohemian town of Český Krumlov, the subject of a tiny, gloomy, autumnal canvas, *Dead Town*. The gallery also owns one of Schiele's most popular female portraits, misleadingly entitled *The Artist's Wife*, an unusually graceful and gentle watercolour of a seated woman in green top and black leggings. In contrast, *Pregnant Woman and Death* is a morbidly bleak painting, in which Schiele depicts himself as both the monk of death and the life-giving mother.

Look out, too, for two canvases by **Edvard Munch**, and for **Oskar Kokoschka**'s typically vigorous landscapes, dating from his brief stay in Prague in the 1930s.

7

Second floor: Czech art 1930–2000

On the second floor, the section covering **Czech art 1930–2000** gives a pretty good introduction to the country's artistic peaks and troughs. First off, there's a wild kinetic-light sculpture by **Zdeněk Pešánek**, a world pioneer in the use of neon in art, who created a stir at the 1937 Paris Expo with a neon fountain. Devětsil, the most important avant-garde art movement in the interwar republic, is represented by **Toyen** (Marie Čermínová) and her lifelong companion **Jindřich Štyrský**, and by abstract photographic works. Avant-garde photography featured strongly in Devětsil's portfolio, and there are several fine abstract works on display, as well as some beautiful "colour tests" and graphics by Vojtěch Preissig, and a few short experimental films from the 1930s.

Fans of Communist kitsch should make their way to the small **socialist realism** section, with works such as the wildly optimistic *We Produce More, We Live Better* and Eduard Stavinoha's cartoon-like *Listening to the Speech of Klement Gottwald, Feb 21, 1948*. There's a great model and drawing of a Tatra 603, the limo of choice for Party apparatchiks in the 1950s. Note, too, the model of Otakar Švec's now demolished Stalin statue, which once dominated central Prague (see box, p.139). Nearby is the allegorical *Large Meal* by Mikuláš Medek, who was banned from exhibiting his works under the Communists. Opposite, there's a section on the **1958 Brussels Expo**, in which Czechoslovakia won several awards.

In the 1960s, **performance art** (*umění akce*) was big in Czechoslovakia, and it, too, has its own section. Inevitably, it's difficult to recapture the original impact of some of the "happenings" – the photographs of Milan Knížak asking passers-by to crow lack the immediacy of the moment. Other photos, such as those of Zorka Ságlová's *Laying out Nappies near Sudoměř*, give you a fair idea of what you missed, and Vladimír Boudník's theory of "explosionalism" would appeal to many small kids.

The gallery owns several works by **Jiří Kolář** – almost pronounced "collage" – who, coincidentally, specializes in collages of random words and reproductions of other people's paintings. The rest of the contemporary Czech art collection is interesting enough, if taken at a canter. **Ivan Kafka**'s phallic installation *Potent Impotency* should raise a smile, and there's the occasional overtly political work such as *Great Dialogue* by Karel Nepraš, in which two red figures lambast each other at close quarters with loudspeakers. It's also worth venturing out onto the balcony, where you'll find, among other things, models of a few of the great landmarks of Czechoslovak Communist architecture and examples from the 1990s, a set design by the innovative **Divadlo Drak** (a puppet company from Hradec Králové) from 1976 and some of **Josef Koudelka**'s famous photographs from the 1968 invasion.

Third floor: nineteenth- and twentieth-century French art

On the third floor is the ever-popular **French art** collection, which features anyone of note who hovered around Paris in the fifty years from 1880 onwards. The collection kicks off with several works by **Auguste Rodin**, particularly appropriate given the ecstatic reception that greeted the Prague exhibition of his work in 1902. Rodin's sculptures are surrounded by works from the advance guard of Impressionism: Courbet, Delacroix, Corot, Sisley and early Monet and Pissarro. There's the characteristically sunny *Provençal Green Wheat* by **Vincent van Gogh**, and *Moulin Rouge* by Toulouse Lautrec with Oscar Wilde looking on. Nearby, the loose brushwork and cool turquoise and emerald hues of **Auguste Renoir**'s *Lovers* are typical of the period of so-called High Impressionism. *Bonjour Monsieur Gauguin* is a tongue-in-cheek tribute to Courbet's painting of a similar name, with **Paul Gauguin** donning a suitably Bohemian beret and overcoat. Also on display is the only known self-portrait by **Henri Rousseau**, at once both confident and comical, the artist depicting himself, palette in hand, against a boat decked with bunting and the recently erected Eiffel Tower.

There's also a surprisingly good collection of works by **Pablo Picasso**, including several paintings and sculptures from his transitional period (1907–08), and lots of examples from the height of his Cubist period in the 1910s; his *Landscape with Bridge* from 1909 uses precisely the kind of prisms and geometric blocks of shading that influenced the Czech Cubist architects. In addition, there are a couple of late paintings by **Paul Cézanne**, a classic *pointilliste* canvas by Georges Seurat and Cubist works by Braque. *Joaquine*, painted by **Henri Matisse** in 1910–11, is a first-rate portrait, in which both Fauvist and Oriental influences are evident. Look out too for **Marc Chagall**'s *The Circus*, a typically mad work from 1927, and a rare painting by **Le Corbusier** himself, which clearly shows the influence of Fernand Léger, one of whose works hangs close by.

7

Third and fourth floors: Czech art 1890–1930

Visitors to the **Czech art 1890–1930** collection are confronted by Otakar Švec's life-sized *Motorcyclist*, a 3D depiction of the optimistic speed of the modern age. Out on the third-floor balcony, there's a feast of architectural drawings, scenography and industrial design from typewriters and vacuum cleaners to wooden aeroplane propellers. Highlights include Josef Čapek's costume and set designs for Janáček's operas, and a model of the Müllerova vila (see p.146).

On the fourth floor are several wood sculptures by **František Bílek**, one of the country's finest sculptors – for a more comprehensive insight into his anguished art, you should visit the Bílkova vila (see p.46). **Jan Preisler**'s mosaics and murals, which feature on Art

---

AN EPIC SLAV TALE

Over the past few years by far the most talked about exhibit at the Veletržní palác is Mucha's **Slav Epic** (*Slovanská epopej*), a series of twenty oversized canvasses painted between 1912 and 1928 following the return of Mucha, who had become the most famous artist of the Art Nouveau period in Paris, to his homeland. The complete set, dramatically depicting monumental events in the tempestuous history of Slavdom with a heavy Czech bias, was first exhibited to the public at the spanking new Veletržní palác in 1928, Mucha having donated the works to the Czech state on the condition that a suitable venue was constructed to house them. Not possessing such a building, the National Gallery found a "temporary" home for the huge paintings in a disused chateau in the sleepy Moravian town of Moravský Krumlov, their unlikely residence throughout the Communist period.

In the early 2000s the city of Prague decided *Slav Epic* belonged in the capital and launched a legal battle to have the canvasses transferred. The authorities argued that more people would see the paintings in Prague than might be prepared to make a special trip to an obscure town in the countryside. Against the move was the Mucha Foundation, run by Mucha's grandson John, who claimed there was no suitable permanent venue for them there. Demonstrations took place in Moravský Krumlov where locals were obviously reluctant to lose their main tourist attraction, but in the end Prague got its way, and the cycle now hangs in the Veletržní palác as a "temporary exhibition". Whether it will be there when you visit is questionable as in the coming years the works are set to be displayed in Asia, a move much protested by the Mucha family. Where the cycle will go from there is anyone's guess.

Nouveau buildings all over Prague, tend to be ethereal and slightly detached, whereas his oil paintings, like the *Black Lake* cycle displayed here, are more typically melancholic. The most successful Czech exponent of moody post-Impressionism was **Antonín Slavíček**, whose depictions of Prague remain perennially popular, as do his landscapes, ranging from the Klimt-like *Birch Mood* to paintings such as *In the Rain*, which are full of foreboding. There are a couple of oils by **Alfons Mucha**, both classic long, narrow poster designs; one is an unfinished version of the *Gismonda* poster for Sarah Bernhardt, which propelled the artist to fame in Paris in 1894.

The fourth-floor collection ends in a foyer area, known rather wonderfully (on each floor) as the Respirium, where sculptures by **Stanislav Sucharda** and **Jan Štursa**, two of the most important Czech Art Nouveau artists, dominate. On the balcony, you can see models and drawings by *fin de siècle* architects such as **Jan Kotěra**, Balšánek, Polívka and Oldřich.

The third floor has a series of works by **František Kupka**, who was Czech by birth, but lived and worked in Paris from 1895 and was one of the first artists in the Western world to exhibit abstract paintings. His seminal *Fugue in Two Colours (Amorpha)*, one of two works he exhibited at the Salon d'Automne in 1912, is displayed here, along with some earlier, pre-abstract paintings (a couple of self-portraits, a family portrait, a≈Matisse-like portrait of a Parisian cabaret actress and *Piano Keys – Lake*, a strange, abstracted, though by no means abstract, work from 1909) plus a pretty comprehensive selection of his later abstract and cosmic works. As you leave the Kupka section, don't miss the small side-room displaying the photography of **František Drtikol**, whose Art Deco nudes made him internationally famous.

The Edvard Munch retrospective exhibited in Prague in 1905 prompted the formation in 1907 of the first Czech modern art movement, **Osma** (The Eight), one of whose leading members was **Emil Filla**, whose *Ace of Hearts* and *Reader of Dostoyevsky* – in which the subject appears to have fallen asleep, though, in fact, he's mind-blown – are both firmly within the Expressionist genre. However, it wasn't long before several of the Osma group were beginning to experiment with Cubism. Filla eventually adopted the style wholesale, helping found the Cubist SVU in 1911. **Bohumil Kubišta**, a member of Osma, refused to follow suit, instead pursuing his own unique blend of Cubo-Expressionism, typified by the wonderful self-portrait *The Smoker*, and by the distinctly Fauvist *Players*.

To round out the Czech Cubist picture, there's furniture and ceramics (and even a Cubist chandelier) by Gočár, Janák and Chochol, as well as sculptures by **Otto Gutfreund**, a member of SVU, whose works range from the Cubo-Expressionist *Anxiety* (1911–12) to the more purely Cubist *Bust* (1913–14). Further on in the gallery there are examples of Gutfreund's later super-realist, technicolour sculptures from the 1920s.

Josef Čapek, brother of the playwright, is another Czech clearly influenced by Cubism, as seen in works such as *Accordion Player*, but, like Kubišta, Čapek found Filla's doctrinaire approach difficult to take, and he left SVU in 1912. Another artist who stands apart from the crowd is **Jan Zrzavy**, who joined SVU, but during a long career pursued his own peculiarly individual style typified by paintings such as his 1909 self-portrait, in which he appears Chinese, and *Valley of Sorrow*, his personal favourite, painted while still a student, and depicting a magical, imaginary and very stylized world.

Výstaviště (Exhibition Grounds)

U Výstaviště • Free • ☎ 702 128 232, ⊕ vystavistepraha.eu • Tram #1, #6, #12, #14 or #17 to Výstaviště Holešovice

Five minutes' walk north from the Veletržní palác lies the **Výstaviště**, a motley assortment of buildings, created for the 1891 Prague Exhibition, which have served as the city's main trade fair arena and funfair ever since. From 1948 until the late 1970s, the Communist Party held its rubber-stamp congresses in the flamboyant stained-glass and wrought-iron **Průmyslový palác** at the centre of the complex.

The grounds are at their busiest at the weekend, particularly in the summer when hordes of Prague families descend on the place to down hot dogs, drink beer and listen to traditional brass band music. The entire complex is slated for a major facelift in coming years so don't be disappointed if some of the following highlights are off limits while that happens.

Planetárium
Mon 8.30am–6pm, Tues–Thurs 8.30am–8pm, Sat 10.30am–8pm, Sun 10.30am–6pm • 50–150Kč • Ⓦ planetarium.cz

Located behind the exhibition grounds on the edge of Stromovka Park, Prague's **Planetárium** has static displays and shows films, but doesn't have telescopes – for those you need to go to the Štefánikova hvězdárna (see p.67).

Maroldovo panorama
April–Oct Tues–Fri 1–5pm, Sat & Sun 10am–5pm • 25Kč

The Výstaviště Exhibition Grounds are home to **Maroldovo panorama**, a giant diorama of the 1434 Battle of Lipany that is the largest such artwork ever created in the Czech Lands, measuring a whopping 11m by 95m. Czech artists Luděk Marold and many helpers, one of them a scenery painter from the National Theatre, assembled the battle scene for an exhibition in 1898; since then the painting has fought its own battles with snow, floods and crumbling pavilions.

Křižíkova fontána (Křižík Fountain)
Ⓦ krizikovafontana.cz

7

Devised for the 1891 Exhibition by the Czech inventor František Křižík, **Křižíkova fontána**, Prague's most famous fountain, puts on hourly evening music and light show performances (with live dancers; 236Kč) to packed audiences. For the schedule, check the website.

Lapidárium
May–Nov Wed 10am–4pm, Thurs–Sun noon–6pm • 50Kč • Ⓦ nm.cz

The only high-brow attraction at the Výstaviště Exhibition Grounds is the National Museum's much overlooked **Lapidárium** (immediately on the right as you enter), official depository for sculptures that were under threat either from demolition, the weather or Prague's acidic air.

The first couple of rooms contain a host of salvaged medieval treasures, such as the slender columns decorated with interlacing from the Romanesque basilica that stood on the site of the city's cathedral. Some of the statues, such as the bronze equestrian statue of **St George**, will be familiar if you've visited Prague Castle; others would be more difficult to inspect close up in their original sites (the figures from the towers of the Charles Bridge, for example). There are copies here, too, such as the busts from the triforium of St Vitus Cathedral.

One of the most outstanding sights is the remains of the **Krocín fountain**, in room 3, an ornate Renaissance work in red marble, which used to grace the Staroměstské náměstí, but failed to hold water and was eventually dismantled in 1862. The angels smiting devils, now displayed in room 5, are all that could be rescued from the **Marian Column**, which also used to stand on Staroměstské náměstí, after it had been attacked as a symbol of Austrian oppression by Czech nationalists in 1918. A plan to return a copy to the square was recently scrapped. Many of the original statues from **Charles Bridge** are in room 6, as well as those that were fished out of the Vltava after the flood of 1890.

Several pompous imperial monuments that were mothballed when the Habsburgs bailed out in 1918 are on display in room 8. One of the first to be removed was the equestrian bronze of **Francis I**, which used to sit under the neo-Gothic baldachin that still stands on Smetanovo nábřeží. By far the most impressive, however, is the statue of **Marshall Radecký**, scourge of the 1848 revolution, carried aloft on a shield by eight Habsburg soldiers, a monument which used to stand on Malostranské náměstí.

Stromovka
Tram #12 or #24 to Výstaviště Holešovice

To the west of Výstaviště lies the *královská obora*, or royal enclosure, more commonly known as **Stromovka**, originally laid out as hunting grounds for the noble occupants of the Hrad, and – thanks to Count Chotek – now Prague's largest and leafiest public park.

If you're heading north to Troja and the city zoo, a stroll through the park is by far the most pleasant approach. If you want to explore a little more, head west, sticking to the park's southern border, and you'll come to a water tunnel built by the court painter Giuseppe Arcimboldo as part of Rudolf II's ambitious horticultural scheme to carry water from the Vltava to the lakes he created a little to the north.

Further west still is Stromovka's main sight, the **Místodržitelský letohrádek**, one of the earliest neo-Gothic structures in the city, begun way back in 1805. Originally conceived as a royal hunting chateau, it served as the seat of the governor of Bohemia until 1918. To continue on to Troja and the zoo, head north under the railway, over the canal and on to the Císařský ostrov (Emperor's Island) – and from there to the right bank of the Vltava.

Troja

Though still well within the city limits, the suburb of **TROJA**, across the river to the north of Holešovice and Bubeneč, still has a distinctly country feel to it. Its most celebrated sight is Prague's only genuine **chateau**, or **zámek**, perfectly situated against a hilly backdrop of vines. Troja's other attraction is the city's excellent **zoo**.

Trojský zámek (Troja chateau)

U Trojského zámku 1 • April–Oct Tues–Thurs, Sat & Sun 10am–6pm, Fri 1–6pm • 120Kč • ☎ 283 851 614, ⓦ ghmp.cz • To get here, walk from Výstaviště, catch bus #112, which runs frequently from metro Nádraží Holešovice, or take a boat (April & Oct Sat & Sun; May–Sept daily; 190Kč; ⓦ paroplavba.cz) from the PPS landing place on Rašínovo nábřeží (metro Karlovo náměstí)

The **Trojský zámek** was designed by Jean-Baptiste Mathey for the powerful Šternberg family towards the end of the seventeenth century. Despite renovation and a rusty red repaint, its plain early Baroque facade is no match for the action-packed, blackened figures of giants and titans who battle it out on the chateau's monumental balustrades. The highlights of the **interior** are the gushing frescoes depicting the victories of the Habsburg Emperor Leopold I (1657–1705) over the Turks, which cover every centimetre of the walls and ceilings of the grand hall. You also get to wander through the chateau's pristine, trend-setting, French-style formal **gardens**, the first of their kind to be created in Bohemia.

The zoo

U Trojského zámku 3 • Daily: March 9am–5pm; April, May, Sept & Oct 9am–6pm; June–Aug 9am–9pm; Nov–Feb 9am–4pm • 200Kč • ☎ 296 112 230, ⓦ zoopraha.cz • To get here, walk from Výstaviště, catch bus #112, which runs frequently from metro Nádraží Holešovice, or take a boat (April & Oct Sat & Sun only; May–Sept daily; 190Kč; ⓦ paroplavba.cz) from the PPS landing place on Rašínovo nábřeží (metro Karlovo náměstí)

Prague's much-respected **zoo** opened in 1931 on the site of one of Troja's numerous hillside vineyards. Since then its 58 hectares (eighty football fields) have seen a lot of investment, especially in the last two decades, with some very imaginative animal enclosures containing the usual occupants – including elephants, hippos, giraffes, zebras, big cats and bears. A bonus in the summer is the fact you can take a **chairlift** (*lanová dráha*) from the duck pond over the enclosures to the top of the hill, where the prize exhibits – a rare breed of miniature horse known as Przewalski – hang out. Other highlights include the red pandas, the giant tortoises, the Komodo dragons and the bats that actually fly past your face in the Twilight Zone.

Botanická zahrada Prahy (Botanic gardens)

Nádvorní 134 • **Gardens** Daily: March & Oct 9am–5pm; April 9am–6pm; May–Aug 9am–8pm; Sept 9am–7pm, Nov–Feb 9am–4pm • 85Kč • **Fata Morgana** Closed Mon • 150Kč • ☎ 234 148 111, ⓦ www.botanicka.cz • To get here, walk from Výstaviště, catch bus #112, which runs frequently from metro Nádraží Holešovice, or take a boat (April & Oct Sat & Sun; May–Sept daily; 190Kč; ⓦ paroplavba.cz) from the PPS landing place on Rašínovo nábřeží (metro Karlovo náměstí)

Hidden in the woods north of the *zámek* is the **Botanická zahrada Prahy**. The botanic gardens feature a vineyard, a Japanese garden, several glasshouses and great views over Prague. A little higher up the hill there's also a spectacularly curvaceous greenhouse, the **Fata Morgana**, with butterflies flitting about amid the desert and tropical plants. Fata Morgana, incidentally, means "mirage" in Czech and the greenhouse certainly seems like one on a freezing winter day.

The northwest suburbs

Spread across the hills to the northwest of the city centre are the leafy garden suburbs of **Dejvice** and neighbouring **Střešovice**, peppered with fashionable modern villas built in the first half of the twentieth century for the upwardly mobile Prague bourgeoisie and commanding magnificent views across the north of the city. Dejvice is short on conventional sights, but interesting to explore all the same; Střešovice has one compelling attraction, the **Müllerova vila**, a restored functionalist dwelling designed by Adolf Loos. Some 4km further west, the **Šárka valley** is about as far as you can get from an urban environment without leaving the city. To the south of Šárka is the battlefield of **Bílá hora**, and **Hvězda**, a beautiful park containing a pretty star-shaped mini-chateau.

Dejvice

DEJVICE was planned and built in the early 1920s for the First Republic's burgeoning community of civil servants and government and military officials. Its oversized, slightly unappealing main square, **Vitězné náměstí** (metro Dejvická, commonly known among locals as Kulaťák), is unavoidable if you're planning to explore any of the western suburbs, as it's a major public transport interchange. There's nothing much of note in this central part of Dejvice, though you can't help but notice the former **Hotel International** (now the *Crowne Plaza*) at the end of Jugoslávských partyzánů, a Stalinist skyscraper that is disturbingly similar to the universally loathed Palace of Culture in Warsaw. For followers of socialist realist chic, however, its workerist motifs merit closer inspection.

Baba

Bus #131 from metro Hradčanská

Dejvice's most intriguing villas are located to the north of Vitězné náměstí in **Baba**, a model neighbourhood of 33 **functionalist houses**, each individually commissioned and built under the guidance of one-time Cubist and born-again functionalist Pavel Janák. A group of leading architects affiliated to the Czech Workers' Alliance, inspired by a similar project in Stuttgart, initiated what was, at the time, a radical housing project to provide simple, single-family villas. The idea was to use space and open-plan techniques rather than expensive materials to create a luxurious living space.

Despite the plans of the builders, the houses were mostly bought up by Prague's artistic and intellectual community. They have stood the test of time better than most utopian architecture, not least because of the fantastic site – facing south and overlooking the city. Some of them remain exactly as they were when first built, others have been radically altered, but as none of them is open to the public you'll have to be content with surreptitious peeping from the following streets: Na ostrohu, Na Babě, Nad Paťankou and Průhledová. To see the inside of a functionalist – albeit luxury – house, you need to head for the Müllerova vila (see p.146).

Muzeum MHD (Transport Museum)

Patočkova 4 • In theory April to mid-Nov Sat & Sun 9am–5pm, but it's worth calling to check • 50Kč • ☎ 296 128 900, ⓦ dpp.cz • Tram #1, #2 or #25 to Vozovna Střešovice

Created in 1993, Prague's public transport museum, **Muzeum MHD**, is housed in a 1909 tram shed on the border of Střešovice and Hradčany. The oldest exhibit is a horse-drawn tram from 1886, but the majority of the vehicles here are municipal trams from the last century, sporting the cream and red livery introduced in 1908. There are one or two buses and trolleybuses too, and an exhibition covering everything from funiculars to the Soviet-built metro.

Müllerova vila (Müller Haus)

Nad hradním vodojemem 14, Střešovice • Guided tours (seven people only per tour) Tues, Thurs, Sat & Sun: April–Oct 9am, 11am, 1pm, 3pm & 5pm; Nov–March 10am, noon, 2pm & 4pm • 300Kč, plus 150Kč extra for an English guide • ☎ 224 312 012, ⓦ muzeumprahy.cz • Tram #2 from metro Malostranská to the Ořechovka stop

Prague has thousands of interwar villas but the most famous must be the **Müllerova vila**, also known as the Loosova vila, southwest of Dejvice. Designed for the incredibly wealthy Müller family by the Brno-born architect, **Adolf Loos** – regarded by many as one of the founders of modern architecture – and Karel Lhota, and completed in 1930 (after planning permission had been refused ten times), it was one of Loos' few commissions, a typically uncompromising box, finished in blank-smooth concrete rendering, its window frames strangely picked out in yellow. It's really nothing to look at from the outside – Loos believed that "a building should be dumb on the outside and reveal its wealth only on the inside" – but if you've any interest in modernist architecture then a trip out here is an absolute must. To visit, it's a good idea to call ahead as only seven people can join each **guided tour**. You can also book online through the City of Prague Museum website (ⓦ muzeumprahy.cz).

Loos's most famous architectural concept was the **Raumplan**, or open-plan design, at its most apparent in the living room, which is overlooked by the dining room on the mezzanine level and, even higher up, by the boudoir, itself a *Raumplan* in miniature. The house is decorated throughout in the rich materials and minimal furnishings that were Loos's hallmark: green and white Cipolino marble columns, with an inset aquarium in the living room and mahogany panelling for the dining room ceiling. The "American kitchen" was state of the art in the 1930s, as was the use of lino for the floor and walls of the children's room, and there are two lifts in the centre of the house – one for people, one for food. Other highlights include the his 'n' hers dressing rooms off the master bedroom and the Japanese-style summer dining room, which opens out onto the roof terrace overlooking Prague Castle.

Šárka

Tram #20 from metro Bořislavka to the last stop ("Divoká Šárka")

If you've had your fill of tourists, touts and ticket takers, hop aboard a tram and walk north down into **Šárka valley**, a peaceful limestone gorge that twists eastwards back towards Dejvice. The first section (Divoká Šárka) is particularly dramatic, with grey-white crags rising up on both sides – it was here that the mythical Šárka (a common Czech girl's name) plunged to her death (see box below). Gradually the valley opens up, with a grassy meadow to picnic on, and an **open-air swimming pool**

ŠÁRKA AND CTIRAD

The Šárka valley takes its name from the Amazonian **Šárka**, who, according to Czech legend, committed suicide here sometime back in the last millennium. The story begins with the death of Libuše, the founder and first ruler of Prague. The women closest to her, who had enjoyed enormous freedom and privilege in her court, refused to submit to the new patriarchy of her husband, Přemysl. Under the leadership of a woman called Vlasta, they left Vyšehrad and set up their own proto-feminist, separatist colony called Děvín, on the opposite bank of the river.

They scored numerous military victories over the men of Vyšehrad, but never managed to finish off the men's leader, a young warrior called **Ctirad**. In the end they decided to ensnare him and tied one of their own warriors naked to a tree, sure in the knowledge that Ctirad would take her to be a maiden in distress and come to her aid. Šárka offered to act as the decoy, luring Ctirad into the ambush, after which he was tortured and killed. However, in her brief meeting with Ctirad, Šárka fell madly in love with him and, overcome with grief at what she had done, threw herself off the aforementioned cliff. Roused by the cruel death of Ctirad, Přemysl and the lads had a final set-to with Vlasta and co., and butchered the lot of them.

nearby (see p.214), both fairly popular with Czechs on summer weekends. There are various points further east from which you can pick up a city bus back into town, depending on how far you want to walk. The full walk to where the Šárka stream flows into the Vltava, just north of Baba, is about 6–7km all told, though none of it is particularly tough going.

Hvězda

Liboc 25c • Tues–Sun: April–Oct 10am–6pm • 75Kč • ⓦ pamatniknarodnihopisemnictvi.cz • Tram #22 or #25 to Obora Hvězda

A couple of kilometres southwest of Dejvice, the **Hvězda** hunting park is one of Prague's most beautiful and peaceful green spaces. Wide avenues of trees radiate from a bizarre star-shaped building (*hvězda* means "star"), which was designed by Archduke Ferdinand of Tyrol for his wife in 1555. Inside, there's a small exhibition on the Battle of Bílá hora, which took place nearby (see box below). It's the building itself, though – decorated with delicate stuccowork and frescoes – that's the real reason for venturing inside; it makes a perfect setting for the chamber music concerts occasionally staged here.

Bílá hora (White Mountain)

To get to Bílá hora from the city centre, take tram #22 from metro Malostranská to the western terminus ("Bílá hora"), then walk 100m further along the main road before turning right into Řepská, from where a path heads across the field

A short distance southwest of Hvězda is the once entirely barren limestone summit of **Bílá hora** (381m), accessible from Hvězda through one of the many holes in the park's southern perimeter wall. It was here in 1620 that the first battle of the Thirty Years' War took place, sealing the fate of the Czech nation for the following three hundred years. In little more than an hour, the Protestant forces of the "Winter King" Frederick of Palatinate were roundly beaten by the Catholic troops of the Habsburg Emperor Ferdinand II. As a more or less direct consequence, the Czechs lost their aristocracy, their religion, their scholars and, most importantly, the remnants of their sovereignty. There's nothing much to see now, apart from the small monument (*mohyla*), and a pilgrims'

7

THE BATTLE OF BÍLÁ HORA

The **Battle of Bílá hora** (White Mountain) may have been a skirmish of minor importance in the Thirty Years' War, but for the Czechs it was to have devastating consequences. The victory of the Catholic forces of Habsburg Emperor **Ferdinand II** in 1620 set the seal on the Czech Lands for the next three hundred years, prompting an emigration of religious and intellectual figures that relegated the country to a cultural backwater until after WWI. The defeat also heralded the decimation of the Bohemian and Moravian aristocracy, which meant that, unlike their immediate neighbours, the Poles and Hungarians, the Czechs had to build their nineteenth-century national revival around writers and composers, rather than counts and warriors.

The 28,000 Catholic soldiers – made up of Bavarians, Spanish, German and French troops (among them the future philosopher, René Descartes) – outnumbered the 21,000-strong Czech, Hungarian and German Protestant army, though the latter occupied the strategic chalky hill to the west of Prague. Shortly after noon on November 8 the imperial troops (under the nominal command of the Virgin Mary) began by attacking the Protestants' left flank, and, after about an hour, prompted a full-scale flight. The Protestant commander, Christian von Anhalt, hotfooted it back to the Hrad, where he met the Czech king, **Frederick of Palatinate**, who was late for the battle, having been delayed during lunch with the English ambassador.

Frederick, dubbed the "Winter King" for his brief reign, had once tossed silver coins to the crowd, and entertained them by swimming naked in the Vltava, while his wife, Elizabeth, daughter of James I of England, had shocked Prague society with her expensive dresses, her outlandish hairdo and her plunging décolletage. Now, abandoned by their allies, the royal couple gathered up the crown jewels and left Prague in such a hurry they almost forgot their youngest son – later to become the dashing Prince Rupert of the English Civil War – who was playing in the nursery. The city had no choice but to surrender to the Catholics, who spent a week looting the place, before executing 27 of the rebellion's leaders on Staroměstské náměstí.

church, just off Nad višňovkou. This was erected by the Catholics to commemorate the victory, which they ascribed to the timely intercession of the Virgin Mary – hence its name, **Panna Maria Vítězná** (St Mary the Victorious). Another attraction here is watching the planes coming in to land at nearby **Václav Havel Airport** – Bílá hora is right under the flight path and jets swoop in low over the hill on their approach to the runway.

Břevnovský klášter

Markétská 1 • Guided tours Sat & Sun: April–Oct 10am (Sun 11am), 2pm & 4pm; Nov–March 10am (Sun 11am) & 2pm • 80Kč • Ⓦ brevnov.cz • Tram #22 or #25 to Břevnovský klášter

The idyllic Baroque monastery of **Břevnovský klášter** was founded as a Benedictine abbey by Boleslav II and St Adalbert, tenth-century bishop of Prague. The myth goes that they met when walking in the forest at a place where a beam (*břevno* in Czech) served as a footbridge across a stream. It was given the full Baroque treatment in the eighteenth century by both Christoph and Kilian Ignaz Dientzenhofer, and bears their characteristic interconnecting ovals, inside and out. They also built the church of sv Markéta, one of the finest chunks of Baroque finery in the capital.

Popmuseum

Bělohorská 150 • Wed & Thurs 4–8pm, Sat 2–6pm or by arrangement • 100Kč • ☎ 605 369 286, Ⓦ popmuseum.cz • Tram #22 or #25 to U Kaštanu

Close to the Břevnovský klášter, on the opposite side of Patočkova, is the compellingly obscure **Popmuseum**. Here, you can sit down and listen to a whole load of scratchy recordings and bootlegs of Czech bands from the late 1950s and 1960s heyday of Czech underground rock (*bigbít*, as it's known in Czech), when, against the odds, the locals fought for the right to party. There's a vast array of memorabilia on display, from old tickets and promo material to a *Daily Mirror* article on Manfred Mann's 1965 Czech tour, and a home-made amp called Samuel, so famous (in Czechoslovakia) it had a band named after it. You can also try out their ancient Czech electric guitars and instruments.

Smíchov

Historically, **SMÍCHOV** is a late nineteenth-century working-class suburb, whose skyline is peppered here and there with satanic chimneys – hardly any of which now belch smoke. It was once home to the Tatra factory that produced trams for the Communist bloc, and still hosts the city's largest brewery, which produces the ubiquitous **Staropramen**. The centre, however, around **metro Anděl**, has been transformed in the past couple of decades, and is endowed with big new glassy malls. To the west, as the suburb gains height, the tenements give way to another of Prague's sought-after villa quarters. To the north, Smíchov borders Malá Strana and, officially at least, takes in a considerable part of the woods of **Petřín**, south of the Hladová zeď.

Downtown Smíchov, around metro Anděl, is now totally dominated by the glasshouse of French architect Jean Nouvel's shopping complex, **Zlatý Anděl**, which has an angel (*anděl*) from Wim Wenders' film *Wings of Desire* etched into the glass. Hidden away behind Zlatý Anděl, up Plzeňská, is Smíchov's former **synagogue**. Built in 1863 to serve the local wealthy Jewish business folk, it was remodelled in the 1930s in functionalist style, and sports unusual crenellations on the roof – only the Hebrew inscription on the ground floor gives any indication of its former use.

Staropramen Brewery

Pivovarská 9 • Daily 10am–6pm; tours in English 10am, 1pm, 4pm Fri–Wed, plus 5pm Mon & Fri • 199Kč • ☎ 273 132 589, Ⓦ centrumstaropramen.cz • Metro Anděl

Though brews from Pilsen steal much of the limelight these days, Prague's main brewery, **Staropramen**, comes a close second at least as far as mass-produced suds are concerned. The company built its first brewhouse in Smíchov in 1869 and it's these historical premises – not the state-of-the-art, clinical plant next door – that are the subject of the fifty-minute audiovisual tour, guiding you through the brewing process and the history of the brewery, and taking in original and mocked-up period scenes from Staropramen's hop-infused past. The tour ends, as all such tours do, with a fizzy jug of froth in the plant's own bar.

Sv Václav

Náměstí 14 Října • Mon–Fri 7.15am–noon, Sat 7.15–11am, Sun 7.30–11am • ☎ 257 317 652 • Metro Anděl

Smíchov's main place of Christian worship is the neo-Renaissance **church of sv Václav**, built in the early 1880s. The style is unusual for the Czech Lands, especially as it was constructed at a time when Josef Mocker was running amok neo-Gothicizing everything in sight. The gloomy interior is a jewel box of Byzantine-style haloed saints, gilded mosaics, huge Ionic pillars of red Swedish granite and a coffered ceiling. The stained-glass windows in the nave feature strikingly tall, colourful portrayals of the Apostles and there's a wonderfully Turkish-looking gilded pulpit with a tent-like canopy.

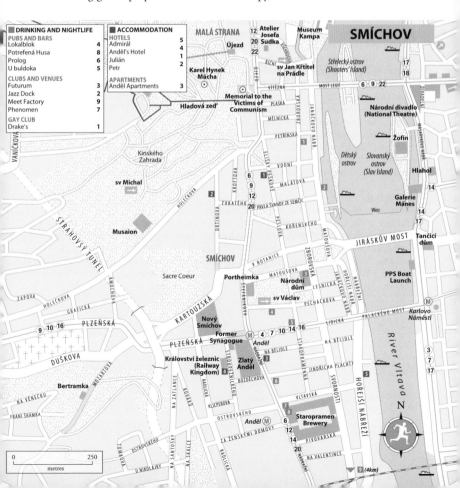

Království Železnic (Railway Kingdom)
Stroupežnického 23 • Daily 9am–7pm • 260Kč • ☎ 257 211 386, ⓦ kralovstvi-zeleznic.cz • Metro Anděl

Since 2009 a group of enthusiasts has been modelling their lives away creating the largest model railway in Eastern Europe, **Království Železnic**. This so-called "Railway Kingdom" is an absolute must for anyone visiting Prague with children and is in fact the capital's most visited museum. When finished, the 1:87 scale model will cover more than 1000 square metres, featuring hundreds of miniature reproductions of junctions, stations, tunnels and well-known sights from across the Czech Republic. At the time of writing the model was almost finished, the remaining spaces taken up by exhibitions of model railway systems produced here and in neighbouring countries. There's lots of railway hardware strewn about the place, kids can let off steam in the playroom and there's an interesting and quite comprehensive exhibition on the history of Czech Railways (sadly in Czech only).

Musaion

7

Letohrádek Kinských, Kinského zahrada 98 • Tues–Sun 10am–6pm • 70Kč • ⓦ nm.cz • Tram #9, #12, #15or #20 to Švandovo divadlo

In the far north of Smíchov, the Kinský family's Neoclassical summer palace, built in 1827, sits on the very southern edge of Petřín hill, and now houses the **Musaion**, the city's beautifully presented and seldom-visited ethnographic museum. For anyone interested in folk costumes and traditions, this is a wonderful destination. The permanent collection, mainly sourced from the Czech Republic's mountainous regions and Moravia, is spread out over eleven rooms on the *piano nobile*, with some of the best costumes in room 4, where the mannequins are decked out in their Sunday best: huge puffed sleeves, ruffs and bows. Some of the most intriguing exhibits are in room 7, which displays fearsome masks and rattles from the pre-Lent Masopust festival, a terrifying Čaramura costume garlanded with eggs and snails, and garlanded *pomlázky*, with which boys lightly whip local girls at Easter. The Christmas section (room 9) is another highlight, with its spectacular *Betlém* (Bethlehem) scene set amid a rocky papier-mâché townscape. Room 11 is given over to a traditional wedding procession, the bride buried in ruffs taking her last journey as a single girl in a small horse-drawn carriage. Moravian folk music is piped gently into all the rooms, heightening the experience, and there are English captions.

Sv Michal
Open only during services • Tram #9, #12, #15 or #20 to Švandovo divadlo

Hidden in the trees uphill from the Musaion is the seventeenth-century shingle-roofed **wooden church of Sv Michal**, which was brought here, log by log, from Carpatho-Ruthenia (now the Ukrainian province of Zakarpattya) in 1929. This is actually the church's third home, the building having been moved from the village of Velke Loucky to Medvedovce in 1793. Timber-built churches are still common in eastern Slovakia, Poland and Ukraine, where they enjoy UNESCO protection.

KARLŠTEJN CASTLE

Day-trips from Prague

Beyond the end of Prague's metro lines rural Bohemia begins, the tourist crowds thin to a trickle and life slows into a timeless rhythm in tune with the seasons. Most of the Czech population dwells in traditional provincial towns, shunning the capital's polluted air and clogged streets for unspoilt tracts of forest, meandering river valleys and fertile plains. Many towns and villages still huddle below the grand residences of their former overlords, their central street layouts little changed since medieval times. These are linked by nineteenth-century railways that take travellers across Bohemia's fairytale landscapes, through the high grass of summer and the heavy snowfalls of the winter months, a world away from Prague's urban sprawl.

> ## DAY-TRIPS FROM PRAGUE HIGHLIGHTS
> **Karlštejn Castle** Built by Emperor Charles IV as a safe box for the imperial crown jewels.
> See p.161
> **Cathedral of St Barbora** One of Bohemia's finest Gothic churches, constructed by local silver miners. See p.159
> **Sedlec Ossuary** The Czech Republic's most ghoulish site, decorated with thousands of human bones. See p.160
> **Konopiště Castle** Erstwhile home to the doomed Archduke Ferdinand whose assassination kicked off WWI. See p.160
> **Terezín** Bohemia's most famous WWII concentration camp. See p.153

To the north of the capital several chateaux grace the banks of the Vltava, including the wine-producing town of **Mělník**, on the Labe (Elbe) plain. Further north is **Terezín**, the wartime Jewish ghetto that is a living testament to the Holocaust. One of the most popular day-trip destinations is to the east of Prague: **Kutná Hora**, a medieval silver-mining town with one of the most beautiful Gothic churches in the country, and a macabre gallery of bones in the suburb of Sedlec.

To the south, the **Konopiště** chateau boasts exceptionally beautiful and expansive grounds. Southwest of Prague, a similar mix of woods and rolling hills cups the popular castle of **Karlštejn**, a gem of Gothic architecture, dramatically situated above the River Berounka. West of Prague, **Lidice**, razed to the ground by the SS, is another location that recalls the horror of Nazi occupation.

8

Mělník

Occupying a spectacular, commanding site at the confluence of the Vltava and Labe rivers, **MĚLNÍK**, 33km north of Prague, lies at the heart of Bohemia's tiny **wine-growing** region. The town's history goes back to the ninth century, when it was handed over to the Přemyslids as part of Ludmila's dowry when she married Prince Bořivoj. From that time until the fifteenth century it became the seat of widowed queens, and it was here that Ludmila introduced her heathen grandson Václav, later to become St Wenceslas

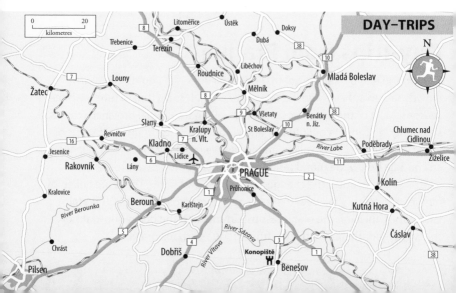

(see box, p.40) to Christianity. Viticulture became the town's economic mainstay when the Emperor Charles IV, aching for a little of the French wine of his youth, introduced grapes from Burgundy (where he was also king). Thanks to its position on the Elbe (Labe in Czech) Mělník's **port** now competes with the vineyards for economic significance.

The zámek

Svatováclavská 19 • Daily: June–Aug 10am–6pm; Sept–May 9.30am–5pm • 130Kč; wine cellars 50Kč • ☎ 315 622 121, ⓦ lobkowicz-melnik.cz

Mělník's greatest monument is its Renaissance chateau, or **zámek**, perched high above the plains and visible for miles around. Apart from during World War II and under the Communists, the building has been owned by the Lobkowicz family since 1753. Visitors get to see the family's magnificently proportioned former living quarters, packed with porcelain, old maps and Old Masters, and affording spectacular views out over the Central Bohemian landscape. The Great Hall is home to several paintings by Škréta, while another highlight is the Baroque altar in the Chapel of St Ludmila. You can also visit the castle **wine cellars**, finishing up with samples of local plonk (extra charge); the **Ludmila white** is Mělník's most popular wine, found on shop shelves across the country in its oddly squat bottles.

Sv Petr and Pavel

Na Vyhlídce 18 • Wed & Thurs 9.30am–12.30pm & 1.15–4pm, Fri & Sat 9.30am–12.30pm & 1.15–5pm, Sun 10.30am–12.30pm & 1.15–5pm • 30Kč • ☎ 315 622 337

Below the *zámek*, vines cling to south-facing terraces as the land plunges down towards the river below. From Mělník's onion-domed **church of sv Petr and Pavel**, next to the chateau, there's an even better view of the rivers' confluence (to the left) and the subsidiary canal (straight ahead), once so congested with vessels that traffic lights had to be introduced to prevent collisions. You can climb the **tower** for an even better view and visit the compellingly macabre **ossuary**, or *kostnice*, filled with the bones of an estimated ten to fifteen thousand medieval plague victims, fashioned into weird and wonderful skeletal shapes in the early nineteenth century.

8

ARRIVAL AND INFORMATION   MĚLNÍK

By train There are very few direct services to Mělník from Prague; take a train from Praha hlavní nádraží and change in Všetaty (8 daily; 1hr).

By bus Regular bus services leave from metro Nádraží Holešovice and metro Ládví (many daily; 35–45min).

Tourist office U Sadů 323 (daily 9am–5pm; ☎ 315 627 503, ⓦ melnik.info).

EATING AND DRINKING

Na Hradbách Náměstí Míru 9 ☎ 315 670 000, ⓦ hradbymelnik.cz. Set under Gothic vaulting on the main square, this popular place serves up meat-heavy mains for around 200Kč. There's a tree-shaded garden. Daily 11am–11pm.

Zámecká restaurace Svatováclavská 19 ☎ 317 070 150. Sample the local wine at source and tuck into hearty Bohemian food at the chateau's light-filled restaurant. The views are as good as the food, but it can get crowded. Daily 11am–8pm.

Terezín

The old road from Prague to Berlin passes through the fortress town of **TEREZÍN** (Theresienstadt), just over 60km northwest of the capital. Purpose-built in the 1780s by the Habsburgs to defend the northern border against Prussia, it was capable of accommodating 14,500 soldiers and hundreds of prisoners. In 1941, the population was ejected and the whole town turned into a **Jewish ghetto**, used as a transit camp for Jews whose final destination was Auschwitz.

Hlavní pevnost (Main Fortress)

Although the **Hlavní pevnost** was put to the test in battle, Terezín remains intact as a garrison town. Today, it's an eerie, soulless place, built to a dour eighteenth-century

EATING
● CAFÉ
Atypik   1

N

▲ Prague

Malá pevnost
(Small Fortress)

National
Cemetery

P

River Ohře

Hlavní pevnost
(Main Fortress)

PRAŽSKÁ

ŽIŽKOVA

MÁCHOVA

Muzeum Ghetta
(Ghetto Museum)

B. NĚMCOVÉ

HAVLÍČKOVA

28. ŘÍNA

KOMENSKÉHO

Church of the
Resurrection
Kostel Vzkříšení
Páně

NÁMĚSTÍ
ČS. ARMÁDY

PALACKÉHO

TYRŠOVA

LEGII

Magdeburská kasárna
(Magdeburg Barracks)

▶ Bohušovice Train Station

0   200
|____|____|
metres

grid plan, its bare streets empty apart from the residual civilian population and visitors making their way between the various museums and memorials. As you enter, the red-brick zigzag fortifications are still an awesome sight, though the huge moat has been given over to allotments.

Muzeum Ghetta (Ghetto Museum)

Máchova 178 • Daily: April–Oct 9am–6pm; Nov–March 9am–5.30pm • 175Kč, combined ticket with other Terezín attractions 215Kč • ☎ 416 782 577, Ⓦ pamatnik-terezin.cz

Tracing the history of the ghetto from its very beginning, the **Muzeum Ghetta**, which opened in a former school in 1991, is the logical place to start your exploration of Terezín. After the war, the Communists followed the consistent Soviet line by deliberately underplaying the Jewish perspective on Terezín. Instead, the emphasis was on the Malá pevnost (see p.156), where the majority of victims were not Jewish, and on the war as an anti-fascist struggle, in which good (Communism and the Soviet Union) had triumphed over evil (fascism and Nazi Germany). The current museum's extremely informative and well-laid-out exhibition attempts to do some justice to the

A BRIEF HISTORY OF THE GHETTO

In October 1941, Reinhard Heydrich and the Nazi high command decided to turn the whole of Terezín into a **Jewish ghetto**. It was an obvious choice: fully fortified, close to the main Prague–Dresden railway line, and with an SS prison already established in the Malá pevnost (Small Fortress) nearby. The original inhabitants of the town – fewer than 3500 people – were moved out, and transports began arriving at Terezín from many parts of central Europe. Within a year, nearly 60,000 Jews were interned here in appallingly overcrowded conditions; the monthly death rate rose to 4000. In October 1942, the first transport left for **Auschwitz**. By the end of the war, 140,000 Jews had passed through Terezín; fewer than 17,500 remained when the ghetto was finally liberated on May 8, 1945. Most of those in the camp when the Red Army arrived had been brought to Terezín on forced marches from other concentration camps. Even after the liberation, typhus killed many who had survived this far.

One of the perverse ironies of Terezín is that it was used by the Nazis as a cover for the real purpose of the **Endlösung**, or "final solution", devised at the Wannsee conference in January 1942 (at which Heydrich was present). The ghetto was made to appear self-governing, with its own council or *Judenrat*, its own bank printing (worthless) ghetto money, its own shops selling goods confiscated from the internees on arrival and even a café on the main square. For a while, a special "Terezín family camp" was even set up in Auschwitz, to continue the deception. The deportees were kept in mixed barracks, allowed to wear civilian clothes and – the main purpose of the whole thing – to send letters back to their loved ones in Terezín telling them they were OK. After six months "quarantine", they were sent to the gas chambers.

Although Terezín was being used by the Nazis as cynical propaganda, the ghetto population turned their **unprecedented freedom** to their own advantage. Since the entire population of the Protectorate (and Jews from many other parts of Europe) passed through Terezín, the ghetto had an enormous number of outstanding Jewish artists, musicians, scholars and writers (many of whom subsequently perished in the camps). Thus, in addition to the officially sponsored activities, countless clandestine cultural events were organized in the cellars and attics of the barracks: teachers gave lessons to children, puppet theatre productions were staged and literary evenings were held.

Towards the end of 1943, the so-called *Verschönerung*, or "**beautification**", of the ghetto was implemented, in preparation for the arrival of the International Red Cross inspectors. Streets were given names instead of numbers, and the whole place was decked out as if it were a spa town. When the **International Red Cross** asked to inspect one of the Nazi camps, delegates were brought here and treated to a week of Jewish cultural events. A circus tent was set up in the main square; a children's pavilion erected in the park; numerous performances of Hans Krása's children's opera *Brundibár* (Bumble Bee) staged; and a jazz band, called the Ghetto Swingers, performed in the bandstand on the main square. The Red Cross visited Terezín twice, once in June 1944, and again in April 1945; both times the delegates filed positive reports.

8

extraordinary and tragic events that took place here between 1941 and 1945, including background displays on the measures that led inexorably to the *Endlösung*. There's also a fascinating twelve-minute film (with English subtitles) showing clips of the Nazi propaganda film shot in Terezín – *Hitler Gives the Jews a Town* – intercut with harrowing interviews with survivors.

Magdeburská kasárna (Magdeburg Barracks)

Tyršova • Daily: April–Oct 9am–6pm; Nov–March 9am–5.30pm • 175Kč; combined ticket with other Terezín attractions 215Kč

South of the ghetto, the **Magdeburská kasárna**, former seat of the Jewish self-governing council, or *Freizeitgestaltung*, has been turned into a fascinating **museum** focusing on Terezín's remarkable artistic life. First off, however, there's a reconstructed women's dormitory with three-tier bunks, full of 1930s luggage and belongings, to give an idea of the cramped living conditions endured by ghetto inhabitants. The first exhibition room has displays on the various Jewish musicians who passed through Terezín, including Pavel Haas, a pupil of Janáček; Hans Krása, a pupil of Zemlinsky; and Karel Ančerl, who survived the Holocaust to become the conductor of the Czech Philharmonic. The final exhibition room concentrates on the writers who contributed to the ghetto's underground magazines. The rooms in between are given over to the work of Terezín's numerous visual artists, many of whom were put to work by the SS, who set up a graphics department here; headed by cartoonist Bedřich Fritta, it produced visual propaganda showing how smoothly the ghetto ran. In addition, there are many clandestine works, ranging from portraits of inmates to disturbing depictions of the cramped dormitories and the transports. These provide some of the most vivid and deeply affecting insights into the reality of ghetto life in the whole of Terezín, and it was for this "propaganda of horror" that several artists, including Fritta, were eventually deported to Auschwitz.

Malá pevnost (Small Fortress)

Principova alej 304 • Daily: April–Oct 8am–6pm; Nov–March 8am–4.30pm • 175Kč; combined ticket with other Terezín attractions 215Kč

Across the River Ohře from the main sights, east along Pražská, the **Malá pevnost** was built as a military prison in the 1780s, the same time as the main fortress. The prison's most famous inmate was the young Bosnian Serb **Gavrilo Princip**, who assassinated Archduke Ferdinand in Sarajevo in 1914, and who was interned and died here during World War I. In 1940 it was turned into an **SS prison** by Heydrich and, after the war, it became the official memorial and museum of Terezín. The majority of the 32,000 inmates who passed through the prison were active in the resistance (and, more often than not, Communists). Some 2500 inmates perished here, while another 8000 died subsequently in the concentration camps. The vast cemetery laid out by the entrance contains the graves of more than 2300 individuals, plus numerous other corpses of unidentified victims, and is rather insensitively dominated by a large Christian cross, plus a smaller Star of David.

Guides (including a dwindling number of Terezín survivors) can show you around, or else you can follow the brief English-language self-guided walking tour. The infamous Nazi refrain *Arbeit Macht Frei* ("Work Brings Freedom") is daubed across the entrance on the left, which leads to the exemplary washrooms, still looking as they did when built for the Red Cross tour of inspection. The rest of the camp has been left empty but intact, and graphically evokes the cramped conditions under which the prisoners were kept, half-starved and badly clothed, subject to indiscriminate cruelty and execution. The main **exhibition** is housed in the SS barracks opposite the luxurious home of the camp *Kommandant* and his family. A short documentary, intelligible in any language, is regularly shown in the cinema that was set up in 1942 to entertain the SS guards.

ARRIVAL AND DEPARTURE | TEREZÍN

By train Trains from Prague's Masarykovo station call at Bohušovice nad Ohří (on the main Prague–Děčín line), 2km south of the fortress (hourly; 1hr).

By bus Buses for Terezín leave from Nádraží Holešovice (up to every 30min; 50min).

EATING

Atypik Máchova 91 ☎416 782 780, ⓦatypik.cz. Just behind the Ghetto Museum, this is the only decent place to eat in town, serving standard Czech food. The cheap lunch menu is a superb deal and most main courses cost less than 100Kč. Mon–Fri 9.30am–9pm, Sat 11am–10pm, Sun 11am–6pm.

Kutná Hora

Thanks to the once rich silver deposits that riddle the local substrata, for around 250 years **KUTNÁ HORA** (Kuttenberg) was one of the most important towns in Bohemia, second only to Prague. At the end of the fourteenth century its population was equal to that of London, its shanty-town suburbs sprawled across what are now green fields, and its ambitious building projects set out to rival those of the capital itself. It's all a bit hard to imagine these days as you wander this small provincial town, with a population of just over 20,000, but the monuments dotted around it, its superb Gothic cathedral and the remarkable monastery and ossuary in the suburb of **Sedlec**, hint at its glory days and make it one of the most worthwhile day-trips from Prague.

Brief history

Kutná Hora's road to prosperity began in the late thirteenth century with the discovery of copper and **silver deposits** in the surrounding area. During the "silver rush" German miners were invited to settle and work the seams, and in around 1300 Václav II founded the royal mint here and sent for Italian craftsmen to run it. It was here that the famous **Prague groschen** (*pražské groše*) was struck, a currency that spread across central Europe because of its stable and reliable silver content. Many of these groschen were used to fund the beautification of Prague, but they also enabled construction of

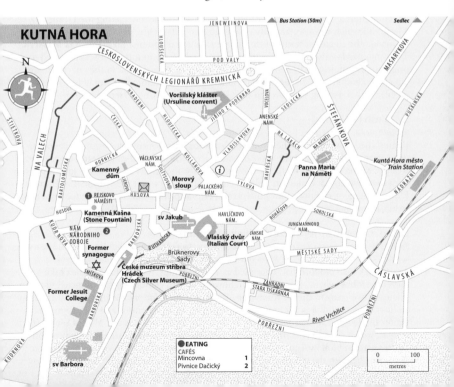

one of the most magnificent churches in central Europe and a number of other prestigious Gothic monuments in Kutná Hora itself.

At the time of the Hussite Wars, the town was mostly German-speaking and staunchly Catholic; local miners used to throw captured Hussites into the deep mine shafts and leave them to die of starvation. Word got out, and the town was besieged and eventually taken by Žižka's fanatical Táborites in 1421, only to be recaptured by Sigismund and his papal forces shortly afterwards, and again by Žižka the following year.

While the silver stocks remained high the town was able to recover its former prosperity, but at the end of the sixteenth century the mines dried up and Kutná Hora's wealth and importance came to an abrupt end – when the Swedes marched on the town during the Thirty Years' War, they had to be bought off with beer rather than silver. The town has never fully recovered, shrivelling to less than a third of its former size, its fate emphatically sealed by a devastating fire in 1770.

Vlašský dvůr (Italian Court)

Havlíčkovo náměstí 552 • Guided tours only: daily: March & Oct 10am–5pm; April–Sept 9am–6pm; Nov–Feb 10am–4pm • 85Kč • ⓣ 327 512 873

Leafy Havličkovo náměstí is home to one of the town's top sights, the **Vlašský dvůr**, originally conceived as a palace by Václav II and for three centuries the town's bottomless purse, where Florentine minters produced the Prague groschen at an incredible rate of two thousand per twelve-hour shift. The building itself has been messed about with over the years, most recently – and most brutally – by nineteenth-century restorers, who left only the fourteenth-century oriel window (capped by an unlikely looking wooden onion dome) and the miners' fountain unmolested. The original workshops of the minters have been bricked in, but the outlines of their little doors and windows are still visible in the courtyard. On the thirty-minute **guided tour** – available in English – you get to see some silver groschen, learn about the minters' hard lives and admire the medieval royal chapel, which shelters a superb full-relief fifteenth-century altarpiece depicting the Death of Mary, and which was spectacularly redecorated in 1904 with Art Nouveau murals.

8

Outside the court is a statue of the country's founder and first president, **T.G. Masaryk**. Twice removed – once by the Nazis and once by the Communists – it was returned to its original position in the 1990s. Before you leave, take a quick look in the court gardens, which descend in steps to the Vrchlice valley. This is undoubtedly Kutná Hora's best profile, with a striking view over to the Cathedral of sv Barbora (see opposite).

Sv Jakub (St James)

Havlíčkovo náměstí

Behind the Vlašský dvůr is the **church of sv Jakub**, the town's oldest, begun a generation or so after the discovery of the silver deposits. Its grand scale indicates clearly quite how wealthy Kutná Hora was by the fourteenth century, though its artistry pales in comparison with the town's other ecclesiastical buildings. The leaning tower is a reminder of Kutná Hora's precarious position, the church's foundations being prone to subsidence from the redundant mines below.

České muzeum stříbra (Czech Silver Museum)

Barborská 28 • Guided tours every 30min: April & Oct Tues–Sun 9am–5pm; May, June & Sept 9am–6pm; July & Aug Tues–Sun 10am–6pm; Nov 10am–4pm • "Town of Silver" (1hr) 70Kč, "Way of Silver" (booking advised; 1hr 30min) 130Kč • ⓣ 733 420 366, ⓦ cms-kh.cz

The **Hrádek** is an old fort that, once used as a second mint, is now home to the **České muzeum stříbra**, where visitors can learn how fourteenth-century miners extracted silver ore. There are two tours to choose from. The "**Town of Silver**" (*Město stříbra*), which takes around an hour, offers a simple scoot around the museum, tracing the history of mining in the region and looking at local geology; more fun, and very popular, is the "**Way of Silver**" (*Cesta stříbra*), which takes thirty minutes longer and skips the museum entirely. Here you don miner's garb and follow a guide through narrow sections of the medieval mines that were discovered beneath the fort in the 1960s – some of which tunnel more than 100m down.

Sv Barbora

Jakubská • Daily: April–Oct 9am–6pm; Nov–March 10am–4pm • 60Kč • ☎ 775 363 938, ⓦ khfarnost.cz

Many claim that Kutná Hora's **Cathedral of sv Barbora** is one of the most spectacular and moving ecclesiastical buildings in central Europe. Not to be outshone by the great monastery at Sedlec (see p.160) or Prague's St Vitus Cathedral, the mineworkers of Kutná Hora began financing the construction of a great Gothic cathedral of their own, dedicated to St Barbara, the patron saint of miners and gunners. The foundations were probably laid by Peter Parler in the 1380s, but it was his son Jan who started construction in earnest. However, work was interrupted by the Hussite Wars, and the church remained unfinished until the late nineteenth century, despite efforts by numerous architects, including Master Hanuš, Matouš Rejsek and Benedikt Ried, in the intervening centuries.

Barborská, the approach road to the cathedral, is lined with a parade of wildly gesticulating Baroque saints and cherubs that almost rival the sculptures on Charles Bridge; on the right-hand side is the palatial seventeenth-century former **Jesuit College**, now an art gallery. The cathedral's exterior bristles with pinnacles, finials and flying buttresses that support its most striking feature, a **roof** of three tent-like towers added in the sixteenth century, culminating in unequal, needle-sharp spires.

The cathedral interior

Inside, cold light streams through the numerous plain-glass windows, illuminating the high-flying **nave** and Ried's playful ribbed vaulting, which forms branches and petals stamped with coats of arms belonging to Václav II and the local miners' guilds. The arching spread of the five-aisled nave is remarkably uncluttered: the multi-tiered tester of the Gothic pulpit – half-wood, half-stone – creeps tastefully up a central pillar, matching black and gold Renaissance confessionals lie discreetly in the north aisle, and, nearby, the filigree work on the original Gothic choir stalls echoes the cathedral's exterior. Look up, and you'll see virtually an entire chamber orchestra of gilded putti disporting themselves over the Baroque organ case.

The **ambulatory** boasts an array of early twentieth-century stained glass, but it's the medieval frescoes preserved in the southernmost chapels that really stand out. In the Smíšek Chapel, there's a wonderful orchestra of angels in the vaulting and a depiction of the Queen of Sheba on one of the walls. Two chapels further along is the Minters' Chapel, its walls decorated with fifteenth-century frescoes showing the Florentines at work.

8

Kamenná kašna (Stone Fountain)

Rejskovo náměstí

On Rejskovo náměstí, the squat, oversize polygonal **Kamenná kašna**, built by Rejsek in 1495, strikes a very odd pose: peppered with finials and replete with blind arcading, it was actually designed as the decorative casing for a reservoir and now houses a shop.

Kamenný dům

Václavské náměstí 183 • Tues–Sun: April & Oct 9am–5pm; May, June & Sept 9am–6pm; July & Aug 10am–6pm; Nov 10am–4pm • 50Kč • ⓦ cms-kh.cz

The **Kamenný dům**, built around 1480, with an oriel window and a steep gable covered in an ornate sculptural icing, now contains a branch of the Czech Silver Museum (see opposite), focusing on the life of the townsfolk between the seventeenth and nineteenth centuries.

Voršilský klášter (Ursuline convent)

Poděbradova 288 • April & Oct Sat & Sun 9am–4pm; May–Sept Tues–Sun 9am–5.30pm • Free

Kutná Hora's Ursuline convent, or **Voršilský klášter**, was begun by Kilian Ignaz Dientzenhofer but remains unfinished to this day. Just three sides of the convent's ambitious pentagonal plan were actually built, its neo-Baroque church being added in the late nineteenth century while sv Barbora (see above) was being restored. The convent was shut down by the Communists in 1950, but the nuns returned here in 1989.

Nanebevzetí Panny Marie

Zámecká 127, Sedlec • April–Oct Mon–Sat 9am–5pm, Sun noon–5pm; Nov–March Mon–Sat 10am–4pm, Sun noon–5pm • 50Kč • ☎ 326 551 049

In the suburb of Sedlec, the fourteenth-century **church of Nanebevzetí Panny Marie** adjoins the defunct eighteenth-century Cistercian monastery (now the largest tobacco factory in Europe, owned by Philip Morris). The building was imaginatively redesigned in the eighteenth century by Santini-Aichl, who specialized in melding Gothic with Baroque – most of his creations are so architecturally unique they have been given World Cultural Heritage status by UNESCO. Here, given a plain French Gothic church gutted during the Hussite Wars, Santini set to work on the vaulting, adding his characteristic sweeping stucco rib patterns, relieved only by the occasional Baroque splash of colour above the chancel steps.

Kostnice (Ossuary)

Zámecká, Sedlec • Daily: March & Oct 9am–5pm; April–Sept 8am–6pm; Nov–Feb 9am–4pm • 90Kč • ☎ 326 551 049, ⓦ ossuary.eu

A good proportion of the crowds boarding trains in Prague are heading to the suburb of Sedlec, to see what lies beneath the **Kostel všech svatých** (All Saints Church) – just one of the town's Santini-Aichl makeovers (see above). This ghoulish **kostnice**, the mother of all ossuaries, full to overflowing with human bones is one of the Czech Republic's top sights. When holy earth from Golgotha was scattered over the graveyard in the twelfth century, all of Bohemia's nobility wanted to be buried here, so when the cemetery was reduced in size in the early nineteenth century, the bones belonging to some forty thousand people were stored inside the church. In 1870, worried about the ever-growing skeleton mountain, the authorities commissioned local woodcarver František Rint to do something creative with them. He rose to the challenge and moulded out of bones four giant bells, one in each corner of the crypt, designed wall-to-ceiling skeletal decorations, including the Schwarzenberg coat of arms, and, as the centrepiece, put together a chandelier made out of every bone in the human body. Rint's signature (in bones) is at the bottom of the steps.

ARRIVAL AND INFORMATION   KUTNÁ HORA

By train Trains leave Prague's hlavní nádraží (every 2hr; 50min) for Kutná Hora hlavní nádraží, the town's main train station. The station is a long way from the centre, near Sedlec; bus #1 will take you into town, or there's usually a shuttle train service ready to leave for the more central but tiny Kutná Hora město spur station.
By bus Buses leave from Prague's Háje metro station at the end of red metro line C (hourly; 1hr 40min).

The bus station is a short walk north of Kutná Hora's historical centre.
Tourist office Palackého náměstí 377 (April–Sept daily 9am–6pm; Oct–March Mon–Fri 9am–5pm, Sat & Sun 10am–4pm; ☎ 327 512 378, ⓦ kutnahora.cz). There's another branch in Sedlec at Zámecká 279 (daily: April–Sept 9am–5pm; Oct–March 9am–4pm; ☎ 326 551 049, ⓦ kutnahora.cz).

EATING AND DRINKING

Mincovna Husova 138 ☎ 327 536 900. "The Mint" is an excellent Czech restaurant within the *Hotel Opat*, near the Kamenná kašna, offering the usual carnivore-friendly menu as well as lots of pastas and vegetarian choices. Mains 150–250Kč. Daily 11am–11pm.

Pivnice Dačický Rakova 8 ☎ 603 434 367, ⓦ dacicky.cz. Large medieval-themed beer hall banging down huge meat platters, wild boar goulash, giant schnitzels and roast ducks with red sauerkraut and fat-speckled dumplings. Mains 160–350Kč. Daily 11am–11pm.

Konopiště

With around a quarter of a million visitors passing through its portcullis every year, the popularity of the **Konopiště** chateau, near the town of Benešov, is surpassed only by the likes of Karlštejn (see opposite). Though Karlštejn looks more dramatic from the outside, Konopiště is the more interesting and varied of the two. Tour groups from across the globe home in on this Gothic pile, which is packed with stuffed animals, weaponry and hunting trophies. Most interesting are its historical associations: King Václav IV was imprisoned by his own nobles in the chateau's distinctive round tower, and **Archduke Franz Ferdinand**, heir to the Habsburg throne, lived here with his wife, Sophie Chotek, until their assassination in Sarajevo in 1914. In addition to remodelling the chateau into its current appearance, the archduke shared his generation's fanatic appetite for hunting, eliminating all animals foolish enough to venture into the grounds. However, he surpassed all his contemporaries by recording, stuffing and displaying a significant number of the 171,537 birds and beasts he shot between the years 1880 and 1906, the details of which are recorded in his *Schuss Liste*, displayed inside – remarkably, only around 1.5 percent of his final bag is displayed. The trigger-happy archduke had certainly amassed some bad karma by the time he took his fateful trip to Bosnia.

Tours of the chateau

There's a choice of four **guided tours**. The first tour, *I okruh*, explores the period interiors, which contain some splendid Renaissance cabinets and lots of Meissen porcelain, while *II okruh* takes you through the chapel, past the stuffed bears and deer teeth. *III okruh*, meanwhile, concentrates on the personal apartments of the archduke and his wife. As Sophie was a mere countess, and not an archduchess, the couple were shunned by the Habsburg court in Vienna and hid themselves away in Konopiště. The *IV okruh* homes in on the huge castle armoury and hunting trophies.

Chateau grounds

In the main courtyard of the chateau, you can pop into the purpose-built **Střelnice** (shooting range; 40Kč), where the archduke would hone his skills as a marksman against moving mechanical targets, all of which have been meticulously restored. Tucked underneath the south terrace is the **Muzeum sv Jiří** (40Kč), which is packed to the gunwales with artefacts from Franz Ferdinand's collection – from paintings to statuettes and trinkets relating to St George, the fictional father of medieval chivalry, with whom the archduke was obsessed. Much the best reason to come to Konopiště, though, is to explore its extensive **zámecký park**, which boasts a marked red path around the largest lake, sundry statuary, an unrivalled rose garden with a café, several greenhouses (*skleníky*; 40Kč) and a deer park.

8

ARRIVAL AND INFORMATION	KONOPIŠTĚ
By bus From Prague's Roztyly metro station, take any bus to Benešov (at least every two hours; 30-40min) then change onto a local bus towards Štěchovice – Konopiště is the second stop.	June–Aug Tues–Sun 10am––5pm; Oct & Nov Sat & Sun 10am–3pm.
By train Trains (frequent; one hour) to Benešov u Prahy leave from Praha hlavní nádraží; the chateau is a 2km walk west of the train station along either the red- or yellow-marked path – the red features more woodland walking.	**Tours** Most tours – *I okruh* (50min; 170Kč), *II okruh* (50min; 170Kč) and *III okruh* (restricted to eight people: 1hr; 240Kč), *IV okruh* (50min; 200Kč) – are in Czech, but there are occasional tours in English, which cost 300Kč/300Kč/420Kč/350Kč extra respectively (ask at the box office or phone ahead).
Opening hours April, May & Sept Tues–Sun 10am–4pm;	**Contact details** ☎ 301 721 366, ⓦ zamek-konopiste.cz.

EATING AND DRINKING	
Stará myslivna Konopiště 2 ☎ 317 700 280, ⓦ stara myslivna.com. The brief menu at the lovely *Old Hunting Lodge*, downhill from the chateau, is straight out of the	archduke's hunting bag, featuring rabbit, venison, pheasant and wild boar. Mains 146–359Kč. Sun–Thurs 11am–9pm, Fri & Sat 11am–10pm.

Karlštejn

Strung out along one of the tributaries of the River Berounka, **KARLŠTEJN** is a small village with a big attraction. The local castle, built specially by Emperor Charles IV to house the imperial crown jewels, is the second most visited in the country after Prague Castle.

The hrad

Castle Feb–June & Sept–Nov Tues–Sun, shorter hours; July & Aug daily 9am–6.30pm; Dec Sat & Sun only; closed Jan **Guided tours** Basic "okruh I" tours (55min; 190Kč); exclusive "okruh II" tours (May–Oct only; 1hr 40min; 330Kč); Great Tower "okruh III" (May–Sept only; 40min; 150Kč) • ☎ 311 681 617, ⓦ hradkarlstejn.cz

Designed in the fourteenth century by Matthias of Arras for Emperor Charles IV, Karlštejn's **hrad** was built as a giant safe, not only for imperial trinkets but also for the emperor's large collection of precious saintly relics. Occupying a defiantly unassailable position high above the village, it quickly became Charles's favourite retreat from the vast city he himself had masterminded. Women were strictly forbidden to enter the castle, and the story of his third wife Anna's successful break-in (in drag) became one of the most popular Czech comedies of the nineteenth century and is the subject of the 1970s Czech film *Noc na Karlštejně* (A Night at Karlštejn).

Ruthlessly and somewhat inaccurately restored in the late nineteenth century by the great neo-Gothicizer Josef Mocker, the castle now looks much better from a distance, with its giant wedge towers rising above a series of castellated walls. Most of the rooms visited on the guided tours contain only the barest of furnishings, the empty spaces taken up by displays on the castle's history. Theoretically, the top two chambers would make the whole trip worthwhile: unfortunately, on the basic guided tour (see above), you can only look into (but not enter) the emperor's residential **Mariánská věž**. It was here that Charles shut himself off from the rest of the world, with any urgent business passed to him through a hole in the wall of the tiny, ornate **chapel of sv Kateřina**.

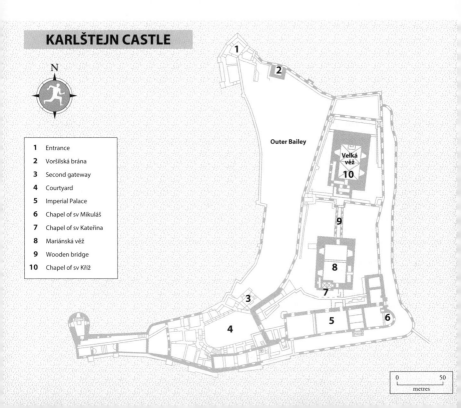

KARLŠTEJN CASTLE

N

1 Entrance
2 Voršilská brána
3 Second gateway
4 Courtyard
5 Imperial Palace
6 Chapel of sv Mikuláš
7 Chapel of sv Kateřina
8 Mariánská věž
9 Wooden bridge
10 Chapel of sv Kříž

Outer Bailey

Velká věž
10

0 ____ 50
metres

Sv Kříž

The castle's finest interior, the **chapel of sv Kříž**, connected by a wooden bridge that leads to the building's highest structure, the **Velká věž**, is only open to visitors who book the longer "exclusive" guided tour in advance. In the emperor's day, only a select few could enter this gilded treasure-house, whose 6m-thick walls contain 2200 semi-precious stones and 128 breathtakingly beautiful fourteenth-century painted panels by the masterful Master Theodoric, Bohemia's greatest fourteenth-century painter (a small selection of his panels are exhibited in Prague's Anežský klášter). The imperial crown jewels, once secured here behind nineteen separate locks, were removed to Hungary after an abortive attack by the Hussites, while the Bohemian jewels are now stashed away in the cathedral in Prague.

ARRIVAL AND DEPARTURE   KARLŠTEJN

By train Trains for Karlštejn depart from Prague's hlavní nádraží (every 30min; 40min). The village is a 10min walk across the river from the station, and it's a further 15–20min climb up to the castle.

EATING

Koruna Karlštejn 13 ☎ 311 681 465, ⓦ korunakarlstejn .cz. Part of *Hotel Koruna*, just down from the castle, this cosy Czech restaurant has surprisingly affordable mains given its location and tourist footfall. The fish comes highly recommended and there's plenty of fried cheese for non-carnivores. Mains 65–290Kč. Daily 11am–11pm.

U Janů Karlštejn 90 ☎ 725 805 965, ⓦ ujanukarlstejn.cz. Bag a table in the sun at this popular lunch spot for a meat and dumplings combo or chicken schnitzel. Mains 90–140Kč. Daily 10am–4pm.

Lidice

The small mining village of **LIDICE**, 18km northwest of Prague, hit world headlines on June 10, 1942, at the moment when it ceased to exist. On the flimsiest pretext, it was chosen as scapegoat for the assassination of the Nazi leader Reinhard Heydrich (see box, p.119). All 173 men from the village were rounded up and shot by the SS, the 198 women were sent to Ravensbrück concentration camp, and the 89 children either went to the camps, or, if they were Aryan enough, were packed off to "good" German homes, while the village itself was burnt to the ground.

After the massacre, the "Lidice shall live" campaign was launched and villages all over the world began to change their name to Lidice. The first was Stern Park Gardens, Illinois, soon followed by villages in Mexico and other Latin American countries. From Coventry to Montevideo, towns twinned themselves with Lidice, so that rather than "wiping a Czech village off the face of the earth" as Hitler had hoped, the Nazis created an international symbol of anti-fascist resistance.

Lidice memorial

10 června 1942 • **Museum** Daily: March 9am–5pm; April–Oct 9am–6pm; Nov–Feb 9am–4pm • 90Kč • ⓦ lidice-memorial.cz • Regular buses to Lidice (16–34min) depart from metros Nádraží Veleslavín and Zličín in Prague.

Knowing the terrible backstory makes the appearance of modern Lidice seem almost perversely unexceptional. At the end of the straight, tree-lined main street, 10 června 1942 (June 10, 1942), there's a dour concrete memorial featuring a small, horrific **museum** where you can watch an eighteen-minute film about the village, including footage shot by the SS themselves as it was burning. The spot where old Lidice used to lie is just south of the memorial, a smooth green pasture punctuated with simple artworks and a chilling bronze memorial depicting the 82 local children who never returned.

8

GUESTROOM, *SAX* HOTEL

Accommodation

When it comes to a place to lay your head, Prague has everything from big multinational chain hotels to attractive and atmospheric Old Town pensions decked out with genuine antiques. However, although you can easily pay a lot or a very little to stay in the city, there is a definite shortage of decent, inexpensive to mid-range places. Partly because of this, some visitors opt for one of the city's many self-catering apartments, which allow you to live like a local for a reasonable price. Unsurprisingly, given the large number of backpackers who hit the city all year round, there are a fair few hostels – and these are supplemented further by a whole host of more transient, high-season-only places. Airbnb-type of accommodation has taken off in a big way in Prague, but city hall is looking at ways of regulating the sector.

9

ACCOMMODATION-BOOKING AGENCIES

There are several **accommodation agencies** that can book you into hotels and pensions, some of which can also help you find a hostel bed or a private room in an apartment. Before agreeing to part with any money, be sure you know exactly where you're staying and check about transport to the centre – some places can be a long way out of town but well linked to the centre by metro or tram.

Apartments in Prague ☎775 588 511, ⒲apartments-in-prague.org. Wide selection of self-catering apartments spread across the Old Town, all with free wi-fi.

AVE ☎251 551 011, ⒲avehotels.cz. A choice of hotels, pensions, apartments and hostel beds. You can book in advance online or by phone (Mon–Fri 8am–6pm).

Bohemia Apartments ☎606 757 284, ⒲bohemia -apartments.com. Beautifully appointed apartments across the city centre, many of them in the New Town.

Prague City Tourism ⒲prague.eu. You can book everything from hotels to hostels in advance online, or reserve through one of the city's tourist offices (see p.30) when you arrive.

RENTeGO ☎224 323 736, ⒲rentego.com. A decent range of self-catering apartments in the Old Town. Book online and get the keys or eCode sent to you.

Stop City Belgická 36, Vinohrady ☎222 521 233, ⒲stopcity.com. Friendly agency that can book you into hotels, pensions and private rooms at very reasonable rates.

ESSENTIALS

Costs Overall, Prague is definitely no longer the bargain it was. If you're looking for a double and can pay around 4000Kč a night, then there's plenty of choice. At the other end of the scale, there are numerous hostels charging as little as 350Kč for a bed in a dorm. Rates are at their very highest over public holidays such as New Year, and drop by as much as a third in July and August, and sometimes by half in the low season between November and February. You can, however, get some very good deals – and undercut the often exorbitant rack rates – by booking online; given that Prague can be busy all year round, it's not a bad idea to book ahead in any case. All prices quoted in the Guide are for the cheapest double room available in high season, which may mean without private bath or shower in the less expensive places – again, these rates may be slashed if you book online in advance. For hostels

we have quoted the cheapest dorm bed in high season.

Facilities The vast majority of rooms in hotels and pensions have en-suite bathrooms and TVs, with continental breakfast either included in the price or offered as an optional extra. Most have free wi-fi, but few have a/c. Even budget hotels out in the suburbs will offer free city maps and some sell public transport tickets.

Neighbourhoods With plenty of centrally located hotels, the only reason you might want to stay out in the suburbs is if you're on a tight budget. The quietest central areas to stay in are on the hilly left bank in Malá Strana and Hradčany, though there's more choice, and more nightlife, in Staré Město and Nové Město.

Camping A very cheap option is to camp. There are several campsites in the Troja district, not particularly far from the city centre. Most are only open from April to October.

HOTELS AND PENSIONS

Despite the difference in name, there's no hard and fast rule as to what constitutes a hotel and what a pension, and it's certainly not reflected in the price. **Standards** overall are still somewhat variable, with sullen service and mild incompetence still encountered here and there.

HRADČANY

★**Domus Henrici** Loretánská 11 ☎220 511 369, ⒲domus-henrici.cz; tram #22 to Pohořelec; map p.34. Stylish, discreet hotel in a fabulous location, with just eight rooms/apartments, some with splendid views. Booking months in advance essential. **4000Kč**

Monastery Strahovské nádvoří 13 ☎233 090 200, ⒲hotelmonastery.cz; tram #22 to Pohořelec; map p.34. Staying within the Strahov Monastery is a great experience, though the room decor, if not the building itself, is disappointingly of this millennium. **3900Kč**

Questenberk Úvoz 15 ☎220 407 600, ⒲questenberk.cz; tram #22 to Pohořelec; map p.34. Created from a Baroque chapel, the *Questenberk* has completely modernized rooms with smart but plain decor and stupendous views from some quarters. **2750Kč**

Savoy Prague Keplerova 6 ☎224 302 430, ⒲hotel savoyprague.com; tram #22 to Pohořelec; map p.34. Super-luxury hotel on the western edge of Hradčany, concealed behind a pretty Art Nouveau facade and well known for its large marble bathrooms. This is one of Prague's finest, and as a result is popular with visiting celebs. **4300Kč**

9

★ **U krále Karla (King Charles)** Úvoz 4 ☎ 257 531 211, ⓦ ukralekarla.cz; tram #22 to Pohořelec; map p.34. Possibly the most tastefully exquisite of all the small luxury hotels in the Hrad district, with beautiful antique furnishings and stained-glass windows. Situated at the top of Nerudova, it's a long, steep slog from the nearest tram stop, however. **3500Kč**

U raka (The Crayfish) Černínská 10 ☎ 220 511 100, ⓦ romantikhotel-uraka.cz; tram #22 to Brusnice; map p.34. The perfect hideaway, with six double rooms in a

WHERE TO STAY?: PRAGUE POSTAL DISTRICTS

If you're thinking of booking a room in advance or planning a long-term stay, it's as well to know a little about the merits, or otherwise, of Prague's various areas and **postal districts**. From 1960 to 1990, Prague was divided into ten districts and most Praguers refer to their area either by name, or by the old postal districts, which still appear on street signs and addresses.

Prague 1 Prague 1 covers all of the old city on both sides of the river, and half of Nové Město, and consequently is generally the most expensive part of the capital in which to sleep. However, anything in this area will be within easy walking distance of the main sights, and will save you a lot of public transport hassle.

Prague 2 Prague 2 is another prime central area, taking in the southern half of Nové Město and western half of Vinohrady, a nineteenth-century des res with good metro connections.

Prague 3 The less salubrious, eastern half of Vinohrady in Prague 3 is well served by the metro; Žižkov, on the other hand, is a grimy, more working-class district, connected to the centre by trams.

Prague 4 Covers a wide area in the southeast of the city, stretching from half-decent, predominantly nineteenth-century suburbs such as Nusle, Podolí and Braník to the grim high-rise *paneláky* of Chodov and Háje. However, even if you find yourself in the latter two areas, you can at least be sure of quick metro connections to the city centre.

Prague 5 Vast area in the hilly southwest of the city, with clean air and attractive family villas predominating and a metro line running through some of it. The area closest to the city is Smíchov, a vibrant, late nineteenth-century district, but there are few bargains to be had here now.

Prague 6 The perfect villa district to the north of the centre, a favourite with foreign embassies and their staff. The metro now runs further into the area, meaning better connections with the centre. It's also the most convenient district for the airport.

Prague 7 The nineteenth-century suburb of Holešovice in the northeast is well served by the metro and trams. Troja, home to numerous ad hoc campsites, is almost bucolic, and correspondingly difficult to get to.

Prague 8 The grid-plan streets of nineteenth-century Karlín are close to the centre and well served by the metro, which extends as far as Libeň; the rest of the area is not so aesthetically pleasing, though the metro reaches out into Kobylisy.

Prague 9 Dominated by factories, Prague's 9th district, in the northeast of the city, is something of a last resort; however, with good metro connections, it's easy enough to get into town at least.

Prague 10 Beware of Prague 10, which extends right into the countryside; areas like Strašnice and Vršovice in the southeast of the city are slightly closer to the centre of things and served, in part, by the metro. Any higher numbers, with the possible exception of the northern reaches of Prague 11 are a long way from the centre and served by bus or regional trains only.

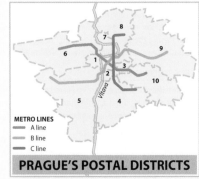

METRO LINES
— A line
— B line
— C line

PRAGUE'S POSTAL DISTRICTS

1 Hradčany, Malá Strana, Staré Město, Josefov and Nové Město
2 Nové Město, Vinohrady, Vyšehrad and Nusle
3 Vinohrady and Žižkov
4 Nusle, Podolí, Braník, Krč and the southeastern suburbs
5 Smíchov and the southwestern suburbs
6 Dejvice, Střešovice, Břevnov and the northwestern suburbs
7 Holešovice, Bubeneč and Troja
8 Karlín, Libeň and the northern suburbs
9 Vysočany and the northeastern suburbs
10 Vršovice, Strašnice and the eastern suburbs

little half-timbered, eighteenth-century cottage in Nový Svět. No children under 12. Reservations essential. <u>**4400Kč**</u>

MALÁ STRANA

Alchymist Grand Hotel Tržiště 19 ☎257 286 011, ⓦalchymisthotel.com; tram #12, #20 or #22 to Malostranské náměstí; map p.56. Over-the-top luxury abounds in this sixteenth-century palace which has been converted into a secluded spa hotel, complete with exotic masseuses and an indoor pool. <u>**6000Kč**</u>

★**Aria** Tržiště 9 ☎225 334 111, ⓦariahotel.net; tram #12, #20 or #22 to Malostranské náměstí; map p.56. Prague's most popular boutique hotel, this superbly stylish, contemporary place has a stunning roof terrace and floors (and rooms) with musical themes from jazz and rock to classical and opera. <u>**5500Kč**</u>

Design Hotel Neruda Nerudova 44 ☎257 535 557, ⓦdesignhotelneruda.com; tram #12, #20 or #22 to Malostranské náměstí; map p.56. Classy hotel, a bit of a march up tourist-clogged Nerudova, with a funky, glass-roofed foyer, lots of natural stone and clean-cut, minimalist decor in the rooms. <u>**3000Kč**</u>

Dientzenhofer Nosticova 2 ☎257 311 319, ⓦdientzenhofer.cz; tram #12, #20 or #22 to Malostranské náměstí; map p.56. Birthplace of the architect Kilian Ignác Dientzenhofer, this is a very popular and unpretentious pension, one of the few reasonably priced places anywhere in Prague to have wheelchair access. <u>**2150Kč**</u>

★**Dům U velké boty (The Big Shoe)** Vlašská 30 ☎257 532 088, ⓦdumuvelkeboty.cz; tram #12, #20 or #22 to Malostranské náměstí; map p.56. The sheer discreetness of this pension, in a lovely old building in the quiet backstreets, is one of its main draws. Run by a very friendly couple, who speak good English, it offers a series of cosy rooms, some en suite, with genuine antiques. Breakfast is extra. <u>**3000Kč**</u>

Lokál Inn Míšenská 12 ☎257 014 800, ⓦlokalinn.cz; tram #12, #20 or #22 to Malostranské náměstí; map p.56. Top-drawer boutique hotel where the original features of the Baroque townhouse have been preserved to provide a backdrop for interesting design features. Superb contemporary restaurant on site. <u>**2800Kč**</u>

Pod Věží Mostecká 2 ☎257 532 041, ⓦpodvezi.com; tram #12, #20 or #22 to Malostranské náměstí; map p.56. One of Prague's best small hotels a few steps from Charles Bridge with understated rooms boasting sumptuous fabrics. Restaurant and creperie on the premises. <u>**4500Kč**</u>

Sax Jánský vršek 3 ☎257 531 268, ⓦhotelsax.cz; tram #12, #20 or #22 to Malostranské náměstí; map p.56. There's nothing square about these funky digs where the groovy 1960s retro styling comes as an unexpected surprise amid the area's Baroque pomp. Something a bit different and very well run. <u>**2400Kč**</u>

U Karlova mostu Na Kampě 15 ☎234 652 808, ⓦarchibald.cz; tram #12, #20 or #22 to Malostranské náměstí; map p.56. Situated on a lovely tree-lined square, just off Charles Bridge, the rooms in this former brewery (now a pub-restaurant) have real character, despite the slick, urban furniture. <u>**3900Kč**</u>

U zlaté studně (The Golden Well) U zlaté studně 4 ☎257 011 213, ⓦgoldenwell.cz; metro Malostranská; map p.56. The location is pretty special: tucked into the hill below Prague Castle, next to the terraced gardens, with incredible views across the roof-tops. The rooms aren't half bad either, with lots of original ceilings, and there's a fine-dining restaurant attached, boasting a marvellous good-weather terrace. <u>**6600Kč**</u>

★**U zlatých nůžek (The Golden Scissors)** Na Kampě 6 ☎257 530 473, ⓦuzlatychnuzek.com; tram #12, #20 or #22 to Malostranské náměstí; map p.56. Ten pleasant rooms with parquet flooring, the odd beam and simple modern furnishings on Kampa island, close to Charles Bridge. <u>**3200Kč**</u>

William Hellichova 5 ☎257 320 242, ⓦsivekhotels.com; tram #12, #20 or #22 to Hellichova; map p.56. The 42 well-maintained, mostly spacious, somewhat unexciting rooms here are a good deal, and breakfast is better than average. Helpful staff. <u>**2000Kč**</u>

STARÉ MĚSTO

Buddha Bar Hotel Jakubská 8 ☎221 776 300, ⓦbuddha-bar-hotel.cz; metro Náměstí Republiky; map p.70. Supremely stylish, expensive boutique hotel with an Eastern slant to the decor and ambience, and all the latest mod cons. <u>**7000Kč**</u>

Černý slon (Black Elephant) Týnská 1 ☎222 321 521, ⓦhotelcernyslon.cz; metro Náměstí Republiky; map p.70. A stunted, ancient building tucked away off Old Town Square by the north portal of the Týn church, now tastefully converted into a very comfortable, if space-poor, hotel. Somehow they've even managed to squeeze a restaurant into the ground-floor space. <u>**3450Kč**</u>

Cloister Inn Konviktská 14 ☎224 211 020, ⓦcloister-inn.com; metro Národní třída; map p.70. Pleasant, well-equipped hotel housed in a former convent in a back street near the main sights; rooms are simply furnished with contemporary fittings. *Unitas* (see p.168) is run by the same people. <u>**2700Kč**</u>

Grand Hotel Bohemia Kralodvorská 4 ☎224 804 111, ⓦgrandhotelbohemia.cz; metro Náměstí Republiky; map p.70. Possibly the most elegant luxury hotel in the Old Town, just behind the Obecní dům. The lovely Art Nouveau decor gives way in the 79 rooms to tasteful beige and brown sophistication and all the amenities you'd expect from a twenty-first-century operation. <u>**5800Kč**</u>

Grand Hotel Praha Staroměstské náměstí 22 ☎221 632 556, ⓦgrandhotelpraha.cz; metro Staroměstská/Můstek; map p.70. If you want a room overlooking the astronomical clock on Old Town Square, then book in here,

9

well in advance. There are beautiful antique furnishings, big oak ceilings, but only a very few rooms, including a single, as well as an attic suite for four. 6700Kč

Haštal Haštalská 16 ☎ 222 314 335, ⓦ hotelhastal prague.com; metro Náměstí Republiky; map p.70. Opposite the sv Haštala church on peaceful Haštalské náměstí, this established hotel offers quite good value for money. Rooms sport dark wood furniture and Prague-themed prints on the walls, and the restaurant is an authentic piece of Art Nouveau. 3500Kč

★**Josef** Rybná 20 ☎ 221 700 111, ⓦ hoteljosef.com; metro Náměstí Republiky; map p.70. Prague's top design hotel exudes hipster-ish professionalism; the lobby is a symphony in off-white efficiency and the rooms continue the crisply maintained minimalist theme with limestone showers and sharply pressed linens. 3400Kč

Lippert Mikulášská 2 ☎ 224 232 250, ⓦ hotel-lippert.cz; metro Staroměstská; map p.70. A pretty good deal virtually on the Old Town Square, the well-appointed bedrooms here all have lovely wooden floors and incredible views of the surrounding blockbuster sights. If you want a bit of quiet, ask for a room at the back of the building. 295000Kč

Pachtův Palace Karoliny Světlé 34 ☎ 234 705 111, ⓦ pachtuvpalace.com; metro Národní třída; map p.70. In the heart of the Old Town, this former Baroque palace is now a luxury hotel, with charming and efficient staff and rooms decked out with a mix of antique and repro furniture. 6950Kč

Paříž U Obecního domu I ☎ 222 195 195, ⓦ hotel-paris .cz; metro Náměstí Republiky; map p.70. Famously the setting for Bohumil Hrabal's novel *I Served the King of England*, this is one of the city's original top-notch hotels, with plenty of *fin-de-siècle* atmosphere still in place. The location has seen much alteration in recent years but this *grande dame* remains the same. 6700Kč

★**Savic** Jilská 7 ☎ 224 248 555, ⓦ savic.eu; metro Národní třída; map p.70. This superb hotel, in the epicentre of the Old Town, flaunts plenty of period features including painted ceilings, leaping vaulting and exposed beams. Staff are as helpful as can be and you'll be looking forward to the excellent buffet breakfast all night. 3900Kč

U Červené židle (The Red Chair) Liliová 4 ☎ 296 180 018, ⓦ redchairhotel.com; tram #17 or #18 to Karlovy lázně; map p.70. Unassuming hotel on a pretty Old Town lane, offering thirteen rooms with green-stained timber furniture, high ceilings and bidets. There's a car park in the courtyard for anyone brave enough to drive into the Old Town's maze of streets. 3800Kč

U medvídků (The Little Bears) Na Perštýně 7 ☎ 224 211 916, ⓦ umedvidku.cz; metro Národní třída; map p.70. The rooms above this famous Prague pub are plain, quiet considering the locale, and something of an Old Town bargain; reservations essential. 2200Kč

U tří bubnů (The Three Drums) U radnice 8–10 ☎ 224 214 855, ⓦ utribubnu.cz; metro Staroměstská; map p.70. Cosy hotel, a short hop from Old Town Square, with five discerningly furnished rooms, either with original fifteenth-century wooden ceilings or lots of exposed beams. No lift but plenty of stairs. 2800Kč

U zlatého jelena (The Golden Stag) Štupartská 6 ☎ 257 531 925, ⓦ goldendeer.cz; metro Náměstí Republiky; map p.70. Every room is different at this relatively inexpensive little pension, though all are spacious and very simply furnished. The location puts you in the thick of the tourist action. 3000Kč

Unitas Bartolomějská 9 ☎ 224 230 533, ⓦ unitas.cz; metro Národní třída; map p.70. Set in a Franciscan convent, the *Unitas* offers simple, slightly over-priced twins here and bargain dorm beds in its *Art Prison* hostel which boasts Prague's oddest room - the cell where Havel was once locked up. 4800Kč

★**Ventana** Celetná 7 ☎ 221 776 600, ⓦ ventana-hotel .net; metro Náměstí Republiky; map p.70. Guests who stay at this super-central luxury boutique hotel rave about the spacious rooms, excellent breakfast and impeccably regimented staff. Add to this Prague's most stylish hotel lobby, gleaming marble-and-tile bathrooms and a library illuminated with crystal chandeliers, and the *Ventana* shapes up as one of Prague's top places to unpack your suitcase. 4800Kč

NOVÉ MĚSTO

★**Alcron** Štěpánská 40 ☎ 222 820 000, ⓦ radissonblu .com; metro Muzeum/Můstek; map p.102. Giant 1930s luxury hotel, just off Wenceslas Square, which has been superbly restored to its former Art Deco glory by the Radisson chain. Double rooms here are without doubt the most luxurious and tasteful you'll find in Nové Město. The restaurant sports a Michelin star, one of only a few in the Czech capital. 4450Kč

Boho Prague Senovážná 4 ☎ 234 622 600, ⓦ hotelboho prague.com; metro Hlavní nádraží; map p.102. Go boho in Bohemia at one of Prague's most stylish hotels where rooms sport shades of grey you never knew existed. There's an inhouse restaurant and wellness facilities. 8000Kč

Boscolo Prague Senovážné náměstí 13 ☎ 224 593 111, ⓦ boscolohotels.com; metro Hlavní nádraží; map p.102. Occupying one of Prague's grandest city-centre palaces, this five-star establishment has some incomparably swish public areas, a remarkable spa, rooms done out with Italian flair and lots of facilities such as a fitness centre and a pool. 8800Kč

Central Hybernská 10 ☎ 225 022 000, ⓦ kkhotels.com; metro Náměstí Republiky; map p.102. Part of the *K+K* group, this once illustrious address has once again been revived and now contains 127 comfortable, mid-range

9

business-standard rooms. A sound choice and well within walking distance of both the old and new towns. **3000Kč**

Dancing House Hotel Jiráskovo náměstí 6 ☎ 720 983 172, ⓦ dancinghousehotel.com; metro Karlovo náměstí; map p.102. Love or hate the *Dancing House*, what former Czech footballer Vladimír Šmicer has achieved by turning the building into one of Prague's more interesting hotels is bound to impress. The Fred Royal and Ginger Royal suites in the building's towers, offering truly awesome views of Prague Castle, are now two of the most desirable hotel rooms in the capital. **3900Kč**

Fusion Hotel Panská 9 ☎ 226 222 800, ⓦ fusionhotels .com; metro Můstek; map p.102. One of the capital's most striking but affordable hotels a schnitzel's throw from Wenceslas Square. Bold interiors blend with artwork to create a memorable hotel experience. **3000Kč**

Grand Hotel Evropa Václavské náměstí 25; metro Muzeum; map p.102. At the time of research this persistently disappointing potential gem of an Art Nouveau hotel was receiving the revamp it had so desperately needed since Havel was addressing the crowds opposite in late 1989. When it reopens (anyone's guess) it's expected to be one of the Nové Město's top places to stay.

Harmony Na Poříčí 31 ☎ 272 114 444, ⓦ hotelharmony .cz; metro Florenc; map p.102. A very sound low-cost option a dumpling's throw from the main sights, suitable for budget travellers who want to sleep, shower, surf the net and eat breakfast. For medieval grandeur, go elsewhere. **2200Kč**

★ **Hotel 16 – U sv Kateřiny** Kateřinská 16 ☎ 224 920 636, ⓦ hotel16.cz; metro Karlovo náměstí; map p.102. The rooms at this family-run hotel are small and plain but it's the exceptionally friendly service you'll remember, and perhaps the complimentary afternoon tea when you arrive back after a day's sightseeing. **3500Kč**

Icon Hotel V celnici 6 ☎ 221 634 100, ⓦ iconhotel.eu; metro Můstek; map p.102. Slick designer hotel, with white-walled rooms containing large, handmade beds and bathrooms in moody slate. The all-day à la carte breakfast, included in the rate, will suit late risers. **3500Kč**

Imperial Na poříčí 15 ☎ 246 011 600, ⓦ hotel -imperial.cz; metro Náměstí Republiky; map p.102. Despite describing itself as Art Deco, this place is definitely more of an Art Nouveau masterpiece. Built in 1914, the public spaces are dripping with period ceramic friezes; the rest of the hotel offers standard twenty-first-century luxury. **4100Kč**

Jungmann Jungmannovo náměstí 2 ☎ 224 219 501, ⓦ antikhotels.com; metro Můstek; map p.102. Small, well-maintained hotel in a very tall, narrow building just a step away from the lower end of Wenceslas Square. Rooms are spacious – especially the suites – and decked out with tasteful modern furnishings. Some have trendy in-room showers, so you'd better know the person you are sharing with pretty well. **4300Kč**

Mánes Myslíkova 20 ☎ 221 516 388, ⓦ hotelmanes.cz; metro Karlovo náměstí; map p.102. Star ratings mean little in the Czech Republic but the *Mánes*, named after the nineteenth-century Czech artist, deserves every one of its four twinklers. The fifty rooms are finished with contemporary panache, the bathrooms are spacious and stylish, and the location near Karlovo náměstí puts you near enough to the main sights. **2400Kč**

Moods Klimentská 28 ☎ 222 330 100, ⓦ hotelmoods .com; metro Náměstí Republiky; map p.102. Located in the little-visited Petrská čtvrt, this design hotel has a definite wow factor, thanks to its wall poetry, concealed neon lighting, minimalist furnishings and modish bathrooms. The uncluttered restaurant is also a hip affair. **3200Kč**

Palace Panská 12 ☎ 224 093 111, ⓦ palacehotel.cz; metro Můstek; map p.102. Luxury five-star hotel just off Wenceslas Square, renowned for its exquisite service and facilities – the sumptuous rooms are immaculately maintained, though the choice of fabrics in some may come as a garish surprise. Excellent breakfast buffet (sometimes included in room rates). **4300Kč**

Salvator Truhlářská 10 ☎ 222 312 234, ⓦ salvator.cz; metro Náměstí Republiky; map p.102. Very good location for the price, just a minute's walk from Náměstí Republiky, with small but clean rooms (the cheaper ones with shared facilities), set around a courtyard. Good buffet breakfast; friendly staff. **2300Kč**

U šuterů Palackého 4 ☎ 728 177 181, ⓦ hotelusuteru.cz; metro Můstek/Národní třída; map p.102. Furnishings and fittings of today blend well with the period architectural features of yesterday at this small good-value pension in a decent location between Národní and Wenceslas Square. Staff are helpful and the downstairs restaurant is a winner. **2300Kč**

U svatého Jana Vyšehradská 28 ☎ 222 560 243, ⓦ hotelusvatehojana.cz; metro Karlovo náměstí; map p.102. Bright and breezy guesthouse next to the Baroque church of St Nepomuk on the Rock. The location may be a bit out of the way, but the rates for the fourteen rooms reflect this. **3000Kč**

TOP 5 BOUTIQUE HOTELS

Aria See p.167
Buddha Bar Hotel See p.167
Lokál Inn See p.167
Moods See above
Ventana See p.168

VYŠEHRAD AND THE EASTERN SUBURBS

Anna Budečská 17, Vinohrady ☎ 222 513 111, ⓦ hotel anna.cz; metro Náměstí Míru; map p.124. Smartly appointed but unimaginative business-standard rooms, friendly staff and a decent location make this a popular Vinohrady choice, with trams and the metro close by. **2100Kč**

Arco Donská 13, Vinohrady ✆271 740 734, ⊕arco guesthouse.com; tram #4 or #22 to Krymská; map p.124. Gay-friendly guesthouse just a short tram ride from the centre of town. Furnishings are cheap, basic and of recent vintage, and all rooms are en suite. 1400Kč

Ehrlich Koněvova 79, Žižkov ✆236 040 555, ⊕hotel ehrlich.cz; tram #9, #10, #11 or #16 to Biskupcova; map p.124. Few tourists would elect to sleep in Žižkov, but perhaps if they saw this spacious, well-maintained hotel on the district's main thoroughfare they might consider the option. Some rooms have baths and a/c and there's a decent café on site. 1900Kč

Galileo Bruselská 3, Vinohrady ✆222 500 222, ⊕hotel galileoprague.com; tram #6 or #11 to Bruselská; map p.124. Ignoring the hideous cladding the owners have added to the nineteenth-century building, this chic hotel is a good choice, furnished with style and offering a vista-rich top-floor restaurant. 3000Kč

Le Palais U Zvonařky 1, Vinohrady ✆234 634 111, ⊕lepalaishotel.eu; tram #6 or #11 to Bruselská; map p.124. Plush late nineteenth-century hotel overlooking the Nusle valley, with the Belle Epoque theme continued throughout the lobby and rooms. Slightly overpriced for the location. 4550Kč

Vítkov Koněvova 114, Žižkov ✆242 453 003, ⊕novum -hotels.de; tram #10, #11, #16 or #29 to Biskupcova; map p.124. One of Prague's best deals, where the spotless, modern rooms tick all the boxes but cost a fraction of those in similar hotels closer to the sights. The location at a busy crossroads isn't great and the breakfast is disappointing, but who cares at these prices? Massive discounts when booked through popular hotel reservation websites. 2200Kč

Vyšehrad Krokova 6, Vyšehrad ✆241 408 455, ⊕pension-vysehrad.cz; tram #6, #7, #18, #22 or #24 to Ostrčilovo náměstí; map p.124. This five-room pension right next to the Vyšehrad fortress offers quiet, respectably furnished rooms with an almost rural Bohemian feel. The breakfast room sports antique furniture. 1500Kč

HOLEŠOVICE AND THE WESTERN SUBURBS

Admirál Hořejší nábřeží, Smíchov ✆257 321 302, ⊕admiral-botel.cz; metro Anděl; map p.149. The best of Prague's "botels" (floating hotels) is moored in Smíchov. Cabins are tiny but fittings are of fairly recent provenance and seasickness is impossible. 2400Kč

Anděl's Hotel Stroupežnického 21, Smíchov ✆296 889 688, ⊕viennahouse.com; metro Anděl; map p.149. This uber-cool 239-room mega-hotel can be found in the heart of gentrified Smíchov. The lobby exudes fashionable designer minimalism, as do the well-equipped chambers; the buffet breakfast is a feast. 5000Kč

TOP 5 LUXURY HOTELS

Alchymist Grand Hotel Koruna See p.167
Boscolo Prague See p.168
Savoy Prague See p.165
Pachtův Palace See p.168
Paříž See p.168

Art Hotel Praha Nad Královskou oborou 53, Bubeneč ✆233 101 331, ⊕arthotel.cz; tram #1, #5, #8, #12, #17, #25 or #26 to Sparta; map p.138. Clean-cut hotel, sprinkled with contemporary art throughout and located in a tranquil neighbourhood, close to Stromovka park and Výstaviště. 2250Kč

Crowne Plaza Koulova 15, Dejvice ✆296 537 111, ⊕crowneplaza.cz; tram 5# or #8 to Podbaba; map p.136. Prague's classic 1950s Stalinist wedding-cake hotel, with its dour socialist realist friezes and large helpings of marble, is now run by capitalist Austrians. This is definitely a business-traveller favourite, though it also attracts tourist groups. 3000Kč

Julián Elišky Peškové 11, Smíchov ✆257 311 144, ⊕julian.cz; tram #6, #9, #12 or #20 to Švandovo divadlo; map p.149. Large, luxurious hotel a short tram ride from Malá Strana. All the usual facilities, plus mini-kitchens and a nice lounge with a real fire. 2900Kč

Karel Mutěnínská 1119/23, Stodůlky ✆235 517 563, ⊕pension-karel.com; bus #142 to Nad Malou Ohradou; not on map. This tiny pension in the far western suburbs offers basic rooms and a no-frill breakfast, but the Ukrainian owners are very friendly, as is the house cat. 1000Kč

Klára Šternberkova 20, Holešovice ✆220 809 009, ⊕prague-accommodation.cz; tram #1, #12, #17, #24 or #25 to Veletržní palác; map p.138. Basic but clean and warm guesthouse just across the road from the Veletržní palác. Above-average breakfast for this price bracket and just a short tram ride to the city centre. 1400Kč

Petr Drtinova 17, Smíchov ✆257 314 068, ⊕hotelpetr .cz; #6, #9, #12 or #20 to Švandovo divadlo; map p.149. Situated on a leafy street at the foot of Petřín hill, close to Malá Strana, this place doesn't look that promising from the outside, but inside are modern, smart and very realistically priced rooms, and helpful staff. 2100Kč

Villa Milada V Šáreckém údolí 10, Dejvice ✆777 688 106, ⊕villamilada.cz; bus #107, #116, #147, #160, #340, #350, #355, #502 or #604 to v Podbabě; map p.136. For a completely different experience from the usual urban hotel, try this rural four-star gem in an Art Nouveau villa at the Vltava end of the Šárka valley. The fifteen rooms are exquisitely decorated in attractive William Morris-style wallpaper and similar fabrics and the location is as peaceful as things get in Prague. Recommended restaurant. 2800Kč

9

APARTMENTS

We've picked out a few of our favourite apartments in Prague below; it is also well worth checking out the options, all around the city, offered by a number of accommodation agencies (see box, p.165). Prices are quoted per night – and you can often rent for just a single night.

MALÁ STRANA

Nosticova Nosticova 1 ☎257 312 513, ⓦnosticova .com; tram #12, #20 or #22 to Malostranské náměstí; map p.56. Baroque house with ten beautifully restored apartments, sleeping between two and four, replete with antique furnishings, sumptuous bathrooms and small kitchens, on a peaceful square not far from Charles Bridge. Prices include breakfast. **6300Kč**

STARÉ MĚSTO

★Residence Řetězová Řetězová 9 ☎222 221 800, ⓦresidenceretezova.com; metro Staroměstská; map

p.70. Attractive apartments, named after the world's most illustrious cities, in all shapes and sizes, sleeping up to four people. Each has a kitchenette, wooden or stone floors, Gothic vaulting or wooden beams and repro furnishings. **3500Kč**

HOLEŠOVICE AND THE WESTERN SUBURBS

Anděl Apartments Nádražní 114, Smíchov ☎257 215 679, ⓦandelapartments.cz; metro Anděl; map p.149. Cheaply furnished mini-apartments with kitchenettes, sleeping up to four people, right opposite Anděl metro in the heart of Smíchov. Spotless and very quiet considering the location. **2650Kč**

HOSTELS

Prague now has tens of hostels, some contemporary design pads, others basic dorms for those who come to party hard and sleep little. Visit ⓦhostelworld.com or ⓦhostelbookers.com to see the whole range and read hostellers' reviews. A tiny handful of places give discounts to HI (Hostelling International; Whihostels.com) and can be booked via the HI's online booking service. All hostels offer free wi-fi, a kitchen and a range of add-on tours, including the ubiquitous pub crawl.

MALÁ STRANA & SMÍCHOV

Adam & Eve Zborovská 50 ☎733 286 804, ⓦadameva hostelprague.com; tram #9, #12, #15 or #20 to Švandovo divadlo; map p.56. Calm, virtually party-free zone in Smíchov with pretty decor, original double doors, kitchens and computers for guest use. Dorms **560Kč**, doubles **1700Kč**

★Charles Bridge Economic Mostecká 4 ☎257 213 420, ⓦcharlesbridgehostel.cz; tram #12, #17, #18, #20 or #22 to Malostranské náměstí; map p.56. As close to Charles Bridge as you can legally sleep, this backpacker hostel has a cool, better-than-average decor, lots of free stuff and tuned-in staff. Dorms **565Kč**

Santini Nerudova 14 ☎257 316 191, ⓦhostelsantini prague.com; tram #12, #17, #18, #20 or #22 to Malostranské náměstí; map p.56. Clean, well-kept hostel in the thick of the tourist action opposite the Romanian embassy in Malá Strana. Possibly the only hostel in the world with authentic Renaissance cassette ceilings, and some of the furniture is antique. Dorms **375Kč**, doubles **1350Kč**

STARÉ MĚSTO

Ritchie's Karlova 9 & 13 ☎222 221 229, ⓦritchies hostel.cz; metro Staroměstská; map p.70. In the midst of the human torrent that is Karlova, this Old Town hostel has no in-house laundry or cooking facilities, but it's clean, with accommodation ranging from en-suite doubles to twelve-bed dorms. Dorms **380Kč**, doubles **1850Kč**

Travellers Hostel Dlouhá 33 ☎777 738 608, ⓦtravellers.cz; metro Náměstí Republiky; map p.70. This very central party hostel situated above the *Roxy* nightclub has been around for years. It's the main booking office for a network of hostels – if there's not enough room here, staff will find you a bed in one of their other central branches. Dorms **540Kč**, doubles **1600Kč**

Týn Týnská 19 ☎224 808 301, ⓦhostelpraguetyn.com; metro Náměstí Republiky; map p.70. Prague's most central hostel is a funky, basic affair, located in a quiet courtyard within staggering distance of Old Town Square. Dorms **375Kč**, doubles **1300Kč**

NOVÉ MĚSTO

MadHouse Spálená 39 ☎222 240 009, ⓦthemadhouse prague.com; metro Můstek; map p.102. The name rather gives the game away at this New Town hostel with its funky hand-painted murals, group dinners and well-equipped kitchen. If party hostels are not your thing, go elsewhere. Dorms **610Kč**

★Miss Sophie's Melounová 3 ☎246 032 621, ⓦmiss -sophies.com; metro I.P. Pavlova; map p.102. A central, slick designer hostel offering everything from cheap dorm beds to fully equipped apartments – certainly not the place for anyone seeking rough-and-ready backpacker digs. The all-you-can-eat breakfast is 150Kč extra. Dorms **610Kč**, doubles **2300Kč**

Rosemary Růžová 5 ☎222 211 124, ⓦpraguecity hostel.cz; metro Můstek or Hlavní nádraží; map p.102. Clean, modern hostel a short walk from the main train station. Three- to twelve-bed mixed dorms, plus doubles with or without en-suite bathrooms. Communal kitchen and free internet. Dorms 370Kč, doubles 1300Kč

VYŠEHRAD AND THE EASTERN SUBURBS

Clown and Bard Bořivojova 102, Žižkov ☎222 716 453, ⓦclownandbard.com; tram #5, #9, #26 or #29 to Husinecká; map p.124. Žižkov hostel that attracts backpackers who like to party. Still, it's clean, undeniably cheap, stages events and has laundry facilities. Breakfast (veggie) costs extra. Dorms 350Kč, doubles 1200Kč

Czech Inn Francouzská 76, Vinohrady ☎267 267 612, ⓦczech-inn.com; tram #4 or #22 to Krymská; map p.124. Upbeat, designer hostel that feels and looks like a hotel, with friendly and helpful staff. The 36-bed cellar dorm is the biggest in the Czech Republic. Dorms 385Kč, doubles 2000Kč

Hostel One Cimburkova 8 ☎222 221 423, ⓦdistrict hostel1.com; metro Hlavní nádraží; map p.124. Part of a European chain, this great chill-out hostel recently moved to a location in Žižkov. Good facilities and a party vibe. Dorms 390Kč, doubles 1300Kč

HOLEŠOVICE AND THE WESTERN SUBURBS

★ **Sir Toby's Hostel** Dělnická 24, Holešovice ☎246 032 611, ⓦsirtobys.com; tram #1, #24 or #25 to Dělnická; map p.138. Out in Holešovice, but among the most welcoming, characterful and efficiently run hostels in the city, just a tram ride away from the centre. Dorms 400Kč, doubles 2200Kč

CAMPSITES

Džbán Nad lávkou 5, Vokovice ☎725 956 457, ⓦcampdzban.eu; tram #2, #20 or #26 to Nad Džbánem; 15min from the tram stop and 4km west of the centre, near the Šárka valley; map p.136. Large field with tent pitches, bungalows, shop, restaurant, tennis courts, lake swimming and gym. Closed Oct–April. Tents 140Kč, plus each adult 130Kč

Herzog Trojská 161, Troja ☎283 850 472, ⓦcamp herzog.cz; bus #112 from metro Nádraží Holešovice to "Kazanka" stop; map p.138. Good location, one of several along the road to Troja chateau, situated in a large, shady back garden. Tents 105Kč, plus each adult 80Kč

Kotva U ledáren 55, Braník ☎244 461 712, ⓦkotva camp.cz; tram #3 or #17 to Nádraží Braník; map p.136. The oldest, and nicest, site, with a riverside location just 20min by tram south of the city. Hostel and caravan accommodation is available too. Tents 138Kč, plus each adult 153Kč

Sokol Troja Trojská 171a, Troja ☎233 542 908, ⓦcamp-sokol-troja.cz; bus #112 from metro Nádraží Holešovice to Čechova škola; map p.138. Larger than _Herzog_ and slightly further away from the Troja chateau and zoo, but well organized, with kitchen, laundry and restaurant on site. Tents 150Kč, plus each adult 150Kč

GRAND CAFÉ ORIENT

Cafés and restaurants

Little has changed on the traditional Czech food front since the 1989 Revolution and anyone who tries to convince you otherwise should be directed without delay to the nearest restaurant and its meat-and-dumpling menu. That's not to say traditional Czech food isn't tasty – on the contrary, dishes using ingredients plucked, picked and hunted from the forests of Bohemia can often be top notch and delicious fresh river fish are a particular speciality. Naturally Prague, as the capital, has the widest variety of places to eat in the country – look hard enough and you can find everything from Afghan to sushi via Vietnamese and Italian food. Should you wish, you could spend an entire week eating out in the city and never go near a dollop of bacon-flecked sauerkraut or a potato dumpling – many do.

CZECH CUISINE

Traditional Czech cuisine has a predilection for pork, gravy, dumplings and pickled cabbage and an aversion to fresh vegetables (other than potatoes) and salads. It may never be going to top the league table of the world's great cuisines, but it is generally tasty and there are several dishes worth looking out for.

Czechs aren't big on starters, with the exception of **soup** (*polévka*), one of the country's culinary strong points. Main dishes are overwhelmingly based on **meat** (*maso*), usually pork (*vepřové*), sometimes beef (*hovězí*). Reading menus, the difficulty lies in decoding names such as *klášterní tajemství* (literally "mystery of the monastery", but actually just a fillet of beef) or even a common dish like *Moravský vrabec* (literally "Moravian sparrow", but actually just roast pork). **Fish** (*ryby*) might be listed with chicken (*drůbez*) and other fowl such as duck (*kachna*). River trout (*pstruh*) and carp (*kapr*) – the traditional dish at Christmas – are the cheapest and most widely available, and are usually served, grilled or roasted, in delicious buttery sauces or breadcrumbs. **Side dishes** (*přílohy*) are usually potatoes (*brambory*), though with meat dishes you'll more often be served **dumplings** (*knedlíky*), one of the mainstays of Bohemian cooking and nothing like English dumplings, more like a heavy white bread. The ubiquitous *obloha* is the Czech version of a **salad**: a bit of tomato, cucumber and lettuce, or cabbage (*zelí*), often swimming in a slightly sweet, watery dressing.

With the exception of *palačinky* (pancakes), filled with chocolate or fruit and cream, Czechs don't go in for **desserts** (*moučníky*). They prefer to eat their ice cream on the street and their cakes in the cafés or cake shops.

At the beginning of the twentieth century, Prague boasted a **café society** to rival that in Vienna or Paris. Communism put paid to that sort of bourgeois nonsense, but happily a handful of grand Habsburg-era haunts have survived – or been resurrected – and have been joined by a whole range of new cafés from designer coffeehouses to rarefied teahouses. Like the Austrians who once ruled over them, the Czechs have a terminally sweet tooth, and the more traditional cafés (*cukrárna*) offer a wide array of cakes and pastries; others offer the familiar gamut of snacks, from soup and sandwiches to rolls and wraps. **Coffee**, once drunk at a *kavárna* (coffeehouse) but now more often at a café, generally attempts to follow the Italian model, but is very hit and miss. **Tea** is drunk weak and without milk, although you'll usually be given a glass of boiling water and a tea bag so you can do your own thing – for milk, say "s mlékem".

ESSENTIALS

Menus Most places now have a (badly translated) English menu. There is a primer for deciphering Czech menus in the Language section of this Guide (see p.248).

Costs and tips Once a real bargain, prices in the city's restaurants are now at or above the EU average due to the strength of the Czech crown and increases in overheads, but the quality of the dining experience, in particular the service, sometimes still has some catching up to do. As in most big tourist cities, places in the most popular areas tend to be aggressively overpriced. Watch out for extras, too: you will often be charged a cover charge for bread, music and for everything you touch, including the stale almonds you thought were courtesy of the house. Venture into the back-streets and you're more likely to find better service, better value and perhaps even better food. Another option is to head for a pub (see p.186), where you can be sure of cheaper, more typical, Czech dishes. When tipping, in restaurants and pubs, simply round the bill up to the nearest 50Kč or 100Kč.

Smoking In 2017 the Czech Republic became the virtually the last country in Europe to introduce a complete smoking ban in pubs, cafés and restaurants. In pubs in particular it will be interesting to see how strictly this is enforced.

HRADČANY

CAFÉS

Kavárna Nový Svet Nový Svět 2 ☎ 242 430 700, ⓦ kavarna.novysvet.net; tram #22 or #23 to Pohořelec; map p.34. Tiny little coffee stop in the delightful Nový Svět district, serving brews, ice cream, snacks and some stronger tipples. Tues–Sun 11am–7pm.

Malý Buddha Úvoz 46; tram #22 or #23 to Pohořelec; map p.34. This teahouse, draped in prayer flags and with a Buddhist altar in one corner, is a tranquil hideout very near Prague Castle. The menu offers mostly vegetarian Vietnamese snacks. Tues–Sun noon–10pm.

10

TOP 5 FINE DINING

Bellevue See p.178
La Dégustation Bohême Bourgeoise
See p.178
Pálffy Palác See p.177
Svatá Klára See p.185
Villa Richter See below

RESTAURANTS

Host Loretánská 15 ☎702 205 108, ⊛hostrestaurant
.cz; tram #22 or #23 to Pohořelec; map p.34. Located
down an inconspicuous flight of steps off Loretánská, this
well-hidden restaurant has stupendous views across Malá
Strana from its glassed front. Expect a mix of Czech and
safe-bet international mains (350–500Kč) and a 175Kč
lunch menu. Mon–Sat 11.30am–10pm, Sun to 9pm.

U císařů (The Emperors) Loretánská 5 ☎ 220 518 484,
⊛ucisaru.cz; tram #22 or #23 to Pohořelec; map p.34.
Upmarket medieval tavern serving a hearty menu of duck,
venison and *guláš* (mains 350–600Kč) as well as Krušovice
in 1L *tupláky* (steins). Admire the Gothic vaulting from your
high-backed leather chair. Daily 10am–midnight.

U ševce Matouše (The Cobbler Matouš) Loretánské
náměstí 4 ☎220 514 536, ⊛usevcematouse.cz; tram
#22 or #23 to Pohořelec; map p.34. Relatively cheap
meat dishes (220–450 Kč) are the speciality at this former
cobbler's, which is one of the few half-decent places to eat
in the castle district – at least Brangelina thought so when
they dined here. Daily 11am–11pm.

Villa Richter Staré zámecké schody 6 ☎702 205 108,
⊛villarichter.cz; metro Malostranská; map p.34. Set amid
the castle vineyards, just outside the Black Tower (Černá věž),
this place has three separate dining spaces, one on top of
the other: the *Piano Nobile* serves classy international mains
(180–500Kč); below, the *Piano Terra* specializes in Italian food
(200–400Kč); and *Panorama Pergola* is the perfect place to
sample Czech wines and soak in the view. Daily 11am–11pm.

MALÁ STRANA

CAFÉS

Bohemia Bagel Lázeňská 19 ☎ 257 218 192, ⊛bohemia
bagel.cz; tram #12, #20 or #22 to Malostranské náměstí;
map p.56. Malá Strana branch, near Charles Bridge, one
of the successful self-service chain (and expat favourite), serving
filled bagels, all-day breakfasts, soup and chilli. Mon–Fri
7.30am–6pm, Sat to 7pm.

★ Café Savoy Vítězná 5 ☎257 311 562, ⊛ambi.cz;
tram #12, #15, #20, #22 or #23 to Újezd; map p.56.
The *Savoy* is a classic, L-shaped Habsburg-era café from
1893 with a superb, neo-Renaissance ceiling; you can just
have a coffee or a snack if you want, but it doubles as a very
good restaurant, with mains (including lots of seafood)
starting at 400Kč. Mon–Fri 8am–10.30pm, Sat & Sun
9am–10.30pm.

Cukrkávalimonáda Lázeňská 7 ☎257 225 396,
⊛cukrkavalimonada.com; tram #12, #20 or #22 to
Malostranské náměstí; map p.56. Very professional and
busy café, serving good brasserie-style dishes, as well as
coffee and croissants, with tables overlooking the church
of Panna Maria pod řetězem. Daily 9am–7pm.

U knoflíčků U Lanové Dráhy 1 ☎777 235 139,
⊛uknoflicku.cz; tram #12, #15, , #20, #22 or #23 to
Hellichova; map p.56. This simple *cukrárna* offers the full
range of ice cream, cakes, coffee and traditional *chlebíčky*
(open sandwiches) at almost countryside prices and is a
great place to put together a 100Kč lunch. No euros and
no cards accepted. Mon–Fri 9am–6.30pm, Sat & Sun
10am–6.30pm.

RESTAURANTS

Bar Bar Všehrdova 17 ☎257 312 246, ⊛bar-bar.cz;
tram #15, #20, #22or #23 to Újezd; map p.56.
Unpretentious cellar restaurant that specializes in pastas,
risottos and Czech meat and fish dishes (around 200Kč).
Mon–Sat 11am–11pm, Sun noon–10pm.

★ Café de Paris Velkopřevorské náměstí 4 ☎603 160
718, ⊛cafedeparis.cz; tram #12, #15, #20, #22 or #23
to Hellichova; map p.56. This cosy, family-run restaurant
is based on the famous *Café de Paris* in Geneva. The
signature dish on the short menu is beef entrecôte (379Kč)
in a creamy secret-recipe sauce (there's a tofu version
available, too). Daily 11.30am–midnight.

Czech Slovak Újezd 20 ☎257 312 523, ⊛czechslovak
.cz; tram #12, #15, #20, #22 or #23 to Újezd; map p.56.
Experience an upmarket return to the halcyon days of
Czechoslovak cuisine with mains (250–350Kč) including
dishes from across the former Czechoslovakia, such as
Slovak *halušky* (gnocchi) and Bohemian *myslivecký guláš*
– hunter's goulash. The hotel restaurant's modern
white and black decor is uplit in neon purple. Daily
noon–11.30pm.

Hergetová cihelna Cihelná 2b ☎296 826 103,
⊛kampagroup.com; metro Malostranská; map p.56.
Slick, smart restaurant with some of the best views of
Charles Bridge, serving Greenland shrimp starters, tasty
pasta and risotto, and the odd traditional Czech dish.
Mains 250–500Kč. Daily noon–1am.

Luka Lu Újezd 33 ☎257 212388, ⊛lukalu.cz; tram #12,
#15, #20, #22 or #23 to Hellichova; map p.56. This Serb
restaurant specializing in grilled Balkan meat dishes (200–
400Kč) is pitching for the most colourful Prague restaurant
award: its knick-knack- and art-filled walls compete with
floorboards, ceiling and various fittings painted in the
brightest of hues. The courtyard is a particularly pleasant
place to dine. Daily 11am–midnight.

Nebozízek (Little Auger) Petřínské sady 14 ☎ 257 515 329, ⓦ nebozizek.cz; Petřín funicular; map p.56. The *Nebozízek* is situated at the halfway stop on the Petřín funicular, so the view is pretty special. There's an outdoor terrace and a traditional Czech menu featuring game dishes from around 200Kč a shot. Daily 11am–11pm.

Noi Újezd 19 ☎ 257 311 411, ⓦ noirestaurant.cz; tram #12, #15, #20, #22 or #23 to Hellichova; map p.56. This stylish, atmospheric restaurant plates up some of the tastiest, spiciest Thai food in Prague (mains 200–300Kč), as well as its famous 600-calorie lunch. There's a lovely courtyard patio round the back. Daily 11am–1am.

Pálffy palác Valdštejnská 14 ☎ 257 530 522, ⓦ palffy .cz; metro Malostranská; map p.56. The restaurant occupies a grand candlelit room on the first floor of an old Baroque palace, and features a wonderful outdoor terrace from where you can survey the red rooftops of Malá Strana. The international menu is renowned for its game and river fish (mains 500–700Kč). Daily 11am–11pm.

U krále Brabantského Thunovská 15 ☎ 257 217 032, ⓦ krcmabrabant.cz; tram #12, #20 or #22 to Malostranské náměstí; map p.56. This rough, medieval tavern claims to be Prague's oldest, banging down platters of meat and jugs of ale since 1375. The guest list might also

be taken with a pinch of sůl, with everyone from King Václav IV to Jaroslav Hášek said to have eaten here. From the look of the façade you'd think there had been a fire inside recently – this is due to the fire shows that take place here in the evenings. Mon 11am–10pm, Tues–Thurs & Sun 11am–11pm, Fri & Sat 11am–midnight.

U sedmi Švábů (The Seven Swabians) Janský vršek 14 ☎ 257 531 455, ⓦ 7svabu.cz; tram #12, #20 or #22 to Malostranské náměstí; map p.56. Named after the Grimm brothers' tale, this torch-lit tavern serves authentically medieval Czech food (165–495Kč) – which theoretically means no potatoes or tomatoes. Fri and Sat nights are the times to be here when the restaurant puts on a fire-breathing, sword-swallowing mini-spectacular for diners. Daily 11am–11pm.

Vegan's Restaurant Nerudova 36 ☎ 735 171 313, ⓦ vegansprague.cz; tram #12, #20 or #22 to Malostranské náměstí; map p.56. A vegan "old Bohemian feast" sounds like an impossible culinary pairing, but the mix of buckwheat, millet, barley, mushrooms and vegetables is tasty and filling. Other meat-free options (175–230Kč) include curries, veggie burgers and fruit dumplings, all served in a simple first-floor dining room under heavy beams. Daily 11.30am–9.30pm.

10

STARÉ MĚSTO

CAFÉS

Au Gourmand Dlouhá 10 ☎ 222 329 060, ⓦ augourmand .cz; metro Náměstí Republiky; map p.70. This beautifully tiled and styled French boulangerie, patisserie and *traiteur*, selling wickedly delicious pastries, is one of the capital's most attractive places to eat. Everything is available for takeaway. Mon–Fri 8am–7pm, Sat 8.30am–7pm, Sun 9am–7pm.

Bakeshop Praha Kozí 1 ☎ 222 316 823, ⓦ bakeshop .cz; metro Náměstí Republiky; map p.70. Three days into a trip to central Europe and already pining for a cupcake or bucket of coffee? Then head to this expat bakery in the very heart of the Old Town. Daily 7am–9pm.

★**Beas** Týnská 19 ☎ 777 165 478, ⓦ beas-dhaba.cz; metro Malostranská/Náměstí Republiky; map p.70. Themeless and utilitarian veggie self-service café through the courtyard off Týnská, offering simple dishes of lentils, chickpeas, heatless curry and rice served on metal canteen trays. You pay by weight – 21.90Kč/100g. Mon–Fri 11am–8pm, Sat noon–8pm, Sun 11am–6pm.

Chez Marcel Haštalská 12 ☎ 222 315 676, ⓦ chez marcel.cz; metro Náměstí Republiky; map p.70. This effortlessly chic French café-bistro is a good place to grab a coffee and a *tarte tatin*, read a French magazine or enjoy some pricey brasserie staples (around 400Kč). Daily 11.30am–11pm.

Country Life Melantrichova 15 ☎ 224 213 366, ⓦ countrylife.cz; metro Můstek; map p.70. Health- and nutrient-obsessed self-service café behind the health-food

shop of the same name: pile up your plate with couscous, lentils, chutney, basmati and salad and pay by weight. There's another branch at Jungmannova 1, Nové Mesto (Mon–Fri only). Mon–Thurs 10.30am–-7.30pm, Fri 10.30am–6pm, Sun noon–6pm.

Crème de la Crème Husova 12 ☎ 732 330 519, ⓦ cremecreme.cz; metro Staroměstská; map p.70. Multinational *gelateria* that serves some of the best ice cream in Prague, containing real fruit and nothing it shouldn't. Mon–Thurs noon–9pm, Fri noon–10pm, Sat 11am–10pm, Sun 11am–9pm.

Den Noc Templová 7 ☎ 775 697 733, ⓦ dennoc.cz; metro Náměstí Republiky; map p.70. Tiny café tucked away in the tourist-free backstreets near the church of St Jakub, serving coffee, homemade cakes and pancakes by day, and Czech wines and tapas by night – hence the name meaning "day night". Tues–Sun 8.30am–3pm; hours vary in the evenings.

Érra Konviktská 11 ☎ 273 136 112, ⓦ cafeerra.cz; metro Národní třída; map p.70. Vaulted cellar café in the

> ### TOP 5 CHEAP EATS
> **Beas** See above
> **Blatouch** See p.184
> **Havelská Koruna** See p.178
> **U knoflíčků** See opposite
> **Velryba** See p.183

TOP 5 BREAKFASTS

Many Czechs get up so early in the morning (often around 6am) that they don't have time to start the day with anything more than a quick cup of coffee. As a result, the whole concept of **breakfast** (*snídaně*) is quite alien for some. Most hotels serve the "continental" basics of tea, coffee, rolls and cold cheese and meat, and there are a few nice cafés where you can pick up a morning snack.

Bakeshop Praha See p.177
Café Savoy See p.176
Cukrávalimonáda See p.176

Louvre See p.183
Obecní dům See p.182

10

backstreets off Betlémské náměstí that's popular with a fashionable mixed straight/gay crowd. Tasty salads and snacks. Daily 11am–midnight.

★ **Grand Café Orient** Ovocný trh 19 ☎ 224 224 240, ⓦ grandcafeorient.cz; metro Náměstí Republiky; map p.70. Relive the swish days of early twentieth-century Prague at this recreated Cubist café from 1911 on the first floor of the House at the Black Madonna (see p.84). The interior, cutlery and views rather outshine the food, so just order a coffee and ogle at your leisure. Mon–Fri 9am–10pm, Sat & Sun 10am–10pm.

★ **Havelská Koruna** Havelská 21 ☎ 224 239 331, ⓦ havelska-koruna.cz; metro Můstek; map p.70. Popular no-frills, self-service Czech *jídelna* (self-service canteen) with some utilitarian bench seating that doesn't allow you to get comfortable. The countryside-style menu runs the gamut of Czech comfort food classics such as *sekaná*, goulash and fruit dumplings, all for under 80Kč; you pay at the exit so don't lose that slip you were given when you entered. Not for the faint-hearted. Daily 10am–8pm.

Kampus Náprstkova 10 ☎ 775 755 143, ⓦ cafekampus .cz; metro Staroměstská; map p.70. Classic, cheap, studenty Czech café, serving good coffee and simple mains for around 100Kč, plus lots of books and newspapers to browse. Mon–Fri 10am–1am, Sat noon–1am, Sun noon–11pm.

Literární kavárna Řetězová 10 ☎ 222 220 681; metro Staroměstská; map p.70. Relaxed, low-lit vaulted café attached to a bookshop in the centre of the Old Town, offering draught beers, cheap food and occasional arty events. Mon–Fri 11am–11pm, Sat & Sun 2–11pm.

Montmartre Řetězová 7 ☎ 602 277 210; metro Staroměstská; map p.70. A classic little barrel-vaulted café, the "*Montík*" was once a famous First Republic dance and cabaret venue, frequented by the likes of Werfel, Jesenská and Hašek. With *echt*-Czech huffy service it's now well off the tourist trail. Mon–Fri 10am–midnight, Sat & Sun 2pm–midnight.

Siva Masná 8 ☎ 222 315 983, ⓦ siva.cajiky.cz; metro Náměstí Republiky; map p.70. A fair stab at a teahouse cellar-den with hookah pipes, scatter cushions, passable Middle Eastern-style coffee and snacks, plus Chinese teas

and Czech white wine. Mon–Fri noon–11.30pm, Sat 2–11.30pm, Sun 2–10pm.

RESTAURANTS

Bellevue Smetanovo nábřeží 18 ☎ 222 221 443, ⓦ bellevuerestaurant.cz; metro Národní třída; map p.70. The view of Charles Bridge and the Hrad is outstanding, the setting is very formal and the international cuisine is imaginative – the only drawbacks are that main courses are 500–1000Kč and you need to book ahead. Daily noon–3pm & 5.30–11pm.

Divinis Týnská 21 ☎ 222 325 440, ⓦ divinis.cz; metro Staroměstská; map p.70. Stylish Italian restaurant where the beautifully presented dishes are exceptionally well prepared but expensive for this type of food (mains around 500Kč). Mon–Fri noon–3pm & 6pm–midnight, Sat 6pm–midnight.

Kabul Krocínova 5 ☎ 224 282 509, ⓦ kabulrestaurant .cz; metro Národní třída; map p.70. This Afghan restaurant is the last to remain open in the Czech capital. Simple grilled and stewed meat dishes, meat-filled dumplings and a lot of vegetarian dishes (mains 90–300Kč) fill the tasty menu here, and somewhat surprisingly there's a full drinks list. Daily 11am–11pm.

La Dégustation Bohême Bourgeoise Haštalská 18 ☎ 222 311 234, ⓦ ladegustation.cz; metro Náměstí Republiky; map p.70. One of Prague's most upmarket restaurants; make sure you're hungry before you make a reservation and choose between three Michelin-starred tasting menus (2500–3500Kč), each consisting of up to eleven courses, all inspired by Czech cuisine. Daily 6pm–midnight.

La Finestra Platnéřská 13 ☎ 222 325 325, ⓦ lafinestra .cz; metro Staroměstská; map p.70. Congenial Italian restaurant, all bare bricks and wooden floors, serving well-crafted traditional dishes (around 500Kč) using fresh seasonal produce. Prices are more Milan than Eastern Europe. Mon–Sat noon–11pm, Sun noon–10pm.

★ **Lehká hlava** Boršov 2 ☎ 222 220 665, ⓦ lehkahlava .cz; metro Národní třída; map p.70. Prague's best vegetarian restaurant has several dining spaces sporting zen-luxe decor. Realistically priced mains (around 225Kč) include meat-free quesadillas, pastas, curries, burgers and roast vegetables. Madly popular, so booking ahead is essential. Mon–Fri 11.30am–11.30pm, Sat & Sun noon–11.30pm.

★ **Lokál** Dlouhá 33 ☎ 222 316 265, ⓦ ambi.cz; metro Náměstí Republiky; map p.70. Vast corridor of a restaurant, smartly decked out in minimalist utilitarian decor and with waiters in formal long white aprons. They serve traditional – but excellent – Czech pub food for between 100Kč and 270Kč, plus various Urquell beers. All dishes are available as takeaways. Mon–Sat 11am–1am, Sun noon–midnight.

Maitrea Týnská ulička 6 ☎ 222 711 631, ⓦ restaurace-maitrea.cz; metro Náměstí Republiky; map p.70. The sister restaurant of *Lehká hlava* (see opposite) is a larger, more luxurious affair, a den of stylish Buddhist calm serving global vegetarian dishes (mains around 225Kč). However, it lacks the vibe of the mother ship and portions here are slightly miserly. Mon–Fri 11.30am–11.30pm, Sat & Sun noon–11.30pm.

Mincovna Staroměstské náměstí 7 ☎ 727 955 669, ⓦ restauracemincovna.cz; metro Staroměstská; map p.70. If you must do your dining on the Old Town Square, this is the least touristy, most reasonably priced and most understatedly Czech restaurant amid the overpriced pizza and beer. Mains such as sirloin in cream sauce and Highlands Region trout land on your table for around 300Kč a plateful. Daily 11am–midnight.

Mlýnec Novotného lávka 9 ☎ 277 000 777, ⓦ mlynec.cz; metro Staroměstská; map p.70. A pricey place (which has garnered the odd Michelin star in the past) with a fabulous riverside terrace overlooking Charles Bridge and the Hrad. Imaginative, international dishes are interspersed with the odd Czech option prepared with unfamiliar ingredients. Mains 500–700Kč. Daily noon–3pm & 5.30–11pm.

Naše Maso Dlouhá 39 T 222 311 378, ⓦ nasemaso .ambi.cz; metro Náměstí Republiky; map p.70. Part of the 1930s Gurmet Pasáž Dlouhá complex, this madly popular hipster butchery and carnivore feasting spot has just six seats (takeaway available), meaning long queues at mealtimes for the superb salamis, meatloaf, hamburgers and sausages. Mains 59–150Kč. Mon–Sat 8.30am–10pm.

Rybárna Masná 1 ☎ 730 870 086, ⓦ bluefjord.cz; metro Náměstí Republiky; map p.70. Offering a guarantee that your order was swimming/crawling in the North Sea/Mediterranean less than 24 hours before it arrived on your plate, this great fishmonger/café serves possibly the freshest seafood in town. Choose your critter and have it cooked as you like for 55Kč extra. Daily 10am–10pm.

Stoleti Karoliny Světlé 21 ☎ 222 220 008, ⓦ stoleti.cz; metro Národní třída; map p.70. Inventive Czech cuisine named after artists, writers, actors and opera singers served in an understatedly stylish dining room with a terracotta floor and basic timber tables. Mains around 250Kč. Daily 11.30am–11.30pm.

U Provaznice Provaznická 3 ☎ 224 232 528, ⓦ uprovaznice.cz; metro Můstek; map p.70. Concealed

10

VEGETARIAN PRAGUE

Czech meat consumption remains high, and **vegetarianism** is still a minority, if increasingly popular, choice. However, vegetarian visitors should have no problem eating well in Prague – there are some excellent veggie restaurants, plenty of pizzerias and a variety of expat places that always have one or two meat-free options.

Even in traditional Czech joints, most menus have a section called **bezmasá jídla** (literally "meals without meat"). Don't take this too literally, though, for it simply means the main ingredient is not dead animal; dishes like *omeleta se šunkou* (ham omelette) still appear in this section. The staple of Czech vegetarianism is **smažený sýr**, a slab of cheese deep-fried in breadcrumbs and served with tartar sauce (*tartarská omačka*) – beware, though, as it sometimes comes with a concealed slice of ham wedged in there. Other types of cheese can also be deep-fried, as can other vegetables: *smažené žampiony* (mushrooms) and *smažený květák* (cauliflower). Emergency veggie standbys, which most Czech pubs will knock up for you without too much fuss, include **knedlíky s vejci** (dumplings and scrambled egg) or **omeleta s hráškem** (pea omelette).

Veggie phrases to remember are "*jsem vegetarián/vegetariánka. Máte něco bez masa?*" (I'm a vegetarian. Is there anything without meat?) For emphasis, you could add "*nejím ani maso ani rybu*" (I don't eat meat or fish).

TOP VEGETARIAN RESTAURANTS

Beas See p.177
Country Life See p.177
Góvinda See p.182
Lehká hlava See opposite

Maitrea See above
Malý Buddha See p.175
Vegan's Restaurant See p.177

10

GURMET PASÁŽ DLOUHÁ

Foodies and street food fans should head to this newly renovated, Functionalist *pasáž* at the eastern end of Dlouhá to experience the **Gurmet Pasáž Dlouhá** (🌐gurmetpasazdlouha.eu), one of the city's newest feeding experiences. So far, ten hip food producers have moved into the arcade selling everything from artisan salamis, sushi, raw food snacks, chocolate creations, fish and cheese. More are expected to take up the remaining shops, creating one of Prague's funkiest food venues.

down a backstreet behind Můstek metro station, this tiled and timbered, virtually tourist-free Czech pub/restaurant plates up no-nonsense Czech favourites at time-warped prices. Daily 11am–midnight.

JOSEFOV

CAFÉS

★**Café 80s** V Kolkovně 6 ☎725 991 924, 🌐cafe80.cz; metro Staroměstská; map p.92. Fun, 1980s-themed café and club with Rubik's Cube sugar sachet holders, *Smash Hits* pop posters, ET riding up the stairs and tables that look like vinyl records. Nostalgic disco nights Wed–Sat. Daily 10.30am–2am.

Mezi řádky Palachovo náměstí 2; metro Staroměstská; map p.92. For a bit of Czech authenticity, join students and professors of Charles University's Humanities Faculty (Filozofická fakulta) at the no-frills uni café deep within the faculty building. Cheap Czech staples (meatloaf, salads drowning in mayonnaise, open sandwiches) plus beer and wine. To find it, enter the building and turn immediately to your right. Mon–Fri 8am–7pm.

Nostress Dušní 10 ☎222 317 007, 🌐nostress.cz; metro Náměstí Republiky; map p.92. This recently revamped café is even more colourful than before with lots of bright cushion space, indoor trees and a resident zebra. Claims to have had Prague's best coffee for two decades – test this alternative fact on a break between synagogues. Mon–Fri 8.30am–midnight, Sat 10am–midnight, Sun 10am–11am.

Rudolfinum Alšovo nábřeží 12 ☎703 181 182, 🌐rudolfinumcafe.cz; metro Staroměstská; map p.92. Splendidly grand nineteenth-century café on the first floor of the Rudolfinum, serving drinks and snacks amid potted palms. It's worth seeing even if you're not thirsty – you don't have to visit the gallery to get in. Tues–Sun 11am–11pm.

RESTAURANTS

Dinitz Bílková 12 ☎222 244 000, 🌐dinitz.cz; metro Staroměstská; map p.92. Situated behind the Spanish synagogue, this kosher restaurant offers a real mixed bag of Middle Eastern snacks, sandwiches, pasta, salads and steaks for firmly Western European prices. Mains 200–500Kč. Mon–Thurs & Sun 11.30am–10.30pm, Fri 11.30am–5pm.

★**James Dean** V Kolkovně 1 ☎606 979 797, 🌐james dean.cz; metro Staroměstská; map p.92. This fun retro American diner has an authentic-looking red-and-white leather interior, monster ketchup and mustard bottles, whirring ceiling fans and waitresses dressed for the part. Portions of burgers and fries are Cadillac sized and the soundtrack is aptly twangy. Mains 200–350Kč. Daily 8am–11pm.

King Solomon Široká 8 ☎224 818 752, 🌐kosher.cz; metro Staroměstská; map p.92. Sophisticated kosher restaurant that serves big helpings of international dishes and traditional Jewish specialities: a three-course set menu (with a beer) costs around 550Kč, but mains are pricey (500–1000Kč). Michelle Obama famously ate here in 2009. Sun–Thurs noon–11pm.

Kolonial Široká 6 ☎224 818 322, 🌐kolonialpub.cz; metro Staroměstská; map p.92. You'll spot this place by the big penny-farthings in the window. The cycling theme continues inside with old enamel bike adverts and bar stools made from saddles. The menu is a mixed pannier, featuring everything from roast pork knee to Caesar salad (mains 200–400Kč). Daily 11am–midnight.

Les Moules Pařížská 19 ☎222 315 022, 🌐lesmoules.cz; metro Staroměstská; map p.92. A wood-panelled Belgian brasserie that flies in fresh mussels and serves them (333Kč/900g) with French fries and Belgian beers. Daily 11.30am–midnight.

Pizzeria Rugantino Dušní 4 ☎222 318 172, 🌐rugantino.cz; metro Staroměstská; map p.92. This authentic Italian (as opposed to Balkan) pizzeria, just off Dlouhá, is the genuine article: an oak-fired oven, gargantuan thin bases and numerous toppings to choose from (110–225Kč), plus Serie A gabbling away on the TV. Mon–Fri 11am–11pm, Sat & Sun noon–11pm.

U Golema Maiselova 8 ☎222 328 165, 🌐restaurantu golema.cz; metro Staroměstská; map p.92. The Golem himself greets diners at this pleasant restaurant in the heart of the Josefov sightseeing zone. The filling meat-themed menu consists mainly of heavy Czech food with a few French elements tossed into the mix (mains 200–400Kč). Daily 10am–11.30pm.

CLOCKWISE FROM TOP *AU GOURMAND* (P.177); *CAFÉ SAVOY* (P.176); *BAKESHOP* PRAHA (P.177) >

NORTHERN NOVÉ MĚSTO AND VÁCLAVSKÉ NÁMĚSTÍ

CAFÉS

Dhaba Beas Na poříčí 26 ☎725 963 536, ⓦbeas-dhaba.cz; metro Náměstí Republiky/Florenc; map p.102. One of a rash of minimalist Indian vegetarian self-service canteens to have opened in Prague in the last decade, this is a very modern affair in a courtyard at the foot of an office block. The food – all pineapple fritters, chickpeas and basmati rice – costs 20.90Kč/100g, so the bill can add up quicker than you think. Mon–Fri 11am–9pm, Sat noon–8pm, Sun noon–6pm.

Dobrá čajovna Václavské náměstí 14 ☎224 231 480; metro Můstek/Muzeum; map p.102. Mellow, rarefied teahouse, with an astonishing variety of teas (and a few Middle Eastern snacks) down an alleyway off Wenceslas Square. Mon–Fri 10am–9.30pm, Sat & Sun 2–9.30pm.

Góvinda Soukenická 27 ☎728 063 747, ⓦgovinda.cz; metro Náměstí Republiky; map p.102. Hare Krishna (Haré Kršna in Czech) restaurant with very basic decor, serving organic Indian veggie dishes for a touch over 100Kč. Mon–Fri 11am–6pm, Sat noon–4pm.

Imperial Na poříčí 15 ☎246 011 440, ⓦcafeimperial.cz; metro Náměstí Republiky; map p.102. Built in 1914, and featuring the most incredible ceramic friezes on its walls, pillars and ceilings, the *Imperial* is a must for fans of outrageously sumptuous Art Nouveau decor. You can come just for a coffee, and they also serve breakfast and light lunches, but the main dishes are slightly overpriced (300–400Kč). Daily 7am–11pm.

★**Lucerna** Vodičkova 36 ☎224 215 495, ⓦlucerna.cz; metro Můstek/Muzeum; map p.102. Wonderfully lugubrious, *fin-de-siècle* café-bar on the first floor, en route to the cinema of the same name, with lots of faux marble and windows overlooking the Lucerna *pasáž*. The bust you pass on the steps up is Václav Havel's grandfather who built the Lucerna. Daily 10am–midnight.

Myšák Vodičkova 31 ☎734 898 607, ⓦmujmysak.cz; metro Můstek; map p.102. Stylish re-creation of a famous *cukrárna* that stood on this spot in the interwar years. Expect high-stacked gateaux and tasty ice cream. Mon–Fri 8am–8pm, Sat & Sun 8.30am–8pm.

★**Obecní dům** Náměstí Republiky 5 ☎222 002 763, ⓦkavarnaod.cz; metro Náměstí Republiky; map p.102. The vast *kavárna* (café), with its famous fountain, is a glittering Art Nouveau period piece – an absolute aesthetic treat. The food is nice enough, but most folk come here for a coffee and a little something from the cake trolley. Daily 7.30am–11pm.

Pekářství Moravec Biskupský dvůr 1 ☎774 706 438; metro Florenc; map p.102. Rural Bohemia-style bakery on a quiet square next to the completely unvisited church of sv Petra. Selling traditional cakes, pastries, ice cream and coffees, it's also a great spot for an early breakfast. Free wi-fi. Mon–Fri 6.30am–6.30pm, Sat 7am–12.30pm.

Tramvaj Václavské náměstí; metro Můstek; map p.102. Two vintage #11 trams stranded in the middle of Wenceslas Square (where they used to run) have been converted into a summer café – a convenient spot for coffee and easy to locate. Mon–Sat 9am–midnight, Sun 10am–midnight.

RESTAURANTS

Francouzská restaurace Náměstí Republiky 5 ☎222 002 770, ⓦfrancouzskarestaurace.cz; metro Náměstí Republiky; map p.102. The Art Nouveau decor in this cavernous Obecní dům restaurant is absolutely stunning, but the French-style main dishes, though proficient enough, are very expensive (600–1000Kč), as are the drinks. Daily noon–11pm.

Hybernia Hybernská 7 ☎224 226 004, ⓦhybernia.cz; metro Náměstí Republiky; map p.102. Proximity to ČSSD headquarters and a couple of ministries means that the hordes of munching bureaucrats might thwart your efforts to bag a table at this extremely popular Urquell restaurant. The menu looks fancy but is made up of stock Czech dishes (150–300Kč) with a few "exotic" ingredients added for effect. Mon–Fri 8am–midnight, Sat & Sun 11am–midnight.

Monarchie Štěpánská 61 ☎296 236 513, ⓦrestaurace-monarchie.cz; metro Můstek/Muzeum; map p.102. Habsburg and other imperial coats of arms line the walls in pompous fashion at this interesting new restaurant in the entrance to the Lucerna pasáž. The Austro-Bohemian menu includes Wiener schnitzel, suckling pig and Pilsen goulash with Carlsbad dumplings. Mains 150–350Kč. Mon–Fri 11am–11pm.

Plzeňská restaurace Obecní dům, náměstí Republiky 5 ☎222 002 780, ⓦplzenskarestaurace.cz; metro Náměstí Republiky; map p.102. Located in the cellar of the Obecní dům, this is the country's most attractive Art Nouveau pub-restaurant with exquisite tiling, wonderful stained glass and huge chandeliers. The mains menu celebrates the best of Czech meat dishes but is slightly overpriced and portions are miserly. Daily 11.30am–11pm.

U sádlů Klimentská 2 ☎224 813 874, ⓦusadlu.cz; metro Náměstí Republiky; map p.102. Deliberately over-the-top themed medieval banqueting hall offering a hearty Czech menu, with classics such as roast pork knuckle and venison goulash (most mains less than 200Kč) swilled down with tankards of foamy Budvar. Mon–Thurs 11am–midnight, Fri & Sat 11am–1am, Sun noon–midnight.

Zvonice (Bell Tower) Jindřišská věž, Jindřišská ☎224 220 009, ⓦrestaurantzvonice.cz; metro Můstek; map p.102. Atmospheric but horrifically expensive restaurant crammed into the woodwork of the sixth and seventh floors of a medieval bell tower. Weekday lunch menu for less than 400Kč; traditional Czech main dishes in the evening from around 750Kč. Daily 11.30am–midnight.

CHEAP EATS AND QUICK SNACKS

The most obvious snack in Prague, sold from kiosks all over the city, is the *párek*, or **hot dog**, a dubious-looking frankfurter (traditionally two – *párek* means a pair), dipped in mustard and rammed into a white roll (*v rohlíku*). The usual multinational burger chains have their outlets splattered all over Prague, too.

Prague's **bakeries** (*pekářství* or *pekárna*) are the places to head for traditional Czech tarts (*koláč* – actually from Moravia), traditionally filled with poppy seed jam (*mákový*), plum jam (*povidlový*) or a kind of sour-sweet curd cheese (*tvarohový*). Traditionally, the Czechs went in for artistically presented open **sandwiches** known as *chlebíčky* – with combinations of gherkins, cheese, salami, ham and aspic – but nowadays the baguette, panini and wrap are in the ascendancy. One reliable city-wide chain is *Paneria* (@paneria.cz), which specializes in providing sandwiches, panini and pastries for hungry office workers; the most central branches are at Kaprova 3 (see p.96) and Maiselova 4 (metro Staroměstská). Whatever the season, Czechs love their daily fix of **ice cream** (*zmrzlina*), traditionally dispensed from window kiosks in the sides of buildings. There are several proper ice-cream parlours, too, some with seating, serving authentic Italian *gelato*.

Markets and **food shops**, including delis, patisseries, bakeries and ice-cream shops, also offer rich pickings when it comes to snacking (see p.209).

10

SOUTHERN NOVÉ MĚSTO AND NÁRODNÍ TŘÍDA

CAFÉS

Café 35 Institut Français, Štěpánská 35 ☎ 221 401 070, @ifp.cz; metro Muzeum; map p.102. Housed in Prague's Institut Français, this café guarantees great coffee and fresh French pastries – plus the chance to pose with a French newspaper. Mon–Fri 8.30am–8pm, Sat 10am–2pm.

Cafétérapie Na Hrobci 3 ☎ 224 916 098, @cafeterapie .cz; tram #2, #3, #7, #17 or #21 to Výtoň; map p.102. Small, simply furnished café that serves nice healthy Mediterranean-influenced salads, sandwiches, toasties and a few hot dishes. Mon–Fri 8.30am–10pm, Sat 9am–10pm, Sun 10am–10pm.

Daruma Trojanova 4 ☎ 603 193 505, @darumatea.cz; metro Karlovo náměstí; map p.102. Sample around fifty types of tea at this cellar teahouse with a homely atmosphere, board games, changing art exhibitions on the walls and laidback staff. Mon–Fri 11am–10pm, Sat & Sun 2–10pm.

★**Friends Coffee House** Palackého 7 ☎ 272 049 665, @milujikavu.cz; metro Můstek; map p.102. Large, modern, multi-spaced coffeehouse with an attractive winter garden, heart-pumping brews, art exhibitions and a library. The location, just off Wenceslas Square, is not bad either. Mon–Fri 9am–9pm, Sat & Sun noon–8pm.

★**Louvre** Národní 22 ☎ 224 930 949, @cafelouvre.cz; metro Národní třída; map p.102. Swish turn-of-the-twentieth-century café with a long pedigree and still a very popular refuelling spot for Prague's shoppers. High ceiling, mirrors, daily papers, decent, inexpensive food, lots of cakes, a billiard hall and window seats over-looking Národní třída. Mon–Fri 8am–11.30pm, Sat & Sun 9am–11.30pm.

Marathon Černá 9 ☎ 777 692 932, @marathoncafe.cz; metro Karlovo náměstí; map p.102. Hidden gem "library café" in the university's 1920s-style religion faculty,

tucked well away from the tourists in the backstreets south of Národní třída. Mon–Fri 10am–midnight, Sat 6pm–midnight.

★**Slavia** Smetanovo nábřeží 2 ☎ 224 218 493, @cafeslavia.cz; metro Národní třída; map p.102. Don't be put off by the big Coca-Cola stickers in the windows here – *Slavia* is still Prague's top café, as it has been since the 1920s. It pulls in a mixed crowd from shoppers and tourists to old-timers and the pre- and post-theatre mob. Come here for a coffee and the view (not the food or the scary service). Mon–Fri 8am–midnight, Sat & Sun 9am–midnight.

Svatováclavská cukrárna Václavská pasáž, Karlovo náměstí 6 ☎ 224 916 774; metro Karlovo náměstí; map p.102. Join the local pensioner posse for a glass of cheap Turkish coffee and a slice of strudel at this busy *cukrárna* within the glass-roofed Václavská pasáž. Daily 8am–7pm.

Velryba (The Whale) Opatovická 24 ☎ 224 931 444, @kavarnavelryba.cz; metro Národní třída; map p.102. For over two and a half decades this funky pub-café has been serving up cheap meals (mains under 200Kč), beer, coffee and art exhibitions to a studenty crowd – and is still going strong. Mon–Fri 11am–11pm, Sat & Sun noon-11pm.

RESTAURANTS

Cicala Žitná 43 ☎ 222 210 375, @trattoria.cz; metro I.P. Pavlova; map p.102. Excellent family-run Italian basement restaurant specializing (mid-week) in fresh seafood (from 380Kč). There's also a wide range of pasta (190–320Kč) and an appetizing antipasto selection. Mon–Sat 11.30am–3pm & 5–10pm.

Dnister Na Moráni 6 ☎ 774 059 788, @restaurace -dnister.cz; metro Karlovo náměstí; map p.102. Take a trip to rural West Ukraine (not as scary as it sounds) at this cellar restaurant where Ukrainian staples such as *deruny*

TOP 5 CAFÉS

Grand Café Orient See p.178
Imperial See p.182
Louvre See p.183
Obecní dům See p.182
Slavia See p.183

10

(potato cakes), *borshch* (beetroot and cabbage soup), *holubtsi* (minced meat and rice wrapped in cabbage leaves) and *vareniki* (filled pasta) can be washed down with Urquell. Mon–Fri 11am–11.30pm, Sat & Sun from noon.

Dynamo Pštrossova 29 ☎224 932 020, ⓦdynamo restaurace.cz; metro Národní třída; map p.102. Fashionable hangout with eye-catching retro-1960s designer decor; inexpensive veggie and pasta dishes (125–150Kč) and steaks and Czech dishes for around 250Kč. Daily 11am–midnight.

Klub Cestovatelů Masarykovo nábřeží 22 ☎734 322 729, ⓦhedvabnastezka.cz; tram #5 to Myslíkova; map p.102. Join fellow nomads at this exotic "Travellers' Club" for some Lebanese food (mains 200–300Kč), hookah pipes, travel-themed photo exhibitions and lectures given by leading Czech travellers. Mon–Sat 11am–11pm, Sun noon–10pm.

Kmotra (The Godmother) V Jirchářích 2 ☎224 934 100, ⓦkmotra.cz; metro Národní třída; map p.102. This inexpensive, brick-vaulted basement pizzeria next to the Mexican embassy is popular, and justifiably so – if possible, book a table in advance. Pizzas 135–188Kč. Daily 11am–midnight.

Miss Saigon Myslíkova 26 ☎257 215 440, ⓦmiss -saigon.cz; metro Karlovo náměstí; map p.102. The Czech Republic has a huge Vietnamese population, a left-over from the Communist period, but their cuisine is virtually unknown, even among Czechs. This simple place tries to put this right with a menu of exotic ingredients (bamboo shoots, oyster sauce, cashew nuts, bean curd) and the staple dish – *pho bo* soup. Mains 49–250Kč. Mon–Fri 10.30am–10.30pm, Sat & Sun 11.30am–11pm.

★**Ryby & Chips** Myslíkova 18 ☎222 519 986, ⓦrybyandchips.cz; metro Karlovo náměstí; map p.102. A London Underground logo bearing the restaurant name as if it were a station welcomes you to Prague's best British fish 'n' chip shop. After all that sugary central European starch, just the smell of this place (it manages to pump out just the right fried-batter-and-vinegar aroma) will have homesick Brits reaching for the pickled eggs. Only the salad option spoils the feel of authenticity. Cod and chips from 109Kč. Daily 10.30am–9.30pm.

U Čiriny Navrátilova 6 ☎222 231 709, ⓦcirina.cz; metro Karlovo náměstí; map p.102. This little family-run place, with just a handful of tables inside and a summer terrace, offers classic Slovak and Hungarian home cooking with dishes such as *halušky* (gnocchi), goulash and *strapačky* (potato dumplings) coming in at around 200Kč a shot. Daily 11am–11pm.

U Šumavy Štěpánská 3 ☎775 555 297, ⓦusumavy.cz; metro Karlovo náměstí; map p.102. Authentically Bohemian restaurant sporting stencilled walls, high ceilings and antique furniture. The menu is a meaty Czech feast of *svíčková* (sirloin in cream sauce), venison, beef goulash and roast pork, all served with fluffy dumplings and tankards of countryside lager. Mains around 200Kč. Daily 11am–midnight.

Žofín Garden Slovanský ostrov 226 ☎774 774 774, ⓦzofingarden.cz; metro Karlovo náměstí; map p.102. On the island nearest the National Theatre, this tranquil place serves beautiful, upmarket Czech food such as venison, pike perch and rabbit (all around 300Kč). Daily 11am–10pm.

VYŠEHRAD AND THE EASTERN SUBURBS

CAFÉS

Blatouch Americká 17, Vinohrady ☎222 328 643, ⓦblatouch.cz; metro Náměstí Míru; map p.124. Unpretentious café in the heart of Vinohrady that predates the flashier establishments all around. Salads, toasted sandwiches, pastas and tortillas, many of them vegetarian, make up the menu, and there's Ferdinand beer from Benešov. Mon–Thurs noon–midnight, Fri noon–1am, Sat 1pm–1am, Sun 1–11pm.

Fialová cukrárna Budečská 40, Vinohrady ☎604 194 182, ⓦfialovacukrarna.cz; tram #11 or #13 to Vinohradská tržnice; map p.124. Cosy little café-bakery with the usual assortment of coffees and cakes and an interior that's all antique furniture and big windows. Mon–Fri 9am–7pm, Sat noon–7pm.

Kaaba Mánesova 20, Vinohrady ☎222 254 021, ⓦkaaba.cz; metro Muzeum; map p.124. This stylish ice-cream parlour/café attracts a young cool crowd with its funky mismatched retro decor. Serves breakfast and light meals. Mon–Fri 8am–midnight, Sat 9am–midnight, Sun 10am–midnight.

Radost FX Café Bělehradská 120, Vinohrady ☎603 193 711, ⓦradostfx.cz; metro I.P. Pavlova; map p.124. The filling veggie dishes at this expat favourite all cost around 200Kč; the decor is decadent and there's a dance soundtrack (with live DJs at the weekend). Despite all this, *Radost* can be a disappointing culinary experience. Mon–Sat 11am–11pm, Sun 11am–3pm.

Roza K Belgická 17, Vinohrady ☎222 544 696; metro Náměstí Míru; map p.124. A cool young crowd hangs out in this deliberately faded, inexpensive café, which puts artworks and photography by local artists on its walls and serves strudel, ice cream, toasts and sandwiches plus lots of drinks. Mon–Fri 11am–11.30pm.

RESTAURANTS

Döner Kebab Žižkov Sladkovského náměstí 3, Žižkov ☎605 156 144, ⓦkebabzizkov.cz; tram #5, #9, #15 or #26 to Lipanská; map p.124. Should the munchies strike in Žižkov, head to this simple kebab joint where the excellent 99Kč boxes contain an entire meal of meat, salad and chips. Mon–Fri 11am–11pm, Sat & Sun noon–11pm.

Las Adelitas Americká 8, Vinohrady ☎222 542 031, ⓦlasadelitas.cz; tram #4, #13 or #22 to Jana Masaryka; map p.124. Prague's tastiest nachos, tacos, enchiladas and quesadillas prepared by Mexican cooks who speak no Czech. Takeaway available. Mains around 200Kč. Mon–Fri 11am–midnight, Sat & Sun noon–midnight.

Mailsi Lipanská 1, Žižkov ☎774 972 010, ⓦmailsi.cz; tram #5, #9, #15 or #26 to Lipanská; map p.124. Friendly Pakistani place that's great for a comfort curry (around 250–500Kč), as hot as you can handle. There's a rare Subcontinental food store next door. Daily noon–3pm & 6–11pm.

Masala Jana Masaryka 36, Vinohrady ☎222 251 601, ⓦmasala.cz; tram #4, #13 or #22 to Jana Masaryka; map p.124. This recently relocated North Indian restaurant is justifiably popular with the local expats. The tandoori kebabs and kormas (around 150Kč) are authentically spicy and the naan bread is home made. Mon–Fri 11.30am–10.30pm, Sat & Sun from 12.30pm.

Mrázek Bělehradská 82, Vinohrady ☎222 514 140; metro I.P. Pavlova; map p.124. Join frugal locals for a meat-sauce-dumpling combo at this traditional *jídelna*

(stand-up self-service canteen). No English spoken. Mains 30–95Kč. Mon–Fri 7am–6pm, Sat 8–noon.

Olše Táboritská 26, Žižkov ☎725 125 324, ⓦrestaurantolse.cz; tram #5, #9, #15 or #26 to Olšanské náměstí; map p.124. Housed in a Communist-era slab, this old-fashioned mass-dining establishment serves level-headed Czech standards at tightly packed, dark-wood tables, occupied at lunchtimes by gossiping office workers. Most mains under 200Kč. Daily 11am–11pm.

Singidunum Bělehradská 92, Vinohrady ☎222 544 113, ⓦsingidunum.cz; metro I.P. Pavlova; map p.124. *Singidunum* is the Latin for Belgrade, and it's the hot-tempered cuisine of the Balkans you'll find at this atmospheric place: *čevapčiči* (kebabs), Adriatic pastas, Croatian *pršut* (ham) plus Macedonian and Montenegrin wines. Mains 150–500Kč. Daily 11am–11pm.

U Slovanské Lípy Tachovské náměstí 6, Žižkov ☎734 743 094, ⓦuslovanskelipy.cz; tram #5, #9, #15 or #26 to Lipanská; map p.124. Žižkov's oldest tavern plates up solid, no-nonsense Prague and Bohemian dishes in a wood-panelled dining room. Interesting guest ales on tap. Mains 100–200Kč. Daily 11am–midnight.

Zanzibar Americká 15, Vinohrady ☎222 520 315, ⓦkavarnazanzibar.cz; metro Náměstí Míru; map p.124. Great neighbourhood bar-restaurant with a long menu of international food and alcohol including Bernard beer. Mains around 180Kč. Mon–Thurs 8am–11pm, Fri 8am–midnight, Sat 10am–midnight, Sun 10am–11pm.

10

HOLEŠOVICE AND THE WESTERN SUBURBS

CAFÉS

★**Café Orange** Puškinovo náměstí 13, Bubeneč ☎725 790 937; metro Dejvická; map p.138. Touting itself as a Tuscan café, this bright place with seats outside by a quiet residential square makes decent pasta, bruschetta, fresh juices and ice cream. Mon–Fri 11am–11pm.

Erhartova cukrárna Milady Horákové 56 Holešovice ☎233 312 148, ⓦerhartovacukrarna.cz; tram #1, #8, #12, #25 or #26 to Letenské náměstí; map p.138. Stylish Czech bakery-café with red leather stools, local clientele and an array of irresistible treats on offer. Daily 10am–7pm.

RESTAURANTS

Domažlická jizba Strossmayerovo náměstí 2, Holešovice ☎607 556 379, ⓦdomazlicka-jizba.cz; tram #1, #12 or #25 to Strossmayerovo náměstí; map p.138. Join lunching locals or instead-of-work Urquell disciples at this traditional olde-worlde, wood-panelled dining room that's been banging down goulash and

chicken schnitzel since 1906. Mains 150–200Kč, lunch menu 120Kč. Daily 11am–midnight.

Hanavský pavilón Letenské sady 173, Letná ☎233 323 641, ⓦhanavsky-pavilon.cz; tram #2, #12, #18, or #20 to Chotkovy sady; map p.138. Wrought-iron Art Nouveau pleasure pavilion above the Vltava, with stunning terrace views; Czech and international mains 300–500Kč. Daily 11am–midnight.

Svatá Klára (St Clare) U Trojského zámku 35, Troja ☎233 540 173, ⓦsvataklara.cz; bus #112 from metro Nádraží Holešovice; map p.138. Formal, evening-only restaurant, first opened in 1679, in a romantic wine-cave setting near the zoo. Specializes in fondue and Czech game dishes from 500Kč. Tues–Sat 6pm–1am.

U Škrétů Milady Horákové 52, Letná ☎223 000 510, ⓦrestaurace-uskretu.cz; tram #1, #8, #12, #25 or #26 to Letenské náměstí; map p.138. Down-to-earth restaurant serving heavy, belly-stretching Czech and Slovak staples and lots of beer from both countries. Mains 100–200Kč. Mon–Fri 11am–10pm, Sat noon–10pm.

Pubs and bars

The Czechs drink more beer than any other nation, downing approximately a pint a day for every man, woman and child in the country. That's a whopping 142 litres a year per person – in fact, more beer is drunk here than water. That said, the smoky old pubs (*pivnice*), traditionally filled with men drinking huge quantities of Czech beer by the half-litre, are a dying breed in Prague; the few that do survive are found way beyond the centre of town, and the 2017 smoking ban has put paid to the fuggy atmosphere. In the centre, the *pivnice* has been brutally gentrified, with smarter decor, prompter service and fancy food. As in most European capitals, the drinking scene in Prague is now enormously diverse, with everything from expat American-style bars and "Irish" pubs to pop-up hipster craft-gin joints.

Pubs and beer halls are about much more than just the beer; most serve **food** as well. Options can range from simple traditional pub grub, such as pickled sausages (*utopence*), potato pancakes (*bramboráky*), *pivný sýr* ("beer cheese" – cottage cheese with beer) and pickled brie (*nakládaný hermelín*) to more sophisticated dishes including venison goulash (*srnčí guláš*), roast pork with dumplings and sauerkraut (*vepřoknedlozelo*) or roast duck (*pečená kachna*). Prague's pubs are particularly good places for a cheap lunch, with menus starting at around 100Kč.

ESSENTIALS

Costs The average price for a half-litre glass of beer is around 30–45Kč.

Opening hours The cooking facilities in pubs usually close around 9pm, but you can often go on drinking a bit after the official closing time, normally 11pm.

Smoking Lighting up in Czech pubs finally became a thing of the past in 2017, the Czech Republic becoming one of the last countries in Europe to implement a complete smoking ban.

DRINKS

Alcohol consumption among Czechs has always been high. It doubled in the 1970s and the population has remained on top of the world league table of beer consumption ever since – though they're quaffing a bit less as every year goes by. That said, violence in pubs is uncommon and the only obvious drunks you're likely to see in public are British stags and hens.

Czech beer Czech beer (*pivo*) ranks among the best on the planet and the country remains the true home of most of the lager drunk around the world today. Beer is served by the half-litre; if you want something smaller, you must specifically ask for a *malé pivo* (0.3l). The average jar is medium strength, usually about 4.2 percent alcohol. Somewhat confusingly, the Czechs class their beers using the Balling scale, which measures the original gravity, calculated according to the amount of malt and dissolved sugar present before fermentation. The most common varieties are 10° (*desítka*), which are generally slightly weaker than 12° (*dvanáctka*). Light beer (*světlé*) is the norm, but many pubs also serve a slightly sweeter dark variety (*tmavé* or *černé*) – or you can have a mixture of the two (*řezané*). *Kvasnicové pivo* is yeast beer, *nefiltrované* is, you guessed it, unfiltered (cloudy) beer. There's also *nepasterované* and *pšeničné* as well as combinations of all the above.

Czech wine Homegrown wine (*víno*) will never win as many prizes as the local beer, but since the import of French and German vines in the fourteenth century a modest selection of medium-quality wines has been produced. Interestingly you won't find Czech wine outside the Czech Republic, as production hardly even covers domestic consumption. The main wine region is South Moravia, though a little is produced around the Bohemian town of Mělník (see p.152). Most domestic wine is pretty drinkable – *Veltlínské zelené* (Grüner Veltliner) is a good, dry white – and rarely much more than 130Kč a bottle in shops, while the best stuff is only available from a good wine shop (see p.209) or private wine cellar, hundreds of which still exist out in the wine-growing regions. A Czech speciality to look out for is *burčák*, a very young, fizzy, sweet, misty wine of varying (and often very strong) alcoholic content.

Brandy The home production of brandies is a national pastime. The most renowned of the lot is *slivovice*, a plum brandy originally from the border hills between Moravia and Slovakia. You'll probably also come across *borovička*, a popular Slovak firewater, made from juniper berries, and *myslivec*, a rough brandy with a firm following. There's also a fair selection of intoxicating herbal concoctions: *fernet* is a dark-brown bitter drink, known as *bavorák* (Bavarian beer) when it's mixed with tonic, while *becherovka* is a supposedly healthy herbal spirit from the Bohemian spa town of Karlovy Vary, with a very unusual, almost medicinal taste.

Absinthe Although illegal in some parts of Europe, absinthe has enjoyed something of a renaissance in Prague. The preferred poison of Parisian painters and poets in the 1920s, absinthe is an evil green spirit made from fermented wormwood – it even gets a biblical mention in Revelation: "and the name of the star is called Wormwood: and the third part of the waters became wormwood; and many men died of the waters, because they were made bitter." St John wasn't wrong: at up to 170 degrees proof, it's dangerous stuff and virtually undrinkable neat. To make it vaguely palatable, you need to set light to an absinthe-soaked spoonful of sugar, and then mix the caramelized mess with the absinthe.

11

HRADČANY

Klášterní pivovar (Monastery brewery) Strahovské nádvoří 1 ☎ 233 353 155, ⊛ klasterni-pivovar.cz; tram #22 or #23 to Pohořelec; map p.34. Tourist-friendly monastic brewery, offering their own pricey light and dark St Norbert beers and Czech pub food. Daily 10am–10pm.

★ **U černého vola (The Black Ox)** Loretánské náměstí 1; tram #22 or #23 to Pohořelec; map p.34. The last surviving ungentrified pub in Hradčany serving Kozel beer in an old mini-palazzo to a few remaining locals and those in the know. Daily 10am–10pm.

PUB MENUS

In pubs and the cheapest restaurants, the **menu** (*jídelní lístek*), which should be displayed outside, is often in Czech only or very badly translated – deciphering it without a grounding in the language can be quite a feat.

These menus are usually divided into sections, beginning with *předkrmy* (starters) or *polévky* (soups), followed by the main courses: *jídla na objednávku* (food to order), *hotová jídla* (ready-made food, which is cheaper and should arrive quickly), *drůbež a ryby* (fowl and fish) and, if you're lucky, *bezmasá jídla* (vegetarian dishes). Side dishes are listed under *přílohy*; puddings, where available, come under the heading *moučníky*.

Bear in mind, too, that in general the right-hand column lists the **prices**, while the far left column often gives the estimated weight of every dish in grams.

MALÁ STRANA

Baráčnická rychta Na tržiště 23 (down a narrow passageway leading south off Nerudova) ☎ 257 286 083, ⓦ baracnickarychta.cz; tram #2, #12, #15, #18, #20, #22 or #23 to Malostranské náměstí; map p.56. *Všebaráčnická rychta* (as it's also known) is a nostalgia-inducing, wood-panelled beer hall dedicated to keeping things traditionally Czech in Malá Strana. One of the few 1930s Modernist buildings in the area, it hosts special events such as Czech balls and *masopust* (carnival) celebrations. Daily 11.30am–11.30pm.

Jo's Bar Malostranské náměstí 7 ☎ 257 531 422, ⓦ josbar.cz; tram #2, #12, #15, #18, #20, #22 or #23 to Malostranské náměstí; map p.56. *Jo's* is the city's original American expat/backpacker hangout. It no longer has quite the vitality it once did but remains a good place to hook up with other travellers. There's also a club, *Jo's Garáž*, downstairs. Daily noon–midnight.

John Lennon Pub Hroznová 6 ☎ 257 214 266; tram #2, #12, #15, #18, #20, #22 or #23 to Hellichova; map p.56. A bespectacled Beatle and a yellow submarine welcome you to this Kampa island pub near the Lennon Wall. The theme isn't overdone inside. Daily noon–1am.

Nicolas Bar Tržiště 10 ☎ 257 225 423, ⓦ nicolasbar.cz; tram #2, #12, #15, #18, #20, #22 or #23 to Malostranské náměstí; map p.56. A well-dressed older crowd of Czechs and expat diplomatic folk come to this small, vaulted cellar bar for live music, pizza and Pilsner. Mon–Thurs noon–midnight, to 2am Fri, Sat & Sun.

U hrocha (The Hippo) Thunovská 10 ☎ 257 533 389; tram #2, #12, #15, #18, #20, #22 or #23 to Malostranské náměstí; map p.56. An old, been-here-forever Czech *pivnice* close to the British embassy, usually full with a close-knit bunch of locals. Daily noon–10.30pm.

U kocoura (The Cat) Nerudova 2 ☎ 257 530 107; tram #2, #12, #15, #18, #20, #22 or #23 to Malostranské náměstí; map p.56. Football scarves and stodgy food confront bewildered foreigners at this old-school Czech pub. An authentic watering-hole catering for Malá Strana's dwindling local drinking community. Daily noon–10.30pm.

★U malého Glena (Little Glenn's) Karmelitská 23 ☎ 257 531 717, ⓦ malyglen.cz; tram #2, #12, #15, #18, #20, #22 or #23 to Malostranské náměstí; map p.56. Smart-looking pub/jazz bar that attracts a fair mixture of Czechs and expats thanks to its better-than-average food and live music in the basement. Daily 11am–2am.

STARÉ MĚSTO

Blatnička Michalská 5; metro Můstek; map p.70. Long-established wine shop where you can drink Moravian reds and whites straight from the barrel, take away or head next door to the popular basement *vinárna* for more wine and inexpensive snacks. Daily 11am–11pm.

Ice Pub Karlovy Lázně, Novotného lávka 5 ⓦ icepub prague.cz; tram #2, #17 or #18 to Karlovy Lázně; map p.70. Pay your 200Kč (entry includes one drink), don your special coat and glasses and enter Prague's chilliest pub (temperature kept permanently at -7°C) where everything, even the shot glasses, is made of ice. Daily noon–5am.

James Joyce U Obecního dvora 4 ☎ 224 818 851, ⓦ jamesjoyceprague.cz; metro Staroměstská; map p.70. The best of Prague's Irish pubs, with Irish staff, an open fire, draught Kilkenny and Guinness and decent Irish-themed food. Mon–Thurs & Sun 11am–12.30am, Fri & Sat 11am–2am.

Kozička Kozí 4 ☎ 224 818 308, ⓦ kozicka.cz; metro Staroměstská; map p.70. Busy, designer bare-brick cellar bar with cheap Czech food, tucked away just a short walk from Staroměstské náměstí. Mon–Thurs 4pm–4am, Fri 5pm–5.30am, Sat 6pm–5.30am, Sun 7pm–3am.

Šenk Vrbovec Skořepka 3 ⓦ senkvrbovec.cz; metro Můstek; map p.70. Once a popular, tiny bolt-hole on Wenceslas Square, this traditional Moravian wine bar moved to bigger and better things in the Old Town a few years ago. Only the best Moravian wines and simple snacks. Mon–Thurs 3pm–midnight, Fri & Sat to 1am, Sun 4–10pm.

FROM TOP *PRAGUE BEER MUSEUM* (P.191); *U MEDVÍDKŮ* (P.190); *VINOHRADSKÝ PARLAMENT* (P.192) >

U medvídků Na Perštýně 7 ☎224 211 916, ⓦumedvidku.cz; metro Národní třída; map p.70. A Prague beer hall going back to the thirteenth century and little changed since then (make sure you turn right when you enter, and avoid the bar to the left). Brews its own series of beer and offers a very cheap lunch menu for central Prague (mains less than 100Kč). Mon–Sat 11.30am–11pm, Sun 11.30am–10pm.

U Vejvodů Jilská 4 ☎224 219 999, ⓦrestauraceu vejvodu.cz; metro Národní třída; map p.70. This atmospheric vaulted beer hall is now one of Pilsner Urquell's very successful chain of pubs, serving expensive upmarket pub food. Mon–Thurs 10am–3am, Fri & Sat 10am–4am, Sun 10am–2am.

★**U zlatého tygra (The Golden Tiger)** Husova 17 ☎222 221 111, ⓦuzlatehotygra.cz; metro Staroměstská; map p.70. Small central *pivnice*, always busy with locals and tourists trying to get a seat; the late writer and bohemian Bohumil Hrabal was a semi-permanent resident and still has a seat reserved for him (he died in 1997). Daily 3–11pm.

JOSEFOV

Kolkovna V kolkovně 8 ☎224 819 701; metro Staroměstská; map p.92. Justifiably popular with passing tourists, this Pilsner Urquell pub has plush decor, excellent pub food and unpasteurized Pilsner on tap. Daily 11am–midnight.

Krčma Kostečná 4 ☎ 725 157 262, ⓦkrcma.cz; metro Staroměstská; map p.92. If you thought the area around Pařížská was a ghetto of gentrification, seek out this cellar tavern for a bit of candle-lit, faux-medieval Czech grit. The Urquell is 35Kč a glass and the old-Bohemian food realistically priced. Daily 11am–11pm.

Tretter's V kolkovně 3 ☎224 811 165, ⓦwww .tretters.cz; metro Staroměstská; map p.92. Smart and sophisticated (but not exclusive) American cocktail bar, with very professional staff and a glamorous ambience. Live jazz on Tues. Mon–Sat 7pm–3am, to 2am Sun.

U Rudolfina Křížovnická 10 ☎222 328 758, ⓦurudolfina.cz; metro Staroměstská; map p.92. A bona-fide Czech *pivnice* very close to Charles Bridge, serving expertly kept Pilsner Urquell and typical meaty pub grub. Daily 11am–11pm.

NOVÉ MĚSTO

American Bar Obecní dům, náměstí Republiky 5 ☎222 002 786, ⓦamerickybar.cz; metro Náměstí Republiky; map p.102. Dating from 1911, this joint in the basement of the Obecní dům might be overpriced, but as one of the city's architectural treasures and its oldest bar, it's still a treat. Daily 11.30am–11pm.

Branický sklípek Vodičkova 26; metro Můstek; map p.102. Convenient downtown pub decked out like a pine furniture showroom, serving typical Czech food and jugs of Prague's Braník beer. The rough-and-ready *Branická formanka* next door opens and closes earlier. Mon–Fri 9am–11pm, Sat & Sun 11am–11pm.

Bredovský dvůr Politických vězňů 13 ☎224 215 427, ⓦrestauracebredovskydvur.cz; metro Hlavní nádraží; map p.102. Virtually tourist-free brick-vaulted city pub, off Wenceslas Square, serving standard pub food helped along with Pilsner Urquell or Velkopopovický kozel beer. Mon–Sat 11am–midnight, Sun 11am–11pm.

Novoměstský pivovar Vodičkova 20 ☎222 232 448, ⓦnpivovar.cz; metro Národní třída; map p.102. Outstanding microbrewery that serves its own well-tapped misty 11° home brew, plus monster portions of Czech sustenance, in a series of twelve sprawling beer halls and rooms, some of which are Gothic affairs deep underground. Mon–Fri 10am–11.30pm, Sat 11.30am–11.30pm, Sun noon–10pm.

★**Pivovarský dům** Ječná 14 ☎296 216 666, ⓦpivovarskydum.com; tram #3, #4, #5, #6, #10, #14, #16, #22 or #23 to Štěpánská; map p.102. Hugely popular wood-panelled microbrewery pub dominated by big shiny copper vats, serving eight types of highly quaffable light, mixed and dark unfiltered beer, plus standard Czech pub dishes. The 89Kč lunch menu is one of the cheapest around. Wi-fi-enabled devices are banned here. Daily 11am–11.30pm.

Potrefená husa Resslova 1 ☎224 918 691; metro Karlovo náměstí; map p.102. Staropramen's chain of smart pubs, serving decent pub food, have proved very popular; this one's in a cosy, brick-lined cellar near the Tančíci dům. Mon–Wed 11am–midnight, Thurs–Sat 11am–1am, Sun 11am–11pm.

U Fleků Křemencova 11 ☎224 934 019, ⓦufleku.cz; metro Karlovo náměstí; map p.102. Prague's most famous medieval brewery where the unique dark 13° beer, Flek, has been brewed and consumed since 1499. It seats more than five hundred tourists at a go, serves short measures (0.4l), slaps on an extra charge for the music and still you might have to queue to get in. The only reason to visit is to sample the beer, which you're best off doing during the day. Daily 10am–11pm.

U havrana (The Crow) Hálkova 8 ☎222 980 750, ⓦrestauraceuhavrana.cz; metro I.P. Pavlova; map p.102. Surprisingly unseedy all-night pub serving food and Pilsen beers throughout the night. Mon–Fri 5pm–5am, Sat 6pm–5am.

U Pinkasů Jungmannovo náměstí 16 ☎221 111 152; ⓦupinkasu.cz; metro Můstek; map p.102. Famous as the pub where Pilsner Urquell was first served in Prague,

A SHORT HISTORY OF BEER

Sugar cubes and Semtex aside, the Czechs' greatest claim to fame is that they invented the world's original **Pilsner beer**. As every Bohemian pub regular knows, by the late 1830s, the German-speaking inhabitants of Plzeň (Pilsen), 90km west of Prague, were disgruntled with the local beer, a top-fermented, dark, cloudy brew of dubious quality. In disgust, they founded the Bürgerliche Brauhaus, and employed a Bavarian brewer, Josef Groll, who, on October 5, 1842, produced the world's first lager, a bottom-fermented beer stored in cool caves. The pale Moravian malt, the Saaz hops and the local soft water produced a clear, golden beer that caused a sensation. At the same time, cheap, mass-produced glass appeared on the market, which showed off the new beer's colour and clarity beautifully. The new rail network meant that the drink could be transported all over central Europe, and Pilsner-style beers became all the rage.

Brewing methods remained traditional until the fall of Communism, after which the larger breweries almost all opted for modernization: pasteurization, de-oxidization, rapid maturation and carbon dioxide injections – which resulted in longer shelf-life, less taste and more fizz. The republic's smaller breweries were either swallowed up or went to the wall. By the mid-1990s, there were just sixty Czech breweries left, with the biggest (except Budvar – still owned by the Czech state) owned by multinationals. However, in the last decade a new breed of family-run breweries and **microbreweries** has sprung up, eschewing modern technology and producing some of the tastiest, most individual brews you'll ever encounter.

11

and still offering excellent unpasteurized beer and classic Czech pub food. Daily 10am–11.30pm.

Výloha Bar Vyšehradská 12 ☎606 762 022, ⓦvyloha bar.cz; tram #3, #10, #14, #16, #18 or #24 to Botanická zahrada; map p.102. Right at the southern end of the

Nové Město, this off-the-beaten-track neighbourhood bar is a superb place to hang out with locals, play darts and watch the Czechs beat the rest of the world at ice hockey. Mon–Thurs 5pm–1am, Fri & Sat 5pm–2am, Sun 5pm–midnight.

VYŠEHRAD AND THE EASTERN SUBURBS

★**Akropolis** Kubelíkova 27, Žižkov ⓦpalacakropolis .cz; tram #5, #9, #15 or #26 to Lipanská; map p.124. Prague's very popular live music venue (see p.195) is also a great place just to have a drink or a bite to eat as well as take in live gigs. Daily 11am–5am.

Demínka Škrétova 1, Vinohrady ☎224 224 915, ⓦdeminka.com; metro Muzeum; map p.124. With much of its original grandiose 1880s decor intact – it is Prague's oldest café – *Demínka* is now run as a pub by Pilsner Urquell, which serves excellent unpasteurized beer, classic Bohemian cuisine and a few central European specialities such as Bavarian *spätzle* (noodles) and Slovak *halušky* (dumplings). Mon–Fri 11am–11pm, Sat & Sun from noon.

Pastička Blanická 25, Vinohrady ☎222 253 228; tram #11 or #13 to Vinohradská tržnice; map p.124. Very popular local Vinohrady pub with cosy wooden booths and a summer beer terrace. Cheap 99Kč lunch menu. Mon–Sat 11am–11.30pm.

★**Prague Beer Museum** Americká 43, Vinohrady ☎775 994 698, ⓦpraguebeermuseum.com; metro Náměstí Míru; map p.124. Too often in Prague beer drinkers are limited to Pilsner Urquell or Staropramen. Not at this no-nonsense temple to the lager gods – oddities rarely seen in the capital such as Bakalář from Rakovník, Konrad from Vratislavice and Ferdinand from Benešov introduce some intriguing variety into the drinking experience. New branch at Smetanovo nábřeží near

Charles Bridge. Mon–Thurs & Sun 11am–2am, Fri & Sat noon–3am.

Riegrovy sady Riegrovy sady, Vinohrady ☎222 717 247, ⓦrestauraceriegrovysady.cz; tram #11 or #13 to Vinohradská tržnice; map p.124. Communist-era park café-pub where the beer terrace is popular with the locals, though the draught beer menu is limited to Urquell and Gambrinus. Daily 11am–midnight.

U Houdků Bořivojova 110, Žižkov ⓦuhoudku.web snadno.cz; tram #5, #9, #15, #26 to Husinecká; map p.124. Old Žižkov boozer with a beer garden, Gambrinus and Kozel on tap and wallet-friendly Czech food. Daily 11am–midnight.

U kroka Vratislavova 12 Vyšehrad ☎775 905 022, ⓦukroka.cz; tram #2, #3, #7, #17or #21 to Výtoň; map p.127. Strangely modern Czech pub – all exposed bricks and brushed stainless steel but serving traditional food and Plzeň beer. Daily 11am–11pm.

U růžového sadu Mánesova 89, Vinohrady ☎222 725 154, ⓦuruzovehosadu.cz; metro Jiřího z Poděbrad; map p.124. A rough countryside pub by Vinohrady standards, featuring enamel signs and nicotine-stained walls, but great for a cheap plate of *guláš* and a Gambrinus on a cold day. Mon–Thurs 10.30am–midnight, Fri 10.30am–1am, Sat 11am–midnight, Sun 11.30am–10.30pm.

Vínečko 33 Budečská 40, Vinohrady ☎222 252 288, ⓦvinecko-33.cz; tram #11 or #13 to Vinohradská tržnice; map p.124. Tiny, off-the-tourist-radar wine cellar offering a few Moravian wines straight from the barrel (30Kč a glass), *slivovice*, smoked meats and venison sausage. Mon–Fri 2–11pm, Sat 4–11pm, Sun 4–10pm.

★**Vinohradský Parlament** Korunní 1, Vinohrady ☎ 224 250 403, ⓦ vinohradskyparlament.cz; metro Náměstí Míru; map p.124. A twenty-first-century version of the Czech pub with imaginative contemporary decor, Staropramen beer and attempts at gourmet-style takes on Czech dishes. Reservations essential in the evening. Mon–Wed 10.45am–midnight, Thurs & Fri 10.45am–1am, Sat 11.30am–1am, Sun 11.30am–11.30pm.

Žluta Pumpa Belgická 11, Vinohrady ☎ 608 184 360, ⓦ zluta-pumpa.info; metro Náměstí Míru; map p.124. Basic watering-hole next to an old yellow pump (hence the name) a short walk from Náměstí Míru, serving obscure regional beers and lots of inexpensive food to soak them

TOP 5 OLD-SCHOOL PUBS

U černého vola See p.187
U hrocha See p.188
U kocoura See p.188
U Rudolfina See p.190
U zlatého tygra See p.190

all up with. Daily 11.30am–12.30am.

Zvonařka Šafaříkova 1, Vinohrady ☎ 224 251 990, ⓦ restauracezvonarka.cz; tram #3, #6, #10, #11, #14 or #16 to Nuselské schody; map p.124. The smart modern pub has a summer terrace with great views over the Nuselské schody and Botič valley, plus reasonably priced food and Gambrinus beer to enjoy as you admire the vistas. Mon–Thurs 11.30am–midnight, Fri 11.30am–1am, Sat noon–midnight, Sun noon–11pm.

HOLEŠOVICE AND THE WESTERN SUBURBS

Fraktal Šmeralova 1, Holešovice ☎ 777 794 094, ⓦ fraktalbar.cz; tram #1, #8, #15, #25 or #26 to Letenské náměstí; map p.138. Much-loved expat cellar hangout with ad hoc funky furnishings, exhibitions and occasional live music, plus a beer garden and kids' play area outside. Daily 11am–midnight.

Klášterní šenk Markétská 1, Břevnov ☎ 220 406 294, ⓦ klasternisenk.cz; tram #22 or #25 to Břevnovský klášter; map p.136. Smart pub within the precincts of Brevnov's Benedictine monastery, with a real fire inside and tables out, plus a menu of classic Czech dishes. Daily 11.30am–11pm.

Letenský zámeček Letenské sady 341, Holešovice ⓦ letenskyzamecek.cz; tram #1, #8, #15, #25 or #26 to Letenské náměstí; map p.138. The beer garden, with its great views down the Vltava, is cheap and popular with the locals; the restaurant inside is upmarket and less remarkable. April–Oct daily 11am–11.30pm.

Lokalblok Náměstí 14 října 10, Smíchov ☎ 251 511 490, ⓦ lokalblok.cz; metro Anděl; map p.149. Opposite the church of St Václav, this hip modernist bar has huge screens that change with the seasons and a climbing wall in the basement. Mon–Thurs 11am–midnight, Fri & Sat 11am–1am.

Na staré kovárně Kamenická 17, Holešovice ☎ 233 371 099, ⓦ pubnakovarne.cz; tram #1, #8, #15, #25 or #26

to Kamenická; map p.138. Ageing, off-the-beaten-track watering-hole with guest beers and cheap Bohemian grub. Mon & Sun 11am–11.30pm, Tues–Sat 11am–1am.

Potrefená Husa Nádražní 90, Smíchov ⓦ phnaverandach.cz; metro Anděl; map p.149. The busy branch of this Staropramen brewery pub is next to the brewery itself and hence could be considered the best place to taste Prague's most popular beer. Mon–Wed 11am–midnight, Thurs–Sat 11am–1am, Sun 11am–11pm.

Prolog Nádražní 108, Smíchov ⓦ prologbar.cz; metro Anděl; map p.149. Incongruously situated next to a grandmas' knicker shop in the grubby southern reaches of Smíchov, this fancy cocktail bar with its gold-and-black decor attempts upmarket exclusivity but prices are actually pretty reasonable. Tues–Sat 2pm–1am.

U buldoka (The Bulldog) Preslova 1, Smíchov ⓦ www .ubuldoka.cz; metro Anděl; map p.149. Great, offbeat pub serving Gambrinus and classic Czech pub food, with live sport and occasional DJ nights and live music in the psychedelic cellar. Mon–Thurs 11am–midnight, Fri 11am–1am, Sat noon–midnight, Sun noon–11pm.

U houbaře Dukelských hrdinů 30; tram #1, #6, #12, #14 or #17 to Veletržní palác; map p.138. Old-style Czech public house directly opposite the Veletržní palác, littered with old radios and TVs. Daily 11am–midnight.

Clubs and live music

Partying into the small hours is a key element of the Prague experience for a dedicated minority of visitors. The city has many late-night drinking-holes (see p.186) and plenty of dance clubs, but where Prague really excels is in its sheer variety of live music venues. Running the gamut from quirky to tacky, these host a range of events, including DJ nights and live gigs – anything from Czech reggae to thrash, with a surprising array of world music bands, some big names from the US and UK and a good crop of home-grown jazz performers. There is also a small but well-established gay and lesbian scene in the city.

ESSENTIALS

Prices Drink prices in clubs and venues are inevitably higher than in pubs, but the hike-up is usually relatively modest and entry to most late-night places is rarely extortionate.

Listings To find out about the city's up-and-coming events, check the listings sections in *Prague Post* and keep your eyes peeled for flyers and posters.

Tickets To buy tickets in advance, try one of the agencies such as Ticketpro, which has a comprehensive listings and ticket website (⊚ ticketpro.cz). Others include Ticketportal (⊚ ticketportal.cz) and Bohemia Ticket (⊚ bohemiaticket.cz).

LARGE LIVE VENUES

Kongresové centrum Praha (Prague Congress Centre) 5 května 65, Nusle ⊚ kcp.cz; metro Vyšehrad; map p.149. Revamped (but still very ugly) 1970s concrete monstrosity used for the old Communist Party congresses but now the venue for conferences and the odd big concert by Western stars.

Lucerna Štěpánská 61, Nové Město ⊚ lucpra.com; metro Můstek; map p.102. Without doubt the best venue in Prague, a gilded old ballroom with balconies, situated in the Lucerna *pasáž*. The programme is a real mixed bag with anybody from Mike and the Mechanics to local "bigbeat" bands.

Malostranská beseda Malostranské náměstí 21, Malá Strana ⊚ malostranska-beseda.cz; tram #12, #20 or #22 to Malostranské náměstí; map p.56. Malá Strana's old town hall attracts a mainly Czech crowd, because of its long history. The programme is a great mixture of rock, roots and jazz, some of which comes in from the sticks. Cover charge 100–250Kč. Gigs usually start at 8.30pm.

02 Arena Ocelářská 2, Libeň ⊚ o2arena.cz; metro Českomoravská; map p.124. This 18,000-capacity indoor arena is used for ice hockey and big-name US and UK artists from Madonna to Mötley Crüe.

Strahovský stadion Strahovská, Břevnov; bus #143 to Koleje Strahov; map p.136. The largest stadium in the world, holding an incredible 250,000 spectators. Has hosted the likes of the Stones but unused in recent years.

Tipsport Arena Za elektrárnou 1, Bubeneč ⊚ tipsport arena-praha.cz; tram #12 or #17 to Výstaviště; map p.138. The sponsors may change, but the awful acoustics don't at this early twentieth-century ice hockey stadium, which doubles as one of Prague's biggest indoor venues.

Výstaviště (Exhibition Grounds) U Výstaviště, Holešovice ☏ 266 727 411; tram #12 or #17 to Výstaviště; map p.138. The 1891 Exhibition Hall at Výstaviště is an atmospheric aircraft hangar of a place to watch a band, even if the acoustics aren't up to much.

CLUBS AND SMALL VENUES

MALÁ STRANA

Popocafépetl @ Újezd Újezd 19 ⊚ popoujezd.cz; tram #12, #15, #20, #22 or #23 to Hellichova; map p.56. One of a chain of popular cafés, this branch is slightly different as it has a dance floor – the programme ranges from DJs spinning retro dance hits to live gypsy bands and Latino nights. Cover charge free–100Kč. Daily 6pm–2am.

Újezd Újezd 18 ⊚ klubujezd.cz; tram #12, #15, #20, #22 or #23 to Újezd; map p.56. Long-standing, popular indie venue with a very small stage. Free entry. Daily until 4am.

STARÉ MĚSTO

Chapeau Rouge Jakubská 2 ⊚ chapeaurouge.cz; metro Náměstí Republiky; map p.70. Centrally located, multifloor, good-time club, with a blood-red bar on the ground floor (free entry) and two dance floors above featuring either DJs or live bands. Cover charge 50–100Kč. Mon–Thurs noon–3am, Fri noon–6am, Sat 4pm–6am, Sun 4pm–2am.

Dejavu Jakubská 6 ☏ 222 311 743, ⊚ dejavuclub.cz; metro Náměstí Republiky; map p.70. Smallish establishment with a bar upstairs and a club in the cellar playing mainstream hits for a mix of tourists and Czechs. Thurs–Sat 8pm–4am.

Karlovy lázně Smetanovo nábřeží 198 ⊚ karlovylazne .cz; metro Staroměstská; map p.70. Central Europe's biggest dance club, spread over five floors of an old bathhouse by Charles Bridge; techno on the top floor, progressively more retro as you descend to the café on the ground floor. Cover charge 180Kč. Daily 9pm–5am.

Klub Lávka Novotného lavka 1 ⊚ lavka.cz; metro Staroměstská; map p.70. Restaurant, theatre and cheesy disco with go-go girls and a great riverside terrace overlooking Charles Bridge and the Hrad. Cover charge from 100Kč (women free). Daily 10pm–5am.

Limonádový Joe Revoluční 1 ☏ 221 803 304, ⊚ klubjoe.cz; metro Náměstí Republiky; map p.70. This easy-going club beneath the Kotva department store has everything from karaoke and oldies nights to fashion shows and Czechoslovak hit discos. Tues–Thurs 5pm–1am, Fri & Sat 5pm–3am.

★ Roxy Dlouhá 33 ⊚ roxy.cz; metro náměstí Republiky; map p.70. The centrally located *Roxy* is a great little venue that's been around since the early 1990s. Housed in a laidback, rambling old theatre, it puts on an interesting programme of events from arty films and exhibitions to exceptional live acts and top DJ nights. Cover charge free–250Kč. Daily from around 8pm.

12

NOVÉ MĚSTO

Lucerna music bar Vodičkova 36 Ⓦ musicbar.cz; metro Můstek; map p.102. Not to be confused with the big venue of the same name, this is an unsophisticated, sweaty cellar bar in the Lucerna *pasáž* that hosts all sorts of gigs as well as themed discos. Cover charge from 100Kč. Daily 8/9pm–3am.

Nebe (Heaven) Křemencova 10 Ⓦ nebepraha.cz; metro Karlovo náměstí; map p.102. A simple formula: a snaking, brick-vaulted cocktail bar with a long drinks menu and DJs pumping out dance music from the last three or four decades. Cover charge from 100Kč. Tues 6pm–3am, Wed & Thurs 6pm–4am, Fri & Sat 6pm–5am.

Studio 54 Hybernská 38 Ⓦ studio54.cz; metro Hlavní Nádraží; map p.102. This late-late after-club venue is a useful place to know about if you want to continue well into the early hours, though the location is rather seedy. Cover charge 100Kč. Thurs 5am–9am, Sat & Sun 5am–1pm.

Vagon Národní třída 25 ☎ 776 446 013; metro Národní třída; map p.102. Great little cellar club rarely visited by foreigners, which specializes in tribute bands: expect imitators of anyone from Jimmy Hendrix to Czech band Olympic. Daily 7pm–6am.

VYSEHRAD AND THE EASTERN SUBURBS

★**Akropolis** Kubelíkova 27, Žižkov Ⓦ palacakropolis .cz; tram #5, #9, #15 or #26 to Lipanská; map p.124. This old Art Deco theatre is Žižkov's most popular club. With some excellent DJ nights and live gigs, it's also a good place to eat and drink. Cover charge from 100Kč. Bar Mon–Thurs 11am–12.30am, Fri 11am–1.30am, Sat & Sun 3pm–12.30am; venue doors open 7pm.

Fatal Rokycanova 29, Žižkov Ⓦ fatalclub.cz; tram #5, #9, #15 or #26 to Lipanská; map p.124. A young Czech crowd flocks to this Žižkov club for the combination of cheap drinks and unfamiliar rock acts from around central Europe. Cover charge 50–100Kč. Mon–Thurs 5pm–2am, Fri & Sat 5pm–3am, Sun 5pm–2am.

Forum Karlín Pernerova 51, Karlín Ⓦ forumkarlin.cz; metro Křižíkova; map p.124. This relatively new and highly impressive venue in the Karlín district north of Žižkov has a programme punctuated with a mixed bag of live music acts. Opening hours dependent on event.

Matrix Koněvova 13, Žižkov Ⓦ matrixklub.cz; tram #5, #9, #15 or #26 to Lipanská; map p.124. No-frills Žižkov club with an inexpensive bar and a basic menu of drum 'n' bass and jungle, but whose programme includes everything from live indie bands to heavy metal. Cover charge free–100Kč. Doors at 8pm.

★**Radost FX** Bělehradská 120, Vinohrady Ⓦ radostfx .cz; metro I.P. Pavlova; map p.124. This spacious, comfortable club is the longest-running all-round dance venue in Prague, with house and techno keeping the expats happy. Cover charge 150–250Kč. Thurs–Sat 10pm–4am.

U vystřelenýho oka (The Shot-Out Eye) U božích bojovníků 3, Žižkov Ⓦ uvoka.cz; tram #5, #9, #15 or #26 to Lipanská; map p.124. Big, loud, heavy-drinking pub just south of Žižkov Hill, off Husitská, with unusually good (occasionally live) indie rock. Free entry. Mon–Sat 4.30pm–1am.

HOLEŠOVICE AND THE WESTERN SUBURBS

Cross Club Plynární 23, Holešovice Ⓦ crossclub.cz; metro Nádraží Holešovice; map p.138. Labyrinthine ad hoc club on several floors, decked out in arty industrial decor, out near Nádraží Holešovice. The DJs on each floor cater to different music tastes from techno to ambient. Be sure to look at the huge, industrial sculptures made from scrap metal outside. Cover charge 50–100Kč. Daily 2pm–2am or later.

★**Futurum** Zborovská 7, Smíchov Ⓦ futurum .musicbar.cz; metro Anděl; map p.149. Smíchov's turn-of-the-century Národní dům is the unlikely home of this impressive, hi-tech club that hosts Czech bands and DJs playing anything from retro to house. Cover charge from 90Kč. Daily 8pm–1am.

★**La Fabrika** Komunardů 28, Holešovice ☎ 604 104 600, Ⓦ lafabrika.cz; tram #6, #12 to U Průhonu; map p.138. In a former factory out in the far-flung reaches of Holešovice, this cultural centre puts on tons of events, including live music. Opening hours dependent on event.

★**Mecca** U Průhonu 3, Holešovice Ⓦ mecca.cz; tram #6 or #12 to U Průhonu; map p.138. Out in the grid-plan industrial streets of Prague 7, this coolly converted factory is one of the most impressive, professional and popular clubs in Prague. Fri & Sat 10pm–6am.

Meet Factory Ke Skláren 15, Smíchov ☎ 251 551 796, Ⓦ meetfactory.cz; tram #4, #5, #12, #16 or #20 to ČSAD Smíchov; map p.149. The co-founder of this multi-purpose venue is artist David Černý and his work features throughout. There are live music concerts here several times a month featuring obscure Czech and overseas acts. Daily 1pm–late.

Phenomen Nádražní 84, Smíchov Ⓦ phenomen.cz; metro Anděl; map p.149. One of Prague's better clubs, with pricey drinks, a glitter-balled dance floor and a party programme starting at 10pm featuring Western European DJs. Tues–Thurs 7pm–3am, Fri & Sat 7pm–4am.

SaSaZu Bubenské nábřeží 38, Holešovice; metro Vltavská; map p.138. Prague's biggest venue is housed in Holešovice's vast market complex and includes a pan-Asian restaurant, a major venue for live gigs and a nightclub. Daily noon–2am.

12

JAZZ CLUBS

Prague has a surprisingly long **indigenous jazz** tradition and is home to a handful of good jazz clubs. With little money to bring in acts from abroad, the performers are almost exclusively Czech and tend to do virtually the entire round of venues each month. The one exception is AghaRTA, which attracts a few big names each year. More often than not it's a good idea to book a table – particularly at AghaRTA and Reduta.

STARÉ MĚSTO

★**AghaRTA Jazz Centrum** Železná 16 ☎222 211 275, ⓦagharta.cz; metro Můstek; map p.70. Probably the best jazz club in Prague, with a mix of Czechs and foreigners and a consistently good programme of gigs, plus a round-the-year festival that brings in some top acts. Cover charge 250–350Kč. Daily 7pm–1am.

Blues sklep Liliová 10 ☎608 848 074, ⓦbluessklep.cz; metro Staroměstská; map p.70. Old Town cellar club that puts on live jazz, flamenco, ragtime and blues from 9pm to midnight. Cover charge free–150Kč. Daily 7pm–2.30am.

Jazz Republic Jilská 1 ☎221 183 552, ⓦjazzrepublic.cz; metro Můstek; map p.70. Recently relocated but still super-central jazz venue with top line-ups and a restaurant. A regular venue for jazz festivals. Daily 8pm–late.

ELSEWHERE IN THE CITY

Jazz Dock Janáčkovo nábřeží 2, Smíchov ☎774 058 838, ⓦjazzdock.cz; tram #9, #12, #15 or #20 to Švandovo divadlo; map p.149. Floating jazz bar with a 10m-long bar, river views and a good variety of music. Gigs begin around 10pm, with jam sessions afterwards. Cover charge 90–200Kč. Mon–Thurs 3pm–4am, Fri & Sat 1pm–4am, Sun 1pm–2am.

Reduta Národní 20, Nové Město ☎224 933 487, ⓦredutajazzclub.cz; metro Národní třída; map p.102. Prague's best-known jazz club – Bill Clinton played sax here in front of Havel – obviously attracts a very touristy crowd, but also some decent acts. Gigs daily from 9.30pm; box office from 10am.

U malého Glena (Little Glen's) Karmelitská 23, Malá Strana ☎257 531 717, ⓦmalyglen.cz; tram #12, #20 or #22 to Malostranské náměstí; map p.56. Tiny downstairs stage worth checking out for its eclectic mix of Latin jazz, be-bop and blues. Live music 9.30pm–2am.

LGBT+ PRAGUE

Prague's **LGBT+ scene** has its spiritual heart in leafy Vinohrady and neighbouring Žižkov. For up-to-date listings check out ⓦprague.gayguide.net and ⓦpraguesaints.cz. You'll also find useful flyers at the places listed below.

STARÉ MĚSTO

Babylonia Martinská 6 ☎224 232 304, ⓦsaunababylonia.cz; metro Národní třída; map p.70. Prague's most centrally located gay sauna, with steam baths, pools and massage on offer. Entry 200–300Kč. Mon–Thurs & Sun 2pm–3am, Fri & Sat 2pm–5am.

Friends Bartolomějská 11 ☎226 211 920, ⓦfriendsclub.cz; metro Národní třída; map p.70. Mixed gay cellar club-bar in the centre of the old town, with regular lesbian nights on Fri. Daily 6pm–3am.

NOVÉ MĚSTO

JampaDampa V tůních ☎704 718 530, ⓦjampadampa.cz; metro Muzeum or I.P. Pavlova; map p.102. Currently the city's most popular and friendly lesbian café/club, with dancing, karaoke and events. Tues–Thurs 6pm–2am, Fri & Sat 6pm–6am.

VYSEHRAD AND THE EASTERN SUBURBS

Bar 21 Římská 21, Vinohrady ☎222 364 720, ⓦklub21.cz; metro Náměstí Míru; map p.124. Small local gay club-bar in a cosy Vinohrady cellar. Entry free. Mon–Sat 6pm–3am, Sun 6pm–1am.

On Club Vinohradská 40, Vinohrady ☎222 520 630, ⓦonclub.cz; metro Náměstí Míru; map p.124. Easily the city's biggest, most popular gay club and now even better after a name change and a complete revamp. Daily 10pm–5am.

Piano Bar Milešovská 10, Žižkov ☎222 969 888; metro Jiřího z Poděbrad; map p.124. Relaxed bar with billiards, a piano and an older, mostly gay, mostly local crowd. Daily 5pm–2am.

The Saints Polská 32, Vinohrady ☎222 250 326, ⓦpraguesaints.cz; metro Náměstí Míru or Jiřího z Poděbrad; map p.124. Small gay bar run by British expats that attracts an older gay crowd (both genders) – a good place to go if you want to find out about the scene. Sun–Thurs 7pm–2am, Fri & Sat 7pm–4am.

Střelec Anglická 2, Vinohrady; metro I.P. Pavlova; map p.124. Out-and-proud, highly visible gay club for older men with a popular "Bear Party" on the last Sat of the month. Daily 5pm–2am.

12

Termix Třebízského 4a, Vinohrady ☎222 710 462, ⓦclub-termix.cz; metro Jiřího z Poděbrad; map p.124. Stylish mixed gay/lesbian club, with lots of dancing, as well as chill-out rooms and darkrooms. Entry free. Wed–Sat 9pm–5.30am.

HOLEŠOVICE AND THE WESTERN SUBURBS
Drake's Zborovská 50, Smíchov ☎257 326 828, ⓦdrakes.cz; tram #9, #12,#15 or #22 to Újezd; map p.149. Very cruisey, labyrinthine gay club with lots of late-night action, strip shows and darkrooms. Entry 500Kč. Daily 24hr.

12

ZRCADLOVÁ KAPLE, KLEMENTINUM

The arts

There's no denying that the Czech capital enjoys a rich cultural life. Classical music wafts through the city, especially in the summer, when the streets, churches, palaces, opera houses, concert halls and even public gardens resonate with high-brow melodies. Mozart had strong links with Prague, and of course the Czechs themselves produced at least four top-drawer classical composers. In addition, Prague boasts three opera houses, five excellent orchestras and a couple of important festivals that attract top-class international artists. There's also a vibrant theatre scene, including mime and puppet theatre, and an impressive array of galleries. Rock, pop and jazz gigs are covered in Chapter 12 (see p.193).

Even if you don't understand Czech, the **theatre** scene in Prague is so diverse that there's usually something worth catching aimed at an English-speaking audience. For a start, the city has a strong tradition of mime, "black light theatre" (see p.201) and puppetry. As for **film**, many cinemas show movies in their original language, and new Czech films often get a showing with English subtitles.

Prague has a fine crop of art **galleries** housing the country's permanent collections from medieval to contemporary art, as well as staging temporary blockbuster exhibitions, with the superb, multi-venue Národní galerie (National Gallery) topping the list in most categories. And in such a photogenic city, it comes as little surprise that there is also an impressive roster of photography galleries.

ESSENTIALS

Tickets and costs If you can obtain tickets online or from the box office (*pokladna*) of the venue concerned, then all well and good. If a performance is sold out (*vyprodáno*), standby tickets are often available at the venue around an hour before the start. Alternatively, you may still be able to get a ticket from one of the city's numerous ticket agencies such as Ticketpro (w ticketpro.cz), which has branches all over Prague, with outlets in the Staroměstská radnice (Old Town Hall), Staroměstské náměstí, Staré Město (daily 9am–7pm), as well as at Rytířská 31, Staré Město (Mon–Fri

10am–6pm), and in the Rokoko *pasáž*, Václavské náměstí 38, Nové Město (daily 9am–2pm & 2.30–8pm). Prices, with a few notable exceptions, are reasonably good value.

Listings The English-language listings in *Prague Post* (w praguepost.com) are selective, but they do at least pick out the events that may be of particular interest to non-Czech speakers, and list all the major venues and their addresses. Also in English is the monthly handout *Culture in Prague* (w ceskakultura.cz) – published in Czech as *Česká kultura* – available from any PIS office (see p.25).

CLASSICAL MUSIC, OPERA AND BALLET

Folk songs, which lie at the heart of Czech music, have found their way into much of the country's traditional repertoire of **classical music**. The Czechs are justifiably proud of their classical music heritage, having produced four composers of international stature – Dvořák, Janáček, Smetana and Martinů – and a fifth, Mahler, who, though German-speaking, was born in Moravia. If the music of Mozart appears rather too often in the city's monthly concert programme, it's not only because the tourists love him, but also because of his special relationship with the city (see p.65). The country continues to produce top-class conductors, a host of singers and virtuoso violinists, and the city's musical heritage ensures a regular supply of international stars. The main **venues** are listed below, but keep an eye out too for concerts in the city's churches and palaces, gardens and courtyards, where evening performances tend to start fairly early (5pm or 7pm). By far the biggest annual event is **Prague Spring** (see p.26), the country's most prestigious **international music** festival.

THE MAJOR VENUES

Prague boasts three large-scale theatres where opera is regularly staged, and has several resident orchestras, the most illustrious of which are the Czech Philharmonic (Česká filharmonie), based at the Rudolfinum, and the Prague Symphony Orchestra (Symfonický orchestr hl. m. Prahy), whose home is the Smetanova síň in the Obecní dům. Note that all the major venues close down for most of July and August.

Národní divadlo (National Theatre) Národní 2, Nové Město ☎ 224 901 448, w narodni-divadlo.cz; metro Národní třída. Prague's grandest nineteenth-century theatre is the living embodiment of the Czech national revival movement, and continues to put on a wide variety of mostly, though by no means exclusively, Czech plays, plus opera and ballet. Worth visiting for the decor alone. The Nová scéna is the theatre's modern second stage. Some productions have English surtitles. Box office daily 10am–6pm.

Obecní dům – Smetanova síň Náměstí Republiky 5,

Nové Město ☎ 222 002 336, w obecni-dum.cz; metro Náměstí Republiky. This fantastically ornate Art Nouveau concert hall is where the Prague Spring festival usually kicks off, and is also home to the excellent Prague Symphony Orchestra (w fok.cz). Box office Mon–Fri 10am–8pm.

Rudolfinum Alšovo nábřeží 12, Staré Město ☎ 227 059 227, w rudolfinum.cz; metro Staroměstská. A stunning neo-Renaissance concert hall from the late nineteenth century that's home base for the Czech Philharmonic (w ceskafilharmonie.cz). The Dvořákova síň is the large hall; the Sukova síň is the chamber concert hall. Box office Mon–Fri 10am–6pm.

Státní opera Praha (Prague State Opera) Wilsonova 4, Nové Město ☎ 224 901 448, w opera.cz; metro Muzeum. A sumptuous nineteenth-century opera house, built by the city's German community, which once attracted star conductors such as Mahler and Zemlinsky. Nowadays, it is part of the National Theatre set-up, but was closed for a much-needed refit at the time of research.

13

Stavovské divadlo (Estates Theatre) Ovocný trh 1, Staré Město ☎ 224 901 448, ⓦ narodni-divadlo.cz; metro Můstek. Prague's oldest opera house, which witnessed the premiere of Mozart's *Don Giovanni*, hosts a mixture of opera, ballet and straight theatre (with simultaneous headphone translation available). Some productions have English surtitles. Box office at Železná 24 open daily 10am–6pm.

OTHER CONCERT VENUES

Anežský klášter (Convent of sv Anežka) U milosrdný 7, Staré Město ☎ 224 810 628; metro Náměstí Republiky. This branch of the Národní galerie puts on regular chamber concerts, often featuring music by the big four Czech composers, in the convent's atmos-pheric Gothic chapel (see p.85).

Atrium na Žižkově Čajkovského 12, Žižkov ☎ 221 721 838, ⓦ atriumzizkov.cz; tram #5, #9, #15 or #26 to Olšanské náměstí. In a most unlikely location, this Baroque chapel sits deep in the heart of Žižkov, staging a regular (though not daily) programme of chamber music.

Bazilika sv Jakub (St James) Malá Štupartská 6, Staré Město ☎ 224 828 816; metro Náměstí Republiky. This church (see p.84), with Prague's finest organ, is a venue for choral church music, sung Mass and regular recitals.

Chrám sv Mikuláše (St Nicholas) Staroměstské náměstí, Staré Město ☎ 224 190 994; metro Staroměstská. Whitewashed Baroque church on the edge of Staroměstské náměstí, used for singing recitals and choral concerts; not to be confused with the church of the same dedication in Malá Strana (see p.82).

Kostel sv Mikuláše (St Nicholas) Malostranské náměstí, Malá Strana ☎ 257 534 215; tram #12 #20 or #22 to Malostranské náměstí. Prague's most sumptuous Baroque church (see p.58) is the perfect setting for choral concerts and organ recitals.

Kostel sv Šimona a Judy (St Simon & Jude) Dušní, Staré Město ☎ 222 321 352; metro Náměstí Republiky. Deconsecrated *trompe l'oeil* church, where the Prague Symphony Orchestra puts on chamber music concerts.

Lichtenštejnský palác (Liechtenstein Palace) Malostranské náměstí 13, Malá Strana ☎ 234 244 136, ⓦ hamu.cz; tram #12 #20 or #22 to Malostranské náměstí. The Czech Academy of Music (HAMU) is based here (see p.55) and puts on chamber concerts and string quartets inside and out in the courtyard.

Lobkovický palác (Lobkowicz Palace) Jiřská 3, Hradčany ☎ 602 108 292, ⓦ lobkowiczevents.cz; metro Malostranská. Baroque and Renaissance concerts as well as other events are held in the palace's main, frescoed

---

CULTURAL INSTITUTES

Various **national cultural institutions** in Prague host a wide variety of artistic offerings throughout the year.

Austrian Cultural Institute (Rakouský kulturní fórum) Jungmannovo náměstí 18, Nové Město ☎ 224 284 001, ⓦ rkfpraha.cz; metro Můstek. Very good exhibitions of Austrian art, plus the odd concert, film and talk. Gallery Mon–Fri 10am–5pm.

British Council (Britská rada) Bredovský dvůr, Politických vězňů 13, Nové Město ☎ 221 991 160, ⓦ britishcouncil.cz; metro Můstek/Muzeum. Various lectures and events all year, plus temporary exhibitions, newspapers, magazines and a reading room. Mon–Thurs 8am–8pm, Fri 8am–5pm, Sat 8.30am–1pm.

Goethe Institut Masarykovo nábřeží 32, Nové Město ☎ 221 962 111, ⓦ goethe.de; metro Národní třída. Weekly German films and frequent lectures; small exhibition space and library. Mon–Thurs 9am–5pm, Fri & Sat 11am–5pm.

Hungarian Cultural Centre (Maďarské kulturní středisko) Rytířská 25–27, Staré Město ☎ 224 222 424, ⓦ praha.balassiintezet.hu; metro Můstek. Weekly film showings and regular exhibitions and concerts. Mon noon–4pm, Tues & Wed 9am–4pm, Thurs 9am–6pm, Fri 9am–1pm.

Institut Français (Francouzský institut) Štěpánská 35, Nové Město ☎ 221 401 011, ⓦ ifp.cz; metro Muzeum. Great exhibitions and a great café, with croissants and *journaux*. Also puts on screenings of classic French films, plus lectures and even the odd concert. Café 35 (see p.183): Mon–Fri 8.30am–8pm, Sat 10am–2pm.

Instituta Italiana di Cultura (Italský kulturní institut) Šporkova 14, Malá Strana ☎ 257 090 681, ⓦ iic-praga.cz; tram #12, #20 or #22 to Malostranské náměstí. Exhibitions, films and events staged in various locations including the wonderful Baroque chapel on Vlašská. Mon–Fri 9am–1pm & 3–6pm, Fri 9am–1pm.

Instituto Cervantes (Španělské kulturní centrum) Na Rybníčku 6, Nové Město ☎ 221 595 211, ⓦ praga .cervantes.es; metro I.P. Pavlova. Regular programme of concerts and films, plus a library. Mon–Thurs 10am–6pm, Fri 10am–4pm.

Polish Institute (Polský institut) Malé náměstí 1, Staré Město ☎ 220 410 410, ⓦ polskyinstitut.cz; metro Můstek. Weekly film showings, occasional concerts and lectures. Tues 2–6pm, Thurs 1–3pm, Fri 11am–3pm.

13

hall at the eastern edge of Prague Castle (see p.45).

Pražský hrad (Prague Castle) Hradčany ☎224 372 434, ⓦ kulturanahrade.cz; tram #22 or #23 to Pražský hrad. There's a regular and varied music programme laid on at the castle, using venues ranging from the Renaissance Míčovna (Ball Game Court) in the Královská zahrada (Royal Gardens) to the spectacularly ornate

Španělský sál (Spanish Hall).

Zrcadlová kaple (Mirrored Chapel) Klementinum, Mariánské náměstí, Staré Město ☎733 129 252, ⓦ klementinum.com; metro Staroměstská. Regular chamber and organ concerts held in the Klementinum's beautifully atmospheric pink Baroque chapel of mirrors (see p.78).

THEATRE

Czech culture has always had a special place for **theatre** (*divadlo*) – the first post-Communist Czech president, Václav Havel, was a playwright – and the scene continues to thrive. With a steady supply of tourists and expats as potential audience, there are now a handful of English-language theatre companies based in Prague. In addition, there's a strong tradition of **mime** and **Černé divadlo** or "black light theatre" (visual trickery created by "invisible" actors dressed all in black) in the city, ranging from the classical style of the late Ladislav Fialka and his troupe to the more experimental work of Boris Polívka. However, along with Prague's long-running multimedia company, Laterna magika, many of these shows are now deliberately geared towards tourists, and can make for disappointing viewing. **Puppet theatre** (*loutkové divadlo*), which also has a long indigenous folk tradition as an art form for both adults and children, is thriving partly thanks to its accessibility to non-Czech audiences. Note that in addition to the venues listed below, the Stavovské divadlo (see p.200) and the Národní divadlo (see p.199) both put on plays as well as opera and ballet.

THEATRE VENUES

Alfred ve dvoře Františka Křížka 36, Holešovice ☎233 376 985, ⓦ alfredvedvore.cz; tram #1, #5, #8, #12, #17, #25 or #26 to Strossmayerovo náměstí. Experimental theatre founded in 1997 by mime theatre guru Ctibor Turba; puts on nonverbal and mime performances and also hosts occasional student dramas.

Black Light Theatre of Prague (Černé divadlo Jiřího Srnce) Na Příkopě 10, Nové Město ☎774 574 475, ⓦ srnectheatre.com; metro Můstek. One of the founders of Laterna magika and inventors of black light theatre, Jiří Srnec still puts on shows, some of which are a cut above the competition. Box office daily 10am–8pm.

Divadlo Archa Na poříčí 26, Nové Město ☎221 716 333, ⓦ divadloarcha.cz; metro Florenc. By far the most exciting, innovative venue in Prague, with two very versatile spaces, plus an art gallery. The programming includes music, dance and theatre, with an emphasis on new and experimental work. English subtitles or translation often available. Box office Mon–Fri 10am–6pm, plus 2hr before performance.

Divadlo Image Národní 25, Nové Město ☎222 314 448, ⓦ imagetheatre.cz; metro Můstek. One of the more innovative and entertaining of Prague's black light theatre venues. Box office daily 10am–8pm.

Divadlo na zábradlí Anenské náměstí 5, Staré Město ☎222 868 870, ⓦ nazabradli.cz; metro Staroměstská. Václav Havel's old haunt and a centre of absurdist theatre back in the 1960s, the Divadlo na zábradlí is still a provocative rep theatre, with a wide variety of shows (in Czech) and a lively bar. Box office Mon–Fri 2–8pm, Sat & Sun 2hr before performance.

Duncan Centre Branická 41, Braník ☎270 006 700, ⓦ duncancentre.cz; tram #2, #3, #17 or #21 to Přístaviště. Occasional dance performances by resident and visiting artists at this theatre based in a school for contemporary dance in the southern suburb of Braník.

Laterna magika (Magic Lantern) Nová scéna, Národní 4, Nové Město ☎224 931 482, ⓦ narodni -divadlo.cz; metro Národní třída. The National Theatre's Nová scéna, one of Prague's most modern and versatile stages, is the main base for Laterna magika, founders of multimedia and black light theatre way back in 1958. Their slick productions continue effortlessly to pull in crowds of tourists. Box office Mon–Fri 9am–6pm, Sat & Sun from 10am.

Ponec Husitská 24a, Žižkov ☎222 721 531, ⓦ divadloponec.cz; metro Hlavní nádraží or Florenc. Former cinema, now an innovative dance venue and centre for the annual Tanec Praha dance festival in May/June. Box office Mon–Fri 5–8pm and 1hr before performance.

Roxy – NoD Dlouhá 33, Staré Město ☎773 25 26 73, ⓦ nod.roxy.cz; metro Náměstí Republiky. Experimental (and often very quirky) theatre staged on the first floor of the Roxy cultural complex. Box office daily 4–8pm.

Švandovo divadlo Štefánikova 57, Smíchov ☎257 318 666, ⓦ svandovodivadlo.cz; tram #9, #12, #15 or #20 to Švandovo divadlo. Pioneering, exciting and experimental, Švandovo is a great place to sample the Prague theatre scene; all productions are in Czech (with English surtitles). There's a great bar and often gigs too. Box office Mon–Fri 2–8pm, Sat & Sun 2hr before performance.

PUPPET THEATRE

When looking for a puppet show, avoid the never-ending performances of Mozart's *Don Giovanni* in period costume, specifically aimed at passing tourists, and sample one of the other companies instead. In 2017, Czech puppetry was listed

13

by UNESCO as a piece of Intangible Cultural Heritage which may mean more traditional shows and better quality as funding is made available.

Divadlo minor Vodičkova 6, Nové Město ☎ 222 231 351, ⓦ minor.cz; metro Karlovo náměstí. The former state puppet theatre puts on children's shows most days, plus adult shows on occasional evenings – sometimes with English subtitles. Box office Mon–Fri 10am–1.30pm & 2.30–8pm, Sat & Sun 11am–6pm.

Divadlo Spejbla a Hurvínka Dejvická 38, Dejvice ☎ 224 316 784, ⓦ spejbl-hurvinek.cz; metro Dejvická/

Hradčanská. Features the indomitable marionette duo, Spejbl and Hurvínek, created by Josef Skupa at one of the few puppets-only theatres in the country. Box office Mon 1–6pm, Tues–Fri 9am–2pm & 3–6pm, Sat & Sun 9.30–11.30am & noon–5pm.

Říše loutek Žatecká 1, Staré Město ☎ 222 324 565, ⓦ riseloutek.cz; metro Staroměstská. This company's rather dull marionette version of Mozart's *Don Giovanni* has been going for years, but it also puts on more interesting kids' shows at the weekends. Closed May to mid-June. Box office Sat & Sun 1–6pm.

FILM

Going to the **cinema** (*kino*) remains relatively inexpensive (around 120–250Kč a ticket) and popular in Prague. Hollywood blockbusters form a large part of the weekly schedule, but the Czech film industry continues to chug along, turning out films that do fairly well domestically, though pale in comparison with the country's output between the 1960s and the mid-1990s. Foreign films are usually shown in their original language with subtitles (*titulky*) – beware dubbed screenings (*dabing*), which are truly dire. Thanks to Prague's expat community, some Czech films are occasionally shown with English subtitles – for a comprehensive rundown of the week's films, see the monthly *Culture in Prague/Česká kultura* (ⓦ ceskakultura.cz). Note that film titles are nearly always translated into Czech, so you'll need to have your wits about you to identify what it is that's actually being shown. The city's main **movie houses** have traditionally been concentrated around Wenceslas Square. The list below is confined to the best screens, plus Prague's art-house film clubs, where you may need to buy an annual membership card (*roční legitimace*) in order to purchase tickets. Keep a look out, too, for films shown at the various foreign cultural institutions around town (see box, p.200), and for the summer-only open-air *letní kino*, which is held on the Střelecký ostrov (ⓦ letnak .cz). The nearest Prague comes to a film festival is the annual **Days of European Film** (ⓦ eurofilmfest.cz), which takes place over two weeks in April.

CINEMAS

Aero Biskupcova 31, Žižkov ☎ 271 771 349, ⓦ kinoaero .cz; tram #9, #10, #11 or #16 to Biskupcova. Crumbling art-house cinema that shows rolling mini-festivals, retrospectives and independent movies.

Bio Konvikt – Ponrepo Bartolomějská 11, Staré Město ☎ 778 522 708; metro Národní třída. Black-and-white classics, some of them very old indeed, dug out from the Czech National Film Archives.

Cinema City Na příkopě 22, Nové Město ☎ 257 181 212, ⓦ cinemacity.cz; metro Můstek. The most central of Prague's multiplex cinemas, regularly showing new Czech releases with English subtitles.

Evald Národní 28, Nové Město ☎ 221 105 225,

ⓦ evald.cz; metro Národní třída. Prague's most centrally located art-house cinema screens a discerning selection of new releases interspersed with plenty of classics.

Kino MAT Karlovo náměstí 19, Nové Město ☎ 224 915 765, ⓦ mat.cz; metro Karlovo náměstí. Tiny café and cinema popular with the film crowd, with an eclectic programme of shorts, documentaries and Czech films with English subtitles. Claims to be the country's smallest cinema.

Lucerna Vodičkova 36, Nové Město ☎ 224 216 972, ⓦ kinolucerna.cz; metro Můstek. Without doubt the most ornate commercial cinema in Prague, with the best café-bar, all decked out in Moorish style by Havel's grandfather, in the *pasáž* the family once owned.

VISUAL ARTS

The **Národní galerie** (National Gallery) runs the city's main **permanent art collections**, in the Anežský klášter (see p.200), Salmovský palác (see p.48), palác Kinských (see p.82), Schwarzenberský palác (see p.49), Šternberský palác (see p.49) and Veletržní palác (see p.139), each of which is described in detail in the Guide. Most of these galleries also give over space for **temporary exhibitions**, and there are several others that only ever stage special exhibitions. *Prague Post* has selective listings, including the foreign cultural institutes that put on regular exhibitions (see box, p.200), but as ever you'll find the fullest listings in the Czech monthly listings magazine *Culture in Prague/Česká kultura*. Dozens of **commercial galleries** have sprung up in the past 25 years or so, only a handful of which can be relied on regularly to show interesting stuff; what follows is a selection of the best. Look out, too, for the various **Prague Biennales** – the city has, in the past, staged more than one in a single year. As in Venice, but on a fraction of the budget, the exhibitions attract contemporary artists and curators from all over the world.

MAJOR EXHIBITION SPACES

České Centrum Rytířská 31, Staré Město ☎ 234 668 501, ⊕ czechcentres.cz; metro Můstek. The mother ship of the state-run globe-spanning Czech Centre network puts on top-notch exhibitions, often with a design/architecture theme. Mon–Fri 11am–6pm, Sat 11am–5pm.

České muzeum výtvarných umění (Czech Museum of Fine Art) Husova 19–21, Staré Město ☎ 222 220 218, ⊕ cmvu.cz; metro Staroměstská. Retrospectives of twentieth-century Czech and (occasionally) foreign artists. Tues–Sun 10am–6pm.

DOX Poupětova 1, Holešovice ☎ 295 568 123, ⊕ dox.cz; tram #6 or #12 to Ortenovo náměstí. Big, privately financed contemporary art gallery in a former metal factory on the industrial east side of Holešovice – expect lots of interesting and provocatively titled shows. Sat–Mon 10am–6pm, Wed & Fri 11am–7pm, Thurs 11am–9pm.

Dům U kamenného zvonu Staroměstské náměstí 13, Staré Město ☎ 224 828 245, ⊕ ghmp.cz; metro Staroměstská. The Prague City Gallery puts on a good range of Czech retrospectives, from Baroque to avant-garde, in the small Gothic rooms and courtyard of this ancient building (see p.82). Tues–Sun 10am–8pm.

Galerie Hollar Smetanovo nábřeží 6, Staré Město ☎ 737 288 310, ⊕ hollar.cz; metro Národní třída. The main exhibition space for Czech graphic artists is situated on the noisy river embankment; but there are plenty of old prints for sale. Tues–Sun 10am–noon & 1–6pm.

Galerie Jaroslava Fragnera Betlémské náměstí 5a, Staré Město ☎ 222 222 157, ⊕ gjf.cz; metro Národní třída. Small gallery that puts on exhibitions on architectural themes. Tues–Sun 11am–7pm.

Mánes Masarykovo nábřeží 250, Nové Město; ⊕ galeriemanes.com; metro Karlovo náměstí. White functionalist building spanning a channel in the Vltava, with an open-plan gallery and a tradition of excellent exhibitions of contemporary art and photography. Hours vary depending on exhibition.

Městská knihovna (Municipal Library) Mariánské náměstí 1, Staré Město ☎ 222 310 489, ⊕ ghmp.cz; metro Staroměstská. The exhibitions at this central Prague City Gallery space, usually devoted to Czech or central European artists and photographers, are well worth checking out. Tues–Sun 10am–6pm, Thurs 10am–8pm.

Obecní dům Náměstí Republiky 5, Nové Město ⊕ obecni-dum.cz; metro Náměstí Republiky. Exhibitions usually on a *fin-de-siècle* theme in the luscious surroundings of the Art Nouveau Obecní dům (see p.109). Daily 10am–6pm.

Pražský hrad (Prague Castle) Hradčany ☎ 224 373 368, ⊕ kulturanahrade.cz; tram #22 to Pražský hrad. Prague Castle has several temporary exhibition spaces, the most impressive of which is the Císařská konírna, Rudolf II's former stables. Tues–Sun 10am–6pm.

Rudolfinum Alšovo nábřeží 12, Staré Město ☎ 227 059 205, ⊕ galerierudolfinum.cz; metro Staroměstská. This magnificent late-nineteenth-century arts complex has one of the few galleries in Prague that can take large-scale international art and photography exhibitions. Tues, Wed & Fri–Sun 10am–6pm, Thurs 10am–8pm.

UPM 17 listopadu 2, Staré Město ☎ 251 093 111, ⊕ upm.cz; metro Staroměstská. The UPM, the city's museum of applied art (see p.99), owns some of the finest Czech art in the world, and will once again put on excellent temporary exhibitions when it reopens in 2018 after rebuilding work.

Valdštejnská jízdárna (Waldstein Stables) Valdštejnská 3, Malá Strana ⊕ ngprague.cz; metro Malostranská. Some of the Národní galerie's most popular exhibitions – from retrospectives of Old Masters to twentieth-century Czech greats – are staged in these former stables by Malostranská metro station. Tues–Sun 10am–6pm.

Veletržní palác Dukelských hrdinů 47, Holešovice ☎ 224 301 122, ⊕ ngprague.cz; tram #6 or #17 to Veletržní palác. Prague's vast modern art museum puts on some of the city's best temporary exhibitions and retrospectives in the galleries on the ground, first and fifth floors (see p.139). Tues–Sun 10am–6pm.

COMMERCIAL GALLERIES

AM 180 Bělehradská 45, Vinohrady ⊕ am180.org; tram #6 #13 or #23 to Bruselská. This youthful arts collective put on exhibitions drawn from their members, and changes every two or three weeks. Mon–Thurs 1–7pm.

Futura Holečkova 49, Smíchov ⊕ futuraproject.cz; tram #9, #10, #15 or #16 to Bertramka. Futura remains at the top of the city's commercial art galleries. The courtyard features David Černý's sculpture *Brownnosers*, and the interior has several exhibition spaces ranging from the classic white cube to atmospheric cellars; there are also separate studios in Karlín. Wed–Sun 11am–6pm.

Galerie Display Bubenská 3, Holešovice ☎ 777 208 186, ⊕ display.cz; metro Vltavská. Excellent contemporary gallery that puts on an experimental range of exhibitions, screens films and encourages artistic debate. Wed–Sun 3–6pm.

Galerie Jiří Švestka Biskupský dvůr 6, Nové Město ☎ 222 311 092, ⊕ jirisvestkagallery.com; metro Náměstí Republiky. Private gallery showcasing young Czech artists and occasionally staging exhibitions by international names. Wed–Fri 2–7pm, Sat 11am–7pm.

Galerie Tvrdohlaví Vodičkova 36, Nové Město ☎ 296 236 491, ⊕ tvrdohlavi.cz; metro Můstek. Situated in the Lucerna *pasáž*, this gallery showcases the work of the Tvrdohlaví (Stubborn Ones), a group of provocative Czech artists born in the 1950s and early 1960s. Daily 10am–10pm.

13

Meetfactory Ke Sklárně 15, Smíchov ☎ 251 551 796, ⓦ meetfactory.cz; tram #4, #5, #12 or #20 to ČSAD Smíchov. Part of David Černý's multi-purpose arts venue, the gallery here puts on cutting-edge exhibitions of contemporary art. Daily 10am–10pm.

PHOTOGRAPHY GALLERIES

Ateliér Josefa Sudka Újezd 30, Malá Strana ☎ 251 510 760, ⓦ sudek-atelier.cz; tram #9, #22, #23 to Újezd. One of three galleries named after the father of Czech photography, this place is worth a visit if only to sneak a look at Sudek's reconstructed studio, where he executed some of his most famous photographic cycles, and which now contains a smattering of Sudek memorabilia. Tues–Sun noon–6pm.

Galerie Josefa Sudka Úvoz 24, Hradčany ☎ 257 531 489, ⓦ upm.cz; tram #22 or #23 to Pohořelec. In the house where Sudek lived and worked from 1959 onwards, this gallery puts on excellent exhibitions organized by the UPM. April–Sept Wed–Sun 11am–7pm; Oct–March Wed–Sun 11am–5pm.

Komorní galerie domu Josefa Sudka Maiselova 2, Josefov ⓦ czechpressphoto.cz; metro Staroměstská. Exhibition space used by Czech Press Photo to put on exhibitions of photojournalism. Tues–Sun 11am–6pm.

Shopping

Prague may not have always been everyone's first choice as a shopping destination, but the days of lumpen electrical goods, bottles of Soviet fizz and surly, pinafore-wearing assistants have long gone. Nowadays there are plenty of flashy malls, exclusive boutiques and the odd quirky independent stores offering a range of temptations – Czech-made glass, ceramics, wooden toys, foodie treats, alcohol, small antique collectibles – to weigh down your bags as you board the flight home. It's worth bearing in mind that the strength of the Czech crown against major currencies has pushed prices high, and many things may actually cost more than they do back home. Though the Czech Republic is still very much a cash economy, the vast majority of shops now accept credit and debit cards.

The backstreets of **Malá Strana**, **Staré Město** and **Nové Město** are happy hunting grounds for interesting little shops, as long as you steer clear of Karlova, Mostecká and Nerudova, where it's strictly puppets, jester hats, Kafka T-shirts, fake Soviet army gear, Mucha merchandise and that most Czech of souvenirs – the Russian *matrioshka* doll. The multinational franchises have staked out Pařížská, Na příkopě and Wenceslas Square, and Prague now has far too many shopping malls for a city of this size, with **Palladium**, on Náměstí Republiky, the mother of them all; more interesting are the old-fashioned, interwar covered **pasáže** on and around Wenceslas Square.

14

ANTIQUES, GLASS AND ARTS & CRAFTS

There are **antique** shops (*starožitnosti*), **secondhand** junk shops (*bazar*) and bric-a-brac outlets all over Prague. Those in the main tourist districts offer few bargains, but elsewhere you may find some inexpensive curios. Shops selling **glass** (*sklo*) are ubiquitous; the difficulty might be finding anything you actually like the look of. For **folk arts** and crafts, you could try the Havelské market (see p.209) or the Manufaktura chain.

HRADČANY

Výbor dobré vůle Zlatá ulička 19; metro Malostranská; map p.36. All the crafts in this tiny shop in the Hrad are made by disabled children; profits go to the Olga Havlová Foundation, set up by Václav Havel's late wife to help them. Hrad ticket required. Daily 9am–5pm.

MALÁ STRANA

Antikvariát Újezd 26; tram #12, #15, #20, #22 or #23 to Újezd; map p.56. Small secondhand bookshop that also sells old film and theatre posters. Mon–Fri 11am–6pm.

Art Puzzle Újezd 33; tram #12, #15, #20, #22 or #23 to Hellichova; map p.56. Tiny private gallery selling handcrafted jigsaw art of all shapes and sizes. Mon–Sat 9am–6pm.

Artěl U Lužického Semináře 7; tram #12, #15, #20 or #22 to Malostranské náměstí; map p.56. Superb design shop offering beautiful lead-free crystal creations and some Czech jewellery. Daily 10am–7pm.

★**Elima** Jánský vršek 5 ☎ 777 580 680, ⓦ elimashop .cz; tram #12, #20 or #22 to Malostranské náměstí; map p.56. This tiny little shop in the backstreets sells beautiful, inexpensive, handmade Polish pottery from Boleslawiec (Bunzlau). Daily 10am–6pm.

Marionety Nerudova 51 ☎ 774 418 236, ⓦ marionettes .cz; metro Malostranská; map p.56. Decent range of marionettes, rod and glove puppets, antique and new. Daily 10am–6pm.

STARÉ MĚSTO

Antik v Dlouhé Dlouhá 37 ☎ 774 431 776, ⓦ antik-v -dlouhe.cz; metro Náměstí Republiky; map p.70. Great antique shop with many authentic items that will fit in a suitcase, though it does specialize in spectacular light fittings and First Republic chrome tube chairs. Mon–Fri 10am–7pm, Sat & Sun noon–6pm.

★**Art Deco** Michalská 21 ☎ 224 815 848; metro Můstek; map p.70. A stylish antique shop crammed with a

wonderful mixture of clothes, hats, mufflers, teapots, glasses, clocks and art from the first half of the twentieth century. Mon–Sat 2–7pm.

★**Bric a Brac** Týnská 7 ☎ 224 815 763; metro Náměstí Republiky; map p.70. Absolutely minute antique store, packed to the rafters with every conceivable trinket. The central location means that prices are very high, but the place is worth visiting for the spectacle alone. The owner also runs a much larger place round the corner. Daily 10am–6pm.

Granát Turnov Dlouhá 28 ⓦ granat.cz; metro Náměstí Republiky; map p.70. The best place to get hold of exquisite Bohemian garnet jewellery made in North Bohemia. Daily 9am–7pm.

★**Kubista** Ovocný trh 19 ☎ 224 236 378, ⓦ kubista.cz; metro Náměstí Republiky; map p.70. Beautiful shop housed in the House of the Black Madonna and selling reproductions of some of the museum's exquisite Cubist ceramics, jewellery and furniture. Tues–Sat 10am–7pm, Sun noon–7pm.

★**Manufaktura** Melantrichova 17 ☎ 601 310 611, ⓦ manufaktura.cz; metro Staroměstská; map p.70. Czech folk-inspired shop with a fantastic array of wooden toys, painted Easter eggs, straw decorations, honeycomb candles and sundry kitchen utensils. Many other branches across the city including at the airport, the main railway station and in the Palladium shopping mall. Daily 10am–8pm.

NOVÉ MĚSTO

Bazar Vyšehradská 8 ☎ 224 912 766; tram #2, #3, #7, #17 or #21 to Výtoň; map p.102. You'll find everything from socialist-era pin badges to 1960s lightshades, 1980s Czechoslovak toy cars to German-built wardrobes at this cheap junk shop south of the city centre. Erratic opening hours.

Moser Na příkopě 12 ☎ 224 211 293; metro Můstek; map p.102. High-class emporium selling the most famous glass and crystal from the West Bohemian spa town of Karlovy Vary. Prices are high. Daily 10am–8pm.

14

BOOKS, MAPS AND GRAPHICS

Sadly many of Prague's English-language bookstores have closed in recent years as expats went online for their reading material. The city does boast several musty **secondhand** bookstores (*antikvariát*), some pricey antiquarian-type places and others cheap, rambling shops; many of these also stock a good selection of old prints and posters.

MALÁ STRANA

Klub Za starou Prahu Mostecká 1 (Karlův most) ☎ 257 530 599; tram #12, #15, #20, #22 or #23 to Malostranské náměstí; map p.56. This small shop at the Malá Strana end of Charles Bridge stocks the city's best collection of books on Prague's intriguing architecture, plus maps and guides. All proceeds go to the Klub Za starou Prahu (Old Prague Club), an organization that lobbies local government to preserve the city you've come to see. Tues–Sat 10am–6pm.

Shakespeare a synové U lužického semináře 10 ☎ 257 531 894, ⓦ shakes.cz; metro Malostranská; map p.56. Don't be deceived by the tiny frontage: this is a wonderful, rambling, well-stocked English-language bookstore in which to while away an afternoon. Daily 11am–7pm.

STARÉ MĚSTO

Kavka Krocínova 5 ☎ 606 030 202, ⓦ kavkaartbooks .com; tram #2, #9, #18, #22 or 23 to Národní divadlo; map p.70. Housed aptly in a thoroughbred functionalist building, this superb store is packed with every conceivable book on the subject of Czech art and photography. Mon–Fri 11am–6pm.

JOSEFOV

Judaica Široká 7 ☎ 222 318 876, ⓦ antikvariat-judaica .cz; metro Staroměstská; map p.92. Probably the best stocked of all the places flogging Jewish books to passing tourists, with books and prints, secondhand and new. Mon–Fri & Sun 10am–6pm.

NOVÉ MĚSTO

Academia Václavské náměstí 34 ⓦ academia.cz; metro Muzeum/Můstek; map p.102. One of the best downtown bookstores for Czech books, with a fair selection of English-language editions and a café on the first floor. Mon–Fri 8.30am–8pm, Sat 9.30am–7pm, Sun 9.30am–6pm.

Antikvariát Dlážděná Dlážděná 7 ☎ 222 243 911; metro Hlavní nádraží or tram #3, #6, #14, #15, #24 or #26 to Masarykovo nádraží; map p.102. This is one of the city centre's longest-established and best secondhand bookstores, but it's the prints and original artwork, some by well-known artists, that many come here for. Mon–Fri 9am–6pm, Sat 9am–1pm.

★ **The Globe** Pštrossova 6 ☎ 224 934 203, ⓦ globe bookstore.cz; metro Národní třída/Karlovo náměstí; map p.102. The expat bookstore *par excellence* – both a social centre and a superbly well-stocked store, with an adjacent café and friendly staff. Mon–Fri 10am–midnight, Fri–Sun 9.30am–1am.

Kant Opatovická 26 ☎ 224 934 219, ⓦ antik-kant.cz; metro Národní třída; map p.102. Lots of old books, including a fair few English-language titles, plus a good display of prints. Tues–Fri 10am–6pm.

THE SUBURBS

Antikvariát Novák Dělnická 45, Holešovice; tram #1, #6, #14, #25 to Maniny; map p.138. You could spend hours clambering and sifting through the old books, paintings, knick-knacks piled high at this scruffy junk shop out in Holešovice. Mon–Fri 9am–7pm, Sat 9am–5pm, Sun 1–5pm.

DEPARTMENT STORES

For most basic goods, and many luxury ones, you're best off heading for one of Prague's **department stores** (*obchodní dům*), which stock most things – including toiletries, stationery and usually an extensive food and drink selection. Prices are quickly catching up with those in Western Europe.

NOVÉ MĚSTO

Kotva Náměstí Republiky 8 ☎ 224 801 300, ⓦ od -kotva.cz; metro Náměstí Republiky; map p.102. A seminal piece of dreadful brown 1970s architecture, Kotva was once *the* department store in Prague, but has since lost a lot of ground to flashier outfits, despite a skin-deep "exclusive" makeover in 2016. It's a classic, though, built by Swedish workers, many of whom carted off Czech brides

when construction was over. Daily 9am–8pm.

Palladium Náměstí Republiky 1 ☎ 225 770 250, ⓦ palladiumpraha.cz; metro Náměstí Republiky; map p.102. The apotheosis of Czech consumerism, with over 200 shops, this is the country's largest shopping mall, occupying the spruced-up former barracks opposite the Obecní dům. Daily 7am–11pm.

FASHION AND COSMETICS

MALÁ STRANA

Ahasver Prokopská 3 ☎ 257 531 404, ⓦ ahasver.com; tram #12, #20 or #22 to Malostranské náměstí; map

p.56. Delightful little shop selling antique gowns and jewellery as well as paintings, porcelain and glass. Tues–Sun 11am–6pm.

STARÉ MĚSTO

★**Botanicus** Týn 3 ☎234 767 446, ⊕botanicus.cz; metro Staroměstská; map p.70. Dried flowers, handmade paper and fancy honey are sold here, alongside natural soaps and shampoos. There's a new branch opposite and several others across the city (and worldwide). Daily 10am–8pm.

Botas66 Skořepka 4; metro Můstek; map p.70. The products of this Communist-era sneaker company have been brought back from the dead, reproduced in lively hues and sold as "retro". Mon–Sat 11am–7pm, Sun 11am–5pm.

Eterno Moderno Benediktská 4; metro Náměstí Republiky; map p.70. Beautifully crafted women's clothes and jewellery, all one-off pieces made by Czech designers and artists. Mon–Fri 11am–7pm.

NOVÉ MĚSTO

Baťa Václavské náměstí 6 ☎221 088 478, ⊕bata.cz; metro Můstek; map p.102. Functionalist flagship store of the Baťa shoe empire, with five floors of footwear on Wenceslas Square. Mon–Sat 9am–9pm, Sun 10am–9pm.

14

MARKETS, FOOD AND DRINK

Prague is surprisingly short of good **markets** (trhy or tržiště) of all types. For bread, butter, cheese, wine and beer, you should simply go to the nearest potraviny or supermarket, although these are still a long way from the superstores of the Western world. Christmas markets have now been firmly re-established, and exist from late November onwards at Wenceslas Square and the Old Town Square. Pricey **farmers' markets** (⊕farmarske-trhy.cz) pop up each week at a different location, most conveniently on náměstí Jiřího z Poděbrad and Vítězné náměstí near Dejvická metro station.

STARÉ MĚSTO

Au Gourmand Dlouhá 10 ☎222 329 060, ⊕augourmand.cz; metro Náměstí Republiky; map p.70. Beautifully tiled French boulangerie, patisserie and traiteur selling delicious pastries. Mon–Fri 8am–7pm, Sat 8.30am–7pm, Sun 9am–7pm.

Blatnička Michalská 6 ☎224 225 860; metro Národní třída; map p.70. A central spot in which to taste and take home Czech sudová vina (wine from the barrel). Mon–Sat 11am–11pm, Sun 11am–10pm.

Country Life Melantrichova 15 ☎224 213 366, ⊕countrylife.cz; metro Můstek; map p.70. Health food shop selling excellent picnic food, organic vegetables, dried fruit and takeaway sandwiches. Mon–Thurs 8.30am–7pm, Fri 8.30am–3/4/6pm, Sun 11am–6pm.

Havelské tržiště Havelská; metro Můstek; map p.70. The only open-air market in the city centre, stretching the full length of arcaded Havelská – much of the fruit and veg has sadly been replaced with souvenir material. Mon–Sat 7am–6.30pm, Sun 8am–6pm.

Monarch Na Perštýně 15 ☎224 239 602; metro Můstek; map p.70. One of Prague's top wine outlets (and wine bars), with Moravian reds and whites and stock from all over the world. Also sells cheese and dried meats. Mon–Sat 5pm–midnight.

NOVÉ MĚSTO

Čajový krámek Národní 20; metro Národní třída; map p.102. Amazing range of teas from all over the tea-growing and tea-drinking world, loose in big glass jars as well as the bagged'n'boxed type. Mon–Fri 9.30am–7pm, Sat 10am–1pm.

Cellarius Štěpánská 61 ☎224 210 979, ⊕cellarius.cz; metro Muzeum; map p.102. Very well-stocked shop in the Lucerna pasáž, where you can taste and take away Czech wines. Also sells period wine glasses and jugs. Mon–Fri 9.30am–9pm, Sat 11am–9pm, Sun 3–7pm.

THE SUBURBS

Galerie piva Krymská 36, Vinohrady ☎777 959 695, ⊕galeriepiva.cz; tram #4, #13 or #22 to Ruská; map p.124. This is a relatively small shop, but it stocks one of the city's most judicious selection of Czech bottled beers. Daily 2.30–9pm.

★**Pivní galerie** U Průhonu 9, Holešovice ☎266 712 763; tram #6 or #12 to U Průhonu; map p.138. The largest selection of bottled Czech beers in the capital, which you can drink in the shop or take away. Also sells beer glasses from all over the Czech Lands. Mon–Fri 11.30am–7pm.

MUSIC

Czech **CDs** are priced a little lower than in the West. Classical buffs will fare best of all, not just with the Czech composers, but with cheap copies of Mozart, Vivaldi and other favourites. Czechoslovak rock from the 1960s to the 1980s is worth checking out, as is Moravian and Slovak folk music. Vinyl has made a big comeback in Prague in recent years.

STARÉ MĚSTO

Hudební nástroje Náprstkova 10 ☎222 221 100, ⊕nastroje-hudebni.cz; metro Národní třída; map p.70. Great place to pick up second-hand Czech instruments, from banjos and mandolins to xylophones

and accordions. Mon 2–6pm, Tues–Fri 11am–6pm, Sat 11am–4pm.

Maximum Underground Jilská 22 ☎724 307 198, ⊕maximum.cz; metro Staroměstská; map p.70. The best indie record shop in town, very strong on dance music, and also reggae, ragga, punk and world music. Mon–Sat 11am–7pm.

NOVÉ MĚSTO

Bontonland Palác Koruna, Václavské náměstí 1 ☎ 601 309 183, ⓦ bontonland.cz; metro Můstek; map p.102. Prague's biggest record store is a subterranean affair at the bottom of Wenceslas Square with three floors of rock, folk, jazz and classical CDs, DVDs and video games. Mon–Fri 9am–8pm, Sat 10am–8pm, Sun 10am–7pm.

Phono.cz Opatovická 24 ☎ 222 521 448, ⓦ phono.cz; metro Národní třída; map p.102. Small retro vinyl shop that stocks the record players, too. Mon–Fri 1pm–7pm.

14 TOYS AND CHILDREN'S GOODS

MALÁ STRANA

Truhlář marionety U lužického semináře 5 ☎ 602 689 918, ⓦ marionety.com; tram #12, #15, #20, #22 or 23 to Malostranské náměstí; map p.56. Prague is awash with cheap, gaudy puppets, but the Truhlář family offers a cut above. Wooden marionettes from around 1600Kč – bespoke from 12,000Kč. Daily 10am–9pm.

STARÉ MĚSTO

Hračky U zlatého lva Celetná 32 ☎ 224 239 469; metro Náměstí Republiky; map p.70. Multi-storey toy shop specializing in wooden playthings, many with a Krteček (Little Mole – the most popular Czech cartoon character) theme. Daily 10am–7pm.

Sparky's Havířská 2 ☎ 777 722 088, ⓦ sparkys.cz; metro Můstek; map p.70. Prague's top *dům hraček* (House of Toys) on four floors, which stocks everything from high-tech gadgets to wooden toys. Daily 9am–8pm.

NOVÉ MĚSTO

Hras Pasáž Rokoko, Václavské náměstí 38 ☎ 224 946 506; metro Můstek; map p.102. A small shop deep inside the Rokoko *pasáž* which stocks some great wooden puzzles and brainteasers (*hlavolamy*), plus board games. Mon–Fri 10am–7pm, Sat & Sun noon–5pm.

THE SUBURBS

Rici Vratislavova 23, Vyšehrad ☎ 724 577 517, ⓦ marionettes-rici.com; tram #2, #3, #7, #17 or #21 to Výtoň; map p.127. Small-scale puppet producer near the Vyšehrad fortress with prices starting around 600Kč. Mon–Fri 9am–4pm.

MISCELLANEOUS SPECIALIST SHOPS

MALÁ STRANA

Analogue Vlašská 10; tram #12, #20 or #22 to Malostranské náměstí; map p.56. The future is analogue at this tiny temple to all things non-digital; they specialize in film photography. Mon–Fri 10am–7pm, Sat noon–6pm.

STARÉ MĚSTO

HUDYsport Na Perštýně 14 ☎ 224 218 600, ⓦ hudy.cz; metro Můstek; map p.70. Outdoor gear shop, ideal if you need to replace your day pack or have come unprepared for the weather. Mon–Fri 10am–7.30pm, Sat 10am–6pm, Sun 11am–4pm.

Sparta Praha Betlémské náměstí 7; metro Národní třída; map p.70. Everything from soccer shirts to ashtrays, mostly for Sparta Praha, but also stocking Slavia Praha, Bohemians and Dukla Praha merchandise. Mon–Thurs 10am–5pm, Fri 10am–4pm.

Unicef Rytířská 31; metro Můstek; map p.70. UNICEF charity shop selling toys, cards, bags and other odds and ends. Mon–Fri 10am–2.30pm & 3–6pm.

NOVÉ MĚSTO

Centrum Fotoškoda Vodičkova 37 ☎ 222 929 029, ⓦ fotoskoda.cz; metro Můstek; map p.102. Big multifloor photography store in the Palác Langhans that has by far the widest range of items in Prague. Mon–Fri 8am–8pm, Sat 11am–6pm.

Česká mincovna Na Příkopě 24, pasáž České národní banky ☎ 224 283 659, ⓦ ceskamincovna.cz; metro Náměstí Republiky; map p.102. The Czech Mint's specialist store selling sets of pristine Czech coins, commemorative sets and real bars of gold. Mon–Fri 9am–6pm

Jan Pazdera Vodičkova 28 ☎ 224 216 197, ⓦ foto pazdera.cz; metro Můstek; map p.102. Truly spectacular selection of old and new cameras, micro-scopes, telescopes, opera glasses and binoculars. Mon–Sat 10am–6pm.

Koh-i-Noor Na Příkopě 24; metro Náměstí Republiky; map p.102. Tiny shop selling the Czechs' famous top-quality Koh-i-Noor pencils, produced since the eighteenth century in the South Bohemian city of České Budějovice. Daily 10am–8pm.

THE SUBURBS

Vinohradská Tržnice Vinohradská 50, Vinohrady ⓦ pavilon.cz; tram #11 or #13 to Vinohradská tržnice; map p.124. The beautiful old market building on Vinohradská třída received a complete twenty first-century refit in 2016, reopening as a high-end furniture and design department store. Also has a decent café and a cheapo Albert supermarket in the basement. Daily 7am–9pm.

Sports

For a nation of ten million souls, the Czechs punch way above their weight when it comes to sporting triumphs: over the past two and a half decades, they have consistently produced world-class tennis players, a strong national football team and several of the world's top ice hockey players. The two sports that pull in the biggest crowds, by far, are football (soccer) and ice hockey. Participating in sports activities is also relatively easy, and over the last decade there has been a boom in running and keep fit. Anyone who likes to pull on a pair of trainers while on holiday should check out RunCzech (ⓦrunczech.cz), which organizes marathons and half marathons across the country.

Getting **tickets** to watch a particular sport is easy (and cheap) enough on the day – only really big matches sell out. To find out about forthcoming sports events, read the sports pages in *Prague* Post, ask at a tourist office or check the website of the given club or venue.

FOOTBALL

The Czech national **football** (*fotbal*; soccer) team has enjoyed mixed fortunes since making the final of Euro '96 and the semi-finals of Euro 2004, failing to qualify for the World Cup in 1998, 2002, 2010 and 2014. As with most of the smaller European nations, the best home-grown players seek fame and fortune abroad. Consequently, domestic teams face a perennial struggle in European competitions.

INFORMATION AND TICKETS

The top-flight league, or První liga, is currently known as the HET liga (Ⓦ hetliga.cz); the seasons run Aug–Nov and March–May, and matches are usually held on Sat. Tickets for domestic games are around 200Kč and four-figure crowds remain the norm. Don't expect the electric atmosphere of other bigger leagues.

TEAMS

Bohemians The "Kangaroos" (*klokani*; Ⓦ bohemians.cz) play in distinctive green-and-white-striped jerseys at the 7500-capacity Ďolíček stadium in Vršovice (tram #3, #6, #7, #17 or #24 to Bohemians). The club's sole league triumph came in 1983.

Dukla Praha The old army team, Dukla Praha (Ⓦ fkdukla .cz) – immortalized in the pop song *All I Want for Christmas is a Dukla Prague Away-Kit* by British band Half Man Half Biscuit – was forced to leave the capital in 1997 and merge with Příbram, 60km southwest of Prague. However, in 2006 Dukla Praha was refounded and is now back in the top flight. They play, in their claret-and-yellow strip, at the 18,000-capacity Na Julisce stadium, Dejvice (tram #8 or

#18 to the Podbaba terminus).

Slavia Praha Prague's second most successful team, Chinese-owned Slavia Praha (Ⓦ slavia.cz), is Sparta Prague's traditional rival, though it's almost a decade since they last won the league (2009). Slavia has traditionally attracted a smaller, more educated, fan base, and is the favourite among the expat community. Their strip is red-and-white shirts with white shorts, and they play in a modern 21,000-seater stadium called Eden, in Vršovice (tram #6, #7, #17, #22 or #24 to Slavia).

Sparta Praha The most successful club in the country, Sparta Praha (Wsparta.cz) has won more league titles than any other club since the Czech league began in 1993. Its traditional working-class fan base is one of the largest in the country and has possibly the worst reputation for racism. They play in claret and white (in honour of Arsenal's original strip) at the 20,000 all-seater Letná stadium (latest sponsor name Generali Arena; 5min walk from metro Hradčanská or take tram #1, #8, #12, #25 or #26 to Sparta); international matches are also regularly played there.

Viktoria Žižkov Viktoria Žižkov (Ⓦ fkvz.cz), based in the traditionally working-class district of Prague 3, won the

---

BATTLE OF THE KANGAROOS

In 1927, the Czech football club **AFK Vršovice** toured Australia and was given two kangaroos as a gift. The kangaroos were kept at Prague zoo, the club renamed itself **Bohemians**, and its nickname (and logo) became **Kangaroos**, or *klokani*. Under the Communists, they attracted a lot of dissident support, and in 1983, the Bohemians enjoyed their finest moment, winning the Czechoslovak league and making it to the semi-finals of the UEFA Cup. However, in 2005, financial mismanagement saw the side relegated to the third tier of Czech football. A club in the northeast of the city, **FC Střížkov**, took a lease out on the name and the distinctive logo, and became **FC Bohemians (Střížkov)**, but when the contract expired refused to give up the Bohemians name, the kangaroo logo or its claim to the club's legacy. Meanwhile, back in Vršovice, the original club was saved by its fans and refounded as **Bohemians 1905**. The five-year dispute came to a head in 2010 when Bohemians 1905 were due to play FC Bohemians (Střížkov) in the first division. FC Bohemians (Střížkov) threatened to boycott the game, but instead vented their anger by quadrupling the ticket prices for the away fans. At the return fixture in Vršovice, Střížkov deliberately failed to turn up for the match – the first time this had ever happened in the history of the league – and had twenty points deducted, relegating them to the second division. Finally, in 2013, a court in Prague handed back the real Bohemians their legacy, though somewhat absurdly Střížkov, a club now playing in the lower leagues, still uses the Bohemians' name and badge.

league championship for the first and only time in 1928. It has won the Czech cup twice in living memory, but is currently languishing in the third division. Viktoria play in red-and-white vertical stripes and their 5600-seater ground is on Seifertova in Žižkov (tram #5, #9, #15 or #26 to Husinecká); they traditionally play their games on Sun mornings.

ICE HOCKEY

Running football a close second as the nation's most popular sport is **ice hockey** (*lední hokej*) – it's not unusual to see kids playing their own form of the game in the street, rather than kicking a football around. The country's best players usually leave to seek fame and fortune in North America's National Hockey League (NHL), but the Czech national team continues to rank among the world's top five hockey nations.

INFORMATION AND TICKETS

Domestic games take place on Sat and can last for anything up to 3hr; they are fast and physical and make for cold but compelling viewing. The season starts at the end of Sept and culminates in the annual World Championships the following summer, when the fortunes of the national side are subject to close scrutiny, especially if pitched against the old enemy Russia, not to mention their former bedmate and new rival, Slovakia. Tickets for domestic games (100–200Kč) can be bought on the day.

TEAMS

Slavia Praha Prague's other big team is Slavia Praha (ⓦ hc-slavia.cz), which has won the league twice, in 2003 and 2008, but was relegated to the second tier of Czech ice hockey in 2015. Slavia play their matches at the Eden ice rink.

Sparta Praha As in football, Sparta Praha (ⓦ hcsparta.cz) is one of the country's most successful teams, having won the Extraliga (ⓦ hokej.cz) four times since 2000. Sparta plays at the Tipsport Arena, next door to the Výstaviště exhibition grounds in Holešovice (metro Nádraží Holešovice).

15

ICE-SKATING

Given the nation's penchant for ice hockey, it's not surprising that **ice-skating** (*bruslení*) is one of Prague's most popular winter activities. Several temporary **rinks** are set up around the city during the Christmas and New Year period, the most central of which is on Staroměstské náměstí. There's also no shortage of permanent rinks (*zimní stadión*) in the city – although public opening hours are often limited to a few hours at the weekend – along with the city's two reservoirs, Hostivář and Šárka, which regularly freeze over in winter. Most rinks are open from October to April; entry costs from 100Kč and skate rental costs around the same.

TENNIS AND SQUASH

For a while, **tennis** was one of the country's most successful exports, with the likes of Martina Navrátilová and Ivan Lendl among the game's all-time greats. The glory days of men's tennis are over but the country still produces world-class women players. If you fancy a quick game yourself, you'll have to bring your own racquet and balls with you, or buy them downtown.

Český Lawn Tennis Klub Ostrov Štvanice, Holešovice ☎ 222 324 601, ⓦ cltk.cz; metro Florenc/Vltavská. Floodlit outdoor clay courts and indoor clay and hard tennis courts. Booking essential. Daily 7am–midnight.

Squash Haštal Hastalská 20, Staré Město ☎ 224 828 561, ⓦ squash-hastal.cz; metro Náměstí Republiky. Six a/c courts in the backstreets of the Old Town. Mon–Thurs 7am–10pm, Fri 7am–9pm, Sat & Sun 9am–9pm.

Tenisové Centrum Olšanská Chelčického 43, Žižkov

☎ 606 810 852, ⓦ tenisolsanska.cz; tram #5, #9, #15 or #26 to Olšanské náměstí. All-weather, illuminated outdoor courts in Žižkov and under a 'bubble' in winter. 24hr.

Tenisový klub Slavia Praha Letenské sady, Holešovice ☎ 233 374 033, ⓦ mujweb.cz/tkslavia; tram #6, #8, #17 or #26 to Strossmayerovo náměstí. Indoor and outdoor floodlit clay tennis courts opposite the Národní technické muzeum. Daily 7am–9/10pm.

HORSE RACING

Horse racing is nowhere near as popular in the Czech Republic as it is in the UK or US, but Prague has the country's main **racecourse**. The biggest steeplechase of the year, the Velká Pardubická – the Czech equivalent of the Grand National – takes place in the Moravian city of Pardubice, about 120km east of the capital.

Velká Chuchle 5km south of the city centre ⓦ velka-chuchle.cz; train from Hlavní nádraží or Smíchov to Praha-Velká Chuchle. Steeplechases and hurdles take place at Prague's main racecourse (*závodiště*) from May to Oct on Sun from 2pm.

SWIMMING

The waters of the Vltava, Beroun and Labe are all pretty murky, and strong currents make for dangerous dips. For a clean swim it's best to head for one of the city's **swimming pools**.

Aquapalace Pražská 138, Průhonice–Čestlice ☎ 271 104 202, ⓦ aquapalace.cz; bus #328 from metro Opatov to Čestlice, Kika-Aquapalace. The biggest aquapark in the Czech Republic can be found in the far southeastern suburbs. Also amazing pools and slides there are myriad saunas and wellness facilities to enjoy, as well as plenty of food. Mon–Fri 10am–10pm, Sat & Sun 9am–10pm.

Divoká Šárka Divoká Šárka 2, Vokovice ☎ 603 723 501, ⓦ koupaliste-sarka.webnode.cz; tram #26 to Divoká Šárka. Idyllically located in a craggy valley to the northwest of Prague, with two small outdoor pools filled with cold, fresh, clean water – great for a full, hot day out. Food and drink and plenty of shade available, too. May to mid-Sept daily 10am–6pm.

Plavecký stadion Podolí Podolská 74, Podolí ☎ 241 433 952, ⓦ pspodoli.cz; tram #2, #3, #17 or #21 to Kublov. Newly refurbished, Prague's most famous swimming complex has indoor and outdoor pools set against a sheltered craggy backdrop. There's also a cheap café that turns into a pub in the evenings. Daily 6am–9.45pm.

GYMS AND SAUNAS

These days there's no shortage of fitness centres and hotels in Prague with good **gyms**, saunas and masseurs. Rates are generally lower outside the swish hotels.

Fitness Galaxie Arkalycká 1, Háje ☎ 608 874 300, ⓦ fitnessgalaxie.cz; metro Háje. Large gym near the metro station at the end of red line C in Prague's southern suburbs. Mon–Fri 7am–10pm, Sat & Sun 9am–10pm.

Health Club & Spa InterContinental Praha Pařížská 30, Staré Město ☎ 296 631 525, ⓦ icfitness.cz; metro Staroměstská. Well-equipped gym and friendly staff in this very central and upmarket hotel. Mon–Fri 6am–10pm, Sat & Sun 7am–10pm.

Hit Fitness Flora Chrudimská 2b, Žižkov ☎ 267 311 447, ⓦ hitfit.cz; metro Flora. Large gym, squash courts, sauna, massage and regular classes – very close to the metro. Mon–Fri 6am–11pm, Sat & Sun 8am–11pm.

YMCA Na poříčí 12, Nové Město ☎ 224 875 811, ⓦ scymca.cz; metro Náměstí Republiky. This modern leisure centre, with gym (*posilovna*), aerobics and pool, is the most central facility in town. Mon–Thurs 6.30am–10pm, Fri 6.30am–9pm, Sat 9am–7pm, Sun 10am–9pm.

PRAGUE SPRING, 1968

Contexts

History

Prague has played a pivotal role in European history – "he who holds Bohemia holds mid-Europe", Bismarck is alleged to have said. As the capital of Bohemia, the city has been fought over and occupied by German, Austrian, French and even Swedish armies. Consequently, it is virtually impossible to write a historical account of Prague without frequent reference to the wider events of European history. Its history as the capital of first Czechoslovakia and now the Czech Republic is, in fact, less than a hundred years old, beginning only with the foundation of the country in 1918. Since then, the country's numerous historical convulsions, mostly focused on Prague, have played out on the world stage at regular intervals, notably in 1938, 1948, 1968 and, most happily, 1989.

Legends

The Czechs have a **legend** for every occasion, and the founding of Bohemia and Prague is no exception. The mythical "mount" Říp, the most prominent of the pimply hills dotting the Labe (Elbe) plain, north of Prague, is where **Čech**, the leader of a band of wandering Slavs, is alleged to have founded his new kingdom, Čechy (Bohemia). His brother Lech, meanwhile, headed further north to found Poland. Some time in the seventh or eighth century AD, **Krok**, a descendant of **Čech**, moved his people south from the plains to the rocky knoll that is now Vyšehrad (literally "High Castle").

Krok was succeeded by his youngest daughter, **Libuše**, the country's first and last female ruler, who, handily enough, was endowed with the gift of prophecy. Falling into a trance one day, she pronounced that the tribe should build a city "whose glory will touch the stars", at the point in the forest where they found an old man constructing the doorstep of his house. He was duly discovered on the Hradčany hill, overlooking the Vltava, and the city was named **Praha**, from the word práh meaning "doorstep". However, it wasn't long before Libuše's subjects began to demand that she take a husband. As Cosmas, the twelfth-century chronicler, put it, "resting on her elbow like one who is giving birth, she lay there on a high pile of soft and embroidered pillows, as is the lasciviously wanton habit of women when they do not have a man at home whom they fear." Again she fell into a trance, this time pronouncing that they should follow her horse to a ploughman, with two oxen, whose descendants (the ploughman's, that is) would rule over them. Sure enough, a man called **Přemysl oráč** (Přemysl the Ploughman) was discovered, and became the mythical founder of the Přemyslid dynasty that ruled Bohemia until the fourteenth century.

Early history

So much for the legend. According to Roman records, the area now covered by Bohemia was inhabited as early as 500 BC by a Celtic tribe, the Boii, who gave their

6th century	7th/8th century
Slavs enter the Elbe plain from the east, pushing out and assimilating Germanic tribes.	According to legend, Krok moves his tribe of Slavs from the Elbe plains to Vyšehrad. Krok's clairvoyant daughter Libuše envisages a city "whose glory will touch the stars".

name to the region. Very little is known about the Boii except that around 100 BC they were driven from their territory by a Germanic tribe, the **Marcomanni**, who occupied Bohemia. The Marcomanni were a semi-nomadic people and later proved awkward opponents for the Roman Empire, which wisely chose to use the River Danube as its natural eastern border, thus leaving Bohemia outside the empire – a fact that has influenced the region ever since.

The disintegration of the Roman Empire in the fifth century AD corresponded with a series of raids into central Europe by eastern tribes: first the **Huns** and later the **Avars**, around the sixth century, settling a vast area including the Hungarian plains and parts of what is now Slovakia. Around the same time, the Marcomanni disappeared from the picture to be replaced by **Slav tribes** who entered Europe from somewhere east of the Carpathian mountains (today's Ukraine). To begin with, at least, they appear to have been subjugated by the Avars. The first successful Slav rebellion against the Avars seems to have taken place in the seventh century, under the Frankish leadership of **Samo**, though the kingdom he created, which probably included Bohemia, died with him around 658 AD.

The Great Moravian Empire

The next written record of the Slavs in the region isn't until the eighth century, when East Frankish (Germanic) chroniclers report a people known as the **Moravians** as having established themselves around the River Morava, a tributary of the Danube. It was an alliance of Moravians and Franks (under Charlemagne) that finally expelled the Avars from central Europe in 796 AD. This cleared the way for the establishment of the **Great Moravian Empire**, which at its peak included Slovakia, Bohemia and parts of Hungary and Poland. Its significance in political terms is that it was the first and last time (until the establishment of Czechoslovakia, for which it served as a useful precedent) that the Czechs and Slovaks were united under one ruler.

The first attested ruler of the empire, **Mojmír I** (c.830–833), found himself at the political and religious crossroads of Europe under pressure from two sides: from the west, where the Franks and Bavarians (both Germanic tribes) were jostling for position with the Roman papacy; and from the east, where the patriarch of Byzantium was keen to extend his influence across eastern Europe. Mojmír's successor, **Rastislav** (846–70), plumped for Byzantium, and invited the missionaries **Cyril and Methodius** (Metoděj) to introduce Christianity, using the Slav liturgy and Eastern rites. Rastislav, however, was ousted by his nephew, **Svatopluk** (871–94), who helped the Germans capture and blind his uncle. Svatopluk himself was then imprisoned, and, on his release, swapped sides, defeating the Germans on several occasions and declaring himself King of Great Moravia. With the death of Methodius in 885, the Great Moravian Empire fell decisively under the influence of the Roman Catholic Church.

Svatopluk died shortly before the **Magyar invasion** of 896, an event that heralded the end of the Great Moravian Empire and a significant break in Czecho-Slovak history. The Slavs to the west of the River Morava (the Czechs) swore allegiance to the Frankish emperor Arnulf, while those to the east (the Slovaks) found themselves under the yoke of the Magyars. This separation, which continued for the next millennium, underlies the social, cultural and political differences between Czechs and Slovaks, which culminated in the separation of the two nations in 1993.

9th century	862	896
Rise of the Great Moravian Empire, which includes Slovakia, Bohemia and parts of Hungary and Poland.	Prince Rastislav invites missionaries Cyril and Methodius to introduce Christianity into the Great Moravian Empire.	The Magyars invade the Great Moravian Empire, heralding a millennium-long split between Czechs and Slovaks.

The Přemyslid dynasty

There is evidence that Bohemian dukes were forced in 806 to pay a yearly tribute of 500 pieces of silver and 120 oxen to the Carolingian empire (a precedent the Nazis were keen to exploit as proof of German hegemony over Bohemia). These early Bohemian dukes "lived like animals, brutal and without knowledge", according to one chronicler. All that was to change when the earliest recorded Přemyslid duke, **Bořivoj** (852/53–888/89), appeared on the scene. The first Christian ruler of Prague, Bořivoj was baptized, along with his wife Ludmila, in the ninth century by the Byzantine missionaries Cyril and Methodius. Other than being the first to build a castle on Hradčany, nothing very certain is known about Bořivoj, nor about any of the other early Premyslid rulers, although there are numerous legends, most famously that of **Prince Václav** (St Wenceslas), who was martyred by his pagan brother Boleslav the Cruel in 929 (see p.40).

Cut off from Byzantium by the Hungarian kingdom, Bohemia lived under the shadow of the **Holy Roman Empire** from the start. In 950, Emperor Otto I led an expedition against Bohemia, making the dukedom officially subject to the empire and its leader one of the seven electors of the emperor. In 973, under Boleslav the Pious (972–99), a bishopric was founded in Prague, subordinate to the archbishopric of Mainz. Thus, by the end of the first millennium, German influence was already beginning to make itself felt in Bohemian history.

The **thirteenth century** was the high point of Přemyslid rule over Bohemia. With Emperor Frederick II preoccupied with Mediterranean affairs and dynastic problems, and the Hungarians and Poles busy trying to repulse the Mongol invasions from 1220 onwards, the Přemyslids were able to assert their independence. In 1212, Otakar I (1192–1230) managed to extract a "**Golden Bull**" (formal edict) from the emperor, securing the royal title for himself and his descendants (who thereafter became kings of Bohemia). Prague prospered, too, benefiting from its position on the central European trade routes. Czechs, Germans, Jews and merchants from all over Europe settled there, and in 1234 the first of Prague's historic five towns, **Staré Město**, was founded to accommodate them.

As a rule, the Přemyslids welcomed **German colonization**, none more so than King Otakar II (1253–78), the most distinguished of the Přemyslid rulers, who systematically encouraged German craftsmen to settle in the kingdom. At the same time, the gradual switch to a monetary economy and the discovery of copper and silver deposits heralded a big shift in population from the countryside to the towns. German immigrants founded settlements in the interior of the country, where German civic rights were guaranteed them, for example Kutná Hora, Mělník and, in 1257, **Malá Strana** in Prague. Through battles, marriage and diplomacy, Otakar expanded his territories so that they stretched (almost) from the Baltic to the Adriatic. In 1278, however, Otakar met his end on the battlefield of Marchfeld, defeated by Rudolf of Habsburg.

The beginning of the fourteenth century saw a series of dynastic disputes – messy even by medieval standards – beginning with the death of Václav II from consumption and excess in 1305. The following year, the murder of his son, the heirless, teenage Václav III, marked the **end of the Přemyslid dynasty** (he had four

Late 9th century	929	950
Přemyslid dynasty ruler Prince Bořivoj builds the first castle on the site of today's Hrad.	Prince Václav (St Wenceslas/ Good King Wenceslas) is murdered by his brother Boleslav the Cruel.	Holy Roman Emperor Otto I invades Bohemia, whose rulers become imperial electors.

PRINCES, KINGS, EMPERORS AND PRESIDENTS

THE PŘEMYSLID DYNASTY
Princes
Bořivoj I d. 895
Spytihněv I 895–905
Vratislav I 905–921
Václav I 921–929
Boleslav I 929–972
Boleslav II 972–999
Boleslav III 999–1002
Vladivoj 1002–03
Jaromir 1003–12
Ulrich 1012–34
Břetislav I 1034–55
Spytihněv II 1055–61
Vratislav II (king from 1086) 1061–92
Břetislav II 1092–1110
Bořivoj II 1110–20
Vladislav I 1120–25
Soběslav I 1125–40
Vladislav II (as king, I) 1140–73
Soběslav II 1173–89
Otho 1189–91
Václav II 1191–92
Otakar I (king from 1212) 1192–1230
Kings
Václav I 1230–53
Otakar II 1253–78
Václav II 1278–1305
Václav III 1305–06

HABSBURGS
Rudolf I 1306–07
Henry of Carinthia 1307–10

THE LUXEMBOURG DYNASTY
John 1310–46
Charles I (as emperor, IV) 1346–78
Václav IV 1378–1419
(Hussite Wars 1419–34)
Sigismund 1436–37

HABSBURGS
Albert 1437–39
Ladislav the Posthumous 1439–57

CZECH HUSSITE
George of Poděbrady 1458–71

THE JAGIELLONIAN DYNASTY
Vladislav II 1471–1516
Louis I 1516–26

THE HABSBURG DYNASTY
Ferdinand I 1526–64
Maximilian 1564–76
Rudolf II 1576–1611
Matthias 1611–19
Ferdinand II 1619–37
Ferdinand III 1637–57
Leopold I 1657–1705
Joseph I 1705–11
Charles II (as emperor, VI) 1711–40
Maria Theresa 1740–80
Joseph II 1780–90
Leopold II 1790–92
Franz 1792–1835
Ferdinand IV (I) 1835–48
Franz Joseph I 1848–1916
Charles III 1916–18

PRESIDENTS
Tomáš Garrigue Masaryk 1918–35
Edvard Beneš 1935–38 & 1945–48
Klement Gottwald 1948–53
Antonín Zápatocký 1953–57
Antonín Novotný 1957–68
Ludvík Svoboda 1968–75
Gustáv Husák 1975–89
Václav Havel 1989–92 & 1993–2003
Václav Klaus 2003–13
Miloš Zeman 2013–18

sisters, but female succession was not recognized in Bohemia). The nobles' first choice of successor, the Habsburg Albert I, was murdered by his own nephew, and when Albert's son, Rudolf I, died of dysentery not long afterwards, Bohemia was once more left without any heirs.

973

The Prague bishopric is established.

1212

Otakar I secures hereditary succession to the Bohemian throne for his descendants.

1234

Prague's Staré Město (Old Town) is founded.

Carolinian Prague

The crisis was finally solved when the Czech nobles offered the throne to **John of Luxembourg** (1310–46), who was married to Václav III's youngest sister. German by birth, but educated in France, King John spent most of his reign participating in foreign wars, with Bohemia footing the bill, and John himself paying first with his sight, and finally with his life, on the field at Crécy in 1346.

His son, **Charles IV** (1346–78), was wounded in the same battle, but thankfully for the Czechs lived to tell the tale. It was Charles – Karel to the Czechs – who ushered in Prague's **golden age**. Although born and bred in France, Charles was a Bohemian at heart (his mother was Czech and his real name was Václav). In 1344, he had wrangled an archbishopric for Prague, independent of Mainz, and two years later he became not only king of Bohemia, but also, by election, Holy Roman Emperor. In the thirty years of his reign, Charles transformed Prague into the new imperial capital. He established institutions and buildings that still survive to this day and founded an entire new town, **Nové Město**, to accommodate the influx of students and clergy. He promoted Czech as the official language alongside Latin and German and, perhaps most importantly of all, presided over a period of peace in central Europe while western Europe was tearing itself apart in the Hundred Years War.

Sadly, Charles's son, **Václav IV** (1378–1419), was no match for such an inheritance. Stories that he roasted an incompetent cook alive on his own spit, shot a monk while hunting and tried his own hand at lopping off people's heads with an axe are almost certainly myths. Nevertheless, he was a legendary drinker, prone to violent outbursts and so unpopular with the powers that be that he was imprisoned twice – once by his own nobles and once by his brother, Sigismund. His reign was also characterized by religious divisions within the Czech Lands and in Europe as a whole, beginning with the **Great Schism** (1378–1417), when rival popes held court in Rome and Avignon. This was a severe blow to Rome's centralizing power, which might otherwise have successfully combated the assault on the Church that was already under way in the Czech Lands towards the end of the fourteenth century.

The Bohemian Reformation

From the start, Prague was at the centre of the **Bohemian Reformation**. The increased influence of the Church, and its independence from Mainz established under Charles, led to a sharp increase in debauchery, petty theft and alcoholism among the clergy – a fertile climate for militant reformers such as Jan Milič of Kroměříž, whose fiery sermons drew crowds to hear him at Prague's Týn church. In Václav's reign, the attack was led by the peasant-born preacher **Jan Hus**, who gave sermons at Prague's Betlémská kaple (see p.87).

Hus's main inspiration was the English reformist theologian John Wycliffe (founder of the Lollard movement), whose heretical works found their way to Bohemia via Václav's sister, Anna, who married King Richard II. Worse still, as far as Church traditionalists were concerned, Hus began to preach in the language of the masses (Czech) against the wealth, corruption and hierarchical tendencies within the Church at the time. A devout, mild-mannered man himself, he became embroiled in a dispute between the conservative clergy, led by Archbishop Zbyněk

Late 13th century	1306	1310
King Otakar II rules over an empire stretching from the Baltic to the Adriatic.	Václav III dies without an heir, bringing the Přemyslid dynasty to an end.	Czech nobles offer the Bohemian throne to John of Luxembourg.

and backed by the pope, and the Wycliffian Czechs at the university. When Archbishop Zbyněk gave the order to burn the books of Wycliffe, Václav backed Hus and his followers for political and personal reasons (Hus was, among other things, the confessor to his wife, Queen Sophie).

There can be little doubt that King Václav used Hus and the Wycliffites to further his own political cause. He had been deposed as Holy Roman Emperor in 1400 and, as a result, bore a grudge against the current emperor, Ruprecht of the Palatinate, and his chief backer, Pope Gregory XII in Rome. His chosen battleground was Prague's university, which was divided into four "nations" with equal voting rights: the Saxons, Poles, Bavarians, who supported Václav's enemies, and the Bohemians, who were mostly Wycliffites. In 1409, Václav issued the **Kutná Hora Decree**, which rigged the voting within the university, giving the Bohemian "nation" three votes, and the rest a total of one. The other "nations", who made up the majority of the students and teachers, left Prague in protest.

Three years later the alliance between the king and the Wycliffites broke down. Widening his attacks on the Church, Hus began to preach against the sale of religious indulgences to fund the inter-papal wars, thus incurring the enmity of Václav, who received a percentage of the sales. In 1412, Hus and his followers were expelled from the university, excommunicated and banished from Prague, and they spent the next two years as itinerant preachers spreading their reformist gospel throughout Bohemia (the countryside is peppered with Hus stones and Hus oaks, places where he said to have addressed the masses). In 1414, Hus was summoned to the **Council of Constance** to answer charges of heresy. Despite a guarantee of safe conduct from Emperor Sigismund, Hus was condemned to death and, having refused to renounce his beliefs, was burned at the stake on July 6, 1415.

Hus's martyrdom sparked off **widespread riots** in Prague, initially uniting virtually all Bohemians – clergy and laity, peasant and noble (including many of Hus's former opponents) – against the decision of the council, and, by inference, against the established Church and its conservative clergy. The Hussites immediately set about reforming Church practices, most famously by administering communion *sub utraque specie* ("in both kinds", bread and wine) to the laity, as opposed to the established practice of reserving the wine for the clergy.

The Hussite Wars: 1419–34

In 1419, Václav inadvertently provoked further large-scale rioting by endorsing the readmission of anti-Hussite priests to their parishes. In the ensuing violence, several councillors (including the mayor) were thrown to their death from the windows of Prague's Novoměstská radnice, in Prague's **first defenestration** (see p.117). Václav himself was so enraged (not to say terrified) by the mob that he suffered a stroke and died, "roaring like a lion", according to a contemporary chronicler. The pope, meanwhile, declared an international crusade against the Czech heretics, under the leadership of Emperor Sigismund, Václav's brother and, since Václav had failed to produce an heir, chief claimant to the Bohemian throne.

Already, though, cracks were appearing in the Hussite camp. The more radical reformers, who became known as the **Táborites** after their south Bohemian base, Tábor, broadened their attacks on the Church hierarchy to include all figures of

1346	Late 14th century	1348
King John's son becomes Charles IV.	As Holy Roman Emperor, Charles IV transforms Prague into a glittering imperial capital.	Charles IV establishes Charles University, the Czech Republic's oldest seat of learning.

authority and privilege. Their message found a ready audience among the oppressed classes in Prague and the Bohemian countryside, who went around eagerly destroying Church property and massacring Catholics. Such actions were deeply disturbing to the Czech nobility and their supporters who backed the more moderate Hussites – known as the **Utraquists** or *utrakvisté* (from the Latin *sub utraque specie*) – who confined their criticisms to religious matters.

For the moment, however, the common Catholic enemy prevented a serious split developing amongst the Hussites, and under the inspirational military leadership of the Táborite **Jan Žižka**, the Hussites' (mostly peasant) army enjoyed some miraculous early victories over the numerically superior "crusaders", most notably at the Battle of Vítkov in Prague in 1420. The Bohemian Diet quickly drew up the **Four Articles of Prague**, a compromise between the two Hussite camps, outlining the basic tenets about which all Hussites could agree, including communion "in both kinds". The Táborites, meanwhile, continued to burn, loot and pillage ecclesiastical institutions from Prague to the far reaches of the kingdom.

At the **Council of Basel** in 1433, Rome reached a compromise with the Utraquists over the Four Articles, in return for ceasing hostilities. The peasant-based Táborites rightly saw the deal as a victory for the Bohemian nobility and the status quo, and vowed to continue the fight. However, the Utraquists, now in cahoots with the Catholic forces, easily defeated the remaining Táborites at the **Battle of Lipany**, outside Kolín, in 1434. The Táborites were forced to withdraw to the fortress town of Tábor. Poor old Sigismund, who had spent the best part of his life fighting the Hussites, was only recognized as king in 1436, and died the following year.

King George of Poděbrady and the Jagiellonian dynasty

Despite the agreement of the Council of Basel, the pope refused to acknowledge the Utraquist Church in Bohemia. The Utraquists nevertheless consolidated their position, electing the gifted **George of Poděbrady** first as regent and then king of Bohemia (1458–71). The first and last Hussite king, George – Jiří to the Czechs – is remembered primarily for his commitment to promoting religious tolerance and for his far-sighted, but ultimately futile, attempts to establish some sort of "Peace Confederation" in Europe.

On George's death, the Bohemian Estates handed the crown over to the **Polish Jagiellonian dynasty**, who ruled *in absentia*, effectively relinquishing the reins of power to the Czech nobility. In 1526, the last of the Jagiellonians, King Louis, was decisively defeated by the Turks at the Battle of Mohács, and died fleeing the battlefield, leaving no heir to the throne.

Enter the Habsburgs

The Roman Catholic Habsburg, Ferdinand I (1526–64), was elected king of Bohemia – and what was left of Hungary – in order to fill the power vacuum, marking the **beginning of Habsburg rule** over what is now the Czech Republic. Ferdinand adroitly secured automatic hereditary succession over the Bohemian throne for his dynasty, in return for which he accepted the agreement laid down at the Council of Basel back in 1433. With the Turks at the gates of Vienna, he had little choice but to compromise, but in 1545 the international situation eased with the establishment of an armistice with the Turks.

1357	Early 15th century	1415
Charles Bridge is begun by Charles IV's architect, Peter Parler.	A period of religious revolt is led by Wycliffian preacher Jan Hus.	Hus is burnt at the stake for heresy at the Council of Constance.

The following year, the Utraquist Bohemian nobility provocatively joined the powerful Protestant Schmalkaldic League in their (ultimately successful) war against the Holy Roman Emperor, Charles V. After a brief armed skirmish in Prague, however, victory initially fell to Ferdinand, who took the opportunity to extend the influence of Catholicism in the Czech Lands, executing several leading Protestant nobles, persecuting the reformist Unity of Czech Brethren, who had figured prominently in the rebellion, and inviting Jesuit missionaries to establish churches and seminaries across the Czech Lands.

Rudolfine Prague

Like Václav IV, **Emperor Rudolf II** (1576–1611), Ferdinand's eventual successor, was moody and wayward, and by the end of his reign Bohemia was again rushing headlong into a major international confrontation. But Rudolf also shared characteristics with Václav's father, Charles, in his genuine love of the arts, and in his passion for Prague, which he re-established as the royal seat of power, in preference to Vienna, which was once more under threat from the Turks. He endowed Prague's galleries with the best Mannerist art in Europe, and invited the respected astronomers Tycho Brahe and Johannes Kepler and the infamous English alchemists John Dee and Edward Kelley, to Prague (see p.44).

Czechs tend to regard Rudolfine Prague as a second golden age, but as far as the Catholic Church was concerned, Rudolf's religious tolerance and indecision were a disaster. In the early 1600s, Rudolf's melancholy began to veer dangerously close to insanity, a condition he had inherited from his Spanish grandmother, Joanna the Mad. And in 1611, the heirless Rudolf was forced by his brother **Matthias** to abdicate, to save the Habsburg house from ruin. Ardently Catholic, but equally heirless, Matthias proposed his cousin **Ferdinand II** as his successor in 1617. This was the last straw for Bohemia's mostly Protestant nobility, and the following year conflict erupted again.

The Thirty Years' War: 1618–48

On May 23, 1618, two Catholic governors appointed by Ferdinand were thrown out of the windows of Prague Castle (along with their secretary) – the country's **second defenestration** (see p.42) – an event that's now taken as the official beginning of the complex religious and dynastic conflicts collectively known as the **Thirty Years War**. Following the defenestration, the Bohemian Diet expelled the Jesuits and elected the youthful Protestant "Winter King", Frederick of the Palatinate, to the throne. In the first decisive set-to of the war, on November 8, 1620, the Czech Protestants were soundly defeated at the **Battle of Bílá hora** or Battle of the White Mountain (see p.147) by the imperial Catholic forces under Count Tilly. In the aftermath, 27 Protestant nobles were executed on Prague's Staroměstské náměstí, and the heads of ten of them displayed on the Charles Bridge.

It wasn't until the Protestant Saxons occupied Prague in 1632 that the heads were finally taken down and given a proper burial. The Catholics eventually drove the Saxons out, but for the last ten years of the war Bohemia became the main battleground between the new champions of the Protestant cause – the Swedes – and the imperial Catholic forces. In 1648, the final battle of the war was fought in Prague, when the Swedes seized Malá Strana, but failed to take Staré Město, thanks to stubborn resistance on Charles Bridge by Prague's Jewish and newly Catholicized student populations.

1419–34	1434	1458
The Hussite Wars ravage Bohemia.	King Sigismund and less radical Hussites defeat the fundamentalist Táborites at the Battle of Lipany.	George of Poděbrady is elected Bohemia's first and last Hussite king.

The Counter-Reformation and the Dark Ages

The Thirty Years War ended with the **Peace of Westphalia**, which, for the Czechs, was as disastrous as the war itself. An estimated five-sixths of the Bohemian nobility went into exile, their properties handed over to loyal Catholic families from Austria, Spain, France and Italy. Bohemia had been devastated, with towns and cities laid waste, and the total population reduced by almost two-thirds; Prague's population halved. On top of all that, Bohemia was now decisively within the Catholic sphere of influence, and the full force of the **Counter-Reformation** was brought to bear on its people. All forms of Protestantism were outlawed, the education system was handed over to the Jesuits and, in 1651 alone, more than two hundred "witches" were burned at the stake in Bohemia.

The next two centuries of Habsburg rule are known to the Czechs as the **Dark Ages**. The focus of the empire shifted firmly back to Vienna and the Habsburgs' absolutist grip over the Czech Lands catapulted the remaining nobility into intensive Germanization, while fresh waves of German immigrants reduced Czech to a despised dialect spoken only by peasants, artisans and servants. The situation was so bad that Prague and most other urban centres became practically German-speaking cities. By the end of the eighteenth century, the Czech language was on the verge of dying out, with government, scholarship and literature carried out exclusively in German. For the newly ensconced Germanized aristocracy, and for the Catholic Church, of course, the good times rolled and Prague was endowed with numerous Baroque palaces, churches, monasteries and monuments, many of which still grace the city today.

The Enlightenment

After a century of iron-fisted Habsburg rule, a dispute arose over the accession of Charles VI's daughter, **Maria Theresa** (1740–80), to the Habsburg throne, and Prague, as usual, found itself at the centre of the battlefield. In November 1741, Prague was easily taken by Bavarian, French and Saxon troops, but the occupation force quickly found itself besieged in turn by a Habsburg army, and in January 1743 was forced to abandon the city. By November 1744, Prague was again besieged, this time by the Prussian army, who bombed the city into submission in a fortnight. After a month of looting, they left the city to escape the advancing Habsburg army. During the Seven Years War, in 1757, Prague was once more besieged and bombarded by the Prussian army, though this time the city held out, and, following their defeat at the Battle of Kolín, the Prussians withdrew.

Maria Theresa's reign also marked the beginning of the **Enlightenment** in the Habsburg Empire. Despite her own personal attachment to the Jesuits, the empress acknowledged the need for reform, and she followed the lead of Spain, Portugal and France in expelling the order from the empire in 1773. But it was her son, **Joseph II** (1780–90), who, in the ten short years of his reign, brought about the most radical changes to the social structure of the Habsburg lands. His 1781 Edict of Tolerance allowed a large degree of freedom of worship for the first time in more than 150 years, and went a long way towards lifting the restrictions on Jews within the empire. The following year, he ordered the dissolution of the monasteries, and embarked upon the abolition of serfdom. Despite all his reforms, Joseph was not universally popular. Catholics – some ninety percent of the Bohemian population by this point – viewed

1490	1526	1576–1611
Master Hanuš crafts the astronomical clock on the side of the Old Town Hall.	Ferdinand I is elected Bohemian king, kicking off four centuries of Habsburg rule.	Rudolf II oversees Prague's second golden age, inviting famous astronomers, alchemists and artists to Prague Castle.

him with disdain, and even forced him to back down when he decreed that Protestants, Jews, unbaptized children and suicide victims should be buried in consecrated Catholic cemeteries. His centralization and bureaucratization of the empire placed power in the hands of the Habsburg civil service, and thus helped entrench the **Germanization** of Bohemia. He also offended the Czechs by breaking with tradition and not bothering to hold an official coronation ceremony in Prague.

The Czech national revival

The Habsburgs' enlightened rule inadvertently provided the basis for the economic prosperity and social changes of the **Industrial Revolution**, which in turn fuelled the Czech national revival of the nineteenth century. The textile, glass, coal and iron industries began to grow, drawing ever more Czechs from the countryside and swamping the hitherto mostly German-speaking towns and cities, including Prague. A Czech working class and even an embryonic Czech bourgeoisie emerged, and, thanks to Maria Theresa's reforms, new educational and economic opportunities were given to the Czech lower classes.

For the first half of the century, the Czech **national revival**, or **národní obrození**, was confined to the new Czech intelligentsia, led by philologists including Josef Dobrovský and Josef Jungmann at Charles University, or Karolinum, in Prague. Language disputes (in schools, universities and public offices) remained at the forefront of Czech nationalism throughout the nineteenth century, only later developing into demands for political autonomy from Vienna. The leading figure of the time was the historian **František Palacký**, a Moravian Protestant who wrote the first history of the Czech nation, rehabilitating Hus and the Czech reformists in the process. He was in many ways typical of the early Czech nationalists – pan-Slavist, virulently anti-German, but not yet entirely anti-Habsburg.

1848 and all that

The fall of the French monarchy in February **1848** prompted a crisis in the German states and in the Habsburg Empire. The new Bohemian bourgeoisie, both Czech and German, began to make political demands: freedom of the press, of assembly, of religious creeds. In March, when news of the revolutionary outbreak in Vienna reached Prague, the city's Czechs and Germans began organizing a joint National Guard, while the students formed an Academic Legion, as had the Viennese. Eventually, a National Committee of Czechs and Germans was formed, and Prague got its own elected mayor.

However, it wasn't long before cracks began to appear in the Czech-German alliance. Palacký and his followers were against the dissolution of the empire and argued instead for a kind of multinational federation. Since the empire contained a majority of non-Germans, Prague's own Germans were utterly opposed to Palacký's scheme, campaigning for unification with Germany to secure their interests. On April 11, Palacký refused an invitation to attend the Pan-German National Assembly in Frankfurt. The Germans immediately withdrew from the National Committee, and Prague's other revolutionary institutions began to divide along linguistic lines. On June 2, Palacký convened a **Pan-Slav Congress**, which met on Prague's Slovanský ostrov, an island in the Vltava. Czechs and Slovaks made up the majority of the delegates, but there were also Poles, Croats, Ukrainians, Slovenes and Serbs in attendance.

1618	1620	1648
Two of Ferdinand II's governors are defenestrated – an event which begins the Thirty Years War.	The Czech Protestants are defeated at the Battle of Bílá hora.	Europe-wide conflict ends in Prague when Catholic students prevent the Protestant Swedes from crossing Charles Bridge.

On June 12, the congress had to adjourn, as fighting had broken out on the streets the previous day between the troops of the local Habsburg commander, **Alfred Prince Windischgrätz**, and Czech protesters. The radicals and students took to the streets of Prague, barricades went up overnight, and martial law was declared. During the night of June 14, Windischgrätz withdrew his troops to the left bank and proceeded to bombard the right bank into submission. On the morning of June 17 the city capitulated – the counter-revolution in Bohemia had begun. The upheavals of 1848 left the absolutist Habsburg Empire shaken but fundamentally unchanged and served to highlight the sharp differences between German and Czech aspirations in Bohemia.

Austria-Hungary: the Dual Monarchy

The Habsburg recovery was, however, short-lived. In 1859, and again in 1866, the new emperor, Franz-Joseph II, suffered humiliating defeats at the hands of the Italians and Prussians, respectively, the latter getting their hands on Prague yet again. In order to buy some more time, the compromise, or *Ausgleich*, of 1867 was drawn up, establishing the so-called **Dual Monarchy** of Austria-Hungary – two independent states united by one ruler.

For the Czechs, the *Ausgleich* came as a bitter disappointment. While the Magyars became the Austrians' equals, the Czechs remained second-class citizens. The Czechs' failure in bending the emperor's ear was no doubt partly due to the absence of a Czech aristocracy that could bring its social weight to bear at the Viennese court. Nevertheless, the *Ausgleich* did mark an end to the absolutism of the immediate post-1848 period, and, compared with the Hungarians, the Austrians were positively enlightened in the wide range of civil liberties they granted, culminating in **universal male suffrage** in 1907.

The Industrial Revolution continued apace in Bohemia, bringing an ever-increasing number of Czechs into the newly founded suburbs of Prague, such as Smíchov and Žižkov. Thanks to the unfair voting system, however, the German-speaking minority managed to hold onto power in the Prague city council until the 1880s. By the turn of the century, German-speakers made up just five percent of the city's population – fewer than the Czechs in Vienna – and of those more than half were Jewish. Nevertheless, German influence in the city remained considerable, far greater than their numbers alone warranted; this was due in part to economic means, and in part to over-all rule from Vienna.

Old Czechs, Young Czechs

Meanwhile the Czech *národní obrození* flourished and, towards the end of the century, Prague was endowed with a number of symbolically significant Czech monuments including the Národní divaldo (National Theatre), the Národní muzeum (National Museum) and the Rudolfinum. Inevitably, the movement also began to splinter, with the liberals and conservatives, known as the **Old Czechs**, advocating working within the existing legislature to achieve their aims, and the more radical **Young Czechs** favouring a policy of non-cooperation. The most famous political figure to emerge from the ranks of the Young Czechs was the Prague university professor **Tomáš Garrigue Masaryk**, who founded his own Realist Party in 1900 and began to put forward the (then rather quirky) concept of closer cooperation between the Czechs and Slovaks.

The Old Czechs, backed by the new Czech industrialists, achieved a number of minor legislative successes, but by the 1890s the Young Czechs had gained the upper hand,

Late 17th century	18th century
The Peace of Westphalia and the Counter-Reformation force Prague's Protestant nobility to abandon the city. The Jesuits are put in charge of education in Bohemia. Protestantism is banned.	The imperial court is shifted to Vienna. Prague gradually turns into a provincial backwater.

and conflict between the Czech and German communities became a daily ritual in the boulevards of the capital – a favourite spot for confrontations being the promenade of Na příkopě. Language was also a volatile issue, often fought out on the shop and street signs of Prague. In 1897, the **Badeni Decrees,** which put Czech on an equal footing with German in all dealings with the state, drove the country to the point of civil war, before being withdrawn by the cautious Austrians.

World War I

At the outbreak of **World War I**, the Czechs and Slovaks showed little enthusiasm for fighting alongside their old enemies, the Austrians and Hungarians, against their Slav brothers, the Russians and Serbs. As the war progressed, large numbers defected to form the **Czechoslovak Legion**, which fought on the Eastern Front against the Austrians. Masaryk travelled to the US to curry favour for a new Czechoslovak state, while his two deputies, the Czech Edvard Beneš and the Slovak Milan Štefánik, did the same in Britain and France.

Meanwhile, the Legion, which by now numbered some 100,000 men, became embroiled in the Russian revolutions of 1917, and, when the Bolsheviks made peace with Germany, found itself cut off from the homeland. The uneasy cooperation between the Reds and the Legion broke down when Trotsky demanded that they hand over their weapons before heading off on their legendary **anabasis**, or march back home, via Vladivostok. The soldiers refused and became further involved in the Civil War, for a while controlling large parts of Siberia and, most importantly, the Trans-Siberian Railway, before arriving back to a tumultuous reception in the new republic.

Meanwhile, during the course of the summer of 1918, the Slovaks finally threw in their lot with the Czechs, and the Allies recognized Masaryk's provisional Czechoslovak government. On October 28, 1918, as the Habsburg Empire began to collapse, the first **Czechoslovak Republic** was declared in Prague. In response, the German-speaking border regions (later to become known as the Sudetenland) declared themselves autonomous provinces of the new republic of Deutsch-Österreich (German-Austria), which, it was hoped, would eventually unite with Germany itself. The new Czechoslovak government was having none of it, but it took the intervention of Czechoslovak troops before control of the border regions was wrested from the secessionists.

Last to opt in favour of the new republic was **Ruthenia** (also known as Sub-Carpathian Rus or Podkarpattya Rus, now the Zakarpattya province of Ukraine), a rural backwater of the old Hungarian Kingdom that became officially part of Czechoslovakia by the Treaty of St Germain in September 1919. Its incorporation was largely due to the campaigning efforts of Ruthenian émigrés in the US. For the new republic this poor province was a strategic bonus, but otherwise a huge drain on resources.

The First Republic

The new nation of Czechoslovakia began postwar life in an enviable economic position – **tenth in the world industrial league table** – having inherited seventy to eighty percent of Austro-Hungary's industry intact. Prague regained its position at the centre of the country's political and cultural life, and in the interwar period was embellished with a

Late 18th century	End 18th century	1780–90
Austrian Empress Maria Theresa introduces compulsory schooling for children and other reforms.	German is by now Prague's dominant language.	Maria Theresa's son Joseph II dissolves the monasteries, ejects the Jesuits from Bohemia and abolishes serfdom.

rich mantle of Bauhaus-style buildings. Less enviable was the diverse make-up of the country's population – a melange of minorities that would in the end prove its downfall. Along with the six million Czechs and two million Slovaks who initially backed the republic, there were more than three million Germans and 600,000 Hungarians, not to mention sundry other Ruthenians (Rusyns), Jews and Poles.

That Czechoslovakia's democracy survived as long as it did is down to the powerful political presence and skill of **Masaryk**, the country's president from 1918 to 1935, who shared executive power with the cabinet. It was his vision of social democracy that was stamped on the nation's new constitution, one of the most liberal of the time (if a little bureaucratic and centralized), aimed at ameliorating any ethnic and class tensions within the republic by means of universal suffrage, land reform and, more specifically, the Language Law, which ensured bilinguality in any area where the minority exceeded twenty percent.

The elections of 1920 reflected the mood of the time, ushering in the left-liberal alliance of the **Pětka** (The Five), a coalition of five parties led by the Agrarian, Antonín Švehla, whose slogan, "we have agreed that we will agree", became the keystone of the republic's consensus politics between the wars. Gradually all the other parties (except the Fascists and the Communists) – including even Andrej Hlinka's Slovak People's Party and most of the Sudeten German parties – began to participate in (or at least not disrupt) parliamentary proceedings. On the eve of the Wall Street Crash, the republic was enjoying an economic boom, a cultural renaissance and a temporary modus vivendi among its minorities.

The 1930s

The 1929 Wall Street Crash plunged the whole country into crisis. Economic hardship was quickly followed by **political instability**. In Slovakia, Hlinka's People's Party fed off the anti-Czech resentment that was fuelled by Prague's manic centralization, consistently polling around thirty percent, with an increasingly nationalist/separatist message. In Ruthenia, the elections of 1935 gave only 37 percent of the vote to parties supporting the republic, the rest going to the Communists, pro-Magyars and other autonomist groups.

But without doubt the most intractable of the minority problems was that of the Sudeten Germans, who lived in the mountainous border regions of Bohemia and Moravia. Nationalist sentiment had always run high in the Sudetenland, many of whose German-speakers resented having been included in the new Slav republic, but it was only after the Crash that the extremist parties began to make significant electoral gains. Encouraged by the rise of Fascism in Austria, Italy and Germany, and aided by rocketing Sudeten German unemployment, the far-right **Sudeten German Party** (SdP), led by a bespectacled gym teacher called Konrad Henlein, was able to win just over sixty percent of the German-speaking vote in the 1935 elections.

Although constantly denying any wish to secede from the republic, the activities of Henlein and the SdP were increasingly funded and directed from Nazi Germany. To make matters worse, the Czechs suffered a severe blow to their morale with the death of Masaryk late in 1937, leaving the country in the less capable hands of his Socialist deputy, **Edvard Beneš**. With the Nazi annexation of Austria (the *Anschluss*) on March 11, 1938, Hitler was free to focus his attention on the Sudetenland, calling Henlein to Berlin on March 28 and instructing him to call for outright autonomy.

19th century	1867	1880s
The arrival of Czech-speaking peasants into the industrializing cities leads to a revival in Czech culture.	The dual monarchy of Austro-Hungary is created, leaving the disillusioned Czechs as junior partners in the empire.	The National Theatre and the National Museum are added to Prague's skyline.

The Munich crisis

On April 24, 1938, the SdP launched its final propaganda offensive in the **Karlsbad Decrees**, demanding (without defining) "complete autonomy". As this would clearly have meant surrendering the entire Czechoslovak border defences, not to mention causing economic havoc, Beneš refused to bow to the SdP's demands. Armed conflict was only narrowly avoided and, by the beginning of September, Beneš was forced to acquiesce to some sort of autonomy. On Hitler's orders, Henlein refused Beneš's offer and called openly for the secession of the Sudetenland to the German Reich.

On September 15, as Henlein fled to Germany, the British prime minister, Neville Chamberlain, flew to Berchtesgaden on his own ill-conceived initiative to "appease" the Führer. A week later, Chamberlain flew again to Germany, this time to Bad Godesburg, vowing to the British public that the country would not go to war (in his famous words) "because of a quarrel in a far-away country between people of whom we know nothing". Nevertheless, the French issued draft papers, the British Navy was mobilized, and the whole of Europe fully expected war. Then, in the early hours of September 30, in one of the most treacherous and self-interested acts of modern European diplomacy, prime ministers Chamberlain (for Britain) and Daladier (for France) signed the **Munich Diktat** with Mussolini and Hitler, agreeing – without consulting the Czechoslovak government – to all of Hitler's demands. The British and French public were genuinely relieved, and Chamberlain flew back to cheering home crowds, waving his famous piece of paper that guaranteed "peace in our time". Naturally the Czechs still feel some bitterness about these events.

The Second Republic

Betrayed by his only Western allies and fearing bloodshed, Beneš capitulated, against the wishes of most Czechs. Had Beneš not given in, however, it's doubtful anything would have come of Czech armed resistance, surrounded as they were by vastly superior hostile powers. Beneš resigned on October 5 and left the country. On October 15, **German troops occupied the Sudetenlands**, to the dismay of those Sudeten Germans who hadn't voted for Henlein (not to mention the half-million Czechs and Jews who lived there). The Poles sneakily took the opportunity to seize a sizeable chunk of North Moravia, while in the short-lived "rump" **Second Republic** (officially known as Czecho-Slovakia), Emil Hácha became president, Slovakia and Ruthenia electing their own autonomous governments.

The Second Republic was not long in existence before it, too, collapsed. On March 15, 1939, Hitler informed Hácha of the imminent Nazi occupation of what was left of the Czech Lands, and persuaded him to demobilize the army, again against the wishes of many Czechs. The Germans encountered no resistance (nor any response from the Second Republic's supposed guarantors, Britain and France) and swiftly set up the Nazi **Protectorate of Bohemia and Moravia**. The Hungarians effortlessly crushed Ruthenia's briefest of independences (one day), while the Slovak People's Party, backed by the Nazis, declared **Slovak independence**, under the leadership of the clerical fascist Jozef Tiso.

Late 19th century	1897	Early 20th century
Political tensions along ethnic lines grow. Prague's Jewish ghetto is gradually demolished and replaced with tall, Art Nouveau tenements.	The Badeni Decrees, putting Czech on a par with German, cause widespread conflict before being withdrawn.	Franz Kafka pens his unsettling novels while working as an insurance clerk in Prague.

World War II

In the first few months of the occupation, left-wing activists were arrested, and Jews were placed under the infamous Nuremberg Laws, but Nazi rule in the Protectorate was not as harsh as it would later become. The relatively benign, conservative aristocrat **Baron von Neurath** was appointed *Reichsprotektor*, though his deputy was the rabid Sudeten German Nazi Karl Hermann Frank. Then, on October 28 (Czechoslovak National Day), during a demonstration against the Nazi occupiers, **Jan Opletal**, a Czech medical student, was fatally wounded; he died in hospital on November 11. Prague's Czech students held a wake in the pub *U Fleků*, after which there were further disturbances. Frank used these as an excuse to close down all Czech institutions of higher education, on November 17, executing a number of student leaders and sending more than a thousand others off to the camps.

The assassination of Heydrich

In 1941, Himmler's deputy in the SS, **Reinhard Heydrich**, was made *Reichsprotektor*. More arrests and deportations followed, prompting the Czech government-in-exile to organize the most audacious assassination to take place in Nazi-occupied Europe. In June 1942, Heydrich was fatally wounded by Czech parachutists on the streets of Prague. The reprisals were swift and brutal, culminating in the destruction of the villages of Lidice and Ležáky (see p.119). Meanwhile, the "final solution" was meted out to the country's remaining Jews, who were transported first to the ghetto in Terezín, and then on to the extermination camps. The rest of the population were frightened into submission – very few acts of active resistance being undertaken in the Czech Lands until the Prague Uprising of May 1945.

The Prague Uprising and liberation

By the end of 1944, Czechoslovak and Russian troops had begun to liberate the country, starting with Ruthenia, which Stalin decided to take as war booty despite having guaranteed to maintain Czechoslovakia's pre-Munich borders. On April 4, 1945, under Beneš's leadership, the provisional National Front, or **Národní fronta**, government – a coalition of Social Democrats, Socialists and Communists – was set up in Košice. By April 18, the US Third Army, under General Patton, had crossed the border in the west, meeting very little German resistance.

On the morning of May 5, the Prague radio station, behind the National Museum, began broadcasting in Czech only. The **Prague Uprising** had officially begun. Luckily for the Czechs, Vlasov's anti-Bolshevik Russian National Liberation Army was in the vicinity and was persuaded to turn on the Germans, successfully resisting the two crack German armoured divisions, not to mention the extremely fanatical SS troops, in and around the capital. Barriers were erected across the city, and an American OSS jeep patrol arrived from Plzeň, which the Third Army were on the point of taking. The Praguers (and Vlasov's men) were pinning their hopes on the Americans. In the end, however, the US military leadership made the politically disastrous decision not to cross the demarcation line that had been agreed between the Allies at Yalta. On May 7, Vlasov's men fled towards the American lines, leaving the Praguers to hold out against the Germans. The following day, a ceasefire was agreed and the Germans retreated, for the most part, and headed, like Vlasov, in the direction of the Americans. The Russians entered the city on May 9, and overcame the last pockets of Nazi resistance.

1909	1914	1914–18
Prague's main railway station opens as Franz-Jozefs Bahnhof.	Archduke Ferdinand d'Este and his Czech wife Žofie Chotková are assassinated in Sarajevo.	During World War I Masaryk, Beneš and Štefánik lobby in the US, Britain and France for an independent Czechoslovakia.

The Third Republic

Violent reprisals against suspected collaborators and the German-speaking population in general began as soon as the country was liberated. All Germans were immediately given the same food rations as the Jews had been given during the war. Starvation, summary executions and worse resulted in the deaths of countless thousands of ethnic Germans. With considerable popular backing and the tacit approval of the Red Army, Beneš began to organize the forced **expulsion of the German-speaking population**, referred to euphemistically by the Czechs as the *odsun* (transfer). Only those German-speakers who could prove their anti-Fascist credentials were permitted to stay – the Czech community was not called on to prove the same – and by the summer of 1947, nearly 2.5 million Germans had been expelled from the country or had fled in fear. On this occasion, Sudeten German objections were brushed aside by the Allies, who had given Beneš the go-ahead for the *odsun* at the postwar Potsdam Conference. Attempts by Beneš to expel the Hungarian-speaking minority from Slovakia in similar fashion, however, proved unsuccessful.

The Communists seize power

On October 28, 1945, in accordance with the leftist programme thrashed out at Košice, sixty percent of the country's industry was nationalized. Confiscated Sudeten German property was handed out by the largely Communist-controlled police force, and in a spirit of optimism and/or opportunism, people began to join the Communist Party (KSČ) in droves; membership more than doubled in less than a year. In the **May 1946 elections**, the Party reaped the rewards of its enthusiastic support for the *odsun*, of Stalin's vocal opposition to Munich and of the recent Soviet liberation, emerging as the strongest single party in the Czech Lands with up to forty percent of the vote (the largest ever for a European Communist Party in a multiparty election). In Slovakia, however, they achieved just thirty percent, thus failing to push the Democrats into second place. President Beneš appointed the KSČ leader, **Klement Gottwald**, prime minister of another Národní fronta coalition, with several strategically important cabinet portfolios going to Party members, including the ministries of the Interior, Finance, Labour and Social Affairs, Agriculture and Information.

Gottwald assured everyone of the KSČ's commitment to parliamentary democracy, and initially at least even agreed to participate in the Americans' **Marshall Plan** (the only Eastern Bloc country to do so). Stalin immediately summoned Gottwald to Moscow, and on his return the KSČ denounced the Plan. By the end of 1947, the Communists were beginning to lose support, as the harvest failed, the economy faltered and malpractices within the Communist-controlled Ministry of the Interior were uncovered. In response, the KSČ began to up the ante, constantly warning the nation of imminent "counter-revolutionary plots", and arguing for greater nationalization and land reform as a safeguard.

Then in February 1948 – once officially known as "**Victorious February**" – the latest in a series of scandals hit the Ministry of the Interior, prompting the twelve non-Communist cabinet ministers to resign en masse in the hope of forcing Beneš to dismiss Gottwald. No attempt was made, however, to rally popular support against the Communists. Beneš received more than five thousand resolutions supporting the Communists and just 150 opposing them. Stalin sent word to Gottwald to take advantage of the crisis and ask for

1918	1918–29	1929
Czechoslovak independence is declared at Prague's Art Nouveau Municipal House.	Multi-ethnic Czechoslovakia enjoys a period of unprecedented economic prosperity.	Prague's St Vitus Cathedral is finally declared completed after almost six centuries of sporadic construction.

military assistance – Soviet troops began massing on the Hungarian border. It was the one time in his life when Gottwald disobeyed Stalin; instead, by exploiting the divisions within the Social Democrats, he was able to maintain his majority in parliament. The KSČ took to the streets (and the airwaves), arming "workers' militia" units to defend the country against counter-revolution, calling a general strike and finally, on February 25, organizing the country's biggest ever demonstration in Prague. The same day Gottwald went to an indecisive (and increasingly ill) Beneš with his new cabinet, all Party members or "fellow travellers". Beneš accepted Gottwald's nominees and the most popular Communist coup in Eastern Europe was complete, without bloodshed and without the direct intervention of the Soviets. In the aftermath of the coup, thousands of Czechs and Slovaks fled abroad.

The People's Republic

Following Victorious February, the Party began to consolidate its position, a relatively easy task given its immense popular support and control of the army, police force, workers' militia and trade unions. A **new constitution** confirming the "leading role" of the Communist Party and the "dictatorship of the proletariat" was passed by parliament on May 9, 1948. President Beneš refused to sign it, resigned in favour of Gottwald, and died (of natural causes) shortly afterwards. Those political parties that were not banned or forcibly merged with the KSČ were prescribed fixed-percentage representation within the so-called "multiparty" Národní fronta.

With the Cold War in full swing, the **Stalinization** of Czechoslovak society was quick to follow. In the Party's first Five Year Plan, ninety percent of industry was nationalized, heavy industry (and in particular the country's defence industry) was given a massive boost and compulsory collectivization forced through. Party membership reached an all-time high of 2.5 million, and "class-conscious" Party cadres were given positions of power, while "class enemies" (and their children) were discriminated against. It wasn't long, too, before the Czechoslovak mining "gulags" began to fill up with the regime's political opponents – "kulaks", priests and "bourgeois oppositionists" – numbering more than 100,000 at their peak.

Having incarcerated most of its non-Party opponents, the KSČ, with a little prompting from Stalin, embarked upon a ruthless period of internal blood-letting. As the economy nose-dived, calls for intensified "class struggle", rumours of impending "counter-revolution" and reports of economic sabotage by fifth columnists filled the press. An atmosphere of fear and Soviet-style paranoia was created to justify **large-scale arrests of Party members** with an "international" background: those with a wartime connection with the West, Spanish Civil War veterans, Jews and Slovak nationalists.

In the early 1950s, the Party organized a series of Stalinist **show trials** in Prague, the most spectacular of which was the trial of Rudolf Slánský, who had been second only to Gottwald in the KSČ before his arrest. Slánský, Vladimír Clementis, the former KSČ foreign minister, and twelve other leading Party members (eleven of them Jewish, including Slánský) were sentenced to death as "Trotskyist-Titoist-Zionists". Hundreds of other minor officials were given long prison sentences, and only a handful of defendants had the strength of will to endure the torture and refuse to sign their "confessions".

Early 1930s	1936	1938
The Wall Street Crash causes an economic downturn that exacerbates tensions between Czechs and Germans.	Future playwright and president, Václav Havel, is born in Prague.	France and Britain sign the Munich Diktat handing the Sudetenlands over to Hitler.

After Stalin

Gottwald died in mysterious circumstances in March 1953, nine days after attending Stalin's funeral in Moscow (some say he drank himself to death). The whole nation heaved a sigh of relief, but the regime seemed as unrepentant as ever. The arrests and show trials continued. Then, on May 30, the new Communist leadership announced a drastic currency devaluation, effectively reducing wages by ten percent, while raising prices. The result was a wave of isolated **workers' demonstrations** and rioting in Plzeň and Prague. Czechoslovak army units called in to suppress the demonstrations proved unreliable, and it was left to the heavily armed workers' militia and police to disperse the crowds and make the predictable arrests and summary executions.

In 1954, in the last of the show trials, Gustáv Husák, the post-1968 president, was given life imprisonment, along with other leading Slovak comrades, though he was one of the few with the strength of will to refuse to sign his confession. So complete were the Party purges of the early 1950s, so sycophantic (and scared) was the surviving leadership, that Khrushchev's 1956 thaw was virtually ignored by the KSČ. An attempted rebellion in the Writers' Union Congress was rebuffed and an enquiry into the show trials made several minor security officials scapegoats for the "malpractices". The genuine mass base of the KSČ remained blindly loyal to the Party for the most part; Prague basked under the largest statue of Stalin in the world, and in 1957 the dull, unreconstructed neo-Stalinist **Antonín Novotný** – subsequently alleged to have been a spy for the Gestapo during the war – became First Secretary and President.

Reformism and invasion

The first rumblings of protest against Czechoslovakia's hardline leadership appeared in the official press in 1963. At first, the criticisms were confined to the country's worsening economic stagnation, but soon developed into more generalized protests against the KSČ leadership. Novotný responded by ordering the belated release and rehabilitation of victims of the 1950s purges, permitting a slight cultural thaw and easing travel restrictions to the West. In effect, he was simply buying time. The half-hearted economic reforms announced in the 1965 **New Economic Model** failed to halt the recession, and the minor political reforms instigated by the KSČ only increased the pressure for greater changes within the Party.

In 1967, Novotný attempted a pre-emptive strike against his opponents. Several leading writers were imprisoned, Slovak Party leaders were branded as "bourgeois nationalists" and the economists were called on to produce results or else forego their reform programme. Instead of eliminating the opposition, though, Novotný unwittingly united them. Despite Novotný's plea to the Soviets, Brezhnev refused to back a leader whom he saw as "Khrushchev's man in Prague", and on January 5, 1968, the young Slovak **Alexander Dubček** replaced Novotný as First Secretary. On March 22, the war hero Ludvík Svoboda dislodged Novotný from the presidency.

1968: the Prague Spring

By inclination, Dubček was a moderate, cautious reformer – the perfect compromise candidate – but he was continually swept along by the sheer force of the reform movement. The virtual **abolition of censorship** was probably the single most significant step Dubček took. It transformed what had been until then an internal Party debate into a

1939		1941
Hitler invades and establishes the Protectorate of Bohemia and Moravia.	Alfons Mucha, the best-known painter of the Art Nouveau period, dies in Prague after being interrogated by the Gestapo.	Czech parachutists trained in Britain assassinate *Reichsprotektor* Reinhard Heydrich in Prague.

popular mass movement. Civil society, for years muffled by the paranoia and strictures of Stalinism, suddenly sprang into life in the dynamic optimism of the first few months of 1968, the so-called **Prague Spring**. In April, the KSČ published their Action Programme, proposing what became popularly known as "socialism with a human face" – federalization, freedom of assembly and expression, and democratization of parliament.

Throughout the spring and summer, the reform movement gathered momentum. The Social Democrat Party (forcibly merged with the KSČ after 1948) re-formed, anti-Soviet polemics appeared in the press and, most famously of all, the writer and lifelong Party member Ludvík Vaculík published his personal manifesto entitled "**Two Thousand Words**", calling for radical de-Stalinization within the Party. Dubček and the moderates denounced the manifesto and reaffirmed the country's support for the Warsaw Pact military alliance.

Soviet-led invasion

Meanwhile, the Soviets and their hardline allies – Gomulka in Poland and Ulbricht in the GDR – viewed the Czechoslovak developments on their doorstep gravely, and began to call for the suppression of "counter-revolutionary elements" and the re-imposition of censorship. As the summer wore on, it became clear that the Soviets were planning military intervention. Warsaw Pact manoeuvres were held in Czechoslovakia in late June, a Warsaw Pact conference (without Czechoslovak participation) was convened in mid-July and, at the beginning of August, the Soviets and the KSČ leadership met for **emergency bilateral talks** at Čierná nad Tisou on the Czechoslovak–Soviet border. Brezhnev's hardline deputy, Alexei Kosygin, made his less than subtle threat that "your border is our border", but did agree to withdraw Soviet troops (stationed in the country since the June manoeuvres) and gave the go-ahead to the KSČ's special Party Congress scheduled for September 9.

In the early hours of August 21, fearing a defeat for the hardliners at the forthcoming KSČ Congress, and claiming to have been invited to provide "fraternal assistance", the Soviets gave the order for the **invasion of Czechoslovakia** to be carried out by all the Warsaw Pact forces (only Romania refused to take part). Dubček and the KSČ reformists immediately condemned the invasion before being arrested and flown to Moscow for "negotiations". President Svoboda refused to condone the formation of a new government under the hardliner Alois Indra, and the people took to the streets in protest, employing every form of non-violent resistance in the book. Individual acts of martyrdom, with the self-immolation of **Jan Palach** on Prague's Wenceslas Square, hit the headlines, but casualties were light compared with the Hungarian uprising of 1956 – the cost over the following twenty years was much greater.

Normalization

In April 1969, StB (secret police) agents provoked anti-Soviet riots during the celebrations of the country's double ice hockey victory over the USSR. On this pretext, another Slovak, **Gustáv Husák**, replaced the broken Dubček as First Secretary, and instigated his infamous policy of "**normalization**". More than 150,000 fled the country before the borders closed, around 500,000 were expelled from the Party, and an estimated one million people lost their jobs or were demoted. Inexorably, the KSČ reasserted its absolute control over the

1945	**1945–47**	**1948**
Czechs rise up against the Nazis in Prague just days before the Red Army liberates the city.	Most of Bohemia's German-speaking population is expelled from the country.	Klement Gottwald leads a Communist coup and seizes power in the "Victorious February".

state and society. The only part of the reform package to survive the invasion was **federalization**, which gave the Slovaks greater freedom from Prague (on paper at least), though even this was severely watered down in 1971. Dubček, like countless others, was forced to give up his job, working for the next twenty years as a minor official in the Slovak forestry commission.

An unwritten social contract was struck between rulers and ruled during the 1970s, whereby the country was guaranteed a tolerable standard of living (second only to that of the GDR in Eastern Europe) in return for its passive collaboration. Husák's security apparatus quashed all forms of dissent during the early 1970s, and it wasn't until the middle of the decade that an organized opposition was strong enough to show its face. In 1976, the punk rock band **The Plastic People of the Universe** were arrested and charged with the familiar "crimes against the state" clause of the penal code. The dissidents who rallied to their defence – a motley assortment of people ranging from former KSČ members to right-wing intellectuals – agreed to form **Charter 77** (*Charta 77* in Czech), with the purpose of monitoring human rights abuses in the country. One of the organization's prime movers and initial spokespeople was the absurdist Czech playwright **Václav Havel**. Havel, along with many others, endured relentless persecution (including long prison sentences) over the next decade in pursuit of Charter 77's ideals. The initial gathering of 243 signatories had increased to more than 1000 by 1980, and caused panic in the moral vacuum of the Party apparatus, but consistently failed to stir a fearful and cynical populace into action.

The 1980s

In the late 1970s and early 1980s, the inefficiencies of the economy prevented the government from fulfilling its side of the social contract, as living standards began to fall. Cynicism, alcoholism, absenteeism and outright dissent became widespread, especially among the younger (post-1968) generation. The **Jazz Section** of the Musicians' Union, who disseminated "subversive" Western pop music (such as pirate copies of "Live Aid"), highlighted the ludicrously harsh nature of the regime when they were arrested and imprisoned in the mid-1980s. Pop concerts, religious pilgrimages and, of course, the anniversary of the Soviet invasion all caused regular confrontations between the security forces and certain sections of the population. Yet still, a mass movement like Poland's Solidarity failed to emerge.

With the advent of **Mikhail Gorbachev**, the KSČ was put in an extremely awkward position, as it tried desperately to separate *perestroika* from comparisons with the reforms of the Prague Spring. Husák and his cronies had prided themselves on being second only to Honecker's GDR as the most stable and orthodox of the Soviet satellites – now the font of orthodoxy, the Soviet Union, was turning against them. In 1987, **Miloš Jakeš**, the hardliner who oversaw Husák's normalization purges, took over from Husák as General (First) Secretary and introduced *přestavba* (restructuring), Czechoslovakia's lukewarm version of *perestroika*.

The Velvet Revolution

Everything appeared to be going swimmingly for the KSČ as it entered **1989**. Under the surface, however, things were becoming more and more strained. As the country's

Early 1950s	1953	1955
Under Gottwald the Communist Party oversees a period of Stalinist terror and show trials.	Stalin and Gottwald die within nine days of each other.	Prague unveils the world's largest Stalin monument.

economic performance worsened, divisions were developing within the KSČ leadership. The protest movement was gathering momentum: even the Catholic Church had begun to voice dissatisfaction, compiling a staggering 500,000 signatures calling for greater freedom of worship. But the twenty-first anniversary of the Soviet invasion produced a demonstration of only 10,000, which was swiftly and violently dispersed by the regime.

During the summer, however, more serious cracks began to appear in Czechoslovakia's staunch hardline ally, the GDR. The trickle of **East Germans fleeing to the West** turned into a mass exodus, with thousands besieging the West German embassy in Prague.

THE PINK TANK

Until 1991, **Tank 23** sat proudly on its plinth in Prague's náměstí Sovětských tankistů (Soviet Tank Drivers' Square), one of a number of obsolete tanks generously donated by the Soviets after World War II to serve as monuments to the 1945 liberation. Tank 23 was special, however, as it was supposedly the first tank to arrive to liberate Prague, on May 9, hotfoot from Berlin.

The real story of the liberation of Prague was rather different. When the Prague Uprising began on May 5, the first offer of assistance actually came from a division of the anti-Communist **Russian National Liberation Army** (**KONR**), under the overall command of **Andrei Vlasov**, a high-ranking former Red Army officer who was instrumental in pushing the Germans back from the gates of Moscow, but who switched sides after being captured by the Nazis in 1942. The Germans were (rightly, as it turned out) highly suspicious of the KONR, and, for the most part, the renegade Russians were kept well away from the real action. In the war's closing stages, the KONR switched sides once more and agreed to fight alongside the Czech resistance, making a crucial intervention against the SS troops who were poised to crush the uprising in Prague. Initially, the Czechs guaranteed Vlasov's men asylum from the advancing Soviets in return for military assistance. In reality, the Czechs were unable to honour their side of the bargain and the KONR finally withdrew from the city late on May 7 and headed west to surrender themselves to the Americans. When the Red Army finally arrived in Prague, many of Vlasov's troops were simply gunned down by the Soviets. Even those in the hands of the Americans were eventually passed over to the Russians and shared the fate of their leader Vlasov who was tried in camera in Moscow and hanged with piano wire on August 2, 1946.

The unsolicited reappearance of Soviet tanks on the streets of Prague in 1968 left most Czechs feeling somewhat ambivalent towards the old monument. And in the summer of 1991, artist **David Černý** painted the tank bubble-gum pink and placed a large phallic finger on top of it, while another mischievous Czech daubed "Vlasov" on the podium. Since the country was at the time engaged in delicate negotiations to end the Soviet military presence in Czechoslovakia, the new regime, despite its mostly dissident leanings, roundly condemned the act as unlawful. Havel, in his characteristically even-handed way, made it clear that he didn't like tanks anywhere, whether on the battlefield or as monuments.

In the end, the tank was hastily repainted khaki green and Černý was arrested under the "crimes against the state" clause of the penal code, which had previously been used by the Communists against several members of the then government. In protest at the arrest of Černý, twelve members of the federal parliament turned up the following day in their overalls and, taking advantage of their legal immunity, repainted the tank pink. Finally, the government gave in, released Černý and removed the tank from public view. There's now no trace of tank, podium or plaque on the square (which has been renamed **náměstí Kinských**). You can, however, still see the tank at the Vojenské technické museum (Military Technical Museum) in Lešany, 40km or so southeast of Prague.

1960s	1962	1968
A gradual political thaw throughout the 1960s leads to the "Prague Spring" of 1968.	Stalin monument dynamited under pressure from the Soviets.	Reforming Slovak Alexander Dubček becomes First Secretary. Concerned by "counter revolution" in Prague, Warsaw Pact countries led by the USSR invade Czechoslovakia.

Honecker, the East German leader, was forced to resign and by the end of October nightly mass demonstrations were taking place on the streets of Leipzig and other German cities. The **fall of the Berlin Wall** on November 9 left Czechoslovakia, Romania and Albania alone on the Eastern European stage still clinging to the old truths.

All eyes were now turned upon Czechoslovakia. Reformists within the KSČ began plotting an internal coup to overthrow Jakeš, in anticipation of a Soviet denunciation of the 1968 invasion. In the end, events overtook whatever plans they may have had. On Friday, **November 17**, a 50,000-strong peaceful demonstration organized by the official Communist youth organization was viciously attacked by the riot police. More than one hundred arrests, five hundred injuries and one death were reported (the fatality was later retracted) in what became popularly known as the *masakr* (massacre). Prague's students immediately began an occupation strike, joined soon after by the city's actors, who together called for an end to the Communist Party's "leading role" and a general strike to be held for two hours on November 27.

Civic Forum and the VPN
On Sunday, November 19, on Václav Havel's initiative, the established opposition groups, including Charter 77, met and agreed to form Občanské fórum, or **Civic Forum**. Their demands were simple: the resignation of the present hardline leadership, including Husák and Jakeš; an enquiry into the police actions of November 17; an amnesty for all political prisoners; and support for the general strike. In Bratislava, a parallel organization, Veřejnosť proti nasiliu, or **People Against Violence** (VPN), was set up to coordinate protests in Slovakia.

On the Monday evening, the first of the really big **nationwide demonstrations** took place – the biggest since the 1968 invasion – with more than 200,000 people pouring into Prague's Wenceslas Square. This time the police held back and rumours of troop deployments proved false. Every night for a week people poured into the main squares in towns and cities across the country, repeating the calls for democracy, freedom and an end to the Party's monopoly of power. As the week dragged on, the Communist media tentatively began to report events, and the KSČ leadership started to splinter under the strain, with the prime minister, **Ladislav Adamec**, alone in sticking his neck out and holding talks with the opposition.

The end of one-party rule
On Friday evening, Dubček, the ousted 1968 leader, appeared alongside Havel, before a crowd of 300,000 in Wenceslas Square, and in a matter of hours the entire Jakeš leadership had resigned. The weekend brought the largest demonstrations the country had ever seen – more than 750,000 people in Prague alone. At the invitation of Civic Forum, Adamec addressed the crowd, only to be booed off the platform. On Monday, November 27, eighty percent of the country's workforce joined the two-hour **general strike**, including many of the Party's previously stalwart allies, such as the miners and engineers. The following day, the Party agreed to an end to one-party rule and the formation of a new "coalition government".

A temporary halt to the nightly demonstrations was called and the country waited expectantly for the "broad coalition" cabinet promised by prime minister Adamec. On December 3, another Communist-dominated line-up was announced by the Party and

1969	1970s	1977
A Slovak, Gustáv Husák, replaces Dubček, who becomes a minor official in the Slovak Forestry Ministry.	Period of "normalization" – when living standards were artificially raised in exchange for the passive cooperation of the populace.	Charter 77 is signed by 243 Czechoslovak dissidents, including Czech playwright Václav Havel.

immediately denounced by Civic Forum and the VPN, who called for a fresh wave of demonstrations and another general strike for December 11. Adamec promptly resigned and was replaced by the Slovak Marián Čalfa. On December 10, one day before the second threatened general strike, Čalfa announced his provisional "**Government of National Understanding**", with Communists in the minority for the first time since 1948 and multiparty elections planned for June 1990. Having sworn in the new government, President Husák, architect of the post-1968 "normalization", finally threw in the towel.

By the time the new Čalfa government was announced, the students and actors had been on strike continuously for more than three weeks. The pace of change surprised everyone involved, but there was still one outstanding issue: the election of a new president. Posters shot up all round the capital urging "**HAVEL NA HRAD**" (Havel to the Castle – the seat of the presidency). The students were determined to see his election through, continuing their occupation strike until Havel was officially elected president by a unanimous vote of the Federal Assembly, and sworn in at the Hrad on December 29.

Early years of freedom

Czechoslovakia started the new decade full of optimism for what the future would bring. On the surface, the country had a lot more going for it than its immediate neighbours (with the possible exception of the GDR). The Communist Party had been swept from power without bloodshed, and, unlike the rest of Eastern Europe, Czechoslovakia had a strong interwar **democratic tradition** with which to identify – Masaryk's First Republic. Despite Communist economic mismanagement, the country still had a relatively high standard of living, a skilled workforce and a manageable foreign debt.

In reality, however, the situation was somewhat different. Not only was the country economically in a worse state than most people had imagined, it was also environmentally devastated, and its people were suffering from what Havel described as "post-prison psychosis" – an inability to think or act for themselves. The country had to go through the painful transition "from being a big fish in a small pond to being a sickly adolescent trout in a hatchery". As a result, it came increasingly to rely on its new-found saviour, the humble playwright-president, Václav Havel.

In most people's eyes, "Saint Václav" could do no wrong, though he himself was not out to woo his electorate. His call for the rapid **withdrawal of Soviet troops** was popular enough, but his apology for the postwar expulsion of Sudeten Germans was deeply resented, as was his generous amnesty that eased the country's overcrowded prisons. The amnesty was blamed by many for the huge **rise in crime** in 1990. Every vice in the book – from racism to homicide – raised its ugly head in the first year of freedom.

In addition, there was still a lot of talk about the possibility of "counter-revolution", given the thousands of unemployed StB (secret police) at large. Inevitably, accusations of previous StB involvement rocked each political party in turn in the run-up to the first elections. The controversial **lustrace** (literally "lustration" or cleansing) law, which barred all those on StB files from public office for the following five years, ended the career of many public figures, often on the basis of highly unreliable StB reports.

1988	1989
Mikhail Gorbachev's policies of *glasnost* and *perestroika* herald a new era of openness in the USSR and lead eventually to the fragmentation of the Soviet Union.	Prague's Velvet Revolution sweeps the Communists from power and Havel to the Hrad.

The 1990 elections

Despite all the inevitable hiccups, and the increasingly vocal Slovak nationalists, Civic Forum/VPN remained high in the opinion polls. The **June 1990 elections** produced a record-breaking 99 percent turnout. With around sixty percent of the vote, Civic Forum/VPN were clear victors (the Communists won thirteen percent, as they still do today) and Havel immediately set about forming a broad "Coalition of National Sacrifice", including everyone from Christian Democrats to former Communists.

The main concern of the new government was how to transform an outdated command-system economy into a **market economy**. The argument over the speed and model of economic reform eventually caused Civic Forum to split into two main camps: the centre-left Občánské hnutí, or Civic Movement (OH), led by the foreign minister and former dissident Jiří Dienstbier, who favoured a more gradualist approach; and Občánská democratická strana, the right-wing **Civic Democratic Party** (ODS), headed by the finance minister **Václav Klaus**, who pronounced that the country should "walk the tightrope to Thatcherism".

One of the first acts of the new government was to pass a **restitution law**, handing back small businesses and property to those from whom it had been expropriated after the 1948 Communist coup. This proved to be a controversial issue, since it excluded Jewish families driven out in 1938 by the Nazis, and, of course, the millions of Sudeten Germans who were forced to flee the country after the war. A law was later passed to cover the Jewish expropriations, but the Sudeten Germans never received a single crown in compensation.

The Slovak crisis

One of the most intractable issues facing post-Communist Czechoslovakia in the years immediately following the Velvet Revolution turned out to be the "**Slovak problem**". Having been the victim of Prague-inspired centralization from Masaryk to Gottwald, the Slovaks were in no mood to suffer second-class citizenship any longer. In the aftermath of 1989, feelings were running high in Slovakia, and more than once the spectre of Slovak independence was threatened by Slovak politicians, who hoped to boost their popularity by appealing to voters' nationalism. Despite the tireless campaigning and negotiating by both sides, a compromise failed to emerge.

The **June 1992 elections** soon became an unofficial referendum on the future of the federation. Events moved rapidly towards the break-up of the republic after the resounding victory of the Movement for a Democratic Slovakia (HZDS), under the wily populist politician Vladimír Mečiar, who, in retrospect, was quite clearly seeking Slovak independence, though he never explicitly said so during the campaign. In the Czech Lands, the right-wing ODS emerged as the largest single party, under Václav Klaus, who – ever the economist – was clearly not going to shed tears over losing the economically backward Slovak half of the country.

Talks between the two sides got nowhere, despite opinion polls in both countries consistently showing majority support for the federation. The HZDS then blocked the re-election of Havel, who had committed himself entirely to the pro-federation cause. Havel promptly resigned, leaving the country president-less and Klaus and Mečiar to talk over the terms of the divorce. On January 1, 1993, after 74 years of troubled existence, **Czechoslovakia** was officially divided into two "new" countries: the Czech Republic and Slovakia.

1990	1992	1993
Czechoslovakia holds its first democratic elections after the fall of Communism.	Following more elections, Czechoslovakia agrees to split into two countries.	Prague becomes the capital of the new Czech Republic.

Czech politics under Klaus

Generally speaking, life was much kinder to the Czechs than the Slovaks in the immediate period following the break-up of Czechoslovakia. While the Slovaks had the misfortune of being led by the increasingly wayward and isolated Mečiar, the Czechs enjoyed a long period of **political stability** under Klaus, with Havel immediately re-elected as Czech president. Under their guidance, the country jumped to the front of the queue for EU and NATO membership, and was held up as a shining example to all other former Eastern Bloc countries. Prague attracted more foreign investment than anywhere else in the country and was transformed beyond all recognition, its main thoroughfares lined with brand-new hotels, shops and restaurants.

Klaus and his party, the ODS, certainly proved themselves the most durable of all the new political forces to emerge in the former Eastern Bloc. Nevertheless, in the **1996 elections**, although the ODS again emerged as the largest single party, they failed to gain an outright majority. They repeated the failure again during the first elections for the Czech Senate, the upper house of the Czech parliament. The electorate was distinctly unenthusiastic about the whole idea of another chamber full of overpaid politicians, and a derisory thirty percent turned out to vote in the second round. In the end, it was – predictably enough – a series of allegations of corruption over the country's privatization that eventually prompted **Klaus's resignation** as prime minister in 1997.

Political stalemate

The **1998 elections** proved that the Czechs had grown sick and tired of Klaus's dry, rather arrogant, style of leadership, but what really did it for Klaus was that for the first time since he took power, the economy had begun to falter. The **ČSSD**, or Social Democrats, under **Miloš Zeman**, emerged as the largest single party, promising to pay more attention to social issues. Unable to form a majority government, Zeman followed the Austrian example, and decided to make an "**opposition agreement**" with the ODS. This Faustian pact was dubbed the "Toleranzpatent" by the press, after the 1781 Edict of Tolerance issued by Joseph II. The Czech public were unimpressed, seeing the whole deal as a cosy stitch-up, and in 2000 thousands turned out in Wenceslas Square for the *Díky a odejděte* (Thank you, now leave) protest, asking for the resignation of both Zeman and Klaus.

Havel stepped down in 2003 after ten years as Czech president, to be replaced by his old sparring partner, Václav Klaus. No Czech president is ever likely to enjoy the same moral stature, though by the end of his tenure even Havel's standing was not what it used to be. His marriage to the actress Dagmar Veškrnová, seventeen years his junior, in 1997, less than a year after his first wife, Olga, died of cancer, was frowned upon by many. And his very public fall-out with his sister-in-law, Olga Havlová, over the family inheritance of the multimillion-crown Lucerna complex in Prague, didn't do his reputation any favours either.

One of the biggest problems to emerge in the 1990s was the issue of **Czech racism towards the Romany minority** within the country. Matters came to a head in 1999 over the planned building of a wall to separate Romanies and non-Romanies in the north Bohemian city of **Ústí nad Labem**. The central government, under pressure from

1990s	1999	2003	2004
Prime minister Václav Klaus implements far-reaching economic reforms.	The Czech Republic joins NATO.	Havel ends his final term as president and hands the keys to the Hrad to Václav Klaus.	The Czech Republic joins the EU along with nine other countries.

the EU, condemned the construction of the wall, and eventually the local council rehoused the white Czechs elsewhere. Since EU accession in 2004, many Romany have left the country, but those who remain still face widespread racism, as do most other minorities.

EU accession and beyond

In June 2003, just 55 percent of the population turned out to vote in the **EU referendum**, with 77 percent voting in favour of joining. On May 1, 2004, the Czech Republic formally joined the EU, along with nine other accession states. Despite their growing cynicism, Czechs genuinely celebrated their entry into the EU; for many, it was the culmination of everything that had been fought for in 1968 and 1989, a final exorcism of the enforced isolation of the Communist period.

EU accession was fairly positive for the Czechs. Their **economy** held up well, so there was no great flight of labour from the country as there was in Poland. Despite the global financial crisis, the conservative Czech financial system remained relatively healthy. If anything, the country suffered from the crown being consistently overvalued, leading to a drop in the number of tourists in 2009 for the first time in twenty years. Numbers have since recovered, however, and the mini-devaluation of the crown by the Czech Central Bank in late 2013 has seen exports up and even more visitors arriving in the capital. Since accession, following the European trend, Czechs have become disillusioned with the EU, though Brexit seems to have tempered this Euroscepticism a bit. In a 2017 survey, over fifty percent of the population saw EU membership as a good thing, well up from previous years.

In recent years, weak coalition governments returned by a divided and apathetic electorate, political scandal and deep-rooted high-level corruption have cast many a cloud over the country, though the economy has performed better than many could have expected. In March 2013, Klaus having served the maximum ten years in office, **Miloš Zeman** made a dramatic return to the political scene when he became the first Czech president to be elected in a popular vote. At the time of writing, it's not yet known whether he will stand in 2018 and there's no clear favourite to occupy the Hrad after him. Meanwhile in 2017 it looked increasingly likely that Andrej Babiš, oligarch, leader of his own ANO movement and, until May 2017, finance minister would form the next government.

Despite the wider country's economic performance, Prague remains an attractive prospect for any young Czech looking to make it big. As more people move in from the sticks, the difference between Czech town and Czech country is likely to grow even further. Prague is the place to be, but it remains to be seen just how much the rest of the Czech Republic will suffer from having such a dominant capital.

2011	2013	2017–18
Havel dies at the age of 75.	Former prime minister Miloš Zeman becomes the first Czech president to be elected in a popular vote.	The Czechs hold crucial parliamentary and presidential elections to decide the future direction the country will take.

Prague personalities

Prague has produced its fair share of world-renowned personalities across a range of fields of human endeavour. Possibly the single most famous person from the city was Franz Kafka, who was ironically not Czech at all but an ethnic German Jew not normally recognized by Czechs as a Czech author. Many others have come here to make their name.

Beneš, Edvard (1884–1948). Hero to some, traitor to others, Beneš was president from 1935 until 1938 – when he resigned, having refused to lead the country into bloodshed over the Munich Crisis – and again from 1945 until 1948, when he acquiesced in the Communist coup.

Brahe, Tycho (1546–1601). Ground-breaking Danish astronomer, who was summoned to Prague by Rudolf II in 1597, only to die from over-drinking in 1601.

Braun, Matthias Bernard (1684–1738). Austrian sculptor who achieved his greatest fame in the Czech Lands, executing sculptures for the city's Baroque palaces, gardens and churches.

Brokoff, Ferdinand Maximilian (1688–1731). Along with Braun, Prague's most famous Baroque sculptor, several of whose works adorn Charles Bridge.

Čapek, Josef (1887–1945). Cubist artist and writer and illustrator of children's books, Josef was older brother to the more famous Karel (see below); he died in Belsen concentration camp.

Čapek, Karel (1890–1938). Czech writer, journalist and unofficial spokesperson for the First Republic. His most famous works are *The Insect Play* and *R.U.R.*, which introduced the word *robot* into the English language.

Dientzenhofer, Kilian Ignác (1689–1751). One of the city's most prolific Baroque architects, whose most famous work is probably the church of sv Mikuláš in Malá Strana.

Dobrovský, Josef (1753–1829). Jesuit-taught pioneer in Czech philology. Wrote the seminal text *The History of Czech Language and Literature*.

Dubček, Alexander (1921–92). Slovak Communist who became First Secretary in January 1968, at the beginning of the Prague Spring. Expelled from the Party in 1969, but returned to become speaker in the federal parliament after 1989, before being killed in a suspicious car crash in 1992.

Dvořák, Antonín (1841–1904). Perhaps the most famous of all Czech composers. His best-known work is the *New World Symphony*, inspired by an extensive sojourn in the US.

Fučík, Julius (1903–43). Communist journalist murdered by the Nazis, whose prison writings, *Notes from the Gallows*, were obligatory reading in the 1950s. Hundreds of streets were named after him, but doubts about the authenticity of the work and general hostility towards the man have made him *persona non grata*.

Gottwald, Klement (1896–1953). One of the founders of the KSČ, general secretary from 1927, prime minister from 1946 to 1948, and president from 1948 to 1953, Gottwald is universally abhorred for his role in the show trials of the 1950s.

Hašek, Jaroslav (1883–1923). Anarchist, dog-breeder, lab assistant, bigamist, cabaret artist and People's Commissar in the Red Army, Hašek was one of prewar Prague's most colourful characters, who wrote the famous *The Good Soldier Švejk* and died from alcohol abuse in 1923.

Havel, Václav (1936–2011). Absurdist playwright of the 1960s, who became a leading dissident and spokesperson of Charter 77 and, following the Velvet Revolution, the country's first post-Communist president.

Havlíček-Borovský, Karel (1821–56). Satirical poet, journalist and nationalist, exiled to the Tyrol by the Austrian authorities after 1848.

Hrabal, Bohumil (1936–97). Writer and bohemian, whose novels were banned under the Communists, but revered worldwide.

Hus, Jan (1370–1415). Rector of Prague University and reformist preacher who was burnt at the stake as a heretic by the Council of Constance.

Husák, Gustáv (1913–91). Slovak Communist who was sentenced to life imprisonment in the show trials of the 1950s. Released in 1960, he eventually became General Secretary and president following the Soviet invasion. Resigned in favour of Havel in December 1989.

Jirásek, Alois (1851–1930). Writer who popularized Czech legends for both children and adults and became a key figure in the Czech national revival.

Jungmann, Josef (1773–1847). Prolific Czech translator and author of the seminal *History of Czech Literature* and the first Czech dictionary.

Kafka, Franz (1883–1924). German-Jewish Praguer who worked as an insurance clerk in Prague for most of his life, and also wrote some of the most influential novels of the twentieth century, most notably *The Trial*.

Kelley, Edward (1555–97). English occultist who was summoned to Prague by Rudolf II, but eventually incurred the wrath of the emperor and was imprisoned in Kokořín castle.

Kepler, Johannes (1571–1630). German Protestant forced to leave Linz for Denmark because of the

Counter-Reformation. Succeeded Tycho Brahe as Rudolf II's chief astronomer. His observations of the planets became the basis of the laws of planetary motion.

Kisch, Egon Erwin (1885–1948). German-Jewish Praguer who became one of the city's most famous investigative journalists.

Klaus, Václav (1941–). Known somewhat bitterly as "Santa Klaus". Prime minister (1992–97), president (2003–13), confirmed Thatcherite, Eurosceptic and driving force behind the economic reforms of the post-Communist period.

Komenský, Jan Amos (1592–1670). Leader of the Protestant Czech Brethren. Forced to flee the country and settle in England during the Counter-Reformation. Better known to English-speakers as Comenius.

Mácha, Karel Hynek (1810–36). Romantic nationalist poet, great admirer of Byron and Keats who, like them, died young. His most famous poem is *Máj*, published just months before his death.

Masaryk, Jan Garrigue (1886–1948). Son of the founder of the republic (see below), foreign minister in the postwar government and the only non-Communist in Gottwald's cabinet when the Communists took over in February 1948. Died ten days after the coup in suspicious circumstances.

Masaryk, Tomáš Garrigue (1850–1937). Professor of philosophy at Prague University, president of the Republic from 1918 to 1935. His name is synonymous with the First Republic and was removed from all street signs after the 1948 coup. Now back with a vengeance.

Mucha, Alfons (1860–1939). Moravian graphic artist and designer whose Art Nouveau posters and artwork for Sarah Bernhardt brought him international fame. After the founding of Czechoslovakia, he returned to the country to design stamps and banknotes, and complete a cycle of giant canvases on Czech nationalist themes.

Němcová, Božena (1820–62). Highly popular writer who became involved with the nationalist movement and shocked many with her unorthodox behaviour. Her most famous book is *Grandmother*.

Neruda, Jan (1834–91). Poet and journalist for the *Národní listy*. Wrote some famous short stories describing Prague's Malá Strana.

Palacký, František (1798–1876). Nationalist historian, Czech MP in Vienna and leading figure in the events of 1848.

Purkyně, Jan Evangelista (1787–1869). Czech doctor, natural scientist and pioneer in experimental physiology who became professor of physiology at Prague and then at Wrocław University.

Rieger, Ladislav (1818–1903). Nineteenth-century Czech politician and one of the leading figures in the events of 1848 and the aftermath.

Rilke, Rainer Maria (1876–1926). Despite having been brought up as a girl for the first six years of his life, Rilke ended up as an officer in the Austrian army, and wrote some of the city's finest German *fin-de-siècle* poetry.

Santini, Jan Blažej (1677–1723). The most unusual architect of his day, Santini was innovative in his use of symbolism and his attempt to fuse Gothic and Baroque elements.

Smetana, Bedřich (1824–84). Popular Czech composer and fervent nationalist whose *Má vlast* (My Homeland) traditionally opens the Prague Spring Music Festival.

Svoboda, Ludvík (1895–1979). Victorious Czech general from World War II, who acquiesced in the 1948 Communist coup and was Communist president from 1968 to 1975.

Tyl, Josef Kajetán (1808–56). Czech playwright and composer of the Czech half of the national anthem, *Where is my Home?*

Werfel, Franz (1890–1945). One of the German Jewish literary circle that included Kafka, Kisch and Brod.

Zeman, Miloš (1944–). Late 1990s prime minister (1998–2002) and third Czech president. A controversial figure for his outbursts, links to China and the Kremlin and alleged alcohol problem.

Žižka, Jan (died 1424). Brilliant, blind military leader of the Táborites, the radical faction of the Hussites.

Books

A great deal of Czech fiction and poetry has been translated into English and is easily available. The key moments in Czech twentieth-century history are also well covered in English. More recently, there have been a whole number of books published in English in Prague, and for these you may need to go to one of the city's English-language bookstores (see p.208). Books marked with the ★ symbol are particularly recommended.

HISTORY, POLITICS AND SOCIETY

Chad Bryant *Prague in Black*. Intriguing scholarly investigation of the roots of Czech nationalism, first under Nazi occupation and then during the lead-up to the 1948 Communist coup.

★ **Peter Demetz** *Prague in Black and Gold: Scenes from the Life of a European City*. Demetz certainly knows his subject, both academically and at first hand, having been brought up in the city before World War II (when his account ends). His style can be a little dry, but he is determinedly un-partisan, and refreshingly anti-nationalist in his reading of history. In *Prague in Danger* the author intersperses his even-handed, objective account of resistance under the Nazi occupation with personal anecdotes of living as a *Mischling*, or "half Jew", in Prague during that period.

R.J.W. Evans *Rudolf II and his World*. First published in 1973, and still the best account of the alchemy-mad emperor, but not as salacious as one might hope.

Jan Kaplan and Krystyna Nosarzewska *Prague: The Turbulent Century*. This is the first real attempt to cover the twentieth-century history of Prague with all its warts. The text isn't as good as it should be, but the book is worth it just for the incredible range of photographs and images.

Karel Kaplan *The Short March: The Communist Takeover in Czechoslovakia, 1945–48*. An excellent account of the electoral rise and rise of the Communists in Czechoslovakia after the war, which culminated in the bloodless coup of February 1948. *Report on the Murder of the General Secretary*

is an incredibly detailed study of the country's brutal Stalinist show trials, and most famously that of Rudolf Slánský, number two in the Party until his arrest.

★ **Callum MacDonald** *The Assassination of Reinhard Heydrich*. Gripping account of the build-up to the most successful and controversial act of wartime resistance, which took place in May 1942, and prompted horrific reprisals by the Nazis on the Czechs.

Peter Marshall *The Theatre of the World: Alchemy, Astrology and Magic in Renaissance Prague*. Detailed account of Rudolf II's court and its famous luminaries: Tycho Brahe, Kepler, Arcimboldo and the magic makers.

Derek Sayer *The Coasts of Bohemia*. A very readable cultural history, concentrating on Bohemia and Prague, which aims to dispel the ignorance shown by the Shakespearean quote of the title, and particularly illuminating on the subject of twentieth-century artists.

Kieran Williams *The Prague Spring and its Aftermath: Czechoslovak Politics, 1968–70*. Drawing on declassified archives, this book analyses the attempted reforms under Dubček and takes a new look at the Prague Spring.

★ **Elizabeth Wiskemann** *Czechs and Germans*. Researched and written in the build-up towards Munich, this is the most fascinating and fair treatment of the Sudeten problem. Meticulous in her detail, vast in her scope, Wiskemann manages to suffuse the weighty text with enough anecdotes to keep you gripped.

ESSAYS, MEMOIRS AND BIOGRAPHIES

Margarete Buber-Neumann *Milena*. A moving biography of Milena Jesenská, one of interwar Prague's most beguiling characters, who befriended the author while they were both interned in Ravensbrück concentration camp.

Karel Čapek *Talks with T.G. Masaryk*. Čapek was a personal (and political) friend of Masaryk, and his diaries, journals, reminiscences and letters give great insights into the man who personified the First Republic.

Helen Epstein *Where She Came From: A Daughter's Search for her Mother's History*. Daughter of a Holocaust survivor, the author traces the effects of anti-Semitism through three generations of women.

Timothy Garton Ash *We The People: The Revolutions of 89*. A personal, anecdotal, eyewitness account of the Velvet Revolution (and the events in Poland, Berlin and Budapest). By far the most compelling of all the post-1989 books. Published as *The Magic Lantern* in the US.

Patricia Hampl *A Romantic Education*. This American author went to Prague in the 1980s in search of her Czech roots and the contrasting cultures of East and West; the book was reissued and updated in 1999 to mark the tenth anniversary of the Velvet Revolution.

Václav Havel The first essay in *Living in Truth* is "Power of the Powerless", Havel's lucid, damning indictment of the inactivity of the Czechoslovak masses in the face of "normalization". *Disturbing the Peace* is probably Havel's most accessible work: a series of autobiographical questions and answers in which he talks interestingly about his childhood, the events of 1968 when he was in Liberec and the path to Charter 77 and beyond (though not including his reactions to being thrust into the role of president).

Václav Havel et al. *Power of the Powerless*. A collection of essays by leading Chartists, kicking off with Havel's seminal title-piece (see above). Other contributors range from the dissident Marxist Petr Uhl to devout Catholics such as Václav Benda.

Miroslav Holub *The Dimension of the Present Moment and other Essays; Shedding Life: Disease, Politics and Other Human Conditions*. Two books of short philosophical musings/essays on life and the universe by this unusual and clever scientist-poet.

John Keane *Václav Havel: A Political Tragedy in Six Acts*. The first book to tell both sides of the Havel story: Havel the dissident playwright and civil rights activist who played a key role in the 1989 Velvet Revolution, and Havel the ageing and increasingly ill president, who, in many people's opinion, stayed on the stage too long.

Benjamin Kuras *Czechs and Balances* and *Is There Life After Marx?* Witty, light, typically Czech takes on national identity and central European politics. *As Golems Go* is a more mystical look at Rabbi Löw's philosophy and the Kabbalah.

Patrick Leigh Fermor *A Time of Gifts*. The first volume of Leigh Fermor's trilogy based on his epic walk along the Rhine and Danube rivers in 1933–34. In the last quarter of the book he reaches Czechoslovakia, indulging in a quick jaunt to Prague before crossing the border into Hungary. Written forty years later in dense, luscious and highly crafted prose, it's an evocative and poignant insight into the culture of *Mitteleuropa* between the wars.

★**Heda Margolius Kovaly** *Prague Farewell*. An auto-biography that starts in the concentration camps of World War II and ends with the author's flight from Czechoslovakia in 1968. Married to Rudolf Margolius, one of the Party officials executed in the 1952 Slánský trial, she tells her story simply and without bitterness. The best account there is of the fear and paranoia whipped up during the Stalinist terror. Published as *Under a Cruel Star* in the US.

Ivan Margolius *Reflections of Prague: Journeys Through the 20th Century*. A moving account of the lives of his parents, Heda and Rudolf Margolius (see above), and the story of his return to Prague to find out the truth about his father.

Nicholas Murray *Kafka*. A superbly researched and very level-headed assessment of the German-Czech writer, who spent almost all of his short life in Prague.

Ota Pavel *How I Came to Know Fish*. Pavel's childhood innocence shines through, particularly when his Jewish father and two brothers are sent to a concentration camp and he and his mother have to scrape a living.

Pressburger and Lappin *The Diary of Petr Ginz: 1941– 1942*. Discovered in 2003, this is the diary of a 15-year-old boy who was taken first to Terezín and then to Auschwitz, where he died. He was exceptionally gifted, compiling a Czech-Esperanto dictionary among other things, and his writing offers parallels with Anne Frank's.

★**Angelo Maria Ripellino** *Magic Prague*. A wide-ranging look at the bizarre array of historical and literary characters who have lived in Prague, from the mad antics of the court of Rudolf II to the escapades of Jaroslav Hašek. Scholarly, rambling, richly and densely written – and unique.

Josef Škvorecký *Talkin' Moscow Blues*. Without doubt the most user-friendly of Škvorecký's works, containing a collection of essays on his wartime childhood, Czech jazz, literature and contemporary politics, all told in his inimitable, irreverent and infuriating way. Published as *Headed for the Blues* in the US.

Ludvík Vaculík *A Cup of Coffee with My Interrogator*. A Party member until 1968, and signatory of Charter 77, Vaculík revived the *feuilleton* – a short political critique once much loved in central Europe. This collection dates from 1968 onwards.

Klaus Wagenbach *Kafka's Prague: A Travel Reader*. Hardback book that takes you through the streets in the footsteps of Kafka.

Zbyněk Zeman *The Masaryks: The Making of Czechoslovakia*. Written in the 1970s while Zeman was in exile, this is a very readable, none-too-sentimental bio-graphy of the country's founder Tomáš Garrigue Masaryk, and his son Jan Masaryk, the postwar foreign minister who died in mysterious circumstances shortly after the 1948 Communist coup.

CZECH FICTION

★**Josef Čapek** *Stories about Doggie and Cat*. Josef Capek (Karel's older brother) was a Cubist artist of some renown, and also a children's writer. These simple stories about a dog and a cat are wonderfully illustrated, and seriously postmodern.

Karel Čapek Karel Čapek was the literary and journalistic spokesperson for Masaryk's First Republic, but he's better known in the West for his plays, such as *The Insect Play* and *R.U.R.*, most of which are to be found in classic collections.

Capek's *Letters from England* had the rare distinction of being banned by both the Nazis and the Communists for its naive admiration of England in the 1920s.

Daniela Fischerová *Fingers Pointing Somewhere Else*. Subtly nuanced, varied collection of short stories from dissident playwright Fischerová.

Ladislav Fuks *Mr Theodore Mundstock*. A very readable novel set in 1942 Prague, as the city's Jews wait to be transported to Terezín.

Jaroslav Hašek *The Good Soldier Švejk*. A rambling, picaresque tale by Bohemia's most bohemian writer of Czechoslovakia's famous fictional fifth columnist, *Švejk*, who wreaks havoc in the Austro-Hungarian army during World War I.

Václav Havel Havel's plays are not renowned for being easy to read (or watch). *The Memorandum*, one of his earliest works, is a classic absurdist drama that, in many ways, sets the tone for much of his later work, of which the *Three Vaněk Plays,* featuring Ferdinand Vaněk, Havel's alter ego, are perhaps the most successful. The 1980s collection includes *Largo Desolato, Temptation* and *Redevelopment*; freedom of thought, Faustian opportunism and town planning as metaphors of life under the Communists. *Leaving* was Havel's last play and is a semi-autobiographical satire about a man giving up the top job.

Nancy Hawker (ed). *Povídky: Short Stories by Czech Women*. Varied collection of stories written by women across the generations, set variously against a background of pre- and post-Communist times.

★**Bohumil Hrabal** Hrabal is a thoroughly mischievous writer. The slim but superb *Closely Observed Trains* is a postwar classic, set in the last days of the war and relentlessly unheroic; it was made into an equally brilliant film by Jiří Menzl. *I Served the King of England* follows the antihero Díte, who works at the *Hotel Paříž*, through the decade after 1938. *Too Loud a Solitude*, about a waste-paper disposer under the Communists, has also been made into a film by Menzl.

Alois Jirásek *Old Czech Legends*. A major figure in the nineteenth-century Czech *národní obrození*, Jirásek popularized Bohemia's legendary past. This collection includes all the classic texts, as well as the story of the founding of the city by the prophetess Libuše.

★**Franz Kafka** A German-Jewish Praguer, Kafka has drawn the darker side of central Europe – its claustrophobia, paranoia and unfathomable bureaucracy – better than anyone else, both in a rural setting, as in *The Castle*, and in an urban one, in one of the great novels of the twentieth century, *The Trial*.

Jan Kaplan *A Traveler's Companion to Prague*. A compilation of memoirs, letters and extracts from diaries and novels, from the medieval to modern, to accompany a stroll round Prague.

Ivan Klíma A survivor of Terezín, Klíma is another writer in the Kundera mould as far as sexual politics goes, but his stories are a lot lighter. *Judge on Trial*, written in the 1970s, is one of his best, concerning the moral dilemmas of a Communist judge. *Waiting for the Dark, Waiting for the Light* is a pessimistic novel set before, during and after the Velvet Revolution of 1989. *The Spirit of Prague* is a very readable collection of biographical and more general essays on subjects ranging from Klíma's childhood experiences in Terezín to 1990s Prague. *No Saints or Angels* is a fairly bleak novel set in post-revolutionary Prague, and exploring three

different generations' reactions to the fall of Communism. *Between Security and Insecurity* takes a look at late twentieth-century values in society and their causes.

Pavel Kohout *Widow Killer* and *I am Snowing: The Confessions of a Woman of Prague*. The latter is set in the uneasy period just after the fall of Communism amid accusations of collaboration. *Widow Killer* is a thriller about a naive Czech detective partnered with a Gestapo agent in the last months of World War II in German-occupied Prague.

★**Milan Kundera** Milan Kundera is the country's most popular writer – at least among non-Czechs. His early books were very obviously "political", particularly *The Book of Laughter and Forgetting*, which led the Communists to revoke Kundera's citizenship. *The Joke*, written while he was still living in Czechoslovakia and in many ways his best work, is set in the very unfunny era of the 1950s. Its clear, humorous style is far removed from the carefully poised posturing of his most famous novel, *The Unbearable Lightness of Being*, set in and after 1968, and successfully turned into a film some twenty years later. *Identity* is a series of slightly detached musings on the human condition and is typical of his later works. *Testaments Betrayed*, on the other hand, is a fascinating series of essays about a range of subjects from the formation of historical reputation to the problems of translations. Kundera now writes in French and is largely ignored in his native land.

Arnošt Lustig *Diamonds of the Night; Night and Hope; A Prayer for Kateřina Horovitová; Waiting for Leah*. A Prague Jew exiled since 1968, Lustig spent World War II in Terezín, Buchenwald and Auschwitz, and his novels and short stories are consistently set amid the horror of the Terezín camp.

Gustav Meyrink Meyrink was another of Prague's weird and wonderful characters. He started out as a bank manager but soon became involved in Kabbala, alchemy and drug experimentation. *The Golem*, based on Rabbi Löw's monster, is one of the classic versions of the tale (see p.93). *The Angel of the West Window* is a historical novel about John Dee, an English alchemist invited to Prague in the late sixteenth century by Rudolf II.

Jan Neruda *Prague Tales*. These are short, bittersweet snapshots of life in Malá Strana at the close of the last century. The author is not to be confused with the Chilean Pablo Neruda (who took his name from the Czech writer).

Karel Poláček *What Ownership's All About*. A darkly comic novel set in a Prague tenement block, dealing with fascism and appeasement, by a Jewish-Czech Praguer who died in the camps in 1944.

Peter Sís *The Three Golden Keys*. Short, hauntingly illustrated children's book set in Prague, by Czech-born American Sís.

Josef Škvorecký A relentless anti-Communist, Škvorecký is typically Bohemian in his bawdy sense of humour and irreverence for all high moralizing. *The Cowards* (which briefly saw the light of day in 1958) is the tale of a group of irresponsible young men in the last days of the war, an antidote to the lofty prose from official authors at the time, but hampered by its dated Americanized translation. *The Miracle Game* enjoys a better translation and is set against the two "miracles" of 1948 and 1968. Less well known (and understandably so) are Škvorecký's detective stories featuring a podgy, depressive Czech cop, Lieutenant Borůvka, which he wrote in the 1960s at a time when his more serious work was banned.

★**Zdena Tomin** *Stalin's Shoe*. The compelling and complex story of a girl coming to terms with her Stalinist childhood. *The Coast of Bohemia* is based on Tomin's experiences of the late 1970s dissident movement, when she was an active member of Charter 77. Although Czech-born, Tomin writes in English (the language of her exile since 1980) and has a style and fluency all her own.

Jáchym Topol *City, Sister, Silver*. Dissident writer and lyricist for Czech rock band Psí vojáci, Topol's first novel to

be translated into English is an inventive take on the alienation and disappointment experienced by the younger generation after the Velvet Revolution.

Ludvík Vaculík *The Guinea Pigs*. This catalogues the slow dehumanization of Czech society in the aftermath of the Soviet invasion. *The Axe* centres on the cultural upheaval of the mid-1960s. Vaculík himself was expelled from the Party during the 1968 Prague Spring and went on to sign Charter 77.

Jiří Weil *Life With a Star; Mendelssohn is on the Roof*. Two novels written just after the war and based on Weil's experiences as a Czech Jew in hiding during the Nazi occupation of Prague.

Paul Wilson (ed.) *Prague: A Traveler's Literary Companion*. A great selection of short stories and snippets on Prague from, among others, Meyrink, Kisch and Čapek, plus contemporary writers such as Jáchym Topol.

POETRY

Petr Borkovec *From the Interior – Poems 1995–2005*. Born in 1970, Borkovec writes poetry that is not political, but personal and lyrical. Translated by Justin Quinn in a dual text, it makes for very accessible reading.

Sylva Fischerová *The Tremor of Racehorses: Selected Poems*. Poet and novelist Fischerová in many ways continues in the Holub tradition. Her poems are by turns powerful, obtuse and personal, and were written in exile in Switzerland and Germany after she fled in 1968.

Josef Hanzlík *Selected Poems*. Refreshingly accessible collection of poems written over the latter half of the 20th century by a poet of Havel's generation.

Miroslav Holub Holub is a scientist and scholar, and his poetry reflects this unique fusion of master poet and chief immunologist. Regularly banned in his own country, he was the Czech poet par excellence – classically trained, erudite, liberal and westward-leaning. The full range of his work, including some previously unpublished poems, is published in *Intensive Care: Selected and New Poems*.

Rainer Maria Rilke *Selected Poetry*. Rilke's upbringing was unexceptional, except that his mother brought him up as a girl until the age of 6. In his adult life, he became one of Prague's leading authors of the interwar period and subsequently probably the best-known Czech poet outside Czechoslovakia.

Marcela Rydlová-Herlich (ed.) *Treasury of Czech Love Poems*. A good way to get a taste of a variety of Czech poetry from more than 33 poets, most of whom are twentieth century.

Jaroslav Seifert *The Poetry of Jaroslav Seifert*. The only Czech writer to win the Nobel Prize for Literature, Seifert was a founder-member of the Communist Party and the avant-garde arts movement Devětsil, later falling from grace and signing the Charter in his old age. His longevity means that his work covers some of the most turbulent times in Czechoslovak history, but his irrepressible lasciviousness has been known to irritate.

LITERATURE BY FOREIGN WRITERS

David Brierley *On Leaving a Prague Window*. A very readable (if dated) thriller set in post-Communist Prague, which shows that past connection with dissidents can still lead to violence.

Bruce Chatwin *Utz*. Chatwin is from the "exotic" school of travel writers, hence this slim, intriguing and mostly true-to-life account of an avid porcelain collector from Prague's Jewish quarter.

Sue Gee *Letters from Prague*. The central character in this book falls in love with a Czech student in England in 1968, but she returns home when the Russians invade. Twenty years later, together with her 10-year-old daughter, she goes in search of him.

Sulamith Ish-Kishor *A Boy of Old Prague*. This story, set

in the Jewish ghetto in the sixteenth century, tells how a poor Christian boy discovers that Jews are not the monsters that he's been told. Aimed at children aged 8 to 11.

Kathy Kacer *Clara's War*. The story of a young girl and her family who are sent from Prague to Terezín in 1943. The horror is played down as the book is aimed at children of 10-plus, but nevertheless it is based on truth.

★**Jill Paton Walsh** *A Desert in Bohemia*. A gripping story set against the aftermath of World War II and the subsequent political upheaval in Czechoslovakia.

Anthony J. Rudel *Imagining Don Giovanni*. Mozart, Da Ponte and Casanova collaborate on the production of *Don Giovanni* with the Marquis de Sade thrown in. An imaginative evocation of the period, which will delight music lovers.

Czech

The official language of the Czech Republic is Czech (čeština), a highly inflected Western Slav tongue regarded as one of the most difficult in the world to learn. Any attempt to speak Czech will be heartily appreciated, though don't be discouraged if people seem not to understand, as most will be unaccustomed to hearing foreigners stumble through their language. English is widely spoken in hotels and restaurants, slightly less universally in shops and museums. Among the older generation at least, German is still the most widely spoken second language.

Pronunciation

English-speakers often find Czech impossibly difficult to pronounce. In fact, it's not half as daunting as it might first appear from the "traffic jams of consonants", as Patrick Leigh Fermor put it, which crop up on the page. An illustration of this is the nonsensical Czech tongue-twister, *strč prst skrz krk* (stick a finger through your neck). Apart from a few special letters, each letter and syllable is pronounced as it's written – the trick is always to **stress the first syllable** of a word, no matter what its length; otherwise you'll render it unintelligible.

Short and long vowels

Czech has both **short and long vowels** (the latter being denoted by an acute accent). The trick here is to lengthen the vowel without affecting the principal stress of the word, which is invariably on the first syllable.

a like the u in c**u**p	**í** or **ý** as in s**ea**t
á as in f**a**ther	**o** as in n**o**t
e as in p**e**t	**ó** as in d**oo**r
é as in f**ai**r	**u** like the oo in b**oo**k
ě like the ye in **ye**s	**ů** or **ú** like the oo in f**oo**l
i or **y** as in p**i**t	

Vowel combinations and diphthongs

There are very few **diphthongs** in Czech, so any combinations of vowels other than those below should be pronounced as two separate syllables.

au like the ou in f**ou**l	**ou** like the oe in f**oe**

A CZECH LANGUAGE GUIDE

There are only a handful of **teach-yourself Czech** courses available and each has drawbacks. *Czech Step by Step* by Lida Hola is more fun than most, but has no accompanying CD; *Colloquial Czech* by James Naughton is good, but a bit fast and furious for most people; *Teach Yourself Czech* is a bit dry. Numerous **Czech phrasebooks** are available, not least the *Czech Rough Guide Phrasebook*, laid out dictionary-style for instant access. A good **website** that will help you learn a little Czech is ⓦ locallingo.com; for an **online dictionary** check ⓦ slovnik.cz. Google Translate generally does a worse job with Czech than with most European languages.

Consonants and accents

There are no silent **consonants**, but it's worth remembering that r and l can form a half-syllable if standing between two other consonants or at the end of a word, as in Brno (Br–no) or Vltava (Vl–ta–va). The consonants listed below are those that differ substantially from the English. **Accents** look daunting – particularly the háček (ˇ), which appears above c, d, n, r, s, t and z – but the only one that causes a lot of problems is ř, possibly the most difficult letter to pronounce in any European language. Even Czech schoolchildren have to be taught how to say it correctly.

c like the **ts** in boats
č like the **ch** in chicken
ch like the **ch** in the Scottish loch
ď like the **d** in duped
g always as in goat, never as in general
h always as in have, but more energetic
j like the **y** in yoke
kd pronounced as **gd**
mě pronounced as mnye

ň like the **n** in nuance
p like the English **p**
r as in rip, but rolled
ř roughly like the sound of **r** and **ž** combined
š like the **sh** in shop
ť like the **t** in tutor
ž like the **s** in pleasure; at the end of a word like the sh in shop

WORDS AND PHRASES

BASICS

Yes	ano
No	ne
Please/excuse me	prosím vás
Don't mention it	není zač
Sorry	pardon
Thank you	děkuju
Bon appétit	dobrou chuť
Bon voyage	šťastnou cestu
Hello/goodbye (informal)	ahoj
Goodbye (formal)	na shledanou
Good day	dobrý den
Good morning	dobré ráno
Good evening	dobrý večer
Good night (when leaving)	dobrou noc
How are you?	jak se máte?
Today	dnes
Yesterday	včera
Tomorrow	zítra
The day after tomorrow	pozítří
Now	hned
Later	později
Leave me alone	dej mi pokoj!
Go away	jdi pryč!
Help!	pomoc!
This one	tento/toto/tato
A little	trochu
Large/small	velký/malý
More/less	více/méně
Good/bad	dobrý/špatný
Hot/cold	horký/studený
With/without	s/bez

GETTING AROUND

Over here	tady
Over there	tam
Left	nalevo
Right	napravo
Straight on	rovně
Where is …?	kde je…?
How do I get to Prague?	jak se dostanu do Prahy?
How do I get to the university?	jak se dostanu k univerzitě?
By bus	autobusem
By train	vlakem
By car	autem
On foot	pěšky
By taxi	taxíkem
Ticket	jízdenka/lístek
Return ticket	zpateční jízdenka
Railway station	nádraží
Bus station	autobusové nádraží
Bus stop	autobusová zastávka
When's the next train to Prague?	kdy jede další vlak do Prahy?
Is it going to Prague?	jede to do Prahy?
Do I have to change?	musím přestupovat?
Do I need a reservation?	musím mit místenku?

QUESTIONS AND ANSWERS

Do you speak English?	mluvíte anglicky?
I don't speak German	nemluvím německy
I don't understand	nerozumím
I understand	rozumím
Speak slowly	mluvte pomalu

THE CZECH ALPHABET

In the Czech alphabet, letters that feature a **háček** (as in the č of the word itself) are considered separate letters and appear in Czech indexes immediately after their more familiar cousins. More confusingly, the consonant combination *ch* is also considered as a separate letter and appears in Czech indexes after the letter *h*. In the index in this book, we use the English system, so words beginning with *c*, *č* and *ch* all appear under *c*.

How do you say that in Czech?	jak se to řekne česky?
Could you write it down for me?	mužete to napsat?
What	co
Where	kde
When	kdy
Why	proč
How much is it?	kolik to stojí?
Is there a room available?	máte volný pokoj?
I would like a double room	chtěl bych dvoulůžkový pokoj
For one night	na jednu noc
With shower	se sprchou
Is this seat free?	je tu volno?
May we (sit down)?	můžeme (se sednout)?
The bill please	zaplatím prosím
Do you have…?	máte…?
We don't have	nemáme
We do have	máme

SOME SIGNS

Entrance	vchod
Exit	východ
Toilets	záchody/toalety
Men	muži
Women	ženy
Ladies	dámy
Gentlemen	pánové
Open	otevřeno
Closed	zavřeno
Danger!	pozor!
Hospital	nemocnice
No smoking	kouření zakázáno
No bathing	koupání zakázáno
No entry	vstup zakázán
Arrival	příjezd
Departure	odjezd
Police	policie

DAYS OF THE WEEK

Monday	pondělí
Tuesday	uterý
Wednesday	středa
Thursday	čtvrtek
Friday	pátek
Saturday	sobota
Sunday	neděle
Day	den
Week	týden

MONTHS OF THE YEAR

Many Slav languages have their own individual systems in which the words for the names of the months are descriptive, beautifully apt nouns.

January	leden	*ice*
February	únor	*hibernation*
March	březen	*birch*
April	duben	*oak*
May	květen	*blossom*
June	červen	*red*
July	červenec	*red*
August	srpen	*sickle*
September	září	*blazing*
October	říjen	*rutting*
November	listopad	*leaves falling*
December	prosinec	*slaughter of pigs*
Month	měsíc	
Year	rok	

NUMBERS

1	jeden
2	dva
3	tři
4	čtyři
5	pět
6	šest
7	sedm
8	osm
9	devět
10	deset
11	jedenáct
12	dvanáct
13	třináct
14	čtrnáct
15	patnáct
16	šestnáct
17	sedmnáct
18	osmnáct
19	devatenáct
20	dvacet
21	dvacetjedna

30	třicet	300	tři sta
40	čtyřicet	400	čtyři sta
50	padesát	500	pět set
60	šedesát	600	šest set
70	sedmdesát	700	sedm set
80	osmdesát	800	osm set
90	devadesát	900	devět set
100	sto	1000	tisíc
101	sto jedna	2000	dva tisíce
155	sto padesát pět	5000	pět tisíc
200	dvě stě		

FOOD AND DRINK TERMS

USEFUL PHRASES

The bill please	zaplatím prosím
Bon appétit	dobrou chuť
Cheers!	na zdraví!
Could I have the menu?	Mohu dostat jídelní lístek?
I don't eat...	Nejím...
I will have...	Dám si...
I'm a vegetarian	Jsem vegetarián/ vegetariánka

BASICS

bezmasá jídla	vegetarian dishes
chléb	bread
chlebíček	(open) sandwich
cukr	sugar
hořčice	mustard
hotová jídla	meals prepared in advance by a restaurant
houska	bap
jídelní lístek	menu
jídla na objednávku	meals made to order
knedlík	dumpling
koláč	tart
křen	horseradish
lžíce	spoon
máslo	butter
maso	meat
med	honey
mléko	milk
moučník	dessert
nápoje	drinks
nůž	knife
oběd	lunch
obloha	garnish – tomato, cucumber and lettuce or cabbage in a thin dressing
ocet	vinegar
ovoce	fruit
palačinky	pancakes

pečivo	pastry
pepř	pepper
polévka	soup
předkrmy	starters
přílohy	side dishes
rohlík	finger roll
(v) rohlíku	in a roll
ryba	fish
rýže	rice
šálek	cup
sklenice	glass
snídaně	breakfast
sůl	salt
talíř	plate
tartarská omáčka	tartare sauce
večeře	evening meal
vejce	eggs
vidlička	fork
zeleniny	vegetables
zmrzlina	ice cream

SOUPS (*POLÉVKY*)

boršč	beetroot soup
bramborová	potato soup
čočková	lentil soup
fazolová	bean soup
hovězí vývar	beef broth
hrachová	pea soup
kuřecí	thin chicken soup
rajská	tomato soup
zeleninová	vegetable soup

FISH (*RYBY*)

kapr	carp
losos	salmon
makrela	mackerel
platýs	flounder
pstruh	trout
rybí filé	fillet of fish
sardinka	sardine
štika	pike

treska	cod
zavináč	herring/rollmop

MEAT (*MASO*)

bažant	pheasant
biftek	beef steak
čevapčiči	spicy meat balls
dršťky	tripe
drůbež	poultry
guláš	goulash
hovězí	beef
husa	goose
játra	liver
jazyk	tongue
kachna	duck
klobása	sausage
kotleta	cutlet
králík	rabbit
kuře	chicken
kýta	leg
ledvinky	kidneys
Moravský vrabec	pork roll
řízek	steak
roštěná	sirloin
salám	salami
sekaná	meat loaf
skopové maso	mutton
slanina	bacon
srnčí	venison
šunka	ham
svíčková	fillet of beef
telecí	veal
vepřový	pork
vepřový řízek	breaded pork cutlet or schnitzel
žebírka	ribs

VEGETABLES (*ZELENINA*)

brambory	potatoes
brokolice	broccoli
celer	celery
cibule	onion
červená řepa	beetroot
česnek	garlic
chřest	asparagus
čočka	lentils
fazole	beans
houby	mushrooms
hranolky	chips, French fries
hrášek	peas
květák	cauliflower
kyselá okurka	pickled gherkin
kyselé zelí	sauerkraut
lečo	ratatouille

lilek	aubergine
mrkev	carrot
okurka	cucumber
pórek	leek
rajče	tomato
ředkvička	radish
špenát	spinach
zelí	cabbage
žampiony	mushrooms

FRUIT, CHEESE AND NUTS (*OVOCE, SÝR, OŘECHY*)

banán	banana
borůvky	blueberries
broskev	peach
brusinky	cranberries
bryndza	goat's cheese in brine
citrón	lemon
grep	grapefruit
hermelín	Czech brie
hrozny	grapes
hruška	pear
jablko	apple
jahody	strawberries
kompot	stewed fruit
maliny	raspberries
mandle	almonds
meruňka	apricot
niva	semi-soft, crumbly blue cheese
oříšky	nuts
ostružiny	blackberries
pivní sýr	cheese flavoured with beer
pomeranč	orange
rozinky	raisins
smažený sýr	fried cheese
švestky	plums
třešně	cherries
tvaroh	fresh curd (cottage) cheese
uzený sýr	smoked cheese
vlašské ořechy	walnuts

COMMON COOKING TERMS

čerstvý	fresh
domácí	home-made
dušený	stew/casserole
grilovaný	roast on the spit
kyselý	sour
na kmíně	with caraway seeds
na roštu	grilled
nadívaný	stuffed
nakládaný	pickled
plněný	stuffed
s povidlem	with jam

s máslem	with butter
s mlékem	with milk
sladký	sweet
slaný	salted
smažený	fried
studený	cold
syrový	raw
sýrový	cheesy
teplý	hot
uzený	smoked
vařený	boiled
(za)pečený	baked/roast

DRINKS

čaj	tea
destiláty	spirits

káva	coffee
koňak	brandy
láhev	bottle
minerální (voda)	mineral (water)
mléko	milk
pivo	beer
presso	espresso
s ledem	with ice
soda	soda
suché víno	dry wine
šumivý	fizzy
svařené víno/svařák	mulled wine
tonik	tonic
vinný střik	white wine with soda
víno	wine

Glossary

brána gate
český Bohemian
chata chalet-type bungalow, country cottage or mountain hut
chrám large church
cukrárna café specializing in cakes and desserts
divadlo theatre
dům house
dům kultury generic term for local arts and social centre; literally "house of culture"
hora mountain
hospoda pub
hostinec tavern
hrad castle
hřbitov cemetery
kaple chapel
katedrála cathedral
kavárna coffeehouse
klášter monastery/convent
kostel church
koupaliště swimming pool
Labe River Elbe
lanovka funicular or cable car
les forest
město town
most bridge

muzeum museum
nábřeží embankment
nádraží train station
náměstí square
ostrov island
palác palace
památník memorial or monument
pasáž indoor shopping mall
pekárna/pekářství bakery
pivnice pub
radnice town hall
restaurace restaurant
sad park
sál room or hall (in a chateau or castle)
schody steps
svatý/svatá saint; often abbreviated to sv
třída avenue
ulice street
věž tower
vinárna wine bar or cellar
Vltava River Moldau (rarely translated these days)
vrchy hills
výstava exhibition
zahrada garden
zámek chateau

Architecture, design and decorative arts terms

Ambulatory Passage round the back of the altar, in continuation of the aisles.

Art Nouveau French term for the sinuous and stylized artistic style dating from 1900 to 1910; known as the *Secese* (Secession) in the Czech Republic (see below) and as Jugendstil in Germany.

Baroque Expansive, exuberant style of the seventeenth and mid-eighteenth centuries, characterized by ornate decoration, complex spatial arrangement and grand vistas.

Chancel The part of the church where the altar is placed, usually at the east end.

Empire Highly decorative Neoclassical style practised in the early 1800s.

Fresco Mural painting applied to wet plaster, so that the colours immediately soak into the wall.

Functionalism Plain, boxy, modernist style, prevalent in the late 1920s and 1930s in Czechoslovakia, often using plate-glass curtain walls and open-plan interiors.

Gothic Architectural style prevalent from the fourteenth to the sixteenth centuries, characterized by pointed arches and ribbed vaulting.

Loggia Covered area on the side of a building, often arcaded.

Nave Main body of a church, usually the western end.

Neoclassical Late eighteenth- and early nineteenth-century style returning to classical Greek and Roman models as a reaction against Baroque and Rococo excesses.

Oriel A bay window, usually projecting from an -upper floor.

Rococo Highly florid, fiddly, though (occasionally) graceful, style forming the last phase of Baroque.

Romanesque Solid style of the late tenth to thirteenth centuries, characterized by round-headed arches and geometrical precision.

Secession Linear and stylized form imported from Vienna as a reaction against the academic establishment.

Sgraffito Monochrome plaster decoration effected by scraping back the first white layer to reveal the black underneath.

Stucco Plaster used for decorative effects.

Trompe l'oeil Painting designed to fool the onlooker into believing that it is actually three-dimensional.

Small print and index

Rough Guide credits

Editor: Neil McQuillian
Layout: Nikhil Agarwal
Cartography: Swati Handoo
Picture editor: Marta Bescos
Proofreader: Jennifer Speake
Managing editor: Monica Woods
Assistant editor: Shasya Goel

Production: Jimmy Lao
Cover photo research: Chloë Roberts
Photographer: Diana Jarvis
Editorial assistant: Aimee White
Senior DTP coordinator: Dan May
Programme manager: Gareth Lowe
Publishing director: Georgina Dee

Publishing information

This tenth edition published January 2018 by
Rough Guides Ltd,
80 Strand, London WC2R 0RL
11, Community Centre, Panchsheel Park,
New Delhi 110017, India
Distributed by Penguin Random House
Penguin Books Ltd, 80 Strand, London WC2R 0RL
Penguin Group (USA), 345 Hudson Street, NY 10014, USA
Penguin Group (Australia), 250 Camberwell Road,
Camberwell, Victoria 3124, Australia
Penguin Group (NZ), 67 Apollo Drive, Mairangi Bay,
Auckland 1310, New Zealand
Penguin Group (South Africa), Block D, Rosebank Office
Park, 181 Jan Smuts Avenue, Parktown North, Gauteng,
South Africa 2193
Rough Guides is represented in Canada by DK Canada, 320
Front Street West, Suite 1400, Toronto, Ontario M5V 3B6
Printed in Singapore
© Rough Guides, 2018
Maps © Rough Guides

272pp includes index
A catalogue record for this book is available from the
British Library
ISBN: 978-0-24130-622-2
The publishers and authors have done their best to
ensure the accuracy and currency of all the information in
The Rough Guide to Prague, however, they can accept
no responsibility for any loss, injury, or inconvenience
sustained by any traveller as a result of information or
advice contained in the guide.
1 3 5 7 9 8 6 4 2

MIX
Paper from
responsible sources
FSC™ C018179
www.fsc.org

Help us update

We've gone to a lot of effort to ensure that the tenth
edition of **The Rough Guide to Prague** is accurate
and up-to-date. However, things change – places get
"discovered", opening hours are notoriously fickle,
restaurants and rooms raise prices or lower standards.
If you feel we've got it wrong or left something out,
we'd like to know, and if you can remember the address,
the price, the hours, the phone number, so much
the better.

Please send your comments with the subject line
"**Rough Guide Prague Update**" to mail@uk.roughguides
.com. We'll credit all contributions and send a copy of the
next edition (or any other Rough Guide if you prefer) for
the very best emails.

ABOUT THE AUTHOR

Marc Di Duca has been a full-time travel guide author for the past decade, covering destinations as diverse as Madeira and Siberia for most major travel publishers. He is a fluent Czech speaker and has lived, worked and played in the country on and off for the past three decades. As well as penning guides, he also works as a translator for various Czech companies, organisations and public bodies.

Acknowledgements

A huge díky moc must go to my parents-in-law for looking after my two sons while I was away in Prague. Many thanks also go to the staff at Prague City Tourism and Czech Tourism as well as Prague friends Paddington Tucker and Honza Rouček. Last but not least big thanks to my wife Tanya for enduring my lengthy absences from home.

Photo credits

Index

Maps are marked in grey

Map index

Listings key

- ■ Accommodation
- ● Eating
- ■ Drinking and nightlife
- ● Shopping

Map symbols

Motorway	✈	International airport	▲	Mountain peak
Road	⊠	Entrance	🐘	Zoo
Pedestrian road	🚢	Boat stop	✡	Synagogue
Steps	✉	Post office		Building
Tram	ⓘ	Information office		Church
Railway	P	Parking		Stadium
Funicular	⊙	Statue/monument		Park
Wall	♔	Castle		Christian cemetery
Ⓜ Metro station	✚	Hospital		Jewish cemetery

City plan

The **city plan** on the pages that follow is divided as shown:

N

0   250
metres

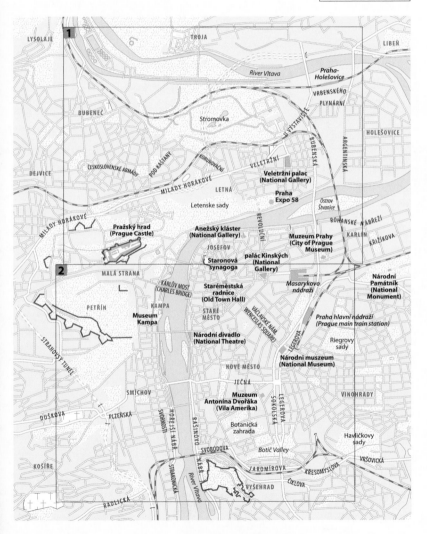

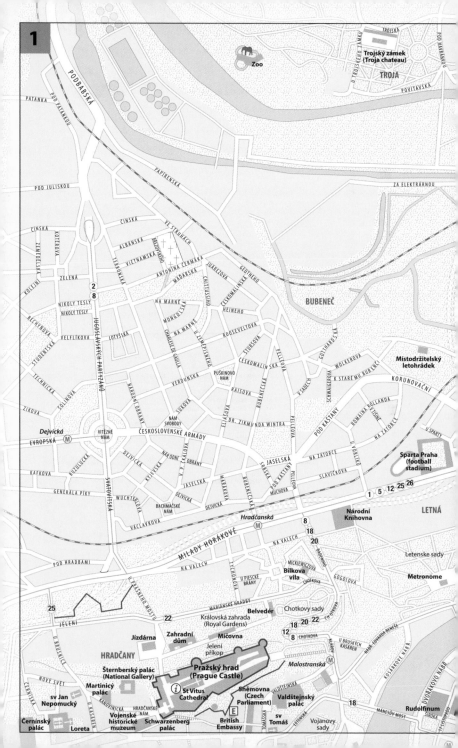

1

PODBABSKÁ

TROJSKÁ

Zoo

Trojský zámek
(Troja chateau)

POD HRABANKOU

TROJA

POVLTAVSKÁ

PATANKA

POD PATANKOU

PAPÍRENSKÁ

POD JULISKOU

ZA ELEKTRÁRNOU

ČÍNSKÁ

ČÍNSKÁ

KOTĚROVA

ZEMĚDĚLSKÁ

ALBÁNSKÁ

 VE STRUHÁCH

BŘEZOVSKÉHO

VIETNAMSKÁ

ZELENÁ

ANTONÍNA ČERMÁKA

JUÁREZOVA

GEOTHEHO

BUBENEČ

2
8

NIKOLY TESLY

NIKOLY TESLY

MAĎARSKÁ

NA MARNĚ

ČESKOMALÍNSKÁ

CHITTUSSIHO

HEINEHO

BĚCHYROVA

STUDENTSKÁ

VELFLÍKOVA

LOTYŠSKÁ

MONGOLSKÁ

NA MARNĚ

ROOSEVELTOVA

ŠTURSOVA

PELLEOVA

GOTTHARDSKÁ

K STARÉMU BUBENČI

Místodržitelský
letohrádek

KORUNOVAČNÍ

TECHNICKÁ

ZIKOVA

ŠOLÍNOVA

NÁRODNÍ OBRANY

JUHOSLÁVSKÝCH PARTIZÁNŮ

CHARLESE DE GAULLA

VERDUNSKÁ

ZEMĚPISNÉHO

PUŠKINOVO
NÁM.

RAISOVA

BUBENEČSKÁ

ČESKOMALÍNSKÁ

POD KAŠTANY

ROMAINA ROLLANDA

VÍTĚZNÁ

NA ZÁTORCE

ROMAINA ROLLANDA

Dejvická

EVROPSKÁ

VÍTĚZNÉ
NÁM.

ČESKOSLOVENSKÉ ARMÁDY

NÁM.
SVOBODY

ELIÁŠOVA

DR. ZIKMUNDA WINTRA

SUKOVA

PELLEOVA

POD KAŠTANY

NA ZÁTORCE

U VORLÍKA

Sparta Praha
(football
stadium)

LETNÁ

KAFKOVA

BUZULUCKÁ

DEJVICKÁ

KYJEVSKÁ

NÁRODNÍ
OBRANY

K. Z. KLÁLOVA

MARÁKOVA

JASELSKÁ

SRBSKÁ

POD KAŠTANY

MUCHOVA

SLAVÍČKOVA

NA ZÁTORCE

1 5 12 25 26

GENERÁLA PIKY

SVATOVÍTSKÁ

WUCHTEROVA

JASELSKÁ

DEJVICKÁ

DEJVICKÁ

BUBENEČSKÁ

Národní
Knihovna

VÁCLAVKOVA

BACHMAČSKÉ
NÁM.

Hradčanská

8

POD HRADBAMI

MILADY HORÁKOVÉ

NA VALECH

18

20

Letenske sady

Metronome

NA VALECH

TYCHONOVA

MICKIEWICZOVA

U PÍSECKÉ
BRÁNY

Bílkova
vila

CHOTKOVA

GOGOLOVA

BADENIHO

25

JELENÍ

U PRAŠNÉHO MOSTU

22

MARIÁNSKÉ HRADBY

Belvedér

Královská zahrada
(Royal Gardens)

Chotkovy sady

18 20 22 CH. OBRNY

12

8 CHOTKOVA

U BRUSKÉ

U PRAŠNÉHO MOSTU

Jízdárna

Zahradní
dům

Míčovna

HRADČANY

Šternberský palác
(National Gallery)

Martinický
palác

sv Jan
Nepomucký

NOVÝ SVĚT

ČERNÍNSKÁ

Černínský
palác

Loreta

KANOVNICKÁ

Vojenské
historické
muzeum

HRADČANSKÉ
NÁM.

Jelení příkop

Pražský hrad
(Prague Castle)

St Vitus
Cathedral

Schwarzenberg
palác

British
Embassy

E

Malostranská

Sněmovna
(Czech
Parliament)

sv
Tomáš

TOMÁŠSKÁ

Valdštejnský
palác

VALDŠTEJNSKÁ

LETENSKÁ

Vojanovy
sady

U BRUSKÝCH
KASÁREN

MÁŠ. EDVARDA BENEŠE

KOSÁRKOVO NÁBŘ.

DVOŘÁKOVO NÁBŘ.

18

Rudolfinum

MÁNESŮV MOST

ŠIROKÁ

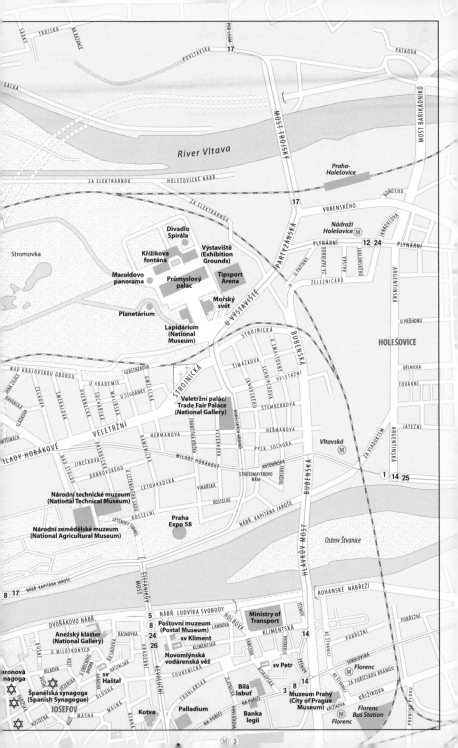

River Vltava

Stromovka

SLÁNKA
TROJSKÁ
MAKAZANKE
DACKA
POVLTAVSKÁ
POD LISEM
PÁTKOVA

MOST TROJSKÝ
MOST BARIKÁDNIKŮ

Praha-Holešovice

ZA ELEKTRÁRNOU
HOLEŠOVICKÉ NÁBŘ.
ZA ELEKTRÁRNOU
BONDYHO

17
VRBENSKÉHO

17

PARTYZÁNSKÁ

Nádraží Holešovice (M)
12 24

Plynární
Plynární

Divadlo Spirála
Křižíkova fontána
Výstaviště (Exhibition Grounds)
Maroldovo panorama
Průmyslový palác
Tipsport Arena
Mořský svět
Planetárium
Lapidárium (National Museum)

JABLONSKÉHO
ŽELEZNIČÁRŮ
ZA PAPÍRNOU
U PAPÍRNY
RÁŠKY

ARGENTINSKÁ

HOLEŠOVICE

U VÝSTAVIŠTĚ
STROJNICKÁ
ŠIMÁČKOVA
U SMALTOVNY
BUBENSKÁ

DĚLNICKÁ
TOVÁRNÍ
U PRŮHONU

STROJNICKÁ

Veletržní palác/ Trade Fair Palace (National Gallery)

ŠIMÁČKOVA
JANOVSKÉHO
SCHNIRCHOVA
VELETRŽNÍ
STEMBERKOVA
HERMANOVA

U STUDÁNKY
NAD KRÁLOVSKOU OBOROU
GERSTNEROVA
U AKADEMIE
UMĚLECKÁ
DUKELSKÝCH HRDINŮ
FRANTIŠKA KŘÍŽKA

JATEČNÍ
ARGENTINSKÁ
ZA VIADUKTEM

NÁMĚSTÍ
SMERALOVA
ČECHOVA
HAVANSKÁ
SELSKÁ
V HÁJÍCH
U AKADEMIE
OVERNECKÁ
SOCHÁŘSKÁ
MALÍRSKÁ
KAMENICKÁ
HERMANOVA
STROSSMAYEROVO NÁM.
FARSKÉHO
ANTONÍNSKÁ
VEVERKOVA

VELETRŽNÍ
MILADY HORÁKOVÉ
Vltavská (M)

TŘÍDY HORÁKOVÉ
NAD ŠTOLOU
JIREČKOVA
OVERNECKÁ
DOBROVSKÉHO
U LETENSKÉHO SADU
LETOHRADSKÁ
PPLK. SOCHORA
VINAŘSKÁ
KOSTELNÍ

BUBENSKÁ

1 14 25

Národní technické muzeum (National Technical Museum)

Praha Expo 58

Ostrov Štvanice

Národní zemědělské muzeum (National Agricultural Museum)

LETENSKÝ TUNNEL
KOSTELNÍ
NÁBŘ. KAPITÁNA JAROŠE

HLÁVKŮV MOST

ROHANSKÉ NÁBŘEŽÍ

8 17
NÁBŘ. KAPITÁNA JAROŠE

DVOŘÁKOVO NÁBŘ.

5
8
24
26

NÁBŘ. LUDVÍKA SVOBODY
Poštovní muzeum (Postal Museum)
sv Kliment
Novomlýnská vodárenská věž

Ministry of Transport

HOLBOVA
LANNOVA
KLIMENTSKÁ
SAMCOVA
ŠTĚPÁNSKÁ

TĚŠNOV

14

POBŘEŽNÍ

PRVNÍHO PLUKU

ŠTEFÁNIKŮV MOST

REVOLUČNÍ

Anežský klášter (National Gallery)
sv Haštal

Španělská synagoga (Spanish Synagoga)
aronová nagoga

JOSEFOV

sv Petr

Florenc (M)
SOKOLOVSKÁ
ZA PORÍČSKOU BRÁNOU

Bílá labuť
Kotva
Palladium
Banka legii

3 8 14
Muzeum Prahy (City of Prague Museum)

KŘIŽÍKOVA
Florenc
Florenc Bus Station

Florenc (M)

DUŠNÍ
U MILOSRDNÝCH
RÁSNOVKA
BÍLKOVA
KOZÍ
ELIŠKY KRÁSNOHORSKÉ
VEZENSKÁ
U OBECNÍHO DVORA
HAŠTALSKÁ
RYBNÁ
KLIMENTSKÁ
SOUKENICKÁ
ZLATNICKÁ
BISKUPSKÁ
NA PORÍČÍ

PAŘÍŽSKÁ
ŠIROKÁ
KOSTEČNÁ
VÍTĚZNÁ
DLOUHÁ
MASNÁ
KRÁLODVORSKÁ
HYBERNSKÁ
TRUHLÁŘSKÁ
PETRSKÁ
NA FLORENCI
KŘIŽÍKOVA

(M) 3

2

LORETÁNSKÉ NÁM.
LORETÁNSKÁ
NERUDOVA

Bretfeldský palác
Institvto Italiano di Cultvra
VLASSKÁ
Liechtenštejnský palác
Schönbornský palác (US Embassy)

sv Mikuláš
MALOSTRANSKÉ NÁM.

sv Josef

Franz Kafka Museum
Staroměstská

Museum of Miniatures

VLAŠSKÁ

Lobkovický palác (German Embassy)
E

Vrtbovská zahrada

MALÁ STRANA

Bridge Tower
MOSTECKÁ

Muzeum Karlova mostu (Charles Bridge Museum)
KARLŮV MOST (CHARLES BRIDGE)

sv František

Strahovský klášter (Strahov Monastery)

VLAŠSKÁ

Panna Maria Vítězná

PROKOPSKÁ
HARANTOVA
MOSTECKÁ

Stare Mesto Bridge Tower

NÁPRSTKOVA

Strahovská zahrada

České muzeum hudby/ Czech Music Museum (National Museum)
HELLICHOVA

KAMPA

Muzeum Bedřicha Smetany (Smetana Museum)

17
18

Petřínská Rozhledna (Petřín Tower)

12
20

Atelier Josefa Sudka

Museum Kampa

Weir

KARLOVA ULICE

SMETANOVO NÁBŘ.

Bludiště

STRAHOVSKÁ

PETŘÍN

22

VŠEHRDOVA

Divadlo na zábradlí
Krannerova kašna

DIVADELNÍ

sv Vavřinec

Funicular Railway

Újezd

Strelecký ostrov (Shooters' Island)

sv Kříž

Nebozízek

Memorial to the Victims of Communism

ŘÍČNÍ

sv Jan Křtitel na Prádle

Pojišťovna Praha

Café Slavia

VANÍČKOVA

OLYMPIJSKÁ

Štefánikova hvězdárna (Observatory)

Karel Hynek Mácha

Hladová zeď

VÍTĚZNÁ

MOST LEGIÍ

6 9 22

Nová scéna

Národní divadlo (National Theatre)

PLÁSKÁ

CHALOUPECKÉHO

MĚLNICKÁ

Žofín

MASARYKOVO NÁBŘ.

JEZDECKÁ

ŠERMÍŘSKÁ

PETŘÍNSKÁ

Dětský ostrov

Slovanský ostrov (Slav Island)

Hlahol

Kinského Zahrada
sv Michal

VODNÍ

MALÁTOVA

Galerie Mánes

14
17

KROFTOVA

6
9
12
20

PAVLA ŠVANDY ZE SEMČIC

Weir

ELIŠKY PEŠKOVÉ

PEŠLOVA

KOŘENSKÉHO

U PLZENKY

U HŘEBENKÁCH
TICHÁ

DRTINOVA

Musaion

ZUBATÉHO

MATOUŠOVA

JIRÁSKŮV MOST

Tančicí dům

RAŠÍNOVO NÁBŘ.

U NESYPKY

ŠVEDSKÁ

ŠVEDSKÁ

STRAHOVSKÝ TUNEL

SMÍCHOV

V BOTANICE

ZBOROVSKÁ

PPS Boat Launch

ZÁPOVA

KMOCHOVA

Sacre Coeur

MATOUŠOVA

Portheimka

Národní dům

JANÁČKOVO NÁBŘ.

Karlovo Náměstí
M

ZÁPOVA

GRAFICKÁ

ERBENOVA

HOLEČKOVA

KARTOUZSKÁ

LESNICKÁ

ŠTEFÁNIKOVA

Palacký Monument

HOŘEJŠÍ NÁBŘ.

PLZEŇSKÁ

PLZEŇSKÁ

sv Václav

PECHÁČKOVA

PALACKÉHO MOST

9 10 16

DUŠKOVA

Nový Smíchov

Former Synagogue

Království železnic (Railway Kingdom)

M
Anděl
4 7 10 14 16

STROUPEŽNICKÉHO

NA BĚLIDLE

LIDICKÁ

3
7
17

Zlatý Anděl

NA BĚLIDLE

NA VENEČKU

FRÁŇ ŠRÁMKA

RADLICKÁ

BOZDĚCHOVA

KOVÁKŮ

JINDŘICHA PLACHTY

SVORNOSTI

OSTROVSKÉHO _Anděl_
M

Staropramen Brewery

VLTAVSKÁ

KLICPEROVA

ZA ŽENSKÝMI DOMOVY

PIVOVARSKÁ

NA VALENTINCE

NÁBŘEŽNÍ

NA ZÁTLANCE

TOMANOVA

OSTROVSKÉHO

U NIKOLAJKY

NA SKALCE

NA SANTOŠCE

NAD SANTOŠKOU

BLELBLOVA

6

12
14
20

STRAKONICKÁ

NA ZÁBRADLÍ

NA CIHLÁŘCE

NA BŘEZINCE

NA VÁCLAVCE

River Vltava

U MRÁZOVKY

NA VÁCLAVCE

NAD ŠVIHANKOU

NÁBŘEŽNÍ

KOTEVNÍ

U SMÍCHOVSKÉHO HŘBITOVA

U KLAVÍRKY

U MALVAZINKY

SANOPZU
U MALVAZINKY

XAVERIOVA

MRÁZOVKA TUNEL

ROZKOŠNÉHO

XAVERIOVA

NA PLÁNI

NA PAVÍM VRCHU

K VODOJEMU

K VODOJEMU

NAD LAUROU

RADLICKÁ

BRANÍKOVÁ

KE KULCE

NA NEKLANCE

M

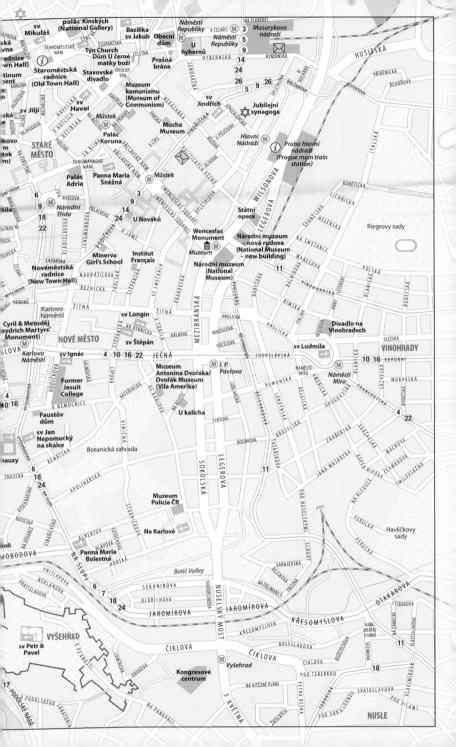

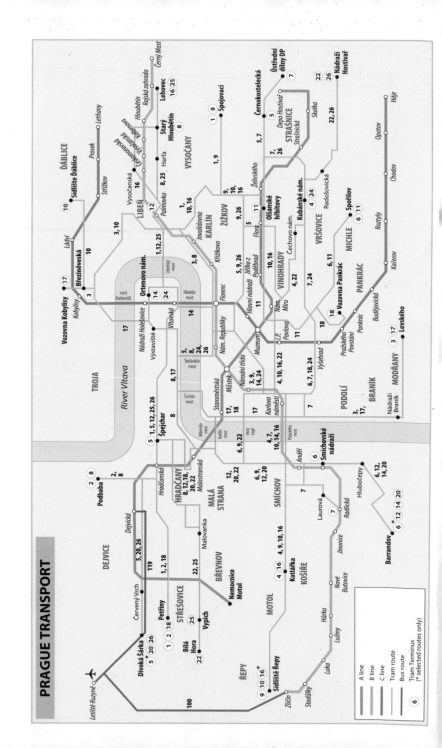

PRAGUE TRANSPORT